DE JIAO

DE JIAO

A Religious Movement in Contemporary China and Overseas: Purple *qi* from the East

Bernard Formoso

NUS PRESS
SINGAPORE

National University of Singapore
AS3-01-02, 3 Arts Link
Singapore 117569

Fax: (65) 6774-0652
E-mail: nusbooks@nus.edu.sg
Website: http://www.nus.edu.sg/nuspress

ISBN 978-9971-69-492-0 (Paper)

National Library Board Singapore Cataloguing in Publication Data

Formoso, Bernard, 1957–
De jiao: a religious movement in contemporary China and overseas: purple *qi* from the East/Bernard Formoso. – Singapore: NUS Press, c2010.
p. cm.
Includes bibliographical references and index.
ISBN-13: 978-9971-69-492-0 (pbk.)

1. Chinese – Foreign countries – Religion. 2. Chinese – Southeast Asia – Religion. 3. Chinese – Foreign countries – Ethnic identity. 4. Southeast Asia – Religion – 20th century. 5. China – Religion – 20th century. I. Title.

BL1950
299.51 — dc22 OCN463350570

Typeset by: Scientifik Graphics
Printed by : Mainland Press Pte Ltd

To

You Qiu Xi and Li Le Zi

CONTENTS

LIST OF TABLES

LIST OF MAPS

LIST OF ILLUSTRATIONS

PREFACE

My interest in De Jiao arose in 1993. At the time, I was doing ethnographic fieldwork amongst Chinese traders of a small town in northeast Thailand, and was led to the temples of this religious movement by the important services its priests provided locally, which included the organization of funerals in accordance with Chinese "tradition". During the next decade, I occasionally visited De Jiao associations in other parts of Thailand and attended some of their rituals.

I collected, however, most of the materials for the present book between 2003 and 2005, thanks to a Senior Fellowship from the Conseil National de la Recherche Scientifique (CNRS, France) and a Research Grant from the Chiang Ching-Kuo Foundation for International Scholarly Exchange. The Chiang Ching-Kuo Foundation also granted publication subsidy to the present book. I am grateful to both institutions for their support, as well as to De Jiao leaders, mediums, and followers for their cooperation. Their answers to what must have seemed to them my incongruous and sometimes irrelevant questions required great patience. Finally, the Asia Research Institute of the National University of Singapore, through a three-month Senior Research Fellowship in 2007, helped me a lot with the editing work.

A NOTE ON CHINESE ROMANIZATION AND THE USE OF PATRONYMIC TERMS

Chinese words or expressions have been romanized according to pinyin. Only when words are widely known in a different orthography have I deviated from this phonetic system. Another exception concerns quotations from other sources, whose words are written according to alternative systems (Wade, EFEO). In such cases, I have added the pinyin romanization in brackets. In the annex, I provide an index and a glossary that includes the Chinese concepts to which I refer throughout the book, together with their respective ideographic scripts, and their pronunciation in the Teochew dialect. With De Jiao outlawed in mainland China at the time of the study, I decided to disguise the names of living De Jiao adepts using acronyms. The intent was indeed to prevent these adepts' identification by police or other repressive forces. On the other hand, the civil or religious identity of promoters or adepts of the movement's earliest stages was given, firstly, because they passed away several years ago and, secondly, to facilitate cross-checking with information from previous studies on the subject.

Fig. 1 The Painting Depicting Yang Rui-De and Yang Ru-Hou as Bodhisattvas

Fig. 2 The Altar of the New Zi Xiang Ge with a Copy of the Original Paintings of Liu Chun-Fang and Yang Jun-Song

Fig. 3 Yang Rui-De

Fig. 4 Ma Gui De

Fig. 5 Wu Zui-Jiao

Fig. 6 The Flag of De Jiao

Fig. 7 A View of Zi Zhen Ge, Bangkok

Fig. 8 An Altar of the Zi Group, Malaysia

Fig. 9 Opening of Restless Ghosts' Jars in Kuala Kurau, Malaysia

Fig. 10 A Couple of Mediums in Malaysia

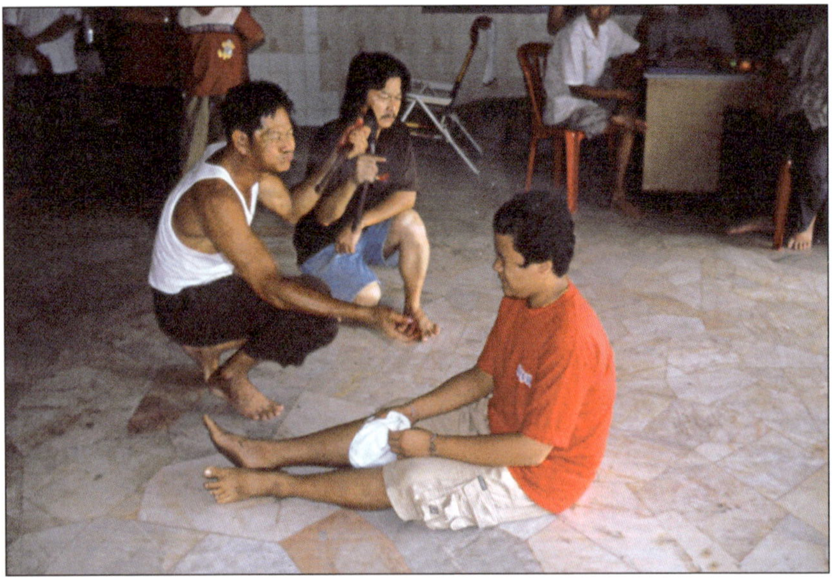

Fig. 11 An Exorcism Through *wu ji* in a Zhen Association

Fig. 12 The Logo of the World Moral Meeting

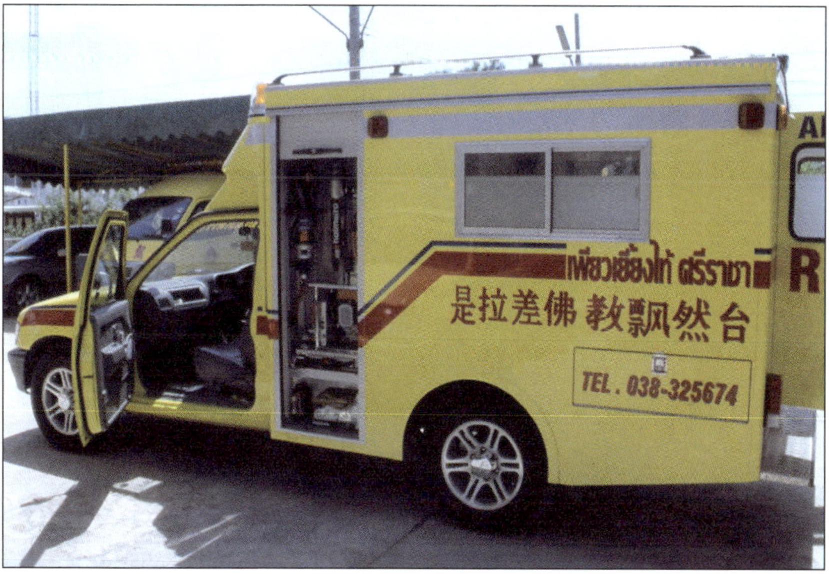

Fig. 13 An Emergency Car, Zi Piao Tan, Siracha, Thailand

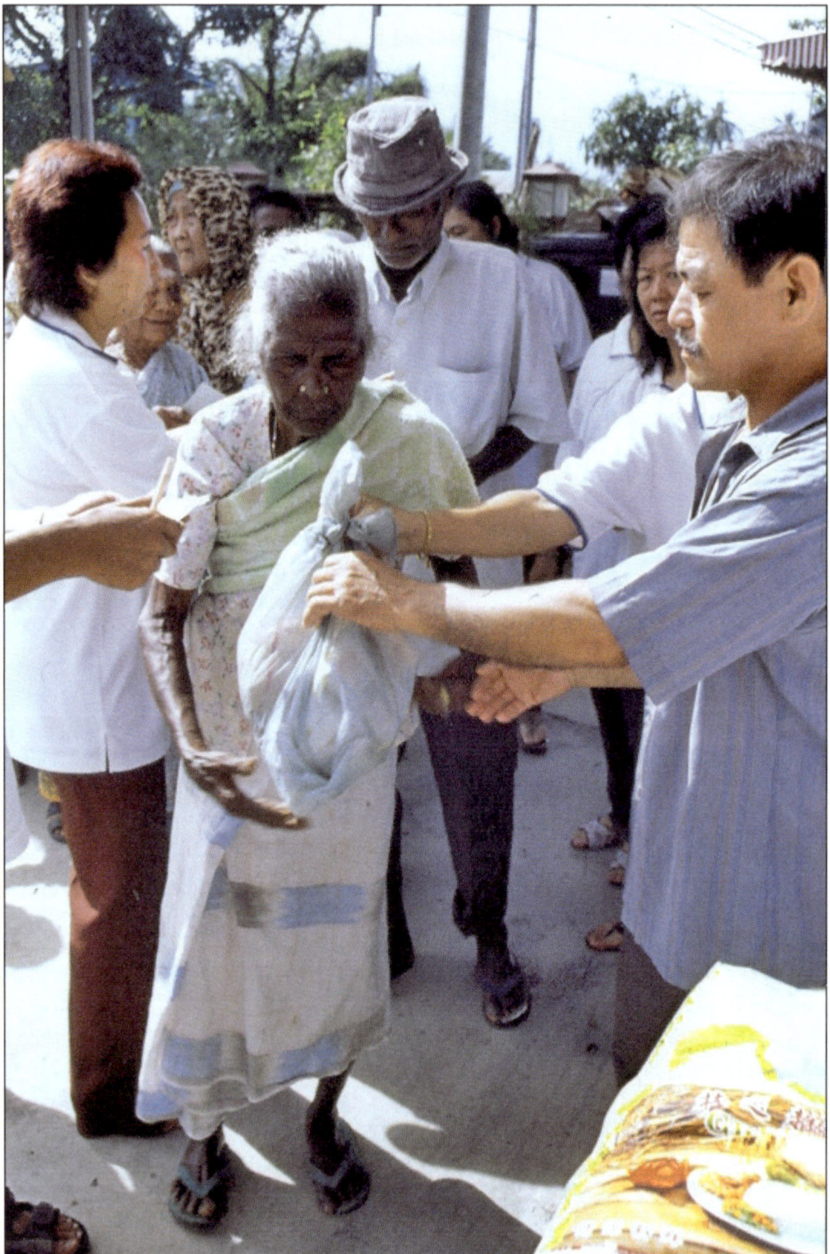

Fig. 14 Distribution of Food to the Poor, Zhen Wen Ge, Parit Buntar, Malaysia

Fig. 15 The Self-portrait of Ji Gong Drawn Through *fu ji* in Zi Hao Ge (1946), and Uncovered in 1998

INTRODUCTION

Compared to other religious movements which came out during the last century, De Jiao is small in size: in 2003 its active membership hardly reaches 230,000.[1] However, the study of a small religious organization may be of great interest from the moment it highlights patterns and dynamics of a wider range. De Jiao, which appeared as a reaction to the Sino-Japanese War and against the emergence in China of secular materialism, is a fascinating example of how people may respond to chaotic conditions or ideological threats by combining local traditions to restore what they believe to be the core values of Chinese civilization. Its founders intended to promote a new synthesis made of Confucian ethics together with Buddhist compassion and Taoist beliefs. To achieve this goal they combined in an original way institutions that had proved their effectiveness in closely related contexts: the philanthropic tradition of *shan tang* ("halls for good deeds"), and the spirit-writing technique of *fu ji* (planchette divination), which allows the reception of messages from deities.

De Jiao is also of special interest because it rapidly spread throughout Southeast Asian Chinese communities after the Second World War, and is the only *shan tang*-like association operating overseas to have acquired an international dimension. At the end of 2004, it had 142 congregations in Malaysia, 74 in Thailand, 11 in Singapore, 16 in the People's Republic of China, 3 in Hong Kong, Laos, and Australia, 2 in the United States, 1 in Taiwan, and another 1 in Japan, with 7 to 10 new chapels being inaugurated each year. This elevated rhythm of creation apart, another sign of dynamism is the fact that top De Jiao leaders in Malaysia, Thailand, and Hong Kong organized regular meetings and raised funds in the mid-1990s to reintroduce the movement in the PRC. Despite a ban imposed by the Beijing government, prompt at the time to equate it with the Falun Gong movement, De Jiao has steadily developed since 1997 small underground congregations of 30 to 60 adepts in different parts of the homeland. Having originated from China, this movement is now returning to its roots. What is particularly significant in this "boomerang process" is the constant adjustment throughout history of De Jiao to cultural "otherness" and political adversity. Built to restore cultural meaning, moral order, and solidarity in a climate of upheaval, De Jiao was later on challenged by either communist persecution or by the segregationist and assimilationist policies conducted by Southeast Asian states against the Hua Qiao (Overseas Chinese). The growth of the movement despite such unfavourable conditions raises questions about the key factors of its adaptability and dynamism.

By analyzing in this book the early history and spread of De Jiao with reference to previous studies and original materials, I assume that the answers to these questions have to do with the organizational pattern of the movement, the structure of its leadership, and the kind of mythological and ritual relationships it entertains with the motherland. One of my arguments is that part of these features result from an evolution overseas which is highly reflective of the ways the Chinese communities of Mainland Southeast Asia adjusted their activities and social structure to local economic conditions and political pressure. By discussing in Chapters II and III the spread of De Jiao throughout Thailand and Malaya, I thus show that its variable strategies of integration and its charitable activities were comprehensive responses to the assimilationist versus segregationist policies of the two states against ethnic Chinese, while reflecting the terms of the contrastive interethnic relationships of this minority with the Thai Buddhists and the Malay Muslims. Further developments make also appear that the criteria for leadership in this religious organization mirror the prominent status given to rich businessmen among the overseas Chinese, and that the strategies and other logics of action underlying its institutional expansion are strongly influenced by the Chinese entrepreneurial ethos.

But De Jiao is not only worth of interest for offering valuable insights into the conditions and changes experienced by the Chinese immigrants in Southeast Asia. Through the boomerang process of its spread and its spirit medium activities, it has also built original bonding with symbols of the Chinese civilization whose greatness it claims to champion from the periphery. Accordingly, a central theme of this study is the role that such a religious movement may play to promote new forms of identification to the motherland as substitutes for loosened genealogical links. De Jiao serves to strengthen the Chinese identity of its followers, mostly Hua Qiao, in several ways that the present book explores. Among them is the link that its pantheon establishes with two major levels of identification, namely the apotheosized figure of the emperor and a specific place of origin.

The fact that Chinese history be periodicized after imperial reigns, and that names for China and the Chinese refer to dynasties (Xia, Han ...) are good indicators of the crucial importance traditionally conferred to the emperor as a prominent symbol of identity. He embodies both the cosmological centre of power and the universally radiating power of the centre. This focus on a sovereign whose overt function is to maintain the unity and the unicity of the country explains that De Jiao, and other religious groups appropriated the millenarian theme of Guan Yu enthroned Jade Emperor, at a time when the political and cultural integrity of China was threatened. According to legendary accounts related in Chapter I, the movement was directly instituted by the new Jade Emperor with the mandate to restore morality on earth. This mandate and the fact that the integration of new members requires a "divine appointment", give the followers the feeling that they are earthly officials of a divine bureaucracy whose Jade Emperor is the supreme leader. The enactments and instructions they receive through the channel of spirit-writing reinforce this belief, which reflects upon their self-perception. Although their settlement outside China was traditionally condemned by the state as a betrayal of the filial piety and of the loyalty due to the emperor (Wang Gungwu, 1988; Thoraval, 2004), they entertain, through mediumship, a close relationship with the heart and hearth of the Chinese civilization identified to the imperial court of heaven. Despite the acculturation of these Hua Qiao to alien contexts, they set themselves up as the bulkwark of this civilization allegedly eroded by centuries of decadence. In other words, they reverse in the realm of fancy their status and the way they are perceived from China, thus arrogating the first role in the uplifting of Chinese authenticity. This self-proclaimed mission explains the recent attempt by adepts, discussed in Chapter VI, to reintroduce De Jiao in mainland China, through the geomantic setting of prospective "nodes of affinity" in potent places.

The pantheon of De Jiao is ruled by icons of the imperial power, but under their leadership, it also incorporates minor Taoist and Buddhist gods who are identified with an ancestral place of origin (see Chapters I and IV). This locus is Chaozhou, a former Prefecture in the northeast of Guangdong province which includes the city of Shantou (Swatow) and is for this reason usually called Chao-Shan, an abbreviation of Chaozhou-Shantou (see Map 1).[2] De Jiao emerged in this area and remained deeply stamped with its local origin. Overseas, its temples are mainly distributed in places where Chinese communities are dominated by the Teochew (the endonym for people from Chao-Shan); the latter still represent today more than 70 per cent of the adepts, and the Teochew dialect is the common idiom in performing rituals. Such regional anchoring indeed constituted

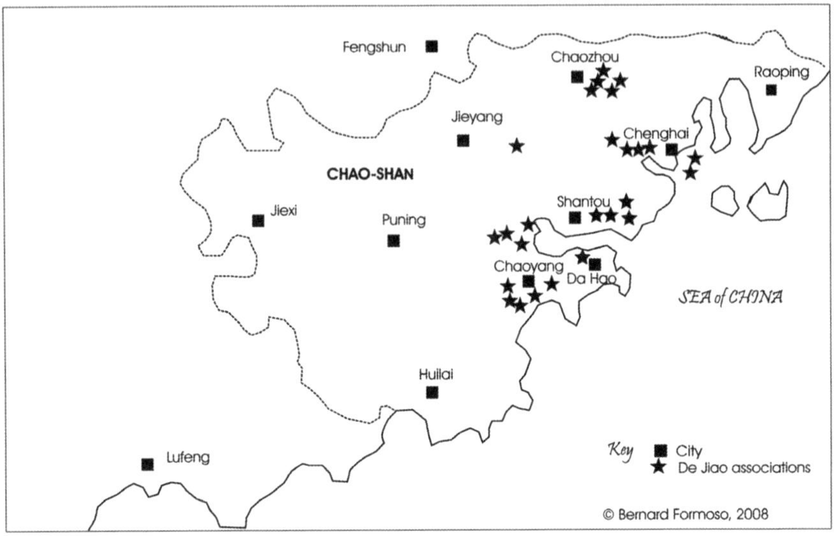

Map 1 The Spatial Distribution of the De Jiao Associations in Chao-Shan Before 1949

an important means to perpetuate abroad a dialectal identity, but it also hampered the extension of the movement to a wider audience. Hence a paradox: whereas De Jiao claims to teach universal values and some of its leaders predict that it will be the great "Chinese religion" of the twenty-first century, it is too locally oriented to really achieve such goals. This discrepancy helps to qualify the so-called instrumentalist theories. Against the utilitarian statements that ethnicity is "a strategy for corporate action" (Cohen, 1969: 27) and that an ethnic group is an "interest group" whose members mobilize opportunely common resources to maximize the achievement of economic and political goals (Glazer and Moynihan, 1975: 8), De Jiao reminds us that overt goals of social action never encompass the whole set of its effects, part of them being unintended consequences.

Besides the integrative mechanisms of what I call the *projective identity*, consisting of building new links with a distant but idealized origin on the ground of nostalgia, the study of De Jiao also offers precious perspectives on another complementary aspect, namely *contrastive identity*. By contrastive identity, I mean the diacritical features that the actors themselves regard as significant and which underlie socially effective boundaries between "us" and "them". Should we remind here that against the etymology of the term identity, the processes it describes are in no way introspective? Rather than constructed with reference to the same, they rest on series of social and symbolic oppositions which discriminate insiders from outsiders. In other words, reflexive consciousness is inseparable of the mirror offered by others.

Although the situationist approach of F. Barth (1969), and the ethnographical works it stimulated have largely documented this mechanism, the present study intends to contribute to the general debate on contrastive identity in two respects. First, it shed light on ambiguities which frequently characterize interethnic relationships, due to their polysemy and multifarious effects. In some situations that De Jiao perfectly illustrates, discrepant, but not necessarily, conflicting issues result from the activities of a community or an institution. The interethnic tensions likely to ensue can be avoided by a social control over the visibility of ambiguous practices, and by outward appearance strategies (Goffman, 1971). The content of Chapters II and III thus reveals that at the same time De Jiao gives ostentatious evidences of its identification with host countries of Southeast Asia, through displays of philanthropy, it discreetly but steadily acts as a promoter of Chinese culture among its followers and a wider circle of Hua Qiao, mostly Teochew, attracted by the various services it offers. Depending on the national contexts, its congregations make generous donations to public hospitals, orphanages, poor villages, or victims of disasters, but they also develop more discriminating activities. They serve as Teochew elders and businessmen clubs, as clinics providing acupuncture and Chinese herbal medicine, as schools teaching the art of calligraphy, Tang poetry, *tai ji quan*, or *qi gong*, or as funeral parlours whose staff perform death rituals according to Chinese customs. In so doing, De Jiao contributes to build a positive image of the Hua Qiao and indirectly makes their social integration easier, but it also strengthens the boundaries separating its followers from non Chinese. Therefore, the study of this religious movement shed light on non paradoxical mechanisms of *counter-assimilationist integration*, likely to apply to other contexts of interaction involving minorities. My argument is that the successful implementation of these mechanisms requires a good familiarity from the minority members with the cultural idiom of the dominant group; it also depends on their political and economic status within the plural society, which conditions their ability to influence the out-groups' attitudes and perceptions. The contrasted ways De Jiao adapted its activities to the Malay and Thai environments support this argument (Chapters II and III).

The second contrastive mechanism of identity that the study of De Jiao discusses concerns internal differentiation. Against the reductionist view of culture as a monolith whose properties could be deciphered through the detailed ethnography of a particle (a local community for instance), the great internal diversification of De Jiao, partly due to its dispersion and adaptation to different cultural contexts, invites us to go thoroughly into the ways social formations may maintain cohesiveness and unicity despite acculturation and internal dynamism. In Chapter IV, by describing various aspects of the De Jiao cults and by analyzing the features of its organization, I reconsider, with reference to recent theories, the relation between unity and diversity in Chinese religion that M. Freedman, A. Wolf and R.P. Weller have debated about.

Diversification within De Jiao is reinforced by a feature common to most of the *fu ji*-based "congregational systems". D. Jordan and D. Overmyer (1986: 82) relevantly pointed out that, in these systems, autonomy of individual units tends to dilute the identity of the whole. De Jiao considered as a whole is a loosely structured aggregate of cult groups. They mainly share moral and charitable goals, and a basic doctrine succinctly exposed into the *De Jiao Xin dian*, a liturgical text of only 346 characters revealed through *fu ji* in 1942. In Chapters II and III, while relating the spread of De Jiao in Southeast Asia, I argue that its high degree of internal differentiation was stressed in Malaysia by competition for leadership and ideological conflicts, while in Thailand it was emphasized by the need of mediums in a context of scarcity and by the correlative incorporation of a heterogeneous set of pre-existing charitable organizations, regardless of their own liturgical patterns. In both cases, however, the outstanding ability of De Jiao to incorporate other forms of cults partly lies in its extensive syncretism. Its pantheon theoretically encompasses under the aegis of the Jade Emperor every god, with none debarred. In Malaysia and Singapore, the Prophet Muhammad and Jesus Christ along with Confucius, Lao Zi, and Śakyamuni are, thus, its five great *shi zun*, or "honourable masters". Another important idea is that each chapel retains as gods to worship those who have chosen this specific place to teach the *de* (virtue). As a new coming "master" expresses *yuan fen* (fate affinity) with local adepts by issuing frequent messages, the pantheon will necessarily extend to him. Consequently, though pantheons may be patterned on the practice of the parent group, they are widely open to idiosyncratic forms. More generally, the compelling force attached to *fu ji* oracles applies to every detail of worship, from temple's architecture and spatial arrangement to ritual agenda, thus contributing to shape the congregations' identity. I show in Chapter IV, which is mostly devoted to doctrine and cults, that aspects of De Jiao such as a temple's committee composition, the content of prayer texts, altars' arrangements, the techniques of *fu ji* to be used, the date of celebrations, and even the nature of the incense to be burned rely on gods' writings. As M. Granet

(1950: 590) observes about Chinese religious practices, "since everything relies on congruencies, everything is a matter of preferences".

The leading function that De Jiao adepts confer to "divine instructions" induces a cult flexibility which in turn largely contributes to the outstanding adaptability of the movement to political contingencies. But the other side of the coin is a noticeable lack of social cohesion and cultural homogeneity. Less than other social formations, De Jiao can be convincingly interpreted through an organic view of community, and a reifying or monolithic approach to tradition. The serializations which, according to B. Anderson (1998: 34), underlie the "imagined communities", either national or diasporic, are in the present case so teeming and partially effective that they confuse the conceptions the adepts have of their own movement.

In relation with its crucial role in the identity's shaping, organization and development of De Jiao and other Chinese religious movements (*pai luan* sects, Yi Guan-Dao ...), *fu ji* spirit-writing mediumship is another important theme of the book. In Chapter V, I deal with the multifarious contexts and aspects of its practice. I then compare several patterns of spirit-writing, which oscillate between two ideal-types named *wen* and *wu ji* (scholars' versus warriors' *ji*). The states of mind of the *ji* practitioners, especially mediums, before, during, and after the performances are also explored by confronting their own spontaneous accounts, published by De Jiao books or magazines, with those accounts derived from interviews. The terms of their revelation and training, as well as the values they should embody are also detailed. Furthermore, I report in this chapter the last-in-date session of the "World Moral Divine Pen Meeting". This event, organized once every three years, is the occasion for mediums and delegates from the different countries were De Jiao is set up, to attend conferences on *fu ji* and to perform spirit-writing together. The session I attended at Kluang, Malaysia, in August 2004, convened during four days more than three thousands adepts and forty-five teams of mediums coming from nine countries. It was for the ethnographer a special occasion to get an overall view of the various styles of *fu ji*. The event, because of its publicity, was also a privileged arena for competing leaders to promote their respective views and interests. The harsh contest for the organization of the next World Meeting which concluded the Kluang session proved to be an interesting case in point to analyze the various leaders' stakes as well as their strategies to concentrate power and fame in such a religious movement.

What is De Jiao? This basic question still lends itself to debate between the adepts and is a factor of dissension. Is De Jiao just a "Moral

Uplifting Society", in accordance with its official English appellation?[3] Is it a "religion" which uses the ambivalent concept of morality as a catch-all subterfuge to spread its truth? In Chapter V, I report the terms of these internal debates and their important consequences in Malaysia, where they led to scission and to the attempt by a minority, inspired by the Christian example, to write a De Jiao "bible". Whereas a majority of followers believe that spirit-writing is a basic feature of De Jiao, and cannot be abandoned, others conversely consider that it should be. Their argument is that it was progressively corrupted by *ren shi wen ti* ("human affairs"), sustains *mi xin* ("superstitions"), and hinders the propagation of De Jiao as a major religion. Ironically, the "bible" that those who stand up for this position have compiled is mainly a collection of spirit-writings!

This paradoxical attitude confirms the *fu ji* techniques as an irreplaceable tool for divine revelation and institutional recognition. But the functions that spirit-writing fulfils are not restricted to these important aspects. D. Jordan and D. Overmeyer (1986: 33–6) report that the tradition of written messages from gods was first developed during the Song Dynasty (960–1279). At the time, it was embraced by the literati as a means of foreknowing both personal fate and topics on the civil service examinations. At the turn of the twentieth century, it became popularly known in Guangdong province as an efficient means to cure opium addicts. Today, among De Jiao congregations, oracular works, healing, charms' delivery, and even ghost-expelling remain the most popular issues of *fu ji*. Dedicated to the solving of individual or family problems, they usually occupy the second half of the séance, the first part being devoted to gods' commands, revelations, and moral injunctions which concern the congregation as a whole.

Finally, by relating the revival of De Jiao in mainland China from 1996 onwards, the last chapter of the book shed light on the role that spirit mediumship plays in the movement's spread, since the concept and details of this process were devised by "honourable masters". Following divine instructions, De Jiao leaders, together with teams of mediums, visited on many occasions the mainland in the late 1990s. There, through outdoor spirit-writing séances, they located the ruins of old Taoist hermitages, as well as supposed primitive De Jiao chapels, and used such "discoveries" to adjust as much as possible the loci of the new temples to be founded with ancient and divine "nodes of virtue". This fascinating archaeological expedition under the gods' guidance gives valuable insights into the role *ji*-wielders may play as "heaven's hands" to legitimize global policies and concrete decisions.

To conclude about *fu ji*, the meaning of the verse-styled messages that deities deliver is often so elliptic that it may look obscure to profane. Although their content can be approached through the mastery of conventions, their exegesis, either issued through collective or individual works, greatly depend on the status, personality, needs, and expectations of those to whom they are addressed, thus opening the door to endless controversies concerning their real meaning, and their corruption by "human affairs". However, the most important revelations of the gods concerning key events or general moral goals are printed out as parts of books and magazines. Tens of volumes of divine moral teaching and commands are thus published each year by the main De Jiao national federations and congregations. I outline in Chapters V and VI the most typical features of this spirit-writing literature, of its distribution and readership. Finally, the still incipient though increasing circulation of news and oracles through the Internet is also taken into account in Chapter VI. I then examine the social profile of the instigators of the De Jiao websites, as well as the kind of information they broadcast in comparison with that conveyed by books and magazines.

Whatever the importance of *fu ji* for this religious movement, De Jiao is not only framed by oracular, prophylactic or curative communication with gods. Charity and welfare are among its highest goals too. It is why in the first chapters of the book, when relating the historical process of its spread in China and Southeast Asia, I detail the movement's specific activities in these fields. The *shan tang* from Chao-Shan whose tradition have influenced De Jiao are deeply rooted in Buddhism. In this respect, they differ from other "halls for good deeds" developed in central or northern China during the nineteenth century and whose ethics were mainly Confucian (Yang, 1961: 335–6; Rowe, 1989: 106). According to local tradition, the first Teochew *shan tang* was created by Song Da-Feng, a Buddhist monk coming from Fujian, who lived during the Song Dynasty and was believed to have been endowed with miraculous powers.

Although the hundreds of *shan tang* that were covering the Teochew area before 1949 and which blossomed again in the 1980s do cultivate a large degree of autonomy, most are organized around the worship of Song Da-Feng and are "younger sisters" through incense sharing of the oldest temple devoted to him in Heping, a Chao-Shan township. The grouping of these *shan tang* under the same saint's banner contributes nowadays as it did it in the past to a basic identity and their close cooperation when facing epidemics, disasters, and even hostile state's policies.[4] In Southeast Asia, the groups they form often combine their efforts for better operational efficiency, while in Chao-Shan more than

150 halls have recently formed a fraternity to satisfy the same goal. Since the early beginning, prominent members of De Jiao have been active in *shan tang* and reciprocally, though the two movements have always been preoccupied with the preservation of their own identities and are actually quite distinct. I analyze the extent, meaning, and mutual effects of such links in Chapters I, II, and III. The latter section is also the occasion to interpret the range of charitable activities that the De Jiao congregations of Malaysia, Singapore, and Thailand undertake as an answer to very contrasting social, religious, and political contexts.

How to Approach a Nebula, and to Deal with Divine Instructions?

At the same time this book discusses *fu ji* spirit-writing as well as the situation and identity of the Southeast Asian Chinese communities through the case study of De Jiao, it also uses the transnational status of this movement to explore and compare forms of folk religiosity in mainland China and overseas. A brief overview of the literature on Chinese "religion" reveals that the ways Buddhist, Taoist and Confucian elements conflate into folk beliefs and liturgies remains a marginal topic, most of the scholarly works emphasizing textual traditions; hence part of my interest for these grass-root synthesis of the *san jiao* ("three teachings"), the other motivation being the fruitful connections that the multi-sites ethnography of De Jiao makes possible. The main originality of the present book by comparison with earlier studies on De jiao or other anthropological approaches of the Chinese culture lies precisely in this multi-sites ethnography. The few researches previously published on De Jiao limited the scope of their enquiry to a country or to closely related national contexts, either Malaysia-Singapore in the case of the book by Tan Chee-Beng (1985) or Thailand in the case of the articles by Kazuo Yoshihara (1987, 1988) and Lin Wu-Shu (2002). Accordingly, their account of the Chinese origin of the movement is based on few written sources. The survey by Tan Chee-Beng of De Jiao in Malaysia and Singapore is undoubtedly a thorough contribution to the knowledge of this religious movement prior to 1985. Based on extensive fieldwork, it provides valuable insights concerning the internal differentiation, competition for leadership and conflicts related to the *fu ji* controversy in the Malay Peninsula. However, it doesn't take into account the ways De Jiao interacts with the Malay environment and the kind of relations it entertains with other national branches of the movement. Kazuo Yoshihara, for his part, mentions interesting connections between De Jiao and Thai political elites, but his account too narrowly focuses on the Bangkok leading congregations, a bias that Lin Wu-Shu reproduces. While updating earlier studies, the present work intends to provide more coverage in relation with the problematic of ethnicity it privileges, and which requires both an enlargement of the research to interethnic relationships and the comparison of several national contexts.

Indeed, to set about the ethnography of a religious movement scattered all over Asia is not an easy task, especially when it has neither a supreme temporal authority to enact unquestionable decrees, nor a spatial core to legitimate a favoured relationship to the gods through pilgrimages. At various occasions, adepts from Malaysia or Thailand told me that if I failed to visit most of the congregations, I would miss the gist of De Jiao. Such assertions reflected the adepts' consciousness of the movement's religious heterogeneity, but the advice was of course impossible for a single researcher to heed. With 252 congregations distributed among eight countries at the end of 2003, De Jiao logistically escapes from a complete and comprehensive overview.

To partly circumvent this problem, I conducted in 1999, 2003, and 2004 extensive surveys among De Jiao congregations in Thailand, Malaysia, Singapore, Hong Kong, and the PRC. I thus visited a total of 86 cult communities, including logically those which at first glance appeared to be the most important from an historical, political, religious, and demographic point of view.[5] The fieldwork comprised interviews of leaders, managers, and mediums about the history, goals, management, and activities of their respective congregations, as well as about the relations they maintain with other De Jiao temples and *shan tang*. Whenever possible I attended rituals, *fu ji* séances, and various celebrations or campaigns of charity. I have also taken the opportunity on this round trip to collect books and periodicals published by the various congregations. More than one hundred journals, magazines, and collections of *fu ji* messages were gathered, and those whose content was the most interesting were partially translated. The comparison of these materials with the results of semi-directed interviews was an attempt to reduce the bias inherent in prompted answers, and to render as accurately as possible the *emic* points of view of the adepts. To make inquiries about a large number of congregations was a complementary method to mirror the polyphony of discourses and the often discordant ideas they convey. Because one of the main hypotheses of the present study is that De Jiao may be considered as a "*shan tang*-like" organization, I have extended the survey to cover Teochew chains of benevolent halls with which De Jiao cooperates, either in Thailand, Malaysia, Singapore, or the PRC.

To conduct a research among devotees, who consider that every aspects of their religious practice, including individual or collective choices, are informed by gods' instructions, raises specific problems concerning the collect of informations. In that case, the transactional relation between the ethnographer and his "objects" of study is virtually extended to a second category of partners, namely gods. In several occasions, informants rebuffed my curiosity by answering that they were simple executioners of the gods' instructions and that the question should be directly addressed to the "honourable masters". They also tried to discover the "true" goals of my research by questioning the gods on the subject. Four times, I thus received personal divine addresses.[6] I must own that I later used some of them as a visa to open closed doors and to elicit comments from followers, especially in mainland China where they were logically more reticent. The content of the messages prompted me to do so; they encouraged the research to be carried out, by proclaiming that it will make De Jiao known to a wider audience and, therefore, will facilitate its worldwide spread. In other words, the study was considered as a useful instrument to promote De Jiao itself. In this perspective, one of the oracles warned me against the danger of publishing inaccurate informations. Later on, in 2005, I was unexpectedly appointed as one of the thirteen foreign honorary councillors of Zi Zhen Ge, the "dragon head" of De Jiao in Thailand. I was informed of this divine appointment by a letter, containing a member's card made of fine gold and specifying my function.

These anecdotes exemplify the kind of takeover attempts by informants that students of religion must frequently face and manage. R. Cresswell (1976: 53) rightly noticed a fundamental difference between the social and biological sciences with respect to the conduct of research. Whereas in the latter it is possible to control unilaterally the conditions of experiments, in the former, the researcher must learn how to to be subjected to them, for the simple reason that he both works on humans and in close cooperation with them. Because of "participating observation" as a basic method of anthropology, the specialist of this discipline depends — in order to obtain reliable information — on the goodwill of other men who inevitably react, with more or less empathy, to his questions, attitudes, or initiatives. These "partners" also try to make sense of the researcher's objectives and to find some advantages with respect to his presence among them. In other words, observers are observed, questioners are questioned, and reciprocal manipulations are inevitably part of the research interaction. In such a context, to compromise between a researcher's own sentiments or ideas and those of the partners in, and subjects of his study is "not a matter of methodological commitment, it is an existential fact" (May, 1993: 78). During my own research, I indeed entered into intersubjective relationships inherent to fieldwork, and, accordingly, displayed outward signs of respect toward De Jiao gods, cults and beliefs. But respect does not mean support and subjection, and whatever the integrative pressure and takeover attempts by adepts, I tried to retain the scientific distance required. This epistemological position needs to be pointed up regarding oracles that I usually report with reference to informants' narratives. These narratives are based on the belief that gods are endowed with superior powers of divination and action and that miraculous events should ensue from their office. Although I assume that to report what is believed to be divine achievements is a good way to introduce the reader to the adepts' theodicy and faith, it must be clear that these vernacular narratives are not considered as explanory statements, but as an aspect of human concerns, expectations strategies, and forms of rationality to interpret.

Is De Jiao a Sectarian Group?

Before going ahead there is a need to characterize more precisely the religious status of De Jiao. According to its basic features, may we define it either as a "religion", a "church", a "sect", or with reference to another concept? This attempt to find an appropriate definition is not just quibbling. It is all the more useful when we consider that the few scholars to have studied De Jiao are either fluctuant or arbitrary in their characterization. For instance, Kazuo Yoshihara (1988) takes for granted that it is a "Chinese religion", whereas Tan Chee-Beng (1985: 1–5), first conflates De Jiao with Chinese syncretic sects based on the "three teachings" (*san jiao*), and later uses the term "church" to define it. Although Tan tries to characterize more precisely the movement in the conclusion of his book, the qualification of De Jiao as "a sect in the neutral sense of denomination" (1985: 70), remains confusing, the features associated to the concepts of sect and denomination being quite distincts in the sociology of religions.

De Jiao literally means the "Teaching [doctrine] of Virtue", *de* being a generic term for virtues and good deeds. According to Ma Gui-De who provided in the 1940s the doctrinal basis for its formation as a religious movement, De Jiao was the original *zong jiao*, or "religion" of China. However, the compound *zong jiao* was created in modern Chinese as a rough equivalent to the western concept of "religion" and could appear controversial when applied to a Chinese religious complex,[7] whose supreme goal is, according to K. Schipper (1982: 15): "to unify humans without dogmatism, profession of faith or doctrinal allegiance".

Actually, depending on the context, *zong jiao* may be translated as "sectarian doctrine", or "ancestors' teaching". In his article, Ma Gui-De (1997: 166–8) refers to the second meaning to argue that De Jiao transcends Confucianism and Taoism and is the supreme ethics that the forefathers of Chinese civilization have bequeathed. Anticipating the critics of Lin Wu-Shu (2002: 1–2), who objects that a sect or a religious movement named De Jiao was never mentioned in the Chronicles or other historical accounts, Ma Gui-De explains that initially the "teaching of virtue — *de jiao*" was not embodied by a specific organization, but was intrinsic to the political order. It was the unifying principle of a Chinese society of the Golden Age, which came to an end with the Three Kingdoms Period (220 AC). For him, the Confucian treatise *Da Xue* ("Great Study"), or the *Dao De Qing* (the Taoist Canon) perfectly reflect *de jiao* as a major means of that time to reach both *zhong yong* ("the happy medium") in family or society's ruling, and *xin fa* ("law of the heart") in human transactions (1997: 167). The reasoning of Ma Gui-De definitely expresses a traditional way of thinking, which echoes the statement of M. Granet (1988: 586) that in China: "Religion is not a differentiated function of the social activity."

Ma Gui-De considers that from the Qin Dynasty (221–207 BC) onwards, a progressive decline of morality undermined Chinese society despite the adoption of Buddhism, so that the people were diverted from the truth and benefits of *de jiao*. He relates (1997: 169–71) successive attempts by Confucians under the Song, Ming, and Qing Dynasties to restore moral order. But their failure and the political chaos caused during the last two centuries by endless revolts and wars created the conditions for a new and stronger reaction. For Ma Gui-De, De Jiao as a modern revival movement was this reaction. The author adds that it is a *zong jiao*, because it fulfils three requirements: (1) it refers to a corpus of "right rules" (*zheng dang de gui ju*); (2) to a well-tried method of education, both rules and method having been experimented upon by ancestors; (3) finally, to the fairness (*dang*) and benevolence (*shan liang*) of its aims. To summarize, the "religion", according to Ma Gui-De (1997: 166): "is 'the ancestors' experience' (*zu zong de jing yan*), which is applicable to everyone and which espouses fair goals".

The *emic* point of view of the earliest promoter of De Jiao is all the most significant. Although Ma Gui-De was a famous *ji*-wielder, he totally evades this activity when depicting the roots and goals of his movement. His argument is then resolutely neo-Confucian, and justifies the further claim of the organization to be a "moral uplifting society". The meaning that he confers to the term "religion" is acceptable, when related to one of the etymologies of *zong jiao*. However, this compound roughly approximates the different meanings of the western concept. Less than other Chinese religious organizations, De Jiao get closer to "religion" as a dogma promoted by a formally organized priesthood through the performance of a standard liturgy. On the contrary, it is firmly rooted in Chinese popular religiosity as it involves openness to a variety of fonts and is fundamentally syncretic. Moreover, as J. Watson and E. Rawski (1988: 4) pointed out, it is the true product of a "ritualistic culture" where the proper performance of rites (set out as "right rules" in the present case) is of paramount importance. Ma Gui-De's emphasis on correctness perfectly illustrates the remark of S. Feuchtwang (1992: 9) that: "Propriety and impropriety (...), order and chaos (...) or harmony and clash (...) in activity, but particularly in ceremony and statement, have been central to Chinese problems of authority and of identification with that authority."

Finally, as a new moral synthesis coming out from the Chinese popular religious complex, and sharing with it most of its basic features, De Jiao cannot be considered as a specific "religion". The label "church" does not suit either if we consider the view of M. Weber (1964: 173, 236) that the church is a sacerdotal and hierarchical institution, closely related to the state and whose membership is fixed by birth, irrespective of the devotees' merits and wishes. Actually, none of these features correspond to De Jiao. It has neither professional priesthood nor full-time missionaries; its membership is elective, it flourishes independently of the state and, like the Weberian sects, prefers spontaneity and innovation to stilted and solemn liturgies. On these aspects it illustrates the general remarks of M. Freedman, according to whom: "Chinese religion was in a sense a civil religion — not austere and cunningly calculated to serve political interests, but based upon a view of the interpenetration of the society and the universe, and upon a conception of authority that in the last analysis would not allow the religious to separate off from the secular." M. Freedman (1974: 40) was, moreover, among the first scholars to doubt the term "church" could apply to the Chinese religious context.

In some respects, De Jiao is close to the so called *pai luan* ("*luan*-bird worship") sects described by D.K. Jordan and D. Overmyer (1986). In both cases, *fu ji* is conceived as a divine charter to contribute to the ethical reformation of humanity. In both cases too, followers believe that they are participating in the central traditions of the Chinese culture. De Jiao and the *pai luan* sects are syncretised, mainly with reference to the *san jiao* (Buddhism, Taoism, and Confucianism). From a sociological point of view, they also share common characteristics. Both recruit at all levels of society, within intellectual or business circles, as well as inside the lower occupational strata. Moreover, partly because of *fu ji* controversy and partly because of rivalry, the internal dynamics of De Jiao and of the *pai luan* sects are fissional. New groups regularly come into existence, and the most powerful among them spawn numerous small congregations that are close in terms of their liturgical tradition, but enjoy a large degree of autonomy. Despite these parallels, however, De Jiao and the *pai luan* groups differ in several aspects.

Among the main differences, there is the fact that De Jiao was not built on the repudiation of Buddhist institutions, but conversely in close cooperation with them, in so far as the political context was favourable. Whereas D. Jordan and D. Overmyer (1988: 10) underline the trend of Taiwan's *pai luan* groups to proudly stress their separateness with contributing traditions, especially Buddhism, by claiming the encompassing status of a "new whole", De Jiao never adopted this position. On the contrary, it emerges from Chapters I and II that its founders were zealous Buddhists, who remained prominent members of Mahayana congregations throughout their life, while overseas sponsorship by Buddhist monasteries was sometimes of crucial importance for De Jiao legalization. Actually, the attitude of the De Jiao members toward Buddhist, Taoist or Confucian institutions is one of deference rather than of competition and mistrust, especially toward the Buddhist *shan tang* worshipping Song Da-Feng. Considered as a supreme religious emblem of the Teochew identity, they deserve emphatic marks of respect. We are here poles apart of the Puritan sects that M. Weber (1963: 134) characterizes with reference to their "insuperable power of resistance". Let us add that overseas, De Jiao congregations are often acknowledged, even by the Chinese *sangha*, for the "Buddhist-like" liturgical offices they offer either during annual festivals (the *Pu Du*, or Universal Salvation Festival, for instance) or during the life cycle rituals (such as funerals), thus palliating the local lack of Chinese Buddhist monks. In connection with its *shan tang* pattern, De Jiao also differs from the *pai luan* sects because of its charity benefiting society without any debarment, whereas the activities of the Taiwan sects are introspective and focus exclusively on spirit-writing.

That De Jiao differs from the *pai luan* sects is not conclusive concerning its religious ascription. Actually, the pervasive analysis of M. Weber (1963, 1964) leads us to conclude that it should not be considered as a sectarian movement. Besides the fact that it does not define itself against the religious traditions from which it stems, it does not practice as well the "universal vocation" that the German sociologist puts forward, a vocation based on the strict and common observance of moral rules, and that opposes the adept of the sect to the member of the church, where one is born and "which makes its mercy shine on the fair as on the unfair persons" (1964: 236). Although some De Jiao members are said to be acknowledged for their high degree of morality by the gods, and consequently receive an elective "name of virtue" (*de hao*) through *fu ji*, they form a minority within the congregations, and there is no procedure for excommunication for those who infringe the rules. Furthermore, the heightened rhythmic creation of new De Jiao congregations, related to their lack of cohesiveness, stand out clearly against the religious life of the sect which, according to Weber, tends to intensity rather than to spreading.

Finally, the concept of cult that American sociologists have adapted to the study of New Religious Movements approximates more to De Jiao realities, in balance with that of denomination. Both cults and denominations occupy a half-way position along the institutional continuum from sect to church. Most of the typical features that define cults, according to G.K. Nelson (1968: 355–6), could characterize De Jiao as well. As further developments in the present study will show, like cults, De Jiao is loosely structured, non-exclusive, and makes few demands on its members. Its boundaries are consequently vague and undefined, and its system of beliefs fluctuating. The philosophy of action of its members pertains, like those of the cult-type groups, to what R. Wallis (1977: 14–5) calls *epistemological individualism*, which he defines as follows: "There are (…) few barriers to doctrinal adaptation and change. Since the determination of doctrine lies with the member, cults cannot command the loyalty of their membership which remains only partially committed. (…) Resources for the control of members are lacking. Members typically move between groups, and between belief systems, adopting components to fit into the body of truth already gleaned. The loyalties of members are thus often shared between ideological collectivities, and this leads to tolerance."

The parallel between De Jiao and cults is also supported by the fact that, unlike sects, cults usually form without breaking off from another religious movement, and rather than advocating a return to pure dogma, they propose embracing something new (in this case, an original synthesis unifying major western and eastern religious doctrines under the same emblem), or embracing something that has been lost (for instance, the virtue as it was professed in the early stages of Chinese civilization). However, De Jiao lacks charismatic leaders around whom cults usually form. The focus on individual achievements and interests which is so characteristic of cults is also less emphasized within De Jiao; loyalties and doctrinal changes are mainly negotiated at the level of local factions or congregations. A parallel can be drawn in this respect with denominations. Another link is the fact that De Jiao tends to build good relationships with the state (especially in the Southeast Asian context as Chapters II and III will illustrate), and to maintain fairly friendly relationships with analogous groups (*shan tang* in the present case, but also several Teochew *shan tang*-like organizations). Other common characteristics lie in its great tolerance to theological diversity and its lack of infatuation with proselytism. Contrary to denomination-type groups, however, this movement is not the result of a schism within a religion or a church and has no professional clergy. Finally, De Jiao should be better considered as a hybrid form between denomination and cult, with possible evolution of certain of its components towards sectarian features, as I shall describe in Chapter V.

To conclude this brief discussion about concepts, let us note that from the beginning, De Jiao congregations never named themselves according to the profuse terminology which renders into Chinese the English word for "temple" (cf. Topley, 1956: 76). They neither referred to the term *si*, denominating Buddhist Chinese altars, nor to the non-Buddhist *miao* places of worshipping, or to the terms *gong* and *dian*, which mean "palace" and "temples for higher deities". In fact, the generic term they use is that of *ge* (*khor*, *kor*, or *kok* depending on the Teochew dialect they relate to), whose most accurate translation is "pavilion", an idiomatic use which emphasizes the receptive function assumed by the De Jiao congregations, through their mediumship activity.

Concerning now the gods to be worshipped, S. Feuchtwang (1992: 3–4) suggests that the term "saint" is preferable to "heroes" and "heroines" to define the Chinese deities who are personified in popular cults, for they are credited with a present effectiveness. That cures, exorcisms, and changes of fortune are sought from Christian saints as well as from the De Jiao gods' own powers tend to substantiate this thesis. Another argument is that both Christians and De Jiao devotees celebrate the annual festival of the deities they worship, and that these gods are an important ingredient of popular beliefs, conceived as belonging to the people, rather than to the clergy. However, the De Jiao's "honourable masters" differ from the Christian and Muslim saints in several aspects. First, they do not personify locality as against the outside world. Indeed, the prominent gods that De Jiao worship are figures of the Chinese folk religion and are not identified with a specific place. For instance, the offerings that De Jiao followers address to Taoist masters such as Lü Dong-Bin, Liu Chun-Fang, Yang Jun-Song or Bai Yun have no link with worship in holy places, nor are they connected with the sacrifice of a life for a faith. As pointed out by S. Feuchtwang (1992: 3), the virtues they exemplify "are not accompanied by a belief in a supreme truth, or by relics of their bodily existence. They were often martyrs, but to a loyalty, not to a faith — loyalty to friends, loyalty to principles of behaviour, loyalty to an emperor or dynasty, loyalty to family line and its honour."

Moreover, De Jiao adepts do not enter into the kind of bargaining often characterized by transactions with the saints, nor do they consider the *shi zun* they venerate as a go-between with supreme gods. Although a formal hierarchy unites members of a common pantheon with the Jade Emperor at the apex, ranking is not a preoccupation for devotees who tend to request gods separately, for powers of their own. Finally, that De Jiao devotees name the gods they worship "honourable masters", whatever their status, is symptomatic of the levelling and personalized relationship they entertain with them.

A Brief Presentation of *fu ji*

Spirit-writing being the main religious activity of De Jiao, it is necessary to provide some preliminary information concerning its symbols, its vocabulary, and basic features. Early in the twentieth century, J.J.M. De Groot (1910: 1294–1300) proposed a general description of the *modus operandi* of *fu ji* séances in Xiamen (Amoy), which does not present any major differences with the contemporary De Jiao spirit-writing performances.

Although *fu ji* may be the commonest compound to be used, De Jiao adepts also refer to the *luan*-bird's metaphor to name spirit-writing. They thus call it *fu luan* ("to wield the *luan*-bird") or *kai luan* ("to open the *luan*-bird") according to contexts. To justify such a metaphor, Malaysian followers explained to me that *luan*-bird is the usual conveyor of the Jade Emperor and of Taoist Immortals, who are the main "honourable masters" to provide oracles. This interpretation is congruent with that of LYT, one of the earliest De Jiao adepts in China (2001: 65), who adds that the *luan*-bird shares with the crane the same subtlety and that both birds are forthcoming Immortals. According to another De Jiao exegesis (Zi Yun Ge, 2001: 64), it is a very auspicious bird, whose chanting brings bliss to human souls.

As noted by J.M. Hargett (1989: 238), most western scholars confuse *luan*-bird with phoenix (*feng*), another fabulous bird popular in Chinese mythology. Although it is undeniable that Chinese poets themselves are prompt to pair *luan* and *feng* images in order to create otherworldly settings in verses, the symbols associated with the two animals are slightly different. According to E.H. Schaffer (1963: 288) the *luan*-bird is an enriched version of the Argus pheasant, and can be translated as *simurgh*, a term used in Persian legends to call a fabulous animal of comparable morphology and character. As for myself, I shall name it in further developments either *luan*-bird or "vermilion bird", incarnadine being its dominant colour.

J.M. Hargett (1989: 253–5) reports that the *luan*-bird appeared in the Taoist literature as early as the first century A.D. and by that time was the favourite mount of Xi Wang Mu, the Queen Mother of the West. It was also associated in poetry with the Confucian ideal of the "princely man" whose moral rectitude puts him high above the common flock. Progressively, its role of aerial courser soaring great distances without difficulty was extended to the transportation of a large range of gods and Taoist Immortals travelling between earth and heaven, hence its close identification with *fu ji*. Another image which also contributed to the association of the *luan*-bird with spirit-writing was its sensitivity to the pitches of musical bells. J.M. Hargett explains that: "When the bells were in proper tune (that is, when government rule was enlightened and virtuous), the *simurgh* would not only sing, but dance as well". We will see in Chapter V that analogically, it is only when the mind of the De Jiao human medium is perfectly pure and virtuous that he can fine-tune to enter into communication with the gods and make the *luan*-bird dance, that is, the divine pen to draw characters.

In practice, the *luan*-bird metaphor applies to a multitude of compounds describing aspects or issues of the *fu ji* activity. In their study of *pai luan* sects, D.K. Jordan and D. Overmyer (1988: 78–9) thus mention *luan tang* ("*luan*-bird's hall") and *luan tan* ("*luan*-bird's chapel") to name the spirit-writing places, or *chiang luan* ("descent of the *luan*-bird"), and *fei luan* ("the flying *luan*-bird") to speak of the activity of receiving divination. For their part, De Jiao adepts speak of *luan tai* ("*luan*-bird's terrace") about their mediums' altars, of *luan bi* ("*luan*-bird's pen") to designate the instrument for spirits to write, or of *sha luan* ("*luan*-bird's sand") to call, on a metonymical way, the wooden platter, sometimes effectively containing sand, which receive the divine messages. The latter are referred either as *luan wen* ("*luan*-bird's writings"), or *luan zhang* ("*luan*-bird's chapters") and *luan yu* ("*luan*-bird's instructions"), depending respectively on the gods' moral injunctions or commands.

A spirit-writing performance starts with an incantation inviting the gods to "descend into the *ji*". While two mediums silently stand by the platter before the temple's main altar, concentrating hard with heads bent and eyes closed, other male members of the congregation, gathered around, strike up the incantation. They enhance the address to the gods by burning incense and invitation messages into the altar's incense pot. Each medium holds one of the two arms of a forked branch, between 1.5 and 2 feet long and made of peach or willow wood. In the latter case it is currently called *liu ji mu* ("willow wood *ji*"). These two species of tree are believed to be very auspicious: both because they are symbols of immortality and fecundity, and because ghosts are known to fear them. Moreover, according to a prominent Malaysian adept of De Jiao, CWB, the willow tree's nodes are usually *ba gua* shaped, thus evoking the universe's charter of the *Yi Jing* divination system. The same writer adds that the willow tree embodies three specific virtues: its stems hang down to the earth, thus suggesting the polite and humble attitude to adopt during rituals; its branches on the contrary point toward the sky as a mark of braveness and straightness; and its roots sink deep into the soil, as a sign of vitality. Finally, he considers the willow as the vegetable emblem of the *Liu Ren*, one of the three divinatory magic of ancient China (2001: 79).[8]

The *ji*-wielders are a pair because they express the *yin/yang* complementary during the process of spirit-writing ritual. The medium who holds one arm of the fork with his right hand, but stands on the left side while facing the altar, is considered as the *yang* and "heaven's hand" (*tian shou*). He is commonly called *zheng ji zhang* ("upright *ji*-palm of the hand") or *qing zhang* ("pure hand's palm"). His fellow who holds the other arm of the fork with his left hand, and stands on the right side while facing the altar is considered as *yin*, and is called *fu ji zhang* ("assistant of the *ji*-palm"). As J.J.M. De Groot (1910: 1297) pointed out, he merely behaves neutrally, abstaining from disturbing the movements of "heaven's hand". When, after prayers and burning incense, the two "*ji* palms" (*ji zhang*), as they are commonly called, begin to shake, and the stick follows their movements by tracing characters, it means that the gods have "opened the *luan*-bird" (*kai luan*), by coming down.

The various supports they use, as well as the ways in which their messages are written down perfectly express the lack of liturgical homogeneity within De Jiao. In some congregations, the tray where the gods' messages are delivered is a square, symbolizing earth, and which is put on the floor with the mediums sitting down to write oracles, whereas elsewhere it is a table and the *ji*-wielders remain standing. In the latter case, the table may be square, circular, or *ba gua* shaped. The material used to write varies accordingly. Though in most cases, characters are traced back on the sand, on incense ashes, or a combination of both; sometimes it is through a thin layer of tea or holy water poured down on the platter that the gods express oracles. These messages, or *shi yu* ("instruction of imperial edicts"), are read by assistants, the *bao yu* ("those reporting the instructions") who stand around the platter and transmit them in a loud voice to clerks, the *ji yu* ("those who write the instructions"), sitting nearby. When sand is used, an assistant is in charge of levelling it after a character has been written. The readers and scribes are educated men, who are able to transcript divine language into legible human writing. However, they sometimes misinterpret the gods' wishes. To prevent mistakes, the scribes submit at the end of each sequence their interpretative work to the gods. If the latter disagree with a word or a sentence, they express their disappointment with vigorous bangs of the tip that they knock down on the tray, and set in motion with the scrawling of the proper characters. Between two sentences there are generally short blanks in the gods' statements, marked by the divine pen standing by or tracing helical circles. The behaviour of the mediums during the séance is supposed to reflect the gods' state of mind or degree of presence. Most of the time, the stick moves fast but smoothly, under the guidance of the gods holding the right hand of the main *ji*-wielder. However, under certain circumstances the "honourable masters" possess the whole medium's body, making him enter into a trance. In that case the gods demonstrate aggressiveness toward spectres or peculiar decisions by making the stick jump up and down, forth and back, and by hammering the tray violently. Conversely, the same acts may be the unexpected consequence of a spectre that takes possession or clings to the soul of the medium who holds it, thus causing the point to write inauspicious oracles. Sometimes too, the main *ji*-wielder reproduces typical behaviours of the god who inhabits him. For instance, some of those who used to be possessed by Ji Gong, the "crazy monk" of the Song Dynasty, endorse the habits of the master by drinking heavily and speaking loudly when they deliver his poems.

These remarks lead us to the question of the identity of the gods who deliver oracles. Although their identity is systematically revealed in the case of De Jiao spirit-writing, the assertion of Tan Chee-Beng (1985: 7) that the name of the deity is mentioned at the end of the message must be qualified. On the contrary, in some congregations the gods start the oracle by giving their names and surnames. Usually, several "honourable masters" come down during the same séance, the average number being two or three. Statements are ordinarily written down by using Chinese script. Indeed, Chinese (either Mandarin or the Teochew dialect) is believed to be the only idiom to render the true commands of the gods', even if messages are sometimes expressed through English, Arabic (in Malaysia), and Thai (in Thailand).

The séances do not exclusively take place in the intimacy of devotees' houses or of congregations' temples. Sometimes, especially when "warriors' *ji*" is performed, mediums shuffle through public spaces, such as urban streets, marketplaces, graveyards, and forests to chase ghosts away. In these cases, or when the purpose is healing, the mediums may use the *ji* not to address messages or prescriptions, but to expel spectres and to cure illness by applying the stick on the patient's body. They are invited to do so by written requests where devotees lay down questions and promises of sacrifice. The letters, which bear the name of the god beseeched, are burned at the altar. The pen's power can be prophylactic as well, when a brush tied to the stump of the forked branch is dipped into vermilion ink to bring happiness, luck, and positive impulse to what it strikes. Finally, the brush is also instrumental to the scrawling of good luck and protective charms on papers and pieces of clothing, either yellow or green.

CHAPTER I

Purple *qi* Coming from the East

According to legend, at the true moment when Lao Zi, straddling his blue unicorn buffalo, was delivering the 81 chapters and 5,000 stances of the *Dao De Jing*, a purple blow (*qi*) crossed the sky by coming from the East. If the title of both the book and the present chapter makes reference to such an omen, it is because this symbol of the Taoist dazzling energy was evocated through *fu ji* at key moments of De Jiao history and became one of its major emblems. The first allusion dates back to the early days of the movement, in 1939, when an oracle attributed to Liu Chun-Fang, a Taoist master of the Tang Dynasty,[1] gave the name Zi Xiang Ge ("the pavilion of the fragrant purple [*qi*]") to the first association to have been created. From this event onwards, *zi* ("purple") served as a generic term to name congregations of the oldest and main De Jiao group. Furthermore, a few months after the establishment of Zi Xiang Ge, Liu Chun-Fang is said to have addressed in this pavilion a poem to Ma Gui-De, the earliest theoretician of De Jiao as a "religion". This poem went with the command to open a congregation named Zi Qing Ge ("pavilion of the pure purple [*qi*]"). The whole message was: "Purple *qi* is coming from the East, and is sending an auspicious branch [the *fu ji* stick?], as well as a beautiful and pure [*qing*] landscape to bodhisattvas. A pavilion must be erected in the Southern breeze and brightness of the good *yang*; from this time on, the virtue will be prized in this world."[2] Implicitly, the divine command was for Ma Gui-De to propagate the *de* throughout the world for the greatest benefit of mankind. A few years after he had fled to Hong Kong to escape Communist repression, he was allegedly confirmed in this mission. Thus, in 1953, at the occasion of a famous spirit-writing *séance*, Liu Chun-Fang invited

Ma Gui-De and another prominent adept, Li Huai-De, to spread De Jiao to Southeast Asia by way of Singapore. Once again the instruction was sealed with reference to "purple *qi*". Slightly differing from the former, the poetic address was: "Purple *qi* is coming from the East, and roots of goodness blossom; it [must] move ahead southward to stand the basis of virtue." More than ten recent De Jiao spirit-writings referring to "purple *qi*" could be mentioned. Most of them encapsulate the same meaning: to propagate virtue to countries of the Southern Seas (*Nan Yang*), where a majority of Overseas Chinese have settled down.

From the metonymical and recurrent reference to "purple *qi*" should we conclude that De Jiao is nothing but a Taoist popular movement? In the introduction, I mentioned that in his writings Ma Gui-De was definitely neo-Confucian because of the moral goals he emphasized. When we take into account the background and religious orientation of the instigators of De Jiao, it appears that it was a true product of the *san jiao* ("three teachings") which characterize popular Chinese religiosity. In the present chapter, I analyze the way these three elements combined through spirit-writing and in close connection with the Teochew *shan tang* tradition, to endow the incipient movement with a specific identity. I also relate the circumstances of its move to Hong Kong and Southeast Asia, and the new turn given to De Jiao as a consequence of the interaction with these new environments. Both steps are documented with reference to De Jiao writings, complemented with oral accounts directly collected in PRC, among the earliest adepts still alive or their family.

Under the Aegis of the Jade Emperor

The movement started on the initiative of two Teochew young men of the same lineage, Yang Rui-Dong (whose adept name is Yang Rui-De) and Yang Ru-Hou, who wanted to relieve their Chaozhou fellow countrymen from the sufferings caused by the Sino-Japanese War. According to interviews that I conducted in 2003 and 2005 with sons, grandsons and cousins of Yang Rui-De, his family were well-to-do in the early 1930s. His father and uncles were active in the tea trade, owning at the time plantations and a small-scale tea conditioning factory in Fujian, as well as tea shops in the city of Chaozhou and in the neighbouring district of Chaoyang. Interestingly, the parents of Yang Ru-Hou were involved in the same business and faced comparable difficulties when, in 1938, both families fled Fujian, due to the Japanese invasion, to take refuge in their hometown of Heping.[3] After the war this move had catastrophic consequences. Because of their inability to prove land ownership, they failed to get back the plantations and thus experienced a severe drop in incomes and status. Thus, in 1947, Yang Rui-De had five children to raise, but his landholding was limited to a farm of 0.4 hectares (6 *mu*).

We can easily imagine that by requesting the gods' help through *fu ji*, the two young men were not only motivated by an altruistic desire to relieve the distress of their Teochew compatriots, but also by the urge to overcome adversity and to reverse their families' ill-fortunes. Yang Rui-De (1912–78) was however a faithful Buddhist. His penchant for involvement in religious affairs became apparent in the early 1930s when, after marriage, he managed one of the family shops near the Kai Yuan temple, a famous Buddhist monastery of Chaozhou. He became one of its active devotees, and the abbot encouraged his vocation through a prediction that he will play an important role in the propagation of the Buddhist faith. For his part, Yan Ru-Hou was ordained a monk in 1944 in Bao Ling-An, a Buddhist monastery in Heping which was renovated due in part to his contributions to the monastery's coffers. Finally, both were locally known as "true" Buddhist believers. Because of this reputation, a local artist who attended their *fu ji* sessions completed a painting in the early 1940s depicting them as bodhisattvas surrounding Śakyamuni, a painting that the sons of Yang Rui-De have kept as a precious relic (Fig. 1). But by attempting in 1939 a communication with the gods through *fu ji* the two young men were not necessarily seeking the help of Buddhist saints. On the contrary, at the time most deities opening the *luan*-bird in Chao-Shan were Immortals or other Taoist masters. Concordant accounts reveal that two or three circles of mediums were concurrently operating in Heping during the Second World War, and the eldest son of Yang Rui-De indicates that his father, before questioning his fate affinity with gods, had attended séances in the neighbourhood.

However, the approach that Yang Rui-De and his friends had of *fu ji* was empiricist. Thus, the first divine pen they used was cut down from a willow tree chosen at random,[4] and for several days pairs of absolute beginners, rotating within a group of eight volunteers, tried without success to get in touch with heaven's gods by chanting incantations extracted from prayers they obtained from books stored in the library of the Yang lineage hall. Finally, after more than twenty hours of inertia, the forked branch, handled by Yang Rui-De and Yang Ru-Hou, started to trace characters. Two Taoist masters of the Tang Dynasty, Liu Chun-Fang and Yang Jun-Song, totally unknown at the time in the Teochew area, are reported to have been the first to heed the devouts' prayers.[5] Their *ji wen* confirmed that China was already in a state of chaos and that the only way to escape it was to restore virtue (*de*), as well as to "wake up and to educate the heart of humans". To achieve this supreme goal they invited the group to create a "pavilion" (*ge*), named Zi Xiang Ge. The gods allegedly indicated a place where to find an auspicious willow tree whose forked branches would be more efficient as the gods' conveyance.

After this event, sessions were regularly organized in the Yang Rui-De house. Other gods came down: some of them frequently, others occasionally. Quickly, a division of divine work was set up: whereas Liu Chun-Fang and Yang Jun-Song were believed to cure cases of misfortune more or less related to geomancy, Hua Tuo, the famous deified physician and surgeon of the Han Dynasty, provided medical prescriptions, and Sun Wu-Kong, the monkey king, hero of the *Journey to the West*, was in charge of exorcisms. Because of its alleged efficiency in these three fields, Zi Xiang Ge became very famous in the Heping area. Thus, between 1939 and 1944 it reportedly cured more than 200 patients affected by madness (RCODJ, 2001: 30). Other miracles contributed to its fame. For instance, during the great starvation and epidemic of plague of 1943 which caused one million fatalities in Chao-Shan (*Chao-Shan bai ke quan shu*, 1994: 756), Zi Xiang Ge organized a *Pu Du* festival.[6] It is said that at this occasion, the two baskets of husked rice which the association used to distribute rations to the poor were constantly replenished, thanks to the gods' magic, to accommodate the needs of a huge populace. For his part, Hua Tuo intervened to produce charms that immunized followers against the plague. The following year, Liu Chun-Fang allegedly predicted through *fu ji* that the Japanese army would occupy Heping for eight months and invited the population to flee. The inhabitants of Yingxi Gang, the small village where Zi Xiang Ge was located, then deserted their houses to take refuge in the mountains nearby. Since 1942 and an oracle message instituting their village as the spearhead of *dao de* in the world, they believed to be the gods' elected community, a status that was reinforced a few months later by the rebuilding of the village's walls according to the geomantic plans drawn by Liu Chun-Fang and Yang Jun-Song.[7]

At the beginning, the small group of men organizing séances at Zi Xiang Ge did not consider themselves as members of an incipient religious movement named De Jiao. They just claimed the humble and common status of *nian fo she* (society for the recitation of Buddhist sutras), in relation with their background and ideals of compassion. However, as their reputation grew, they quickly attracted newcomers whose experience and motivations were different. Among them, a man whose birth name was Ma Han-Ru, and with an adept name of Ma Gui-De, played a key role in furthering the development of the association.

Ma Gui-De (1914–83) was born in Miancheng, a town close to Heping and belonged to the Ma lineage, prominent in the area.[8] Whereas Yang Rui-De was a member of a family of rural traders and his level of education was limited to four years of primary school, Ma Gui-De was born into a family belonging to the urban upper middle class, and attended secondary school. His father was an influential lawyer in Shantou and for several years was the secretary of the Shantou Chamber of Commerce. Significantly, the education of Ma Gui-De included an ecclectic mix of private Confucian studies (*si shu*), training in traditional Chinese medicine, and western-style programs imposed by the Republican government. In the late 1930s, he became headmaster of a private primary school in Shantou, and because of his background and of this position became more conscious than others about the rapid and important ideological changes which marked the first decades of post-imperial China. The neo-Confucian inflexion that he gave to De Jiao was the result of his negative assessment of such changes on the morality of the young generations.

Ma Gui-De began to attend the *fu ji* séances of Zi Xiang Ge a few months after its creation. The *Bamboo Bridge Collection*, an anthology of the main *fu ji* messages proclaimed in the earliest pavilions, reports that at the occasion of his first visit, he received the revelation from Song Da-Feng that Yang Rui-De and him were tied together by a strong "fate affinity" (*yuan fen*) (Li Huai-De, 1955: 248). According to the same source, Ma Gui-De had contracted a bad disease in 1936 and was near death, when he received the following dream-like message: "Nine purple lights have illuminated the day when the Virtue spread all over the world". The purple lights were later interpreted as the nine pavilions he founded in the Chao-Shan area. However, his real involvement dates back to the spring of 1940 when, according to the oracle I mentioned earlier, Liu Chun-Fang is said to have instructed him to open a new pavilion, Zi Qing Ge (紫清閣 – "pavilion of the pure purple"), and to propagate the virtue of the purple *qi* southward. Having received at the same time the revelation to become "heaven's hand" (*qing zhang*), Ma Gui-De took powder from the incense burner of Zi Xiang Ge to open his own association in Miancheng.[9] Through the "incense fire" ritual (*xiang huo*), a chain of affiliated "purple pavilions" worshipping the same gods was founded, but this new group had neither a common denomination nor a doctrine and liturgy.

Between 1940 and 1942 Ma Gui-De endeavoured to fill this gap. Tan Chee-Beng (1985: 18) reveals that, as early as 1940, the founder and president of Zi Qing Ge had already published an article entitled *Zhong guo yuan shi zong jiao* (中國原始宗教 – *The Original Religion of China*).[10]

In this article, the characters *de* and *jiao* were combined for the first time to name what the author considered to be the original religion of China. The focus of Ma Gui-De on the moral and educational aspects perfectly emerges from his way of interpreting the compound *zong jiao* ("religion") as the "ancestors' teachings".[11] He describes these teachings as the sum of thousands of years of experience and local practices crystallized into "well-matched rules of virtue" (*dang de gui ju* – 当的规矩) (1997: 166). According to him, the supreme goal of the believers should be to adapt such rules to the material conditions and habits of the present time, in order to promote, through education, values such as fairness, goodness, and honesty. His emphasis on teaching is also expressed in the portrait he draws of Confucius, "who never was a clergyman (*zong jiao jia* – 宗教家), but an instructor (*jiao yu jia* – 教育家) and a statesman (*zheng zhi jia* – 政治家)" (1997: 167).

Although the author refers to a wide corpus of Confucian texts mentioning the characters *de* and *jiao*,[12] he is the first to observe that the two terms were never applied in Chinese classics to a specific religious organization. His essentialist explanation is that in the early age of Chinese civilization the "teaching of virtue" was coextensive to the art of ruling, as part of a Chinese natural order of human relationships. This golden age of Chinese civilization ended with the Three Kingdoms Period (220–65 AC), that opened a long era of political instability, moral obscurantism, and cultural decadence. It is because of this secular breaking off that there is a need for "the enlightened ones" to institutionalize a religious movement whose doctrine, centred on the teaching of virtue, can challenge that of Christianity and Islam. Ma Gui-De concludes his essay by suggesting a method to propagate *de jiao*. This method is mainly based on the teaching of Confucian morality through the various levels of the educational system (primary and secondary schools, university) (1997: 178). Accordingly, one of his first initiatives after the creation of Zi Qing Ge was to collect funds among the gentry of Miancheng to open a local evening class devoted to the teaching of Chinese traditional morality (Li Huai-De, 1955: 1).

At the time however, his writings and local initiatives lacked the legitimacy that the gods would provide. Two years later, in 1942, this gap was filled during a *fu ji* séance organized into a new pavilion, named Zi He Ge (紫和閣 – "purple pavilion of those who join in singing"), that he had just created in the city of Shantou with the help of friends. More precisely, on the 22nd day of the fifth lunar month, the "Buddhas and Immortals" (*zhu fo xian zun*) went down, astride on the *luan*-bird, to proclaim the *De Jiao Xin Dian*, or "Canon of De Jiao". This *fu ji* text of only 346 characters is divided into four parts (see appendix 1). The introduction (composed of 40 characters) is called *Zhu xiang ci*, or "Incense prayer". Since 1942, followers of most De Jiao associations use to strike it up as a song in order to open a communication link with the gods at the beginning of ceremonies or during spirit-writing sessions. It ends with the following eulogy chanted three times: *Na mo tian yun hai hui zhu xian zhen* (南无天云海会诸仙真 – "We pledge allegiance to all the deities who reside on clouds and islands").

The next part is called *Qi Zan*, or "Invocation" (79 characters), which sets out the cosmology and pantheon of the incipient religious movement, starting with the fundamental complementarities of *yin* and *yang*, and sun and moon. It also mentions the "immense force" of the five elements, the deities of the five orients and the omnipotent virtue (*di de*) of the Jade Emperor "who fills the whole world and gives life to all living things". Lastly, the *Qi Zan* invites a specific divine association named *de de she* ("virtue-virtue association") to patronize the organization's rituals. According to congruent exegesis that various De Jiao pavilions have published in Malaysia (Ji Cheng Ge, 1998: 18; Zi Yun Ge, 2001: 158), the *de de* association of gods was founded by Xuan Min Gao Shang Di (a deferential name for the Jade Emperor), together with the founders of Taoism, Buddhism, Confucianism, Christianity, and Islam, as well as the deities in heaven. The Jade Emperor is the supreme leader of the association, with Guan Ping Shao-Di as the master-in-charge (*zhu cai*). The objective of the whole group is to unite the "five [great] doctrines" (*wu jiao*) in order to spread the teachings of De Jiao throughout the world so that all humanity would be united into one great family.

The third and central part of the *De Jiao Xin Dian* is the *Jing Wen* ("Scriptures"). Huang Xia-Nian (2003: 60) considers this section of 222 characters as the quintessence of the Canon. It expresses the deep compassion of the Jade Emperor who spreads his great teaching to prevent quarrels, epidemic, sickness, and suffering among humans. The teachings consist of six commandments: to refrain from cheating, falsehood, greed, rashness, arrogance, and laziness. In order to rescue all living things from suffering and misfortune, pious followers must adhere to the commandments and read constantly the "Holy Scripture". It is also the way in which they attain "enlightenment, wisdom, Buddha-hood, and immortality". The scripture ends with a eulogy, chanted three times, whose meaning is to pledge allegiance to the community of gods who take malevolent spirits away. Finally, in the "epilogue" section (*Shou jing ci*), Buddhas and Immortals praise the "immeasurable merits" of the Jade Emperor, who has established the teaching of the "purple virtue" (*zi de*) as a privileged way to gain access to paradise. Once again, this part ends with eulogies chanted three times and addressed to the *de de she*.

The structure and content of the *De Jiao Xin Dian* having been described, let us add some comments. First, the text is located within the tradition of the *shan shu*. These morality books were written through *fu ji*, and prospered from the end of the Qing Dynasty onwards (cf. You Zi-An, 1994; Song Guang-Yu, 1997; Fan Chun-Wu, 1999). They usually comprised an invocation and a presentation of the cosmogony and of the pantheon, as well as a succession of moral lectures from a wide panel of gods. The oldest *shan shu* text identified into the Chaoyang area was written in 1941 (one year before the *De Jiao Xin Dian*). It had been enacted at Ru Zong Tan (儒宗坛), the most prominent among the few local Confucian *shan tang*. This benevolent hall had been created in 1928, in the port city of Haimen, near Heping. Possibly, Ma Gui-De, as a Confucian activist, attended some of its spirit-writing sessions. Reinforcing such an hypothesis is the fact that both the Haimen *shan tang* and the Ma Gui-De's association call the Jade Emperor *Xuan Min Gao Shang Di Yu Huang Da Tian Zun* ("The most High God Jade Emperor, the Heavenly Respected One"), a quite uncommon title to assign to him. More fundamentally, the two associations adhere to the legend of the "Father Guan Yu having been enthroned Jade Emperor".[13]

According to this legend, Guan Sheng Di-Jun, also known as Guan Di-Ye, a deity who was initially a prominent warrior during the Three Kingdoms period in China by the name Guan Yu, succeeded the old Jade Emperor. The latter is said to have abdicated because he was enraged to see people being lustful and greedy, and felt powerless to cleanse humanity of its vices. Portrayed in Chinese folklore as the epitome of loyalty, courage and righteousness, usually pictured with a halberd in one hand and a Confucian treatise in the other as symbols of balance between the *wen* and *wu* facets of power, Guan Yu was an ideal candidate for his succession. D.K. Jordan and D.L. Overmyer (1986: 60) report that in many contemporary Taiwan *pai luan* groups (but this interpretation certainly applies to Mainland China too) Guan Yu is credited with appealing to the Jade Emperor to allow him to establish *fu ji* divination as a last attempt to save humanity from divine displeasure.

More recently, Wang Jian-Chuan and Li Shi-Wei (2000) investigated the origin of the story of "Guan Yu having been enthroned Jade Emperor" and its spread through Mainland China and Taiwan. They identify three possible literary sources of it. All are *fu ji* texts that *shan tang* of the southwest of China produced in the early 1920s. Among them, the one entitled *Zhong wai pu du huang jing* (中外普渡皇经 –

Sutra for the Universal Salvation of China and Abroad)[14] probably exerted a great influence on the *shan tang* of Haimen. First, because to name Guan Yu it uses a specific colloquial, *xuan min* ("heaven's vault") that Ru Zong Tan had incorporated into its own denomination of the Jade Emperor. And second, because the *shan shu* that both associations edited were entitled "Sutra for the universal salvation". Although recent De Jiao articles (Zi Zhen Ge, 1997, Li Guang-Zhao, 2003: 163) suggest that the early adepts of the movement could have learned the story from a popular millenarian book published in the second half of the 1920s entitled *Dong ming ji* (洞冥记 – "Notes on the Hell"), Ma Gui-De, Li Huai-De, and other adepts of the first generation never mentioned this document in their writings.

Wang Jiang-Chuan and Li Shi-Wei (2000: 216) suggest that the rapid propagation of the legend throughout southern China resulted from the great audience of *fu ji* texts at the time. However, the main reason for such popularity certainly ensued from its millenarian content. The legend not only legitimizes the practice of *fu ji*, it also makes *fu ji* a major instrument of governance in the hands of a strong heavenly ruler in charge to restore the moral and political order that, according to widespread opinion, the late Qing emperors and Republican governments failed to preserve. In such a context, De Jiao may be understood as an attempt to revive the prosperity of China under the spiritual guidance of a newly enthroned emperor of heaven, and through the model provided by an incipient society of virtuous devotees. Despite his increased involvement in human affairs, the Jade Emperor remains however a distant figure. Although in most De Jiao pavilions around the world, he sits on the celestial throne and occupies the highest position on the altars, receiving abundant offerings, especially on his birthday, the ninth day of the first lunar month, he usually conveys his commands to worshippers through his two chief assistants, Guan Ping and Lü Dong-Bin, and less frequently through other gods. Moreover, he never directly addresses the personal requests of individuals, whatever their status may be.

To conclude with the *De Jiao Xin Dian*, its promulgation may be considered as a decisive step toward the institutionalization of the new religious movement. From this event onward, the pavilions were not only united through a core pantheon composed of Liu Chun-Fang and Yang Jun-Song, and by a naming system based on the generic cluster *Zi-Ge*, but also by a shared liturgy. From then on, all of the congregations began their rituals and *fu ji* séances by reciting the *Xin Dian*, with the exception of Zi Xiang Ge which maintained its own invocation text. Because of its status of "eldest brother" association, it could hardly acknowledge the leadership that Ma Gui-De was implicitly claiming through his various initiatives. The promulgation of the *Xin Dian* also contributed to promote the concept of *de jiao*, without however making it salient enough to identify the movement. Such a reference came later, when Ma Gui-De moved to Hong Kong in the late 1940s. Meanwhile, the movement was usually named through the compound *Yang Liu Xian*, with *Yang* referring to Yang Jun-Song, *Liu* to Liu Chun-Fang, and *Xian* (先) to the whole community of "honourable masters".

Under the Patronage of Ji Gong, into the Fold of *shan tang*

I have suggested that the "Book of virtue" of a local Confucian *shan tang* may have influenced the content of the *Canon of De Jiao*. More tangible facts prove that since the earliest times the *Yang Liu Xian* associations expanded in close connection with urban "benevolent halls" managed by the local gentry. Thus was the case for Zi Cheng Ge (紫澄閣), the fourth association to have been created. In 1942, few months after the promulgation of the *De Jiao Xin Dian,* members of Zi He Ge who were natives of the Chenghai district received the divine command to establish this new pavilion in their hometown. Their leader, a Confucian named Wu Cheng-De (吴澄德), then tried to enlarge the number of followers and to find financial support. To this end, he got in touch with acquaintances of Ming Yang Shan She (铭阳善社), a *shan tang* created by local businessmen in 1931. Although this benevolent hall worshipped Song Da-Feng, its members shared with Ma Gui-De the same will to uplift morality. To serve this goal they had opened in 1936 a school teaching Confucian virtue and providing free books to students, the Ming De Xue Xiao (明德学校). It is said that by introducing them to the *De Jiao Xin Dian*, Wu Cheng-De attracted several Ming members to his newly created pavilion (Li Huai-De, 1955: 2). In 1945, a famine that struck Chenghai gave the two organizations the opportunity to strengthen their links. The president of Ming Yang Shan She and Ma Gui-De, carrying out a god's instructions, went to Hong Kong to raise relief funds. One month later, in Chenghai, they were able to supply food to more than six thousand people per day, while many physicians of the district obeyed the De Jiao "honourable masters", who asked them to serve as volunteers and to provide free medication to the needy. Finally, in 1948 Song Da-Feng asked the members of the *shan tang* to write a biography of Lü Dong-Bin, one of the prominent Taoist masters of the Yang Liu Xian pavilions. This message was interpreted as an order to merge the charitable activities of both associations (Zi Xin Ge, 2000: 99).

After the establishment of Zi Cheng Ge, 23 more pavilions were founded before the end of 1944.[15] This rapid growth, despite the religious restrictions imposed by the Japanese, demonstrates the great dynamism of the movement at the time, and its increasing popularity in Chao-Shan. Because of war shortages, the decorations in the shrines were far from grandiose. LXW, one of the earliest adepts, reports that the sacred items of many pavilions were reduced to an incense burner, without any statues or paintings of gods. In most cases, the identities of the latter were written on sheets of paper stuck above the altars. The pavilions were part of ordinary houses, which either belonged to followers or were rented premises. No outward, overt architectural features indicated that such buildings were being used for religious purposes. Despite this strategy of invisibility, the spirit-writing sessions usually attracted a crowd of men and women of every age and social condition. According to LXW, even Japanese soldiers sometimes disobeyed their hierarchy and attended the sessions, looking for oracles or seeking healing.

Among the associations created in 1944, four require comments. In the first one, named Zi Yang Ge (紫陽阁), an important document was proclaimed, the *De Jiao Yi Shi*, or "Consciousness of De Jiao", while in the second, Zi Hao Ge (紫濠阁 – "Pavilion of the Purple Hao"[16]), Ji Gong, the "crazy monk", appeared for the first time to De Jiao followers. As for the third and the fourth ones, Zi Yuan Ge (紫垣阁) and Zi Xiong Ge (紫雄阁), the "honourable masters" chose them on several occasions to deliver major oracles.

Zi Yang Ge opened during the spring of 1944 in Longqi, a small town in the Chao'an district. Its founder, Li Huai-De, was a locally born petty official working for the administration of a neighbouring county. As Tan Chee-Beng (1985: 16) rightly noticed, Li Huai-De became with Ma Gui-De a key figure in the spread of De Jiao not only in mainland China but also in Southeast Asia. In a paper that he wrote together with Ma Gui-De in the 1950s he describes himself as a mystic, looking for the Taoist *Xuan* (the "Unfathomable") and for the highest forms of spirituality (Li Huai-De and Ma Gui-De, 1954: 2). Among his few friends still alive, those I interviewed in 2003 confirm that he was mainly Taoist in mind and aspirations, thus counterbalancing the neo-Confucianism of Ma Gui-De.

According to the *The Bamboo Bridge Collection*, Li Huai-De attended his first spirit-writing session during the Spring Festival of 1944 (Li Huai-De, 1955: 260). The séance was organized at Zi Qing Ge, the association of Ma Gui-De. Despite his complete lack of experience, he received a divine command to hold the willow stick from that day onward. Through a mysterious numerical combination based on his age, the *ji wen* also suggested that he will be later the instigator of a "double nine".[17] It was also at Zi Qing Ge that he received few months later the instruction from Liu Chun-Fang to establish Zi Yang Ge. A pavilion which should be under the special patronage of Lao Zi must be established, the *fu ji* message concluded. Before the end of 1944, the oracle found an outstanding illustration when the same Liu Chun-Fang reportedly proclaimed, on behalf of Lao Zi, a 81-page synthesis of the *Dao De Jing*,[18] entitled *De Jiao Yi Shi*, "The Consciousness of De Jiao". A careful analysis of this document reveals that it remains very close in structure and content to the book attributed to Lao Zi. The only changes regarding the original version concern some references to the present time. Unlike the *Xin Dian*, the *Yi Shi* did not arouse *emic* comments or exegesis which could help us understand the meaning that the adepts attach to it. It may however be interpreted as an attempt to appropriate the main Taoist work through its symbolic reshaping. Significantly, Li Huai-De, after his move to Hong Kong, promoted the idea that De Jiao was invested by the Jade Emperor with the divine mission to federate under his flag the *wu jiao*, the five doctrines, namely: Buddhism, Taoism, Confucianism, Christianity, and Islam. Such an idea was, for example, expressed in the preface he wrote to the second edition of the *Yi Shi* (Li Huai-De, 1948). Later on, in the 1970s, Malaysian *de you*, or "friends in virtue", followed this view by providing a "Bible" which put together digests of the five doctrines' main holy books (see Chapter V).

The Taoist leanings of Zi Yang Ge were not incompatible with the pursuit of charitable goals. On the contrary, they allowed close interactions with *shan tang*. A *fu ji* message attributed to Liu Chun-Fang and addressed to the members of the association on the thirteenth day of the sixth lunar month of 1945 proves it. The *ji wen* proclaimed that the final chaos (*mo jie*) will not be long in coming, and urged the people to prevent it by a moral burst of great magnitude and the creation of benevolent halls (*shan she*). Reports mention the consecutive creation of several benevolent halls in Chenghai and Chaoyang districts (Li Huai-De, 1955: 276).

De Jiao developed as a religious movement and increased its social basis by producing its own Canon, and by taking over as well as reshaping the holy books of major religions. But another factor in its relative success was to incorporate into its own pantheon very famous gods of the Chinese popular complex of beliefs. Such was the case for Ji Gong (also called Dao Ji), the Buddhist "crazy monk". Recently, Meir Shahar (1998) demonstrated that this historical figure, who lived near Hangzhou, the southern Song capital, between the late twelfth and early thirteenth centuries, became after his death the subject of a large volume of writing, as a miracle worker. According to the author's thesis, Ji Gong became a very popular god, because during his lifetime he developed an exceptional and non-standard set of behaviours. He was a Buddhist monk, a fine literati, and a master in poetry, but was also insubordinate, used to drinking alcohol and visiting whorehouses. His outstanding power partly results of his ability to overlap and finally transcend most of moral, social, and political categories, as well as boundaries between the beliefs of the learned and of the people, thus allowing many social and religious groups to variously interpret his image to suit their own ideological agendas. For instance, Shahar (1998: XIV) observes that: "Whereas rebels and outlaws have highlighted Daoji's rebellious traits, authors of 'morality books' (*shan shu*) have used him as a mouthpiece for conservative values." He also notices that the popularity of Ji Gong increased continuously from the seventeenth century onward, because of the great success achieved by several novels depicting his legendary achievements.

Compared to other gods, Ji Gong came forward to De Jiao in a very specific way. Zi Hao Ge, where he appeared for the first time, is also atypical, since it merged very early with a *shan tang*, thus offering an utmost expression of the close links uniting at the time these charitable associations with the "purple pavilions". Zi Hao Ge was created soon after Zi Yang Ge, more precisely the eighteenth day of the fourth lunar month of 1944. His founder and first president was an old friend of Li Huai-De, named Wu Zui-Jiao (吴醉樵). He was a prominent member of the most influential lineage established in the harbour of Da Hao. He successfully passed the *ming shi*, a high graduation in the mandarin exam system, and occupied high positions in the territorial administration up to the end of the 1920s. Afterwards, he managed the businesses and real estates of his family. According to what his last son told me, he was both a pious Buddhist and a fervent supporter of Confucian doctrine. In 1939 he created a benevolent hall named Cong De Shan Tang. This association, located in a natural area of Da Hao called the "Eighteen Caves", provided food, free medical care, and coffins to the victims of disasters. In 1943, during the famine which caused one million casualties in the Shantou area, Mr. Wu distributed rice bags and other basic necessities to thousands of people. Later on, he opened an orphanage with a primary school that received over 200 children.

Because of his ties with Li Huai-De, Wu Zui-Jiao regularly attended *fu ji* sessions at Zi Yang Ge. It is there that he received the gods' instruction to found Zi Hao Ge. After a few months, the house they had rented to settle the association was sold and they moved their headquarters to Cong De Shan Tang. Then, the two associations, which already shared the same president, decided to merge their activities, *fu ji* teams, and pantheons. The cult that Cong De Shan Tang devoted to Song Da-Feng and Ji Gong was therefore enlarged to Taoist deities including the Jade Emperor, Liu Chun-Fang, Yang Jun-Song, and other Immortals. In fact, Cong de Shan Tang was at the time one of the few benevolent halls of the Chao-Shan area to worship Ji Gong. Its members had started the cult in the early 1940s, after the reported miraculous curing of one of their leaders by the Buddhist saint.

However, the patronage of Ji Gong remained insignificant up to the eighteenth day of the first lunar month of 1945. On that day, a message attributed to him denounced the privative accumulation of wealth. The *ji wen* also encouraged Zi Hao Ge to sponsor new pavilions, as well as every kind of good deeds to improve life on earth (Zi Xin Ge, 1955: 272–3). But his most famous appearance occurred on the ninth day of the ninth month of 1946. A *ji wen* from Song Da-Feng had previously informed followers that Ji Gong will show himself. On the indicated date he reportedly appeared, standing on a cloud, directly above a hill, west of the outdoor spot where the adepts were gathered. According to the last witness still alive, LLZ, the second president of Zi Hao Ge, spirit-writing was immediately performed. LLZ reports that Ji Gong expressed the wish to paint a self-portrait and asked for rice paper, ink, and brushes. He started to paint his picture, but after a while he suddenly interrupted his work. The mediums asked what the matter was. He answered by indicating the colours that should be used in the painting and their layout to complete the painting. In the context of Communist repression of the 1950s, a member of the association kept the precious painting concealed in his house. In 1998, LLZ uncovered it and distributed hundreds of printed copies overseas, among the De Jiao associations and temples worshipping Ji Gong (Fig. 15).

Crazy Ji is one of the few Chinese gods to have sparked collective visions in modern times, and the only one that I know who is believed to have made his own portrait through *fu ji*. In 1933, the same Ji Gong appeared to a man through a dream, indicating that his portrait had been drawn in a cave near Hangzhou. The man visited the cave with a photographer who took pictures at random in the cave's darkness. When the film was processed, the god's form was miraculously observed on one of the pictures. The fact that since the Ming dynasty folktales about Ji Gong depict him as a non-conformist monk, who shared the imperfections of ordinary folk and lived the life of the poor made him a more approachable and more "human" god than others. That devotees pretend to observe him under certain circumstances is therefore not surprising. In the same way, some people in contemporary China claim to be a reincarnation of Ji Gong. Among them, a man whose religious name is LD must be briefly mentioned. In the early 2000s his organization developed a close relationship with De Jiao associations overseas, and he refers to the Ji Gong painting of Zi Hao Ge to legitimate his claim to be a "living Ji Gong".

According to his autobiography, LD was born in 1928 in Chongshan, the hometown of Sun Ya-Tsen. The first dreamlike message he received from Ji Gong dates back to the Cultural Revolution, and concerned the preservation of a precious statue of Buddha. At the time, however, he lived as a beggar, and in the late 1980s came very close to death because of a brain stroke. Then, according to his claim, Dao Ji miraculously cured him. In exchange for this favor, he was instructed to nurture charitable activities in the Pearl River area. Some time later, he secretly moved to Macao and from there to Hong Kong. Acknowledged for his oracles and miraculous healings, he managed to raise funds that he used either to build large religious centres (the biggest, located on a hill near Chongshan, has 10,000 statues of arahant) or to finance charitable activities, especially in mainland China where he sponsored the building of schools.

In 2000, LD fortuitously got in touch with the main De Jiao association of Thailand, Zi Zhen Ge. At the time, one of his assistants visited a friend of hers in Bangkok who was a member of Zi Zhen Ge. During her stay, they attended there a weekly *fu ji* session. The Hong Kong lady was very impressed by the performance of the main *ji*-wielder who regularly embodies Dao Ji. Two years later, she received from the same medium the message that "Ji Gong is LD and LD is Ji Gong". Because of the great fame of this medium from Thailand to Taiwan, such an oracle was an important factor of the legitimization for LD in his claim to be the "living Ji Gong". Another argument was a malformation he has on his right wrist and which was similar to the very specific wrists that Ji Gong had revealed on the Zi Hao Ge painting (Fig. 15). These "proofs", that LD plays up with great skill, have logically led to a close cooperation between his organization, Dong Kai Yuan, and some De Jiao associations.

In revisiting the history of Zi Hao Ge, it should be noted that a year after the episode of the Ji Gong self-portrait, Wu Zui-Jiao passed away. A few months before his death, a *ji wen* addressed to him was interpreted *a posteriori* as a tribute from Ji Gong to his charitable work, and an allusion to his forthcoming departure to heaven. Later on, the poem was carved on stones surrounding the terrace where the mediums had brushed the master's portrait. It can still be seen in the Eighteen Caves. LLZ replaced him as president of the association. He was the son of a rich businessman of Da Hao, managing both fisheries and stone carving, and had worked between 1935 and 1940 as a broker in Vietnam. A few months after his return, he involved himself in Cong De Shan Tang, and from there in Zi Hao Ge. His life as a follower was a tragedy, but he played a key role in articulating the early history of De Jiao in China through research on its origins that overseas adepts implemented in the late 1990s. For this reason, I shall come back to him later.

Finally, Zi Hao Ge anticipated further trends of De Jiao, by proving to be very adaptable to local conditions and by incorporating new figures into its pantheon. These gods, as it happened, were not only "members of the team", they also assumed locally the divine leadership, thus inflecting new developments. Whereas Ma Gui-De promoted neo-Confucianism, and Yang Rui-De, Li Huai-De, or others favoured Taoist cults, Wu Zui-Jiao and his fellows put in the limelight saints of the popular Buddhism, such as Song Da-Feng and Ji Gong. It is also during one of the spirit-writing séances of this congregation that a *ji wen* mentioned Christianity for the first time, by teaching that all the religions come from the same source (Li Huai-De, 1955: 264).

Interestingly, Liu Chun-Fang is said to have instituted an influential member of Zi Yuan Ge, the next De Jiao association to be examined, as "spirit of the Eighteen Caves" after his death. This man, who had passed the *ju ren* of the classic exam system, used to teach Confucian precepts to the members of his lineage. He was a very close friend of Zhang Xiang-Yao, the first president of Zi Yuan Ge. This latter was a business tycoon of the Teochew township of Gezhou who had successfully expanded his activities to Vietnam and, at the end of his life, was devoting a lot of time and money to philanthropy. The pavilion was established on the first day of the sixth lunar month of 1944. Two years later, in 1946, Li Huai-De visited this association several times: on the first occasion to organize the succession of Zhang, and on the second occasion because he had received a divine instruction to found a *shan tang* named Ming De in Gezhou. He succeeded on account of the financial support of leaders and worthies of three towns. The benevolent hall began to provide food, coffins, and free medical care to the poor.

At the occasion of one of these visits, he was performing spirit-writing together with Ma Gui-De when suddenly their Y-shaped willow stick split into two. This extraordinary incident was variably interpreted, depending on events that adepts were willing to emphasize. For certain Singaporean and Malaysian followers, the splitting of the willow stick was the forerunner of the ban on the practice of *fu ji* that Lü Dong-Bin imposed to them 20 years later.[19] However, for most "brothers in virtue", the message confirmed that Ma Gui-De and Li Huai-De will separate soon, and that they will promote De Jiao overseas through different ways. They refer to an earlier revelation, made in 1945 at Zi Xing Ge (Chenghai), according to which Ma Gui-De should be responsible for spreading De Jiao in Hong Kong, and Li Huai-De for the same work in Southeast Asia (Li Huai-De, 1955: 3).[20]

Finally, Ma Gui-De moved in 1947 to Hong Kong, where he founded a new pavilion with the help of local Teochew businessmen. As for Li Huai-De, at the end of 1946 he stayed for three months in Vietnam with the new president of Zi Yuan Ge to collect funds on behalf of the *shan tang* of Gezhou, and from Saigon he migrated to Singapore. A few years later, he established there the first local De Jiao association, which afterwards served as a bridgehead to spread the movement throughout Malaysia.

Zi Yuan Ge apart, another association played an important role to prophesy the spread of De Jiao toward Southeast Asia. Its name was Zi Xiong Ge. This association had been founded in Shantou by Ma Gui-De and members of the local Chamber of Commerce during 1944. One of its first and most famous spirit-writing sessions was organized for the thirteenth day of the fifth lunar month of 1944. That day "honourable masters" reportedly drew, through *fu ji*, 20 pictures of cocks whose task was to sing for peace (Li Huai-De, 1955: 266). Another important revelation occurred one year later when Confucius, Śakyamuni, and Lao Zi straddled the *luan*-bird, and allegedly asked Zi Qin Ge (Ma Gui-De) and Zi Yang Ge (Li Huai-De) to spread the teaching of *de* to Singapore, Malaysia, and Thailand. The masters added that Ma Gui-De and another adept, Zhang De-Ze, would play a key role in propagating the virtue in Hong Kong.

Among the earliest members of Zi Xiong Ge, two individuals require attention. When I conducted the enquiry, both were still alive, and I was fortunate enough to collect their accounts. LYT, the first one, fled to Hong Kong in 1953 to escape the Communist repression. In 1976 he founded in Kowloon a pavilion whose name, Zi He Ge, was the resumption of the one where *De Jiao Xin Dian* had been proclaimed in 1942. Later, between 1990 and 2003, he proved to be very active in reviving De Jiao in the PRC. I shall deal with his history and initiatives in more detail later. As for the second, LXW (his name of adept being LDeW), he was the man who introduced the movement in Thailand. He was born in Siam in 1913, from a Teochew father and a Siamese mother.

The father was an export wholesaler of preserved seafood and owned a small canning factory in Bangkok. According to a strategy recurrent among Chinese immigrants of that time (Formoso, 2000), he sent his son to Chao-Shan and entrusted the young boy to the care of the Chinese wife that his lineage had prompted him to marry before leaving. The idea was to ensure him a good Chinese education. Because of this decision and of successive wars, LXW remained in Chao-Shan from 1918 to 1945. During the Japanese occupation and its attendant tragedies, he had a moral awakening and got involved in the charitable activities of various *shan tang*. When Zi Xiong Ge was created in the urban district of Shantou where he was living, he attended its spirit-writing sessions. In 1945, he was getting ready to embark on the first ship about to sail from Shantou to Bangkok when the Taoist master Bai Yun (White Cloud) sent him the order to develop the teaching of virtue, and to promote charity in Thailand. The "heaven's hand" who received the divine message was a 13-year-old boy. This young medium drew a picture of Bai Yun and wrote divine poetry. LXW should bring with him these religious paraphernalia and incense powder in order to open in Bangkok a temple named Zi Chen Ge (紫辰阁). By his own recollection, LXW dreaded the heavy responsibility that the gods entrusted to him, and demonstrated his reluctance to do it. But the "honourable masters" are said to have made his fear disappear by asserting that they would take care of everything. They added that if necessary Bai Yun would appear under the form of a white wild goose to help him. At the beginning, LXW devoted a room of the family's back-shop to the cult of Bai Yun, Liu Chun-Fang, Yang Jun-Song, and Wu Meng-Wu, another Taoist master who had expressed the wish to be worshipped in the new pavilion.[21] But it was only when he hired immigrants, native of his village in China, that the cult gained in importance. Fortunately, among them there was an illiterate man, named XLC, who proved to be an inspired *ji*-wielder. His outstanding ability in this aspect was interpreted with reference to divine intervention.

Communist Repression and Redeployment to the British Colonies

During the turbulent times which followed the end of the Second World War in China, the situation of De Jiao was necessarily precarious. The failure of a coalition government and the consecutive resumption of civil war at the end of 1946 weakened De Jiao's position. By speaking in favour of a utopian society based on the strict observance of Confucian values and whose model was to be found in the "great imperial China" of ancient times, the theoreticians of the movement were endorsing positions totally antithetic with the orientations of the Chinese Communist Party, whose political agenda involved erasing all traces of the *ancient régime*. They were not in agreement as well with the occidentalism that a majority of the Guomingdang leaders professed. Such ideological divergences had terrible consequences for some adepts after 1949. "Brothers in virtue" who did not flee Chao-Shan paid a heavy toll during the counter-revolutionary campaigns of 1951. Several of them perished in the "rehabilitation camps" where they had been imprisoned, while others saw their lives irreparably changed. Such was the case for the founder of the movement, Yang Rui-De. Charged as a landowner and a purveyor of superstitions, he was a victim of the campaign "to break the four kinds of archaisms" (*po si jiu*). His family was subjected to public séances of criticism (*pi dou*), and during one such session his wife died because of excessive harshness. In 1956 he was assigned to a cooperative as an agricultural worker. Finally, after decollectivization he received a tiny plot of one *mu* of agricultural land for his livelihood.

Even more tragic was the destiny of LLZ, the second and last president of Zi Hao Ge (Da Hao). He was the youngest among a group of six brothers and inherited part of the businesses that his father managed before his death in 1946 (stone carving, fisheries, and salt trade). He was a rich man with assets abroad, but was also a religious activist, and one of his brothers was a member of Yi Guan-Dao. They were considered *di zhu fan dong hui dao men* (地主反动会道门 – "revisionist landlords involved in superstitious activities"). In 1951, when the counter-revolutionary campaigns began, both were imprisoned in the north of Guangdong province. At the time, LLZ was married and was the father of three sons. Malnutrition and illness killed two of them during his internment, and his brother, the aforementioned member of Yi Guan-Dao, perished as a consequence of ill-treatment. Furthermore, in 1957, the same year he was transferred to a reeducation camp, his wife passed away. LLZ remained in this camp for twelve years and from there moved to a cooperative of the district of Puning (Chao-Shan). Finally, he was released in 1979, at the age of 60. He had been deprived of his freedom for more than 30 years, had lost four close members of his family, and was economically ruined.

Very early, Ma Gui-De and Li Huai-De, the two instigators of the movement, understood that the situation in China was becoming progressively unbearable, and decided to leave the country. Ma Gui-De moved to Hong Kong in 1947. Officially it was just a temporary stay to establish Zi Yuan Ge (紫苑阁), a new association that Liu Chun-Fang had ordered him to found on Victoria Island. But he quickly got a resident permit sorted out, due to the help of influential local businessmen. He also set himself up as a specialist of traditional Chinese medicine in Hong Kong, a skill that he had acquired in his young age and which was in high demand, especially when the practitioner was a famous medium. The move was actually for him a new start. Significantly, before leaving Chao-Shan he took bags of incense powder from both Zi Xiang Ge (the Yang Rui-De association) and Zi Qing Ge (the first pavilion he had himself founded). By this symbolic gesture and the "incense fire" rituals it anticipated, he guaranteed a link of consubstantiality between the endangered institutional roots of the movements and the next overseas associations to come.

The *fu ji* sessions of Zi Yuan Ge attracted many members of the Teochew community in Hong Kong and, after few months, it raised enough funds to supply the poor with cotton clothes and to manage a dispensary providing them with free medical care (Li Huai-De, 1955: 4). One year later, in 1948, an umbrella organization was created which was in congruence with Hong Kong regulation on associations. Its designation, Xiang Gang De Jiao Hui (香港德教會 – "De Jiao Association of Hong Kong" or XGDJH) marked a turning point in the structuring of the movement. It was the first time that one of its institutions was called De Jiao. Henceforth, the designation of the whole movement referred to a universalistic ambition: the teaching of "virtue". During the succeeding decades, the organizations whose main goal was to federate the pavilions at a national or international level systematically used De Jiao as a unitary label.

Whereas Ma Gui-De and his fellows promoted such a shift in ambition and scale, other leaders tried to transfer the institutional roots of the movement from China to Hong Kong. The first such attempt occurred in 1952. At the time, some of the XGDJH members, due to differences in opinion over financial matters, broke away and formed an association whose name, Zi Xiang Ge, was identical to that of the Yang Rui-De pavilion. To legitimize the "transfer" abroad of the oldest "purple pavilion", they indeed put forward a supreme gods' instruction. They also actuated their shrine with incense powder that they had obtained directly from the Yingxi Gang mother-temple a few weeks before its closure by the Communists. The resort to the notion of "transfer" follows closely the compound *ban jia* (搬家 – "to move"), that my informants used to name the process. Such a move is exceptional and implies a special permission of the gods who instructed the foundation of the initial *ge* and patronized it afterwards. Each new pavilion is supposed to receive from its heaven's patrons a specific name acting as its fundamental identity. A shared naming would augur ill for both associations, because of the chaotic merging of their respective fates that such appellations would entail. It is why the De Jiao associations never share their names with other affiliated associations from the past and the present. I have mentioned one exception to this rule. The second and last one also took place in Hong Kong. In 1976, Liu Chun-Fang reportedly asked for the move to Hong Kong of Zi He Ge, the association where the *De Jiao Xin Dian* had been promulgated in 1942 and which had ceased activities in the early 1950s. With this double move, Hong Kong became for De Jiao the substitutive heartland of both its *spiritus* (i.e., the flow of virtue the gods insufflate) and *doxa* (the canon they teach). The fact that none among the congregations of Southeast Asia challenged this role proves that they unanimously recognized Hong Kong as a substitute homeland. The only breach to this consensus occurred in 1997 when a group of prominent leaders of De Jiao from Malaysia and Thailand supported the "rebirth" of Zi Xiang Ge in Yingxi Gang. But in this particular case, it was heralded as a symbolic act involving a return to De Jiao's roots in mainland China. Lending credence to this move was the fact that the president of this new Zi Xiang Ge was one of the Yang Rui-De grandsons.

The continuity with the historical roots of the movement that the move to Hong Kong ensured was strengthened by the influx in the British colony of many adepts between 1947 and 1952. For instance, the president of Zi Cheng De and of Ming De Shan She in Chenghai, Wu Cheng-De (吳澄德), was going to be arrested when he fled to Hong Kong with his family in 1952. His son, WMY was a founder of Zi Jing Ge (紫靖阁), one of the three De Jiao congregations still active in Hong Kong, and is up to now its main *ji*-wielder. LYT, who was secretary of Zi Xiong Ge in Shantou, is another example. He arrived in 1950 and is now president of Zi He Ge in Kowloon. Even Li Huai-De stayed in the colony for several months, after his trip to Vietnam and before his move to Singapore in 1948.

A high proportion of these refugees were *ji*-wielders. Thus, they reproduced in Hong Kong the mushrooming of mediums' circles and related pavilions which characterized the early spread of the movement in China. One of the main purposes of the XGDJH was precisely to federate and to channel the activities of these small congregations. Kazuo Yoshiwara (1988: 201) reports that, in the early 1950s, 20 to 30 associations belonged to the organization. Most of them have disappeared since. That period was a privileged moment of introspection because of the gathering in one place of most of the instigators and early leaders of the movement, and because of the trauma and breaking off due to Communist repression. Records reveal that Ma Gui-De, Li Huai-De, Wu Cheng-De and others had frequent talks about the future of the movement, and took initiatives which inflected heavily its new orientations. The adaptation of some prominent adepts to the Singaporean political and cultural context also contributed to this change. Between 1948 and 1953 more than 20 "brothers in virtue" moved from Hong Kong to the biggest harbour in Southeast Asia. Among them, three young *ji*-wielders played a key role in spreading the movement locally. These three men were: Li Huai-De, Zheng Chang-Jia (郑长家), and CLJ, who was a former secretary of Zi Cheng Ge, the association of Chenghai. All three settled down in Singapore in the same year, 1948. Li Huai-De worked as a general broker for a trading company based in Hong Kong, while CLJ started a brilliant career as a physician and specialist in Chinese medicine. Because of this occupation that he shared with Ma Gui-De, both men maintained close relations, the former relying partly on the latter for his medication stores. According to reports, Ma Gui-De shuttled back and forth between Hong Kong and Singapore several times yearly in the 1950s, thus creating the conditions for regular meetings with Li Huai-De and his colleagues.

At the beginning, the three mediums maintained communication with "honourable masters" through spirit-writing séances they regularly performed in Li Huai-De's house. Oracles and healing sessions were provided to satisfy increasing popular demand. However, it was only at the end of 1952 that the first pavilion of Singapore and Malaysia was founded: Zi Xin Ge (紫新阁 – "New Purple Pavilion"). A few weeks before, Li Huai-De made a business trip which took him to Thailand and Hong Kong. In Bangkok, he visited LXW and his friends who had, like him, practised informal spirit-writing for years, but had inaugurated Zi Chen Ge a few months earlier. Thinking about founding his own pavilion in Singapore, he sought advice from them and in view of such a possibility took incense powder from their altar. In Hong Kong, Ma Gui-De referred to the prophecy of the broken willow stick and encouraged him. Back in Singapore a planchette session delivered a divine instruction, while the same day a *fu ji* session organized at XGDJH, in Hong Kong, specified the name of the forthcoming association and the date of its opening ceremony. At this occasion, a *ji wen* attributed to Liu Chun-Fang referred to the "purple *qi* coming from the East".[22] Interestingly, that opening day, incense powders coming from the XGDJH and from Bangkok were mixed together to give life to the shrine. In the following years, Zi Xin Ge served as the mother-temple for the new pavilions to be created in Malaysia and Singapore. It also participated actively in the new impetus given to the movement in the early 1950s. At the time, Ma Gui-De, Li Huai-De, and their colleagues were facing a twofold challenge: to preserve the unity of the organization overseas, but also to introduce new objectives for it, if not a new dimension. Indeed, the dream of Ma Gui-De to reinstate Confucian morality and through it the great civilization of the forefathers had less chance than ever of being fulfilled. The Communist takeover had swept away any such prospect. Consequently, other supreme goals had to be found. A strong sense of unity and uniqueness also had to be instilled among "brothers in virtue" to make up for uprooting and scattering.

Out of their Teochew homeland, Ma Gui-De and his friends discovered another more urban, cosmopolitan, and westernized China. In Hong Kong and Singapore, Chinese communities were thriving under British rule, while the adepts of several religions lived together peacefully. Democracy seduced Ma Gui-De. In a paper entitled "Introduction to De Jiao", he wrote: "in the world of the twentieth century, democracy has developed so far that all the ideas which hamper freedom, equality and justice can not dominate anymore." He added that: "Everybody needs freedom and equality, but the freedom of some cannot hinder that of others." The true freedom, according to him and with reference to the Confucian concept of self-rule (*jie gui*): "consists in showing respect for the others' choices" (1997: 173).

To take an interest in Christianity and Islam was all the more necessary in Hong Kong, Singapore, and Malaysia, where the rulers and natives were in large part believers of one of these two religions. Going deeper into the knowledge of their respective values, moral dictates, and taboos, as well as their history, philosophy, and soteriology could provide keys for a better integration in the host country. Ma Gui-De and his fellows were also willing to grasp the features which made possible the worldwide spread of these "great religions". The purpose was to adapt such characteristics to their own religious movement in order to strengthen its unity and to enlarge its audience. One of the main features that Ma Gui-De identified is the "elevated doctrine" that Buddhism, Christianity, and Islam preach "to strengthen confidence and faith among their adepts" (1997: 174). From the beginning the doctrine of De Jiao had been formulated in the hazy terms of "the teaching of virtue". In China, depending on adepts, the focus concerning "virtue" was on Confucian morality, Buddhist compassion, or Taoist immanent *dao de*. But whatever the *doxa* emphasized, the beliefs remained "particularistic" in the sense that they exclusively referred to the Chinese religious complex. Overseas, the theoreticians of the movement remained faithful to the concept of *de jiao* ("teaching of virtue"). The latter even became the name of the "religion" they were proclaiming. This label, because of its vague content, was perfect in the sense that it could facilitate the introduction of changes under the appearance of continuity.

Toward a New Ambition?

Along this line, Ma Gui-De and his fellows broadened the religious scope of the movement. More precisely, they developed its supreme goals from a particularistic concern toward an overt universal ambition. The "virtue" that De Jiao acknowledged was henceforth extended to Christianity, a religion that Ma Gui-De considered to be at the vanguard of universal love, and to Islam which he thought to be to the forefront of merciful pity (1997: 174). From a syncretism limited to the *san jiao* (Taoism, Confucianism, and Buddhism), he thus attempted to shift to another one, more encompassing, which included the monotheist religions of the West, and was called *wu jiao* ("five doctrines"). One possible covert goal of this augmentation of doctrinal breadth was to provide an opportunity for recent immigrants who were De Jiao adherents to offset their status of soon-to-be-integrated aliens by symbolically amalgamating with their own system of beliefs religious ideals from the host societies. Interestingly, the shift from *san* to *wu jiao* never found an echo outside the places where it was politically functional: Hong Kong, Singapore, and Malaysia. Even in these places the western doctrines, although formally recognized by the congregations, were never taught and were taken into account only marginally for the conduct of rituals. As Tan Chee-Beng (1985: 2) had already pointed out 20 years ago: "There was the additional worship of Jesus Christ and Prophet Muhammad as deities, but the Christian and Islamic doctrines were hardly adopted."

Indeed, Ma Gui-De had to justify such an extension. He argued that De Jiao is transcendent (*chao zong jiao* – 超宗教). Its true significance would be to spread the teaching of good deeds among the people whatever the idiomatic dogma they refer to. According to his point of view, humanism is the common basis of the five great religions and to act accordingly is "to satisfy the 'heaven's heart' (*shang wei tian xin* – 上慰天心)" (1997: 186). But few are those who fit this requirement. In a *fu ji* oracle promulgated in 1944 at Zi Hao Ge, the "honourable masters" regretted that each religion "stands at its own gate" (*ge li men hu* – 各立门户) (Li Huai-De, 1955: 265). Against this trend, the divine mission of

De Jiao would be to guarantee the "great universal harmony" (*da tong* – 大同). To achieve this end, four main objectives were identified in the early 1950s. They are usually enunciated as a preface to the *De Jiao Xin Dian* in the booklet given to the followers, especially in Malaysia and Singapore. These objectives are: (1) to believe in the holy sages of the five principal religions; (2) to carry out educational activities with the object of guiding the people towards benevolence and high morality, and teaching them to cultivate their character and to practise the *dao*; (3) to organize social charity and welfare works with a view to relieving the people in poverty and distress; (4) to work for the welfare of the members of De Jiao and to instill in them a congenial passion for building up morality.

The syncretism extended to western religions that De Jiao displays is far from unique in the Asian context. On the contrary, it is one of the latest attempts of this kind, and Ma Gui-De certainly drew his inspiration from a number of Chinese religious "sects" founded on such a basis in the first half of the twentieth century. Among them, let us briefly mention the Dao-De She (Society of the Way and Its Virtue). It was grounded among local gentry and high officials of the Shandong province around 1916. Just like De Jiao later, its followers emphasized charity and used spirit-writing for oracles and healing (Prasenjit, 2003). It promoted the worship of the "Most Sacred Venerable Patriarch of Former Heaven" (*Zhi Sheng Xian Tian Lao Zi*) as well as the founders of the "five teachings". Later, it changed its name to Hong Wan-Zi Hui (World Red Swastika Society). Today, De Jiao congregations in Hong Kong, Singapore, and several towns in Malaysia coexist with the temples of this religious body. Another interesting sect is Wu Shan-She (Society for Enlightenment to Goodness). It was founded around 1915 in Szechuan and claims to follow the teachings of Taoism, Buddhism, Confucianism, Christianity, Islam, and even Judaism (de Witt Twinem, 1925: 463–82).

Yi Guan-Dao (the "way to unity" sect) is certainly the best known of these organizations, because of the large number of its adepts in contemporary Taiwan. It was created as an independent organization around 1928 (Li Shi-Yü, 1948: 32–7), and worships Tian Ji Lao-Mu (the "Ancient Mother of Limitless Heaven"), the high being who transcends all the "lesser gods", including Jesus Christ and Allah. Like in the other organizations mentioned above, its followers use *fu ji* as a medium to enter into communication with the gods (Jordan and Overmyer, 1986: 213–36; Clart, 2003). They believe that mankind is now in the third stage of the "final chaos" and can be saved only through the mercy of

Tian Ji Lao-Mu, who uses other gods and their teachings as vehicle for salvation. Finally, on the fringe of the Chinese world let us mention as another syncretistic movement Cao Đài ("High place"), which was founded in the south of Vietnam in 1926. Its supreme goal, proclaimed through revelation by his transcendent god (Cao Đài Tiên Ông Đai Bô Ta Ma Ha Tat), a Vietnamese avatar of the Jade Emperor, is to combine and transcend Buddhism, Taoism, Confucianism, Christianity, Islam, Hinduism, and Spiritualism. The "saints" who relay through spirit-writing (*có bút*) the commands of the transcendent god may be Jesus Christ, Buddha, Lao Zi, and Confucius, but may also include Joan of Arc, Victor Hugo, Sun Ya-Tsen, or Alan Kardec, the founder of Spiritualism.

With regard to the other changes that Ma Gui-De introduced to allow De Jiao to become a "great religion", he emphasizes the necessity of specific places and times allotted to rituals. According to him, De Jiao must look at the example set by the Christian churches and the Muslim mosques in developing its own network of associations (*hui*), which can be used for the meeting of "enthusiastic and faithful devotees" (1997: 179). He also suggests choosing the first and the fifteenth day of each lunar month, which are usual days for regular offerings to gods in traditional China, as equivalent to the Sunday of the Christians or the Friday of the Muslims. These two days would be mainly devoted to the communion with the gods through the performance of religious services. But implicitly, because of the ideas of simultaneity and serialisation they underlie, they are all the most useful in fomenting a strong feeling of unity between adepts scattered in many countries. The sharing of a common pantheon and a common liturgy should considerably strengthen such sentiments of unanimity. But the variations on these aspects are great from place to place or from a sub-group to another. For most of the congregations of the Purple line, the liturgical unity is limited to the use of the canon of De Jiao as a prayer text.

Another important factor in stoking unity lies in the respect of basic precepts to apply in daily life, and which distinguishes the community of true and faithful adepts from others. In the early 1950s, Ma Gui-De and his fellows published a basic creed of five tenets, the *De Jiao xin tiao*, as well as a list of Ten Virtues and Eight Rules (*shi zhang ba ze*) that De Jiao followers should observe. Later on, in the 1960s, two other tenets were added to the creed, through oracles from Lü Dong-Bin. Both *De Jiao xin tiao* and *shi zhang ba ze* are printed in most De Jiao publications, together with the Canon. In the last part of his article entitled "*De Jiao jiang shu*" ("an account on De Jiao") which was first published in Hong Kong around 1949, Ma Gui-De comments on the Ten Virtues, mainly with reference to Confucian treatises. Although there is no evidence that the precepts and rules were proclaimed *per se* during any *fu ji* session, most of them are recurrent in the moral stanzas addressed to the devotees through *fu ji*. Thus, the first four of the basic creed's seven tenets were mentioned in the *De Jiao Xin Dian*. According to the English translation of them that offers Ji Cheng Ge, the main De Jiao publishing house of Malaysia (1998: 4), they are as follows:

(1) To follow the religion of De Jiao, one must adhere to *de* (morality); and to practise morality, one must be sincere.
(2) Cheat not and fake not; do not be covetous; do not be presumptuous; do not be arrogant; do not be indolent.
(3) Do not encroach on each other's rights. Do not be involved in recrimination and litigation.
(4) Hold fast to your will to stay clean; enjoy the bliss of contentedness.
(5) Be a kind father and a filial son; be an affectionate elder brother and a respectful younger brother. Be a righteous husband, while a wife should be obedient.
(6) Abstain from liquor, licentiousness, gambling and smoking.
(7) Set yourself to the task of practising *dao* and you will be remembered in posterity.

The Ten Virtues are also borrowed from Confucian ethics, wherein respect distinguishes the gentleman (*jun zi*). They are as follows: (1) filial piety (*xiao* – 孝) ; (2) brotherly love (*ti* – 悌); (3) loyalty and faithfulness (*zhong* – 忠); (4) faith and sincerity (*xin* – 信) ; (5) propriety or courtesy (*li* – 礼) ; (6) righteousness (*yi* – 义); (7) integrity and honesty (*lian* – 廉) ; (8) consciousness of shame (*chi* – 耻) ; (9) benevolence (*ren* – 仁), which is actually the keynote of Confucian ethics; (10) wisdom (*zhi* – 智). Significantly, the first eight of these virtues are also being professed by Yi Guan-Dao. While the Ten Virtues are for the adepts to pursue, the Eight "Rules" are for them to avoid. They are as follows: refrain from cheating (*bu qi* – 不欺); from falsehood (*bu wei* – 不伪); from greed (*bu tan* – 不贪); from recklessness (*bu wang* – 不妄); from arrogance (*bu jiao* – 不骄); from laziness (*bu dai* – 不怠); from spitefulness (*bu yuan* – 不怨); from hatred (*bu wu* – 不恶).

Apart from supreme goals, basic tenets, and unifying times or places, another requirement to become a largely acknowledged religious movement is having common concepts to be shared by devotees. The *Canon of De Jiao*, published in 1942, had already provided some of them, such as *de de she* (the society of gods under the leadership of Jade Emperor), or *tian zun* ("heaven's masters"). The word *ge* ("pavilion") which was applied from the beginning onward to the worshipping places is also very specific. However, after 1950 new notions appeared in *fu ji* messages and other De Jiao writings. Interestingly, most of them hinge on "virtue", related or not to "teaching". Thus, the gods are called either *tian zun* ("heaven's masters") or *shi zun* ("honourable masters"), while, within the context of the gods' relationship with their followers, the devotees are called *de sheng* ("students of virtue"). The expression of this hierarchical relation apart, the adepts call themselves alternately *de xiong* ("elder brothers in virtue"), *de you* ("friends in virtue"), or *tong de* ("similar in virtue"), which rather stresses their horizontal brotherhood of faith. Nevertheless, within the larger community of devotees, there is a smaller and hierarchically elevated subset, composed of the "blessed" disciples who received the revelation of a "fate affinity" with the gods. For them too, specific categories apply. They claim the title of *yuan zi* ("sons of affinity"), and enjoy the special privilege of a "name of virtue" (*de hao*), which necessarily incorporates the generic word *de* (Ma Gui-*De*, Li Huai-*De*, and so on).

A distinct flag and a specific anthem are also among the criteria of religious distinctiveness created in the 1950s. The principle of having a group identity represented by a flag is not new among the Chinese syncretic movements. For example, Yi Guan-Dao and the World Red Swastika Society had designed their own emblem before. The De Jiao flag was created in 1953 during a *fu ji* séance organized in Singapore. For the occasion Li Huai-De and Ma Gui-De acted as mediums. Later on, the symbolism of such an item aroused few exegesis. I refer here to that proposed by the United Moral Uplifting Society of Malaysia in 2003. Before analyzing flag-related symbolism, let us describe the flag. It is made of a white earth's globe with five red parallels and three meridians of the same colour. Within this globe the word *de* (德) is written. The globe is located in the middle of a rectangle, surrounded by a yellow background crossed by three horizontal blue stripes (Fig. 6). The yellow colour, according to this exegesis, expresses purity, whereas red is the symbol of vitality, and blue is the colour of the adepts' loyalty to their motherland, China. Concerning the five red parallels, they illustrate the *wu jiao*, the five doctrines, with the middle one having unity as an additional meaning. The three meridians represent basic Confucian relationships: (1) between the Emperor and his subjects; (2) between a father and his sons; and (3) between a husband and his wife. Finally, the three blue stripes symbolize the cosmological and fecund combination of heaven, earth, and mankind.

The flag is hung on the front of most De Jiao buildings throughout the world, except in the PRC were the movement is illegal. This emblem is also used as a distinctive logo for the publications and other items that De Jiao produces to promote its cause. As for the anthem, the idea was certainly borrowed from a modern Malaysian tradition, according to which each state of the Federation, but also functional organizations such as Boy Scouts, Girl Guides, or Rotary's Club may create their own one. They are allowed to play it, after the national hymn at the occasion of their main ceremonies (inaugurations, congregations' birthday, and the like). The De Jiao hymn is called *De Jiao hui hui ge* (德教会会歌 – "song of the De Jiao associations"). Ma Gui-De wrote its lyrics, while another adept, Qu Luo-Hun, composed the melody.[23] Significantly, this anthem is rarely sung by adepts outside Malaysia and Singapore.

***

Whereas De Jiao presents a prophetic character by conveying the gods' commands through spirit-writing, it does not announce the imminent "coming down" of a divine messenger and consequently has no messianic content. Moreover, contrary to other so-called "syncretistic" religious movements (such as Yi Guan-Dao and Cao Đài), De Jiao never had a Pope or a Patriarch who was recognized as a revealed leader during his lifetime, and was deified after his death. Neither Yang Rui-De nor Ma Gui-De became objects of worship, and whatever the crucial role the latter played to build and spread De Jiao, one can hardly find his biography and picture in the hundreds of books and magazines that the movement has so far printed out. Indeed, his articles have been brought out again by prominent congregations, but there is no cult of personality concerning him and others. More fundamentally, competition for leadership positions exists within De Jiao like in any other organization, but it never resulted in a steady hierarchy. On the contrary, as the next chapter will show, De Jiao's main organizational feature is a flexible institutional segmentarity.[24] Indeed, if we consider the genealogical order instituted by successive "incense fire" rituals, the structuring of the movement is arborescent. But an analysis of the movement's historical process in Malaysia and Singapore, presented in Chapter III, reveals that the legitimacy of new groups does not narrowly rest on the descent instituted by incense sharing. Moreover, symbolic ties of this kind have a very limited effect on the links that congregations establish with others. Rather than pyramidal, the organizational structure of De Jiao looks like the "a-centred" systems that P. Rosenstiehl and J. Petitot describe. In these kind of systems, multilateral relationships between neighbours prevail and local operations are combined to build collective strategies or institutional bonds, apart from any central authority (1974: 45–62). As for the neighbours, they may belong formally to the same organization or to different ones. A good example of the second alternative is given by the very close links that some pavilions, such as Zi Cheng Ge or Zi Hao Ge, established with *shan tang* in the early times of the movement, which had important consequences on their cults. The spatial structuring of De Jiao is also consistent with the proprieties of the a-centred systems. It has no holy place or headquarters which could serve as a rallying point for the community of believers. Although, as I have argued, Hong Kong became after 1949 its substitutive heartland, De Jiao remains without any sacred place for pilgrims to visit.

If we may consider De Jiao as a syncretistic movement, since it results from a counter-acculturative process implying the manipulation of exogenous symbols and principles of action, the religious synthesis it proposes is limited and not very original. Its theology is rooted deeply in the *san jiao* complex of ideas and beliefs. Like many other Chinese religious movements before it, De Jiao appears as a specific variation on the common idiom of basic conceptions, symbols, and ritual forms that provide the ancient and tight embedding of Buddhism, Taoism, and Confucianism. Heirs to this long syncretistic tradition, the instigators of De Jiao were "naturally" disposed to shift from one set of "teachings" to another, without any dogmatism or sentiment of discrepancy. It is for example the faithful Buddhist Yang Rui-De who enters into a relation of "fate affinity" with Taoist masters through *fu ji* just like Ma Gui-De, notwithstanding his Confucian enthusiasm. Such a cultural aptitude to syncretism mainly applied to the components of the Chinese religious complex, but worked as well for Christianity and Islam when formal ecumenicalism proved effectual in easing social integration overseas.

In this context, the specificity of De Jiao that reveals its early history rests on the gods it puts in the limelight (for instance, Yang Jun-Song who was almost unknown in the Teochew area before 1939), and on a special terminology used to name its gods and institutions (*de de she* for the heaven's assembly, *shi zun* for the deities, *ge* or "pavilion" to define the worshipping places, and so on). Another aspect is the conflation of Taoist-oriented spirit-writing with all-over charitable activities it realizes, and correlatively the close cooperation it entertains with *shan tang* whose *fu ji*, when practised, is mainly turned toward Buddhist saints. Finally, we must mention the emphasis it puts on a few key concepts. Among them, the notion of *de* ("virtue") is of special importance.

I have argued that because of its hazy content, the concept of *de* was most facilitative in allowing changes of orientation under the appearance of continuity. Thus, whereas the primitive goal of De Jiao was to restore an idealized Chinese civilization ruled according to Confucian ethics, overseas the movement's priorities necessarily changed. In Southeast Asian contexts where immigrants had to cope with natives' ostracism and eventually with policies of assimilation, De Jiao's agenda was to preserve the cohesiveness and the cultural identity of the local Chinese communities. The family unit was conceived as a microcosmic Chinese society and the main stronghold abroad of its cultural achievements, and also became the focus *par excellence* of the "teaching of virtue". The prospect was henceforth to promote the five cardinal relationships (*wu lun*), and mostly the relations between father and son, husband and wife, elder and younger brothers and between friends, with, in the latter case, a special emphasis on the "brotherhood in virtue" uniting the adepts.

In that context of cultural uprooting, the implicit meaning of the term "virtue" significantly changed. Exegesis of *fu ji* texts produced overseas suggest that *de* was then frequently conceived with nostalgia, as the moral and spiritual digest of a distant but forever cherished motherland. Consequently, the "teaching of virtue" could appear as an ideal way to insure harmonious and long-lasting relationships between generations, as well as between the Hua Qiao and the ancestors' homeland. Following the distinction made by E. Castells between forms and origins of identity building, we could say that during the process of its transfer from China to Nanyang, De Jiao shifted from a *resistance identity* against the chaotic conditions generated by the war to a *project identity*, characterized by a redefinition of its position in society, and an attempt to uplift the Confucian morality within Chinese communities overseas.[25]

When we compare such a meaning of *de* with what Ma Gui-De and Li Huai-De were pushing forward at the same time, which incorporated aspects of western religions, the paradox is glaring. However, the analysis in the following two chapters of the way De Jiao spread to Southeast Asia reveals that the contradiction is more apparent than real. Although there is no reason to doubt the sincerity of Ma and Li when they intended to create a universal fraternity under the De Jiao flag, such a project was a practice limited to the manipulation of symbols and had no theological effects. In other words, it never went beyond the stage of outward appearances. However, experience shows that the tactical resort to the *wu jiao* doctrine was of great utility in certain tense political situations to gain the benevolence of the authorities, and to cultivate among the adepts an illusory feeling of power and control over external forces. In that particular case, the claim of the fundamental unity of mankind's supreme religious goals proved to be a very efficient tool to shade the preservation of Chinese cultural uniqueness it actually contributed to serve. The fact that the new *de de she* line-up incorporating Jesus Christ and the Prophet Muhammad was conceived as remaining under the supreme command of a Chinese divine ruler — namely the Jade Emperor — is highly evocative of the attempt by Ma Gui-De and his colleagues to contain, in the realm of fancy, the threat represented by the pervasive spread of western ideas and values within the Chinese communities of Hong Kong, Singapore, and Malaysia.

CHAPTER II

Spread to the Southern Seas: The Buddhist Horizon

The main assumption I support in this chapter and the following is that the strategies, activities, and organizational patterns developed by De Jiao in the various Southeast Asian countries where it spread highly reflect the political situation of the Chinese in those national contexts, as well as the main features of their acculturation, and of their interactions with the host society. Such adequacy is indicative of an adaptability whose main characteristics will be specified.

When the existence of the movement was threatened in China, most of its leaders fled to Hong Kong and, from there, De Jiao quickly spread toward Southeast Asia. As indicated before, the spreading to Nanyang (Southern Seas) followed two paths: one directly from Shantou to Thailand and another from Hong Kong to Singapore and Malaysia. During a 40-year period the creation of new agencies in Southeast Asia was limited to these three countries. Such a spatial limitation may be explained by the waves of Chinese diaspora in Asia, and more specifically, the Teochew demography overseas. Whereas in 1950, just after the ban on emigration imposed by Beijing, the proportion of Chinese in Burma, Cambodia, Laos, Vietnam, Indonesia, and the Philippines did not exceed 4 per cent of the total population of these countries — a critical mass apparently insufficient to allow the local blooming of a religious organization like De Jiao — it reached 78.1 per cent in Singapore, 38.4 per cent in the Federation of Malaya, and 16.7 per cent in Thailand (Skinner, 1951: 79). Moreover, in the latter country the Teochew counted at that time for more than 50 per cent of the local Chinese population (Skinner, 1954: 258).

Although in Malaysia and Singapore the proportion of people originating from Chao-Shan is lower,[1] they control a large part of the rubber plantations and have very wealthy and influent businessmen within their ranks.

The comparison between these three national contexts in the light of De Jiao's adaptation is all the most interesting since the political situation of the Chinese in Thailand, Malaysia, and Singapore is not only sharply contrasted, but also illustrates major alternatives concerning minorities' rights and policies. In previous works (Formoso, 2000a, 2000b), I argued that the ideals of tolerance and material detachment that Theravada Buddhism promotes among natives made the socio-economic integration of the Chinese in Thailand easier. Because they emphasize Buddhist devotion to improve their *karma* in view of prospects of better rebirth, the Thai do not challenge seriously the claim of the Thailand-born Chinese to control national industry, trade, and banking. On the contrary, the Muslim faith perfectly fits the Malay cultural propensity to commerce and has even stimulated it between the fifteenth and seventeenth centuries.[2] We only have to recall that Malay merchants (including Indonesians) reigned over the sea trade between India and China for centuries. Consequently, during colonial times when British rulers gave strong impetus to the inflow of coolies in the Malay States, a harsh competition for economic power quickly resulted in the deterioration of the relationship between Malay and newcomers. This rivalry and the fear of the natives of being outnumbered by the Chinese led to interethnic conflicts and tensions. Another closely related effect was indeed to underscore communal identities and to enhance the turning in on themselves of both communities. In 1971, the Malaysian government, through its New Economic Policy, tried to inflect the balance of power in favour of the *Bumiputra* ("sons of the soil", i.e., Malay natives) by implementing steps for positive discrimination (De Koninck, 1994: 170). For instance, 80 per cent of the positions in the police, army, and civil administration should henceforth be reserved to *Bumiputra*, and these latter had privileged access to public health and welfare services. In return, the authorities tolerated the creation of schools, clinics, and other institutions managed by Chinese "for Chinese". In other words, the government let the Chinese assume an important part of their own needs. This policy was equivalent to pursuing in another way the special provisions for ethnic customs that the British colonial power had instituted during the nineteenth century (Hall, 1986: 546, 549). It had very important consequences in the field of education, since generations of local-born Chinese were educated in private schools and colleges using Mandarin as the main teaching language.

Finally, whereas the young Federation of Malaysia, as a true heir to British colonial policy, placed the emphasis on issues relating to minorities and ethnic communities within society, Thailand, on the other hand, came into a process of assimilation by quelling Chinese identity and otherness. The first landmark of this policy was the promulgation in 1918 of the Private School Act which made compulsory the registration of private schools with the Ministry of Education. The Chinese teachers were required to demonstrate good proficiency in the Thai language, for they had to teach in the national idiom at least four hours a week. As noted by W. Skinner (1954: 280), the Thai government of that period imposed more restrictions to the creation of Chinese schools than the colonial rulers in Malaya or Indonesia.

The political pressure on the Chinese reached its apex in the late 1930s. Thailand was then living under the dictatorship of Field Marshall Phibun Songkhram (1938–44 and 1948–57), an ardent nationalist whose favourite slogan was "Thailand for the Thai". According to Garth Alexander (1973: 35), Chinese immigrants assumed at that time a catalytic function: on the one hand, they were stigmatized as tools of a foreign power threatening national security, but on the other hand, they were acknowledged as skillful businessmen worthy of emulation. Between 1938 and 1939 Phibun's administration enacted a comprehensive series of anti-Chinese laws and decrees. It formed a state corporation to compete with the Chinese in the rice trade and to take over the production of basic commodities (salt, petroleum, tobacco, and the like). More than 20 occupations were forbidden to non-citizens. A new revenue code sharply increased taxes on commerce, while an alien registration fee was introduced. Moreover, a majority of non-citizens could not buy land in the kingdom anymore, and Chinese commercial signs were heavily taxed. Lastly, the use of the Chinese language was limited to two hours a week in Chinese schools and most of them, as well as Chinese-language newspapers, were closed down (Wyatt, 1984: 254). A few years after the end of the Second World War, Phibun began a new anti-Chinese campaign, on the fallacious pretext of a possible fifth column of subversion on behalf of Communist China. The annual quota of Chinese immigrants was drastically reduced,[3] as was the maximum number of Chinese schools and ethnic associations authorized for the whole kingdom (Coughlin, 1960: 150). These discriminatory steps virtually halted Chinese immigration, but failed to curb Chinese entrepreneurship. However, they led most Chinese to get Thai citizenship and to change their patronymics for Thai-like surnames. Another consequence was a dramatic drop in Chinese proficiency among the young generations. As for prominent businessmen, they extended their alliances to the Thai elite and incorporated in their boards of trustees military and police high officers to "insure" their businesses and to enlarge their influence (Skinner, 1954: 650–52).

Finally, the anti-Chinese campaigns that Phibun and his supporters orchestrated did not elicit a significant response among the Thai people. Whatever the strength of the locals' prejudices against the Chinese, such prejudices could not jeopardize the economic hegemony of the Chinese. In the early 1980s, ethnic Chinese owned two-thirds of the top one hundred national enterprises, while five prominent Chinese bankers controlled, directly or indirectly, more than 50 per cent of the private sector (Girling, 1985: 78). This steady rise in economic supremacy could have resulted in a new repressive impetus from the authorities, but such was not the case. When Thailand, backed by the United States, developed significantly its infrastructure base in the 1960s, the so-called "Chinese problem" lost its acuteness. The Thai government was then fixated by the Communist insurgency at the periphery and the claim of the urban middle class for democratization. Although most of the laws and decrees promulgated during the Phibun era still apply today, from the 1970s onward the Thai government loosened its grip on the Chinese.

Under the *shan tangs'* Shadow

In the previous chapter I have indicated that the first De Jiao pavilion in Thailand was created a few months after the end of the Second World War. Its instigator was a local businessman named LXW, who had spent nearly 30 years in Shantou to get a Chinese education. During this stay, he regularly attended De Jiao *fu ji* sessions. During one such session he received a command from the Taoist master Bai Yun to open in Bangkok a pavilion named Zi Chen Ge. At the beginning, he set a small shrine in the family's shop located in the heart of Bangkok's Chinatown.[4] Obeying divine instructions, LXW indeed worshipped the heavenly founders of De Jiao, Liu Chun-Fang and Yang Jun-Song, but also Bai Yun and Wu Meng-Wu, two other Taoist masters. He thus instituted a basic pantheon that De Jiao pavilions of Thailand will adopt and which is specific to them. When, after a few years of private worshipping in Bangkok, he invited inspired mediums from Chao-Shan to come and assist him, the cult became very popular and the need to transfer Zi Chen Ge to new and larger premises could not be ignored. Such a move took place in 1951.

At the time, the Thai Government severely controlled the registration of new Chinese associations, especially those whose stated purpose involved religious activities. Consequently, for a couple of years, LXW and his colleagues pursued their activities underground in the new premises of Saphan Khao (Bangkok downtown). Meanwhile, a "brother in virtue" and medium called CDeT, who had recently migrated from Chao-Shan, established in Bangkok another pavilion named Zi Xuan Ge (紫玄阁). Its identity was revealed at Zi Chen Ge, and it is also from there that incense powder was taken to animate the new shrine. In 1953 the two pavilions merged their names, staff, and activities to form the Xuan Chen Shan Tang (玄辰善堂 – "Benevolent Hall of the Abstruse Stars" – XCST), whose true De Jiao appellation was Zi Zhen Ge (紫真阁 – "Pavilion of the True Purple").

This new association deserves some comment. First, it opportunely claimed affiliation with the circle of *shan tang*, or "halls for good deeds". In the Thailand of the 1950s, the registration of new Chinese associations was usually rejected, except for *shan tang* whose charitable activities benefited poor peoples, irrespective of their ethnic origin. Secondly, to reduce the risks of their application to be turned down, the leaders of XCST used a famous Buddhist monastery in Bangkok as a Trojan horse. This monastery of the Mahayana tradition, called Wat Sommanan Borihan (Jing Fu Si, 景福寺 in Chinese), was under royal patronage, and its abbot, a monk of Vietnamese ancestry, was highly renowned for his magical powers. Because he was a friend of a prominent member of Zi Chen Ge, he used to attend spirit-writing sessions. It is during one such session that he received the revelation to "lodge" De Jiao. Although this support contributed to the official recognition of XCST, assistance from an unexpected quarter proved to be much more efficient. I refer here to the mother-in-law of Prime Minister Phibun Songkhram, a Teochew woman, who had become a fervent supporter of De Jiao after a miraculous healing. Due to such backing, the association was easily registered, and it even received the rare honour to be inaugurated by King Bhumibol himself on 25 February 1953.

Despite such an honour, the association had no special privileges in conducting its religious activities. Long-time devotees remember that in the early 1950s a curfew had been imposed in Bangkok after a coup, and that meetings of more than five people were forbidden. It made it difficult to held *fu ji* séances. To circumvent the difficulty, a "liaison officer" visited followers' homes, often riding a bicycle, to gather questions addressed to the "honourable masters". An important part of the oracles concerned healing. Followers received the gods' prescriptions through *fu ji*. Fair copies of them were made on association-headed bills, and by presenting them to herbalist shops in Bangkok's Chinatown the patient, whatever his economic status, could get free medicine, the cost of such to be taken care of by the *shan tang*.

This system of free oracular medications and series of accurate prophecies contributed to the fame of the association. In a context where proficient *ji*-wielders were very few, XCST was progressively known in the 1950–60s as the best Chinese spirit-writing circle in Bangkok. Its séances attracted major figures within the Chinese and Thai-Chinese elite. Among them was Li Zhi-Mian (李之绵), who became a leader of the organization. According to Kazuo Yoshihara (1988: 202), he was an influential businessman, having held posts such as chief director of the Rice Exporter Association and vice-chairman of the Chinese Chamber of Commerce. Important donations by such tycoons made the XCST one of the most prosperous and active philanthropic organizations in the Thai capital. Its charitable activities extended to a wide range of services, including free provision of food, coffins, and clothes to the poor and victims of disasters. It opened in the Si Phraya district of Bangkok the Tai Hua Hospital, a middle-scale structure with 40 beds and a staff of 26, including 16 nurses and 4 doctors. In 1956 it also bought a large piece of land in Saraburi to establish a cemetery offering good *feng shui* for low-cost graves. It met such success that it became the largest Chinese cemetery in Thailand, a rank which remains unchallenged up to now.[5]

Few years after the establishment of XCST, De Jiao began to spread throughout Thailand. Twenty-three more agencies were created between 1955 and 1972 (Map 2). Each of them received a set of statues and incense powder from XCST, which acted as a mother-temple. Interestingly, their geographical distribution reflects that of the Chinese community at the time, with a high concentration in Greater Bangkok and in the provinces bordering the Gulf of Siam (17),[6] and a few agencies in the north (4), and the northeast (2). All of these pavilions but one were officially registered as *munithi kan kuson song khrô* ("charitable association for good deeds" in Thai) and a majority claimed the title of *shan tang*, their "purple" name serving mainly for identification within the De Jiao network. For example, Zi Chong Ge (紫崇阁), the association of Phitsanulok, was also known as Chong Cheng Shan Tang (崇成善堂), while Zi Nan Ge (紫南阁) of Hat Yai was officially named Nan Bang Shan Tang (南邦善堂). Among the first associations to have been created, Zi Feng Ge (紫峯阁) and Zi Wei Ge (紫微阁) deserve full attention. They perfectly illustrate the close links between political and economic powers as well as between Thai and Chinese elites which were essential for the establishment of new pavilions at that time. They also embody two different orientations,

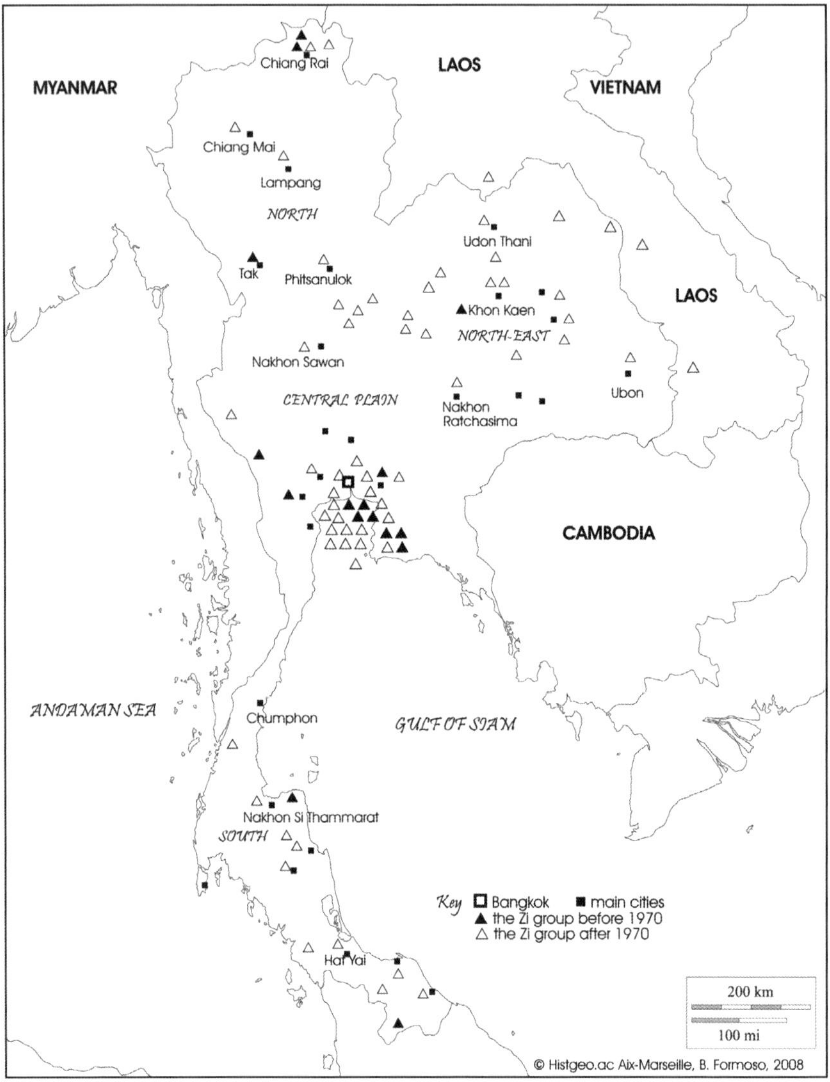

Map 2 The Spatial Distribution of De Jiao Pavilions in Thailand

thus giving an insight on how various the goals and activities of De Jiao can be within the same national context.

Zi Feng Ge started its activities unofficially in 1951, and was in fact the third De Jiao association to have been created in Thailand. Chonburi, the province where it was located, contained an important part of the Chinese living in the kingdom. Following a common pattern, the first step was the organization of *fu ji* sessions. Zi Feng Ge was lucky enough to have its own "celestial hand", a Chaozhou-born merchant who discovered his vocation by attending séances at Zi Chen Ge. However, it is less the modest fame of this medium than the Zi Feng Ge's location in a sightseeing spot which made its prosperity and determined its particular orientation. Initially the place, on the slope of a hill overhanging the Chonburi seaside, had been acquired by a wealthy old Teochew with the prospect of building his graveyard. This man sometimes attended spirit-writing sessions at Zi Chen Ge, and one day he asked the "honourable masters" about the suitability of the place. Wu Meng-Wu and Yang Jun-Song replied that the place's *feng shui* was so exceptional that: "it could not be for men, but for gods' rest". The businessman then gave the plot to the incipient Zi Feng Ge association, with the proviso that it constructs a temple on the site. The masters revealed that it should be mainly devoted to Buddha and his saints. Soon after, leaders of Zi Feng Ge invited into their premises the king's councillor and president of the Buddhist Association of Thailand, Sannya Thammasat.[7] Impressed by the tranquillity of the place, by the charitable goals of the group, and seemingly acknowledging the truth of the masters' message, he accepted to become its patron. Thus, in 1955, Zi Feng Ge could be registered, not as a *munithi* or *shan tang*, but as a Buddhist organization named in Thai language *Phut Samakhom Chi Hong Haen Prathet Thai* ("Zi Feng Buddhist Association of Thailand").

Year after year, by developing the site and by skillfully combining *fu ji* activities with the great events in the Chinese religious calendar, the Committee of Zi Feng Ge succeeded in making it an attractive place for tourists and pilgrims. Both categories of visitors (more than 50,000 annually) enjoy the view, the quiet atmosphere of the nature reserve, and walk within it from one shrine to another to make devotions. Progressively, the association has built more than ten pagoda or halls which contain the icons of a wide range of deities, including Buddhist saints, Taoist masters and other popular gods (Sun Si-Miao, Hua Tuo, Sun Wu-Kong, Guan Yu). Finally, the managerial board of Zi Feng Ge is more involved in the tourism business than in charitable activities, the latter being reduced to gifts to the needy at the occasion of the Universal Salvation Festival (*Pu Du*).

Compared to Zi Feng Ge, Zi Wei Ge better reflects the activities of most De Jiao agencies in Thailand. This pavilion, the fourth in chronological order, was officially created in 1961. The official reason was the XCST's large number of followers, making the establishment of a second agency in Bangkok necessary. But conflicts within the Xuan Chen's directorial board may eventually be the main cause. The committee members of Zi Wei Ge maintain to have brought the incense powder for their "incense fire" ritual from Shantou, despite evidence that they received it together with a set of statues from XCST. Like the latter and Zi Feng Ge, the association benefited from the patronage of people belonging to the highest sphere of political power. Thus, one of its founders was the father-in-law of General Thanom Kittikachorn, secretary of state in the Field Marshall Sarit Thanarat cabinet (1957–62) and future prime minister (1963–73) (Yoshiwara, 1988: 202). Due to this support, the association could register as a *munithi/shan tang*; it chose to call itself Charity Foundation for the Promotion of Culture (*Munithi Song Soem Watanatham* in Thai, 泰国世觉善堂 – *Tai Guo Shi Jue Shan Tang*, in Chinese).[8] Since the beginning of Zi Wei Ge, a China-born Teochew is in charge of its regular spirit-writing activities. In 2003 he was over 70 years old. Unlike Xuan Chen, Shi Jue Shan Tang never managed a hospital. It made the choice to develop smaller structures through the progressive establishment of three western medicine clinics offering free diagnoses and drugs. Located in Bangkok and its suburb, they have a staff of three doctors who deliver a total of about 20,000 prescriptions annually. Among other charitable activities, the association provides free clothes, blankets, food, or coffins to the poor and victims of disasters. It also makes donations to orphanages, hospices and Thai hospitals. Lastly, it support Chinese schools, and has given in 1992 one million baht (about US$25,000) in contribution to the building of the Hua Qiao Chalem Prakiat University, a private Chinese university managed by Bao De Shan Tang, the oldest and biggest *shan tang* in Thailand. The current president of Shi Jue Shan Tang, the senator YHQ, owner of the world's largest crocodile farm, is one of the wealthiest businessmen in Thailand and Southeast Asia as well.

Because of their comparable and important level of activities, Shi Jue and Xuan Chen integrated the "Big Five Benevolent Halls" (*Wu Da Shang Tang*), a syndicate that Bao De Shan Tang formed under its leadership at the end of the 1960s. The covert goal of the cartel is to reduce the harsh rivalry for fame and influence of the powerful tycoons who control the major Chinese charitable organizations of Bangkok. More prosaically, the syndicate also coordinates the means and logistics of partners in order to improve the efficiency of their large-scale charitable operations. For that purpose the managers of the "Big Five" meet twice a year, before the Spring Festival and the *Pu du*, two major events of the Chinese calendar at the occasion of which large amounts of money and food are distributed to the needy. Emergency meetings are also organized in case of disasters (floods, fires, landslides, train derailments, and the like). Each *shan tang* has its own team of volunteers, and Bao De Shan Tang even employs squads of professional firemen and rescuers. Consequently, their deployment on the field of operations has to be coordinated.

As I have shown elsewhere (Formoso, 2003a: 846–7), the mutual-help structure that this syndicate has established is hierarchical, with Bao De Shan Tang taking advantage of its seniority and unchallenged prosperity to act as a patron.[9] Significant of this status is the fact that it imposed on the others the cult of Song Da-Feng, the Buddhist saint of the Song Dynasty, who is believed to be the legendary instigator of the first Teochew *shan tang* in history.[10] Shi Jue and Xuan Shen Shan Tang "enlarged" the gods they worship accordingly. They also raise funds annually for Bao De Shan Tang, in return of a share of them, depending on the latter's appraisal of the importance of their humanitarian projects.

The Turn of the 1970s

By the early 1970s, the conjunction of several factors changed both the situation and the general goals of De Jiao in Thailand. First, the political context became less restrictive for ethnic Chinese. It was the consequence of the democratic revolution of 1973, which ended nearly 30 years of the primacy of ultra-nationalist policy. During the next decades, the growing political consciousness of an urban middle class largely composed of Chinese or Thai-Chinese made it all the more necessary for Thailand's rulers to take into account both their interests and their values. The 1970s is also the period when the policy of opening up the regions through the introduction of transport facilities began to yield some results. As a result, the deployment of the Chinese to the hinterlands, which was already under way, gained in importance.

At the same time, De Jiao was facing in its microsphere a set of changes and challenges so striking that its present leaders mark the 1970s as the main turning point in the local history of the movement. The first change corresponds to the death in 1974 of Xiong Lu-Cheng, the main medium of XCST. This man had not only contributed to the fame of the association, he also had "given life" to most of the De Jiao agencies in the provinces during the 1960s. A majority of them had no *ji*-wielders of their own, and relied on him to organize spirit-writing sessions, which were of vital importance to enlarge the circle of their followers. His occupation of commercial traveller gave him the opportunity to fit more or less their expectations. Although Xiong Lu-Cheng had trained some followers to succeed him, they were considered less experienced and accurate. His death was all the more felt that the demand for good mediums was exploding in a context of rapid growth.

Indeed, the let-up of the political control on Chinese religious activities, which accompanied the process of democratization, gave an unprecedented impetus to the creation of new temples and to the spread of religious organizations. De Jiao followers, who were moving in great numbers from Bangkok to the north, northeast, or southern part of the country, seized this opportunity to open new pavilions, often in a rush. The economic boom of the 1980s to the 1990s amplified the phenomenon. Whereas 24 De Jiao purple pavilions had been created between 1953 and 1972, an additional 50 were established from 1973 to 2003. Due to the easing of restrictions, the great majority of them dropped the "*shan tang* mask" to claim overtly and sometimes ostensibly their De Jiao identity.

The strong impetus for the creation of new shrines concerned not only De Jiao, but also two other *shan tang*-like organizations, namely Peng Lai and Ming-Jip Tan. I have presented these two chains of temples in more detail in other publications (Formoso 1996a, 1996b, 2003a, 2004). Like De Jiao, the Teochew founded and largely dominate them. Their agencies are linked together and ordered through the "incense fire" ritual, while their cults find their sources in the *san jiao* tradition, and revolve around the practice of *fu ji*. Their charitable activities also reproduce the *shan tang* pattern. However, they are different from De Jiao on several important points. They do not stress moral goals as De Jiao does, they never existed as a line of cults in China, and their influence is limited to Thailand. Lastly, the gods their cults focus on are more specific. In the case of Ming and Jip Tan,[11] the basic pantheon is formed by the *Ba Xian*, the Eight Immortals of the Taoist mythology, whereas in the case of Peng Lai, the prominent figure is He Ye-Yun, a Taoist geomancer famous in some parts of Chao-Shan.[12]

While Ming Tan and Peng Lai established their first shrines in Thailand earlier than De Jiao (Ming in 1925, and Peng Lai in 1950), the rhythm of creation of new agencies proved to be slower in their case. In 2003, Ming-Jip Tan had only 47 agencies and Peng Lai no more than 28. Altogether, the two organizations barely outnumbered De Jiao associations at the time. The main explanation for this relatively slow growth lies in the fact that they are more demanding about the motivations of the applicant cult community, its charitable projects, and the presence within it of incipient *ji*-wielders. To give its approval for the establishment of a new temple, the Ming Tan national council requires its patronage by two congregations, and takes a final decision on the basis of their feasibility report. Peng Lai calls for the organization by local Chinese of a costly *xiu gu gu* (修孤骨), or "repairing of orphaned bones". If the sponsorship of very wealthy tycoons acting from Bangkok suffices to open a new De Jiao pavilion, the two other organizations have always given precedence to local initiatives and skills. Consequently, their local anchorage is stronger, and they attract most of the few mediums proficient enough in Chinese to assume the function. Herein lies the main challenge they impose to De Jiao. Whereas most of the Ming-Jip Tan or Peng Lai agencies have *ji*-wielders, only ten of the 74 De Jiao associations of Thailand had a regular spirit-writing activity in 2003. Furthermore, half of them depend on foreigners, since a medium travels between Hong Kong and Bangkok to serve alternately three associations, while two others depend on a team coming from Malaysia. Finally, five teams of local mediums remain, but among them a defector from Ming Tan can be found.

This case of defection, which shows how far De Jiao may incorporate religious otherness if need be, concerns Zi Piao Tan (紫飘壇). This association was founded in 1993 in Siracha (Chonburi). It resulted from a conflict which pitted the president of the oldest Ming temple of Thailand,[13] also located in Siracha, against his main *ji*-wielder, JTX. The latter, due to his fame, won over followers and sponsors to create a new association. JTX intended to remain faithful to the Eight Immortals worship, but could not stay any longer into the Ming fold, nor integrate Jip Tan, though they worship the Ba Xian. He was in conflict with the leaders of this line as well. Peng Lai, on its hand, already had a temple in Siracha. Consequently, he sought out De Jiao to discuss his change of affiliation. Because they had few pavilions in Chonburi province and were in need of good mediums, an agreement was easily reached. The medium could remain faithful to the Eight Immortals and to the Ming liturgy, including specific invocations to do *fu ji*, but he should work for the spread of De Jiao as much as possible. Zi Piao Tan, the name of the new association, perfectly reflects the terms of the compromise. *Zi* is the generic name for the De Jiao associations of the Purple line; *piao* refers to Piao Ran Tai (飘然台),[14] the temple in Puning (Chao-Shan) where the incense powder to open Zi Piao Tan came and which is actually the mother-temple of the whole Ming line; finally, *tan* is the generic name for the shrines of this line. Interestingly, in 1994, the president of Piao Ran Tai received *fu ji* poetry from Ji Gong in a temple that De Jiao had just opened in Fengshun, a township of Chaozhou. The divine command was for this man to establish in his hometown a pavilion named Zi Pu Ge ("Purple pavilion of Pu [ning]"). According to witnesses, when the divine order was promulgated, the man was totally unknown to the De Jiao delegation visiting China. Later, back in Thailand and through information provided by JTX, the person was identified as the president of Piao Ran Tai. With the support of adepts from Thailand, he bought premises, and after years of preparation he opened Zi Pu Ge in 2002. The symbolism of the event is consistent with that of the Zi Piao Tan's creation: De Jiao, in its claim of ascendancy and to increase significantly its own influence, derived strength from both China's and Thailand's roots of the Ming line, the oldest *shan tang*-like organization of Thailand.

The catch-all strategy that Zi Piao Tan illustrates started in the 1970s. It partly explains the rapid growth of De Jiao from that time onwards, since around ten charitable associations coming from various horizons have been so far incorporated into the movement.[15] Another tactic to improve the local influence of De Jiao was to open its pantheon to very popular deities. Following divine oracles it thus progressively adopted the cult of Guan Yin, Ji Gong, Song Da-Feng, Lü Dong-Bin, and He Ye-Yun. Also, in the early 1970s, De Jiao began to organize *xiu gu gu*. At least two reasons explain its keen interest for this festival. First, at that time the movement began to spread in areas which had so far been neglected by teams of bone gatherers working for Peng Lai and Ming-Jip Tan. Second, this festival provides opportunities to perform very good deeds, thus bolstering the prestige of its organizers in the community. It is also the main symbol of Teochew religious identity.

In fact, *xiu gu gu* appears to be a very singular adaptation by the Teochew of the so-called second burial, traditionally performed in rural areas of Guangdong province.[16] The aim of the festival is to look after the "orphaned" dead. It is believed that since there is nobody to take care of them, they will become angry and hungry restless ghosts, haunting the physical world and threatening the social order as well as the individual. In Chao-Shan, the orphaned dead may be unidentified victims of disasters initially buried in a great hurry, corpses from shipwrecks, or occupants of old graveyards which must be moved to another place. The aim of *xiu gu gu* is twofold: to rid the country of these malevolent ghosts, and to convert them into benevolent spirits through propitious geomancy and outstanding tokens of Buddhist compassion. These spirits shall therefore draw good fortune towards the members of their adoptive family (a village, a group of villages, and most frequently a *shan tang*), this in return for regular worshipping. According to legend, Song Da-Feng devised *xiu gu gu* at the time of a plague which ravaged Shantou, somewhere during the twelfth century. Although so far neglected by scholars, the festival has remained a very popular institution up to now in Chao-Shan. It was one of the very few religious activities that Red Guards tolerated during the Cultural Revolution period. At the time, the local government pragmatically used this custom to its own ends. In a context of increasing land pressure, it was an ideal means to remove old graves cluttering up the fields without endorsing the political and economic cost of the shift.

Notably, in Thailand, the *xiu gu gu* festival was welcomed, save for a few liturgical changes.[17] The reason lies in a fascinating approach to interethnic co-operation based on common goals and the congruence of certain Thai and Chinese religious beliefs. I have described the terms of this co-operation elsewhere (Formoso, 1996a). Let us recall however that the Thai conceive of the unfortunate dead as persons whose destiny was shortened by untimely death, violent or otherwise. Just like the Chinese, they believe that these dead eventually become malevolent spirits haunting the world, and they usually bury them without ceremony in the deep forests. But, whereas the Teochew believe that the restless ghosts of the dead are like pitiful beggars and believe that through *xiu gu gu* their bones may be changed into "gold", thus bringing fortune and wealth, the unfortunate dead awaken an unambiguous feeling of fear among the local people who readily abandon them and their burial sites. The aforementioned approach to interethnic cooperation rests on these divergent interpretations. The Thai, without any notion of being affronted, let the Chinese have power over the remains of the unfortunate dead. Therefore, each year the *shan tang* and *shan tang*-like organizations take charge of thousands of corpses at the request of hospitals, coroners, and poor Thai families. For instance, Bao De Shan Tang has "processed", through ten *xiu gu gu*, 153,000 corpses between 1910 and 1999.

To involve itself in the organization of this festival presented many advantages for De Jiao.[18] At the level of each pavilion, it was a means to perform good deeds on behalf of the whole cult community and to reinforce its cohesiveness through works' sharing. The festival, as an attempt to rid the country of malevolent ghosts, is also demonstrative of the movement's philanthropy and identification with the national community. Also, the activities associated with the festival go well with, and even complement, the rescue services that most associations provide, since an important part of the dead that are "processed" are victims of traffic accidents or of major disasters that the De Jiao volunteers "rescue". Lastly, it is an advantageous means to strengthen the bonds between the De Jiao associations in Thailand. In actuality, whatever its size and economic status, a single pavilion cannot hope to organize and orchestrate such an event alone. In the provinces, the search for skeletons in the forests and graveyards usually lasts for two or three months and requires hundreds of bone gatherers working everyday. When a pavilion has collected enough funds to organize a *xiu gu gu*, it asks other De Jiao associations for volunteers. They provide manpower and ritual expertise, while the De Jiao teams of mediums take turn to perform spirit-writing which come with most of the ritual stages. Some of these sessions enter the category of *wu ji* ("warrior's *ji*"), since their aim is either to chase devils out or to indicate with the forked branch the spots where the prospectors will find skeletons.

The co-operation of most De Jiao agencies in conducting this festival proved to be a very useful cohesive factor at a time when the number of pavilions increased significantly, and with it the risks of internal segmentation. In the early 1970s, several events threatened the continuation of the movement's unity. The most damaging among such episodes was the emergence of irreconcilable differences between two prominent leaders of XCST, which led to the division of the mother-temple into two distinct associations. One of the several grounds for conflict was the location of the *shan tang*. Whereas one faction was willing to keep it within the fold of the Wat Sommanan Borihan, and consequently under royal patronage, the other, taking into account the new political context and an increasing volume of charitable activities, sought to separate the association from the Buddhist monastery both spatially and institutionally. Finally, the two organizations that emerged from the clash left the Wat Sommanan Borihan, and after several parallel moves, bought distinct plots of land for their own headquarters. Whereas one retained the name of Xuan Chen Shan Tang and kept the management of both the hospital and the cemetery, the other, more open to the influence of the host society, maintained Zi Zhen Ge as its name, registered itself as a Buddhist charitable association, and kept the insignia of Thai royal patronage and the privileges that such patronage conveyed. As for LXW, the instigator of De Jiao in Thailand who had taken a stand in the above-described conflict, he opportunely received a *fu ji* message from Bai Yun ordering him to remain detached from these "human affairs" (*ren shi wen ti*). He then decided to stay for two years in Hong Kong where he learned *tai ji quan*. Back in Thailand, he became a renowned master in this art of longevity.

Among the other events which challenged the unity of Thailand's Purple pavilions in the early 1970s, let us mention the growing influence in the Pattani province of Ji Yang Ge (濟陽閣 – "Pavilion of the [Dao] Ji's Sun"), an association in the neighbouring Malaysian state of Kedah. Ji Yang Ge was originally the result of a joint venture between Ji Xi and Zan Hua, two local-born De Jiao sub-groups. At the time, De Jiao organizations in Thailand and Malaysia had few interactions with each other; furthermore, Zan Hua claimed to reform the whole De Jiao movement under its own leadership. Consequently, the spread of Ji Yang Ge in Pattani, a region where Malay and Thai powers fought for supremacy over the centuries, was considered an attack on the sovereignty of the Purple line over Thailand, as well as a transgression against the roots of De Jiao in Mainland China. Although Ji Yang Ge was initially established in Thailand in 1965, the opening in that year of Zi Hong Ge (紫虹閣 – "Pavilion of the Purple Rainbow") in the small border town of Betong had gone unnoticed. Six years later, when the movement reached Hat Yai, the biggest city in the south, the leaders of the Bangkok-based associations realized the danger. The pavilion in Hat Yai, named Zi Nan Ge (紫南閣 – "Purple Pavilion of the Southern Wind"), had to inevitably exercise great influence on the provinces of the south (Songkhla, Pattani, Narathiwat, Yala, Satun, Nakhon Si Thammarat), since the pavilion's founder and president, CXD, was the mayor of the city and also a prominent Hainanese tycoon in the south.

The circumstances which led to the creation of Zi Nan Ge confirm the observation of J. Cushman about a famous Hokkien tin-mining dynasty: national boundaries are of little importance in this part of Southeast Asia regarding the strength of kinship ties between Chinese (Cushman, 1991). If CXD became a member of De Jiao, it is mainly because he was convinced to join the movement by his cousin, CDE, a leading businessman in the Malaysian state of Kedah who was president of Ji Yang Ge. The incense powder used to "open" Zi Nan Ge was taken from this pavilion and from a closely related agency in Perlis (Kedah), whose name was Zi Yang Ge (紫陽閣). It is also these two Malaysian agencies that provide, until the present time, teams of *ji*-wielders who organize Zi Nan Ge's spirit-writing sessions.

The Galactic Policy

To overcome internal conflicts and threats from within, the leaders of De Jiao took steps which show how far the local Chinese have assimilated patterns typical of the Thai political system. Before discussing them, we should briefly mention the outstanding development of Zi Zhen Ge in the late 1970s. Due to the patronage of the royal family and the support of very influential businessmen, and also because it managed to replace its first generation of talented *ji*-wielders by another, more famous one, Zi Zhen Ge progressively established itself at the top of the national movement. In 2003, followers considered it as the unchallenged "dragon head pavilion" (*long tou ge*) for the whole country (Lin Wu-Shu, 2002: 5). At the time, its members numbered around 1,500, whereas its main challengers, XCST and Shi Jue Shan Tang, claimed 450 and 500 members respectively. Moreover, the proportion of wealthy entrepreneurs among its adherents is much higher than in the other De Jiao associations in Thailand. Its board of directors was thus composed in the early 2000s of 229 businessmen, including honorary members. Among the latter were the four leaders of the Hua Qiao of Thailand (Lin Wu-Shu, 2002: 5).

In 1973, after purchasing its own building, it began to publish the periodical *Zi Ying Chuan Zhen* (紫影传真 – "Purple Reflection of the True Teaching"). This stern-looking quarterly, entirely written in Chinese, without any pictures or photographs, contains both news from the movement, and the main *fu ji* texts proclaimed by pavilions of Thailand. Historically, it was the first De Jiao periodical to be published overseas and its wide distribution brought Zi Zhen Ge fame abroad.[19] In 1991, the association built its new headquarters on the right bank of the Chao Praya River (Thonburi). A series of miracles suggested the plot as a place blessed by the gods.[20] Blueprints and designs of the buildings were drawn by a renowned contractor from Chonburi. A majority of followers see in this creation a masterpiece of Chinese religious architecture (Fig. 7). Princess Sirindhorn presided over the opening ceremony held on 27 April 1993. Ten years later, in 2003, a nine-storey pagoda, called "Great stupa to celebrate the Thai-Chinese harmony", was built to coincide both with the six-cycle birthday celebration of King Bhumibol (he was 72 years old at the time: 6 × 12), and the fiftieth anniversary of the founding of Zi Zhen Ge. Its opening ceremony was presided over by the supreme patriarch of Thailand's Buddhist clergy.

Interestingly, Zi Zhen Ge worked its way up to the top of the movement's hierarchy not because of its charitable activities, though they are considerable,[21] but as a consequence of its missionary zeal. Since the early 1980s, it has steadily instigated, year after year, the creation in Thailand and abroad of more than thirty "Purple pavilions". It assumes a leading role in this activity, with Ji Yang Ge of Alor Setar (Kedah) acting as its main assistant. The creation of new pavilions apart, the proselytism of Zi Zhen Ge found in its publishing activities another way of expression. We have already mentioned the quarterly publication it has regularly issued since 1973. The association also acts as the publishing house of the Federation of the Moral Uplifting Societies of Thailand. In that capacity, it publishes the latter's quarterly, *De Xun* (德讯 – "Information on Virtue"). This magazine, richly illustrated with colour photographs, was started in 1999 and has a print run of 3,000. It contains abstracts of *fu ji* texts, obituaries, and reports on great events (such as *xiu gu gu*, or opening ceremonies). Although most of the content is written in Chinese, Thai translations are provided with regard to important news. Zi Zhen Ge also prints, reprints, and sometimes translates from Chinese to Thai certain morality books, articles by De Jiao leaders (such as those written by Ma Gui-De), *fu ji* anthologies, and even exegesis of Buddhist and Taoist texts. Complementing such publishing and editorial activities is the library that the association manages, which, in addition to the precious Buddhist and Taoist books it contains, provides the most comprehensive collection of extant De Jiao publications. Because it controls most of the information on the movement's activities in Thailand through the two aforementioned quarterlies, Zi Zhen Ge necessarily exerts great influence on the other De Jiao agencies in the country. This ascendancy is reinforced by the fact that two-thirds of the 74 agencies at the national level received their name and incense powder from Zi Zhen Ge (acting alone or within the fold of XCST). Moreover, almost twenty pavilions rely on its mediums for their occasional spirit-writing sessions.

But more interestingly, this association has attained its dominant position by adapting for its own purposes the so-called model of "galactic polity", which is typical of the pre-national Southeast Asian states. Being the only De Jiao association to be under Thai royal patronage, it seems to have perfectly integrated into its galactic polity model the main aspects of the Thai kingship's pattern of power. According to S.J. Tambiah (1976: 113), the most characteristic features of the galactic model are: "a central planet surrounded by differentiated satellites, which are more or less 'autonomous' entities held in orbit and within the sphere of influence of the center".

If we admit that such a parallel exists, Zi Zhen Ge acts as the exemplary centre, while the other pavilions, held in orbit, are for the most part satellites established on the fringe of the national territory. They prove to be more or less autonomous, but reproduce at their scale the pantheon of the centre, as well as its basic religious doctrine, liturgy, and *shan tang*-like system of charitable activities. In return for their relative autonomy, the centre asks for material help if needed and for unfailing loyalty. It is along this line of conduct that the Zi Nan Ge's problem was solved. A few months after members of Ji Yang Ge instigated the creation of this pavilion in Hat Yai, its president was approached by a delegation from Bangkok. At the time Ji Yang Ge had become embroiled in conflict with the Zan Hua group and could not offer a satisfying alternative. Consequently, an agreement advantageous for both parties was easily found. It stipulated that Zi Nan Ge would have full scope to develop De Jiao in the south of the country. In other words, it could act as a principality, sovereign in the administration of its domain. But, in return for such a grant, it should be faithful to the Thailand's organization, and take an active part in its activities. Later, the gods strengthened opportunely this pact by "appointing" the president of Zi Nan Ge vice-chairman of the Federation of the Moral Uplifting Associations of Thailand, and by casting him in the role of ambassador to the brother-associations in Malaysia and Singapore. Zi Nan Ge effectively took very important initiatives in the 1980s to make the pavilions on the two sides of the border work together. Nevertheless, its role in the management of foreign affairs remained minor compared to that of Zi Zhen Ge, and we can risk here another parallel with the royal prerogative in pre-modern Siam, since at the time, the king had official monopoly on conducting transactions with foreign countries. If Zi Zhen Ge had made obvious its ambition to lead the national movement, a majority of pavilions should have rejected its claim. It is by steadily championing the cause of unity, efficiency, common interest, and spread of the faith that the association's leadership obtained legitimacy and primacy. The main initiative it took in the name of these principles commenced in 1979, when Zi Zhen Ge worked actively to create a national federation gathering all of the De Jiao associations in Thailand.[22] The primary objective was to maintain unity through cult standardization and fair rules of representation.

One of the first actions of the federation was to obtain from the house of LXW the incense burner he brought from China to establish De Jiao in Thailand. It is from this pot, now located in the Federation's headquarters, that incense is taken to give life to new pavilions. The pictures of Liu Chun-Fang, Yan Jun-Song, Wu Meng-Wu, and Bai Yun were designed through *fu ji*. Sets of statues reproducing these pictures were cast and distributed to every pavilion in order for them to have exactly the same icons on their altars. Although this distribution enhanced the unity and uniqueness of the Thailand branch, it did not entail uniformity, with each agency adding its own choice of statues and gods to the basic set.

At the occasion of the first general meeting, the members defined the rules of the federation. It was decided that an executive committee, elected by the whole assembly for a four-year term, will be composed of representatives of the 25 agencies having received the most votes. In turn, this committee should elect its president through secret ballot. Experience proved that, similar to national polls results, the man chosen to be chairman was inevitably the wealthiest among the candidates. Thus, the last four mandates were held twice by YHQ, the owner of the world's biggest crocodile farm and president of Shi Jue Shan Tang, and twice by SZM, the president of Zi Zhen Ge, a prominent entrepreneur in the building materials business in Thailand. The president of the committee, whose identity is confirmed through *fu ji*, is powerful, since he makes most of the decisions. Once a year he is supposed to visit every association, but no leader has done so in recent history. An annual meeting of the committee also takes place in the premises of a host association chosen by the "honourable masters".

Despite the egalitarian principles which underlie these rules, hierarchy, either based on economic differences or on other criteria, remains present in practice, thus introducing discrepancies which sometimes call for arbitration by the gods. The way the federation solved the problem of the agencies' numbering system offers a good example of the latter solution. Until 1992, the custom within De Jiao in Thailand was to refer to the agencies in the order of their creation. For instance, an association called "pavilion no. 20" was the 20th to have been created under Thailand's Purple line. This number was part of the identity of each temple in the same way that its "purple name" serves as an identifier. However, such a numbering system also served to designate an association's place in the hierarchy, since the elder associations enjoyed precedence and ritual prerogatives in collective ceremonies. The hierarchical principle was widely practiced and accepted, but a key dilemma emerged after the division of the first officially created pavilion into two new agencies, XCST and Zi Zhen Ge, with each of them claiming the status of pavilion number one. After the establishment of the federation, the numbering controversy lasted for more than ten years. Finally, Zi Zhen Ge contacted its partisans who had become dominant in the federation, to demand that the conflict be settled forever through judgment of the gods. The "honourable masters" then ordered the splitting up of XCST, which they apparently considered to be too big, into two pavilions: one, Zi Xuan Ge, which was actually the primitive purple name of the association, should correspond to the *shan tang* managing the hospital; whereas a new label, Zi Yuan Ge (紫元阁 – "Pavilion of the Purple Chinese Money") should apply to the cemetery of Saraburi. XCST was not very keen with this latter name, which made evident the utilitarian aspect of the cemetery. Furthermore the gods ordered that the rank of "number one" pavilion be determined by drawing lots.

The lot-drawing yielded unexpected results. The association which ranked first was a recently created vegetarian temple of Nakhon Pathom (a city of the Central Plain), whereas Zi Zhen Ge got the number 41, and Zi Xuan Ge came in last, with the rank of number 52. Although there was no proof of cheating, the leaders of the latter considered the grading as an affront. They then chose to stand aloof from the federation's executive committee, thus letting Zi Zhen Ge rule supreme over the whole movement. In 2003, the president of Zi Zhen Ge strengthened the hegemony of his association by offering to the federation a plot of land in the suburb of Bangkok for building its headquarters. In the new premises, which were under construction at the time of the study, the federation plans to develop several services, such as a vegetarian canteen, a research institute on De Jiao together with a library, classes to teach Buddhist and Taoist philosophies, and meditation training courses. The proclaimed ambition of the forthcoming centre is to become the fountain-head for the propagation of De Jiao throughout the world.

Extroverted Charity

To conclude this short presentation of De Jiao in Thailand we should briefly consider the welfare and relief services its agencies have so far developed. Interestingly, such activities reproduce the missions of assistance to victims of disasters and to the unfortunate dead which contributed to the popular success of *shan tang* in China during the late Qing Dynasty.[23] Because it mainly benefits the locals, the carrying out of Chinese charitable activities reinforces the belief of the Thai elites that their policy of assimilation succeeded, whereas it reinforces the belief of philanthropic businessmen that they are the true, though informal, patrons of national society. In other words, these activities largely contribute to the collective delusion on which rests the smooth social integration of ethnic Chinese in Thailand.

A brief overview of De Jiao charity in Thailand reveals that it is less diversified than in Malaysia and Singapore. A sharp contrast also exists in terms of degree of involvement between the areas presenting high concentrations of ethnic Chinese (Bangkok Metropolis and the Gulf of Siam), and the rest of the Kingdom. In the latter case the competition between De Jiao, Ming, and Pong Lai associations magnifies the resource constraints attributable to the small size of local Chinese communities. Accordingly, the prosperity and dynamism of the big *shan tang*-like associations in Bangkok, such as Zi Zhen Ge, Shi Jue Shan Tang, and XCST, should not conceal the modest level of operations of the others.

The fact that the charitable activities being implemented by De Jiao in Thailand mainly benefits the Thai population is attributable to the wish of the Hua Qiao to give proof of social integration in positive reply to the national policy of minorities' assimilation, and also stems from the relative prosperity achieved by most adherents and from the absence of cultural barriers which may conceivably prevent access to the resources and services the associations offer. Thus, the restrictive concept of *halal*, which governs the food consumption among Malay Muslims, finds no equivalent among Thai Buddhists. Charity directed at the Thai populace takes several forms. The main one consists in the supply of rice and other basic commodities to the poor at the occasion of major events of the Chinese calendar. Every pavilion to some extent distributes rice to the needy during the *Pu Du* festival, while many pavilions send red paper bags containing small amounts of money to the residents of orphanages and poorhouses during the Spring Festival. Serving as patrons of schools and hospitals located in poor urban districts or remote rural areas is also a frequent practice among the economically well-off associations. For instance, Zi Nan Ge of Hat Yai provides financial support to several primary schools, including a school conducting lessons in Braille, located in poor villages of the province of Pattani; meanwhile, XCST sends more than 200,000 baht yearly to primary schools located in the vicinity of its cemetery in Saraburi; and so on.

Following the *shan tang* example, a majority of De Jiao associations in Thailand provide emergency relief services to compensate for the country's deficiency in public rescue teams. Although the pavilions limit their involvement to the provision of clothes, food, and money to victims of disasters, in some cases they can provide teams of volunteers, who have undergone some training to assist the police, the firefighters, and the medical emergency services. Zi Piao Tan, located in Siracha, certainly has the most efficient rescue service organization among the De Jiao associations in the country. It can rely on 200 well-trained volunteers who are organized in four squads rotating on a 24-hour watch, and whose radios are in permanent contact with the police. The volunteers have received training in basic medical treatment, traffic regulation, and forensic medicine. They are fitted out with seven pick-ups and three ambulances, among which a high-tech polyvalent one equipped with hydraulic spread-cutters, and an intensive care unit. Zi Qing Ge (紫青閣) of Chumpae also has a well-trained rescue team fitted out with five vehicles. When the December 2004 tsunami devastated Phu Khet Island, both associations sent personnel to assist the rescuers. This tragic event served as a catalyst for an unprecedented level of coordination among De Jiao pavilions of Thailand, since they succeeded in collecting millions of baht to help the victims.

From the followers' point of view, relief activities undertaken to alleviate the plight of the poor or the victims of disasters follow the same lines as the taking charge of the remains of unfortunate dead. The *xiu gu gu*, as a ritual process aimed at converting wandering ghosts into benevolent ancestors-like souls, is believed to be the most effective way to "rescue" those dead. I have already mentioned that many pavilions in the provinces periodically allotted important amounts of money to the celebration of this festival. In preparation for such an event, they usually take charge of the unclaimed corpses they store in their cemeteries. In contrast with the practice in Malaysia and Singapore, wherein the cremation of dead bodies has become the rule, in Thailand the free supply of coffins to the poor still remains a basic activity of Chinese charitable organizations, including De Jiao. On the other hand, services linked to ancestor worship are either absent or reduced to a minimum among De Jiao associations in the country. Here we touch on a major difference with the practice in Malaysia and Singapore wherein these services, mainly oriented toward prosperous Chinese families, remain a major source of income. Such a difference may be partly explained by a high proportion of intermarriages with native women in Thailand, as well as by the disappearance of most lineage associations because of the institutional limitations imposed by Thai nationalist policymakers for decades. The result is that, in contrast with customs in Malaysia, the associations in Thailand do not manage tablets halls and rely on the religious staff of other organizations to perform funerals in accordance with Chinese tradition.

More generally, the Thai policy of assimilation succeeded in reducing activities directed toward the preservation of Chinese culture. Whereas in Malaysia most De Jiao agencies sponsor local Chinese schools, none but two do so in Thailand.[24] Moreover, no pavilion organizes classes in Chinese poetry or calligraphy, and the practice of *tai ji quan*, *qi gong*, and *wai tan gong* which is very popular among Malaysian followers is totally ignored in Thailand, except in Zi Wei Ge where LXW and his disciples run a class of *tai ji quan*. Lastly, the associations in Thailand do not provide any services pertaining to Chinese medicine, although some of them manage daily or occasionally a vegetarian canteen.

CHAPTER III

Spread to the Southern Seas: Facing the Malay Muslims

In comparison with the movement's experience in Thailand, the spread of De Jiao in the Malay Peninsula was of a totally different kind. Whereas in the former the movement succeeded in maintaining formal unity, regardless of the struggles for leadership between its members, in Malaysia and Singapore De Jiao continually expanded since the beginning through the parallel development of several groups. Although the Purple line, originating from mainland China, remained the mainstream body when it began to spread in Malaysia during the 1950s, two other groups, Ji Xi and Zan Hua, emerged locally, both claiming to belong to De Jiao. Later, in the early 1970s a fourth group, Zhen Xi, appeared because of a controversy concerning the practice of *fu ji*.

Here we are encountering another major difference with Thailand, namely the profusion of *ji*-wielders in Malaysia, which partly explains the hatching of several challenging groups. Because of the government's emphasis on issues relating to minorities within Malaysian society, most Hua Qiao of Malaysia are proficient at Chinese, and consequently the proportion of people able to master the poetical style of language required to do *fu ji* is higher compared to the proportion of people with such capabilities in Thailand. The great number of mediums, the lack of central authority regulating their activities, and the frequent discrepancies in their messages amplify the dilemma of so-called "problematic spirit-writing" which is articulated around the central question of the divine messengers' legitimacy and accuracy.

Finally, another significant difference between De Jiao associations in Thailand and Malaysia concerns their basic pantheons. Although in the case of the Zi group, Liu Chun-Fang and Yang Jun-Song are present in both cases, Wu Meng-Wu and Bai Yun are of little significance in Malaysia and Singapore. In these two countries, the pavilions of the Purple line share copies of the same painting on their altars. Li Huai-De commissioned a professional painter to depict the image in 1952. His idea was to represent the gods who were the first to appear at Zi Xin Ge, the oldest De Jiao pavilion in the Malay Peninsula. These gods are Lao Zi, placed in the highest position, and one step below him are the founders of De Jiao: Liu Chun-Fang on the right and Yang Jun-Song on the left. The Eight Immortals surround this holy Taoist trinity (Fig. 8). On the altars of the Purple pavilions, at least three statues are also found: that of Guan Yu enthroned as the Jade Emperor in the centre, that of Lü Dong-Bin, one of the Eight Immortals on the left, and on the right side the icon of another prominent god, whose identity changes from one association to the other (the most recurrent are Guan Yin, Ji Gong Huo-Fo, and Guan Ping Shao-Di). In contrast with the association's experience in Thailand, where he sends messages only very occasionally, Lü Dong-Bin, commonly named Fu You Da-Di or Lü Chun-Yang, is indisputably the most active *shi zun* among the Zi, Zan Hua, and Zhen groups in Malaysia. Because of his prevalence, some of the devotees consider him as the prime minister of the Jade Emperor.[1] Although the order to create Zi Xin Ge came from Liu Chun-Fang, oracles attributed to Lü Dong-Bin exerted a decisive influence on the destiny of this pavilion and of its offshoots. Between 1954 and 1957, eight De Jiao associations of the Zi group were created in the Federation of Malaya (which then included Singapore).[2] All of them were established as a result of *fu ji* revelations at Zi Xin Ge, Lü Dong-Bin delivering their names in some cases. More fundamentally, Fu You Da-Di allegedly determined their number and rhythm of establishment according to the "principle of number" (*shu li*).

"First" and "Second Nine"

The first time Lü Dong-Bin reportedly mentioned this principle was on the ninth day of the first lunar month of 1957. A *ji wen* then commanded the leaders of the Zi group to respect the "first nine" (*jiu yi*), arguing that the line had now come to full maturity. Let us recall here that in Chinese numerology the figure "nine" symbolizes the "supreme absolute" or the "perfect totality" (Granet, 1988: 137–46). By strict adherence to this idea, the first De Jiao adepts of Malaysia could not imagine the establishment of pavilions beyond the "first nine" but by doubling the figure, and made it depend on new divine instructions.

Two years after the Zi group received the oracle, the Ji group, which worships Ji Gong, also reached its "first nine". The first Ji pavilion, Ji De Ge (濟德閣) of Ipoh (Perak) had been founded in 1952, just six months after the association of Li Huai-De. It was followed by the successive creation of branches in Singapore (1953), Muar (1954), Petaling Jaya (1955), Port Weld (1956), Taiping (1957), Seremban (1958), and Alor Setar (1959). Ling Yin Si, a Singaporean temple devoted to Ji Gong, was considered as the ninth pavilion. In 1959, the leaders of the Ji group received a *ji wen* from Lü Zu whose meaning was similar to the oracle previously addressed to the Purple line. He allegedly ordered them to stop the founding of new pavilions, since they had already "succeeded in completing the circle". They obeyed this instruction for 40 years. It was only in 1999 that Ji Gong is said to have given his approval for them to start a "second nine" (*jiu er*).[3] In the meantime, three other important oracles were attributed to Lü Dong-Bin. The first one concerned the mother temple of the Zan Hua group whose founding he had ordered in 1957 (significantly the ninth day of the ninth lunar month). One year later, three associations of the Zi group received messages attributed to Fu You Da-Di suggesting that Zan Hua Ge should play an important role among the De Jiao associations in Malaysia and Singapore. The most explicit *fu ji* script came from Zi Shu Ge (紫書阁) of Johor Bahru. It instructed that instead of two houses Master Lü should have only one named Zan Hua, whose vocation was to become the "common roof" and "supreme ultimate of the two rites"(*tai ji liang yi* – 太极两仪). In other words, the divine function of Zan Hua was to unify the Zi and Ji groups (the two rites) under its own authority. As noted by Tan Chee-Beng (1985: 44), some leaders of the two groups were understandably unhappy about such a prophecy, and thus contested its accuracy.

The second important "revelation" of Lü Dong-Bin, which was more easily accepted, came in 1961. The master is said to have authorized the Purple line to create a "second nine" (*jiu er*). Consequently, between 1961 and 1964, another series of nine Zi associations was established. It gave to the main group the opportunity to spread in areas of the Federation of Malaysia that De Jiao had so far neglected. The first pavilion of the new generation was thus founded in 1961, in the insular State of Sarawak (Kuching), while two associations were opened on the eastern coast of peninsular Malaysia, one in Kota Tinggi in 1962, and the other in Trengganu, in 1964.[4] After the foundation of the last association of the "second nine", no more pavilions of the Purple line were created in

Malaysia and Singapore for eight years. The third and last important message concerning the number nine was delivered in 1967 at Li Shan Ge (立善閣), an association of the Zan Hua group. It blessed the completion of a "third nine" (*jiu san*) under the authority of Zan Hua Ge. The poem referred implicitly to the two "first nine" of the Zi and Ji groups and to the uniting as well as transcendent function imparted to Zan Hua. Its own "first nine" whose process had started in 1960 was presented as the very highest achievement which will make the *luan*-bird "breathe the Imperial Canon".[5] According to a key passage of the *fu ji* text, "the numerology 9 × 3 is a very fecund *yang*" and "the summit [i.e., Zan Hua] is covered with old venerable pine trees [symbols of longevity]" (Li Guang-Zhao, 1995: 91). In accordance with the oracle, Zan Hua stopped its institutional development and endeavoured to produce an Imperial Canon, known as the "Bible of Bukit Mertajam".

Finally, the spread of De Jiao in Malaysia and Singapore between 1952 and 1970 alternated short intervals of quick expansion with long periods of inertia. In contrast with the unremitting but slow process which characterized the spread of De Jiao in Thailand, its growth in Malaysia and Singapore was much more erratic and dynamic, since 44 associations were created between 1952 and 1972 in these two countries *vis-à-vis* only 24 in Thailand during the same period. We have shown that the Ultimate Absolute (*tai ji*) whose numerological emblem is "nine" served as a kind of "open sesame" spell for the dissemination process in Malaysia, with Lü Dong-Bin acting as a divine lockkeeper. Although the "principle of numbers" was known among the adepts of China, Hong Kong, and Thailand, it was never utilized as a facilitative "switch" within these national contexts, thus bringing into question its political function.

Interestingly, the completion of the Zi and Ji "first nine" coincided with a period of political uncertainty in the Malay Peninsula. The independence of Malaysia in 1957, as well as the self-governing status obtained by Singapore in 1959 and the onset of violent confrontations between the Malay and the Chinese which lasted until the independence of Singapore in 1965, created a very inauspicious climate for the local spread of De Jiao. To adopt a wait-and-see attitude was then a realistic choice, especially for a religious movement whose organization was overlapping both territories. Significantly, when, in the early 1960s, oracles attributed to Lü Dong-Bin authorized the Zi and Zan Hua groups to expand again, the foundation of their new agencies was restricted to Malaysia, the territory that had the best potential for further development. This move thus served to dispel the unease of the Malaysian authorities who otherwise would have raised questions about the political loyalties of De Jiao followers. As another example of adaptation let us mention the cessation in the late 1960s of the De Jiao expansion (no associations were created between 1967 and 1970). Such a pause was consistent with and coincided with the aims of the First Malaysian Plan (1966–70), a program that initiated the pro-Malay policy of later periods, and whose implementation was characterized by a severe renewal of interethnic confrontations.

In this fraught situation, the display of respect for the "five great religions" became all the more functional. Whereas in Thailand the *wu jiao* ideology and its symbols are totally ignored, in Singapore and Malaysia the De Jiao pavilions, except those of the Ji group, hang in their prayer hall, generally in a conspicuous place, pictures of Confucius, Lao Zi, Buddha, Jesus Christ, and the symbol representing Prophet Mohammad. Historically, the first to display them was Zi Xin Ge, the association that Li Huai-De founded in Singapore. Although the founders of the five religions are represented in the same row, an implicit hierarchy is however perceptible to those who are familiar with Chinese symbolism. Thus, the central symbol for Lao Zi is flanked on the left by those of Confucius and Buddha and on the right by those of Jesus Christ and Prophet Muhammad. Since the left is the seat of honour in Chinese ritual context, it means that Confucius and Buddha are more prominent than Jesus Christ and Prophet Muhammad. As for the central position of Lao Zi, it emphasizes the leading position of Taoism for the Zi, Zhan Hua, and Zhen associations which display the *wu jiao* symbols. The informants confirm this interpretation by commonly considering Lao Zi, Buddha and Confucius as the three "great honorable masters" (*da shi zun*) of the movement.

If the respect for Islam that the ideology of the *wu jiao* conveys should logically suit the local people, it can hardly be the case for the *shan tang* activities. As a result of the cultural and religious barriers separating Chinese and Malay Muslims and due to the segregationist policy of the Malaysian government, the charitable activities of these organizations mainly benefits the in-groups and, in stark contrast with the situation in Thailand, cannot be used as a tool to promote political integration. It appears that in Singapore and Malaysia, the De Jiao associations entertain few relations with the network of *shan tang*, and notably with the Blue Cross Charitable Institution, an all-encompassing organization that the "halls for good deeds" had constituted at the end of the Second World War.

What Status for the Groups Born Overseas?

By presenting them as "rooms under the same roof", the poetic texts that devotees attribute to Lü Dong-Bin largely contributed to legitimate the Ji and Zan Hua groups in the view of members of the Purple line. Another evidence of the uncontroversial legitimacy of these overseas' "sprouts" lies in the fact that, early on, the leaders of the Ji, Zi and Zan Hua groups tried to cooperate with each other. Most attempts in this sense failed, but for reasons that had more to do with precedence and etiquette than with the legitimacy of the protagonists. Tan Chee-Beng (1985: 38–9) documents in details the earliest attempt. In the early 1950s, following a divine instruction that "Zi and Ji belong to one family" (*Zi Ji yi jia* – 紫濟一家), Zi Xin Ge and Ji De Ge collaborated to found new pavilions. They thus worked together to form Ji Yun Ge (Singapore), Zi Chang Ge (Malacca), and Ji Xin Ge (Muar). But the co-operation ceased after the establishment of Ji Xin Ge (1954), because of rivalry and quibbling.[6]

Although undeniable, the legitimacy of the groups born overseas does not solve the problem of their status. In this sense, the way they interpret their origins and function, as well as the way the other De Jiao groups react to such views, is particularly instructive. Thus, according to a semi-legendary account written in 2002 by a vice-chairman of Ji De Ge, the revelation to establish the Ji group came in 1952. At the time, Ji Gong is said to have travelled in the neighbourhood of Ipoh, the main city of the Perak state (Map 3). This trip was allegedly made in response to Song Da-Feng, whose intention was to spread the Buddhist faith in the area. Once on the spot, Ji Gong judged the *feng shui* of the place very good but the level of morality of the people deplorable. To remedy the situation, he asked two Taoist masters, Bai Yun and Zhang Xuan-Tong to act on two local Teochew entrepreneurs, Ma Shi-Ying and Wen Ying-Chai, who were going to Penang for business. Due to to this divine intervention, they met during their stay a De Jiao *ji*-wielder who had been a member of Zi Xiang Ge, the association of Yang Rui-De, and who had fled China a few months earlier. Miraculously, heavy rains fell on the city for a full week, so that the three men had plenty of time available to chat about De Jiao and spirit-writing. According to the legendary account, Zhou Xiu-Wen, the adept from Chaozhou succeeded in converting Ma and Wen, and taught them some of the rudiments of *fu ji*, including the invocation prayer of the *De Jiao Xin Dian*.

Back in Ipoh, the two businessmen met with some friends at the house of Ma Shi-Ying and improvised a planchette session with Ma acting as main *ji*-wielder. Immediately after they started singing the invocation

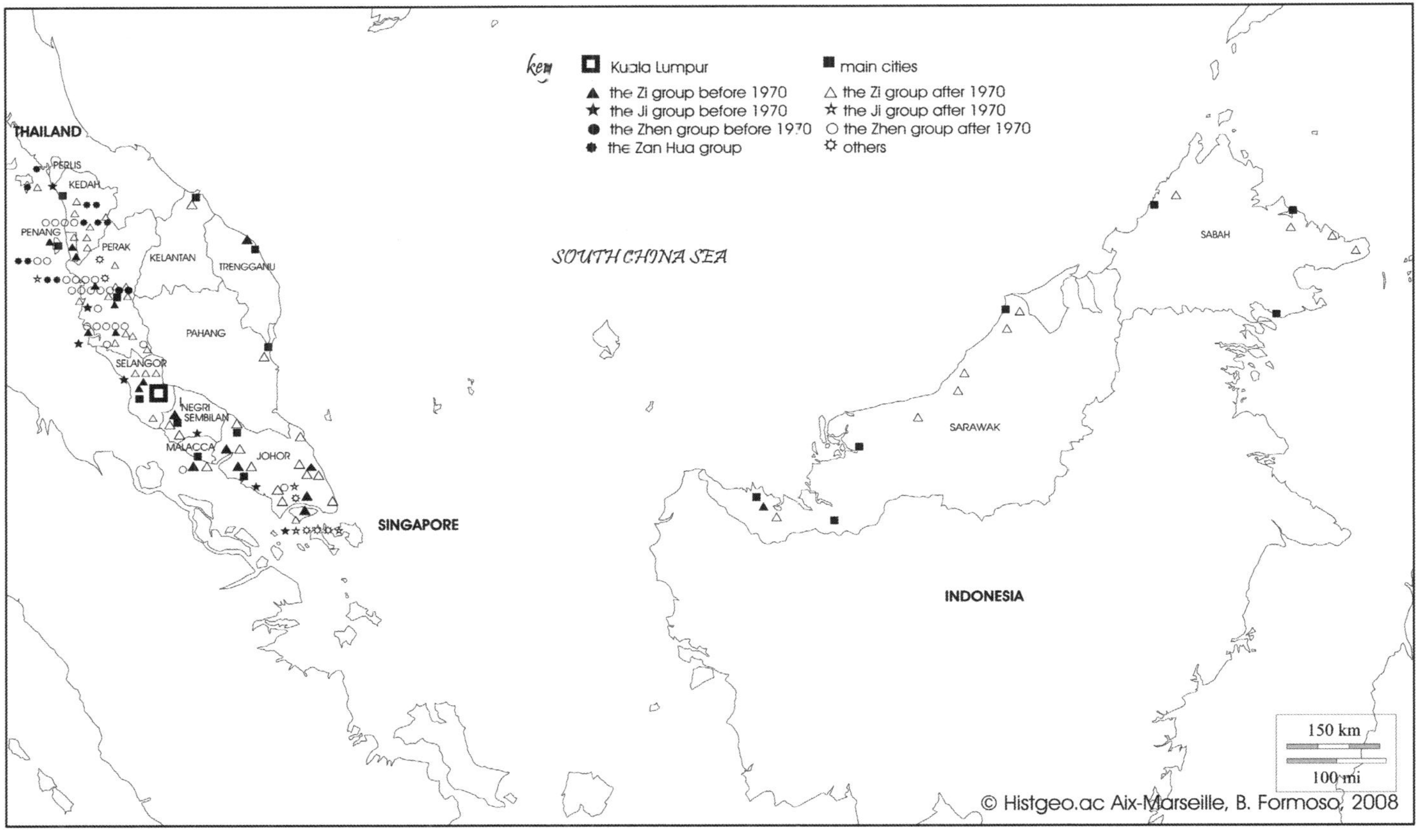

Map 3 Distribution of the De Jiao Denominational Groups in Malaysia and Singapore, Before and After 1970

prayer, a moral poetry attributed to Ji Gong came down. During the following weeks, Ma Shi-Ying, Wen Ying-Cai, and their friends multiplied the séances and oracles. The number of followers increased accordingly. Ji Gong reportedly appointed a group of ten persons known for their high degree of morality which later became the committee of the first Ji association. The order to found this pavilion came on the fourth day of the fourth lunar month of 1952. Ji Gong named it Pi Li Ji De Ge (霹雳濟德阁 – "Pavilion of the Ji [Gong] virtue's thunderclap"), abbreviated as Ji De Ge ("Pavilion of the Ji Gong virtue"). The goals Dao Ji is said to have assigned to the association were manifold: to uplift the morality of the society as a whole and within it the morality of the youth, and to support the old, the poor, and the weak through charitable activities. According to the subsequent exegesis that Ji followers made of both the congregation's name and the oracle, Ji Gong intended to make of the incipient group the spearhead of his renewed teaching. In other words his objective was to make Ji De Ge a "thunderclap of morality", inaugurating a new era (Guo Qing-Gao, 1997: 214–5).

Finally, the account emphasizes the fact that Ji De Ge was directly founded from the first De Jiao pavilion in history, Zi Xiang Ge. Although it did not get its censer from it, the association of Ipoh was allegedly endowed by the gods with the rare privilege to receive its *fu ji* technique as well as the *De Jiao Xin Dian* from the sources of the movement. This specific process made it an equal of Zi Xin Ge, the Zi association founded in Singapore by Li Huai-De. This idea of equivalence is supported by the fact that the new "pavilion of virtue" received from the *fu luan* a specific generic name, *ji*, which thus avoided its subordination to a mother-temple of the Purple line. Furthermore, it has its own "gods' society", the *de de she ji*, that parallels the *de de she* of the Zi group. Also significant is the fact that the 1990s' spread of De Jiao back in China was instigated and led conjointly by a Ji association in Malaysia, Ji Yang Ge of Alor Setar, and a Zi association in Thailand, Zi Zhen Ge of Bangkok. At the time, the Ji group conducted in the PRC research trips on the origin of De Jiao independently of those organized by the Zi group. The parity with the latter that Ji claims and that the Purple line partly admits goes together with divine patronages which are complementary. If the supreme goals that the deities assigned to the two groups are similar (to uplift the moral standard of contemporaries and to provide health care and material support to the needy), the revelation to fulfil their achievement came from Taoist masters in one case, and from a prominent saint of popular Buddhism in another. Because of this endowment, the two groups complement each other in the emphasis they place on the Buddhist and Taoist aspects of the De Jiao virtue.

On the contrary, Zan Hua relies on its own historiography to challenge the leadership of the Purple line. According to oral accounts that I recorded in 2003, completed by the report of a follower, Li Guang-Zhao (1995: 90–5), a Teochew native of the Chaoyang district migrated to Penang in 1918 and brought with him a statue of Lü Dong-Bin worshipped by his family for generations. This man, named Tang Zi-Huan (唐子欢), acting as "celestial hand", established a small shrine in the town of Bukit Mertajam to communicate through *fu ji* with Lü Zu. Because the place proved to be of "good affinity with the god" (善缘德因 – *shan yuan de yin*), the circle of devotees got progressively wider. Tang Zi-Huan passed away in 1937, the very day of Lü Dong-Bin's birthday celebration (an evident sign of divine election). Two years later, in 1939, while his descendants were imploring the help of the Immortals to restore peace, with one of his nephews, Tang Xi-Ru, acting as *ji*-wielder, Lü Zu allegedly sent a message predicting the imminent rise of De Jiao in China. At the occasion of this oracle, later known as the *Qi Dao Shang Cang* ("Heavenly Prayer"), he provided information on the philosophy of the forthcoming movement (concerning the *wu jiao* particularly), as well as on its basic pantheon. He referred to Guan Yu as the new Jade Emperor and designated himself, Lü Dong-Bin, as the intermediary between men and heaven. The master is said to have concluded his message by asking the Tang family to broadcast the new faith throughout Malaysia and by announcing the imminent end of the war. The Tang interpreted the oracle as a divine order to become the privileged messengers of the god and to assume a leading role to propagate the new faith in Malaya. From 1939 to 1957, Lü Dong-Bin sent other similar instructions to the Tang Xi-Ru's group (Bukit Mertajam Bible, 1986: 37–8). Finally, in 1957 he asked this group to found a pavilion bearing the name of his legendary hermitage, Zan Hua. I have already mentioned that, in 1958, associations of the Purple line received messages from Lü Zu suggesting that this new association should become the roof covering the Zi and Ji groups. These *ji* texts reinforced the conviction of Tang Xi-Ru and his fellows that they had been chosen by the Jade Emperor to assume the leadership of De Jiao.

The way they have structured the altar of Zan Hua Ge in 1960 is highly revealing of such an ambition. According to the description of Tan Chee-Beng (1985: 44), which remains valid for 2003, a marble tablet symbolizing Zan Hua Ge and 18 smaller tablets representing the first nine Zi and Ji associations are erected on the altar of the association of Bukit Mertajam. Also erected are eight bigger tablets bearing the name of the Jade Emperor (Guan Gong), the five "founders of religions" as well as Lü Zu and Ji Gong. The tablet for the Jade Emperor is the biggest and is placed at the highest level of the altar. The tablets for the "five founders of religions" are in the next lower row, followed by those of Lü Dong-Bin (on the left, which is the seat of honour) and Ji Gong (on the right) in the third row. As for the tablet symbolizing Zan Hua, it is in the fourth row, flanked by the tablets of the first four Zi associations on its left and those of the first four Ji associations on its right. The last and lowest row consists of five Zi tablets on the left and five Ji tablets on the right. Tan Chee-Beng pertinently notices that the unilateral decision to erect tablets bearing the name of the Zi and Ji pavilions as well as the greater prominence of its own tablet led to the accusation that Zan Hua Ge aimed at heading the De Jiao associations in Malaysia and Singapore.

From the point of view of the Purple line, further unease was stimulated by the fact that most of the Zan Hua associations claimed the generic term *zi* as part of their name. Moreover, Tang Xi-Ru maintained that his group, though born overseas, had been endowed with an upstream and heading position by the Jade Emperor, since Lü Zu had allegedly informed him of the forthcoming birth of De Jiao before it was effectively set up. The motivations and circumstances which led to the creation of both groups were also comparable, with a handful of "men of virtue" (*zhong shan zi*) imploring in 1939 heaven's gods to relieve the Chinese of the torments of the Sino-Japanese War, and the deities compassionately supporting their efforts through *fu ji*.

In 1959, Lü Dong-Bin is said to have advised Zan Hua to join the Federation of the De Jiao associations of Malaysia and Singapore (Nan Zong) that had just been founded. However, the temple of Bukit Mertajam could hardly submit to the authority of this organization largely dominated by the Purple line. The adhesion failed because of questions of precedence. Thus, Nan Zong wanted Zan Hua to adopt the logo of the Zi group, but its leaders refused, pointing out that their own logo had been attributed by Lü Dong-Bin and so should not be changed. Another stumbling block was a planchette script from Lü Dong-Bin which enjoined all the associations of the Zi group to stop having *fu ji* sessions permanently. The instruction was revealed on the eighteenth day of the ninth lunar month of 1967, at Zi Peng Ge of Teluk Intan, an association of the Zi group. It specified that the 18 associations of the Purple line should simultaneously burn their planchette sticks at nine o'clock on the morning of the 29th day. Very few pavilions obeyed, though they gave up the practice of *fu ji* for a while (Tan Chee-Beng, 1985: 27). In fact, the problem reappeared in 1971 when Zan Hua Ge received the same command and decided to cease spirit-writing forever. When a majority of Zi associations resumed it few years later, those which remained faithful to the Lü Zu instruction, allied together with Zan Hua, giving a new twist to the crisis undermining the Purple line.

How to Do Without "Flying *Luan*-Bird"?

Several interpretations were given by followers regarding the interruption of *fu ji*. The main ones were: that very few people had attained the moral state to be reliable mediums, that undue invocations were bothering the peace of the gods, and that the latter were not willing to interfere anymore in the conflicts affecting the cohesiveness of De Jiao associations. Men should henceforth solve their problems by themselves, suggested a *wen ji* attibuted to Lü Zu sent in 1968 to a group of doubtful devotees, during a séance at Zi Xin Ge.[7] In other words, an excess of *fu ji* was going to kill *fu ji* because of the discrepancies and confusions it created. The seeming confirmation by Lü Zu of his earlier command led most of the 18 Zi associations of Singapore and Malaysia to suspend for ten years their *fu ji* activities. Therefore, those in favour of ceasing the practice of spirit-writing won the day and the 16 ideograms attributed to Lü Zu are frequently quoted as divine legitimacy. The few Zi associations which maintained planchette sessions were nevertheless headed by Zi Chang Ge of Melaka, the oldest pavilion in Malaysia.

Four years later, in 1971, a similar instruction attributed to Lü Dong Bin and delivered at Zan Hua Ge, reinforced the determination of the supporters of the interruption, but led to conflict within the Zan Hua group. Eventually, three pavilions interpreted the instruction as a human intention (*ren yi*) rather than a divine revelation. They decided to carry on planchette sessions and broke off all relations with Zan Hua Ge. Both Ji Yang Ge and Zi Yang Ge which had seceded earlier also continued holding *fu ji* sessions. As for the others, they brought all their planchette sticks to Zan Hua Ge where they were kept stored for years in a locked room. In 1977, when the associations of the Zi group resumed the practice of *fu ji*, the planchettes and divine pens were burnt in the temple's courtyard to dissuade members of the group from following this path. In the meantime Zan Hua Ge had hanged at the gate of its prayer hall a marble tablet predicting the exhaustion of fortune and the breaking off in the continuity of generations for those who would infringe on the ban imposed by Lü Zu. In early 2000 the tablet mysteriously disappeared.

Ji Gong is said to have never confirmed the Lü Zu's oracle and consequently the Ji group maintained its regular spirit-writing sessions as though nothing was amiss. As a reaction to the ban, another local "De Jiao" group called Zhen Xi emerged in the late 1960s. Its original centre was the northern part of Perak state where most of its pavilions remain concentrated today. An important part of its pantheon and ritual are derived from Ming Shan She (明善社), a group of "benevolent altars" which emerged in 1958, also in the north of Perak state (more precisely in Began Serai).[8] Herein lies the main contribution of the *shan tang* tradition to the spread of De Jiao in Malaysia.

Both Ming and Zhen groups share the same basic pantheon, composed of Song Da-Feng, Li Dao-Ming (Li Tie-Guai), one of the Eight Immortals whose recognized emblem is a bottle-gourd, and Song Chao-Yue (Song Chan), a Teochew Taoist geomancer and physician of the Ming Dynasty.[9] In the specific case of Zhen, two other main gods have been added: Zhong Li-Quan, another member of the Eight Immortals' group, and Ji Gong. According to the oral account of a prominent member, Song Chan attributed the name *zhen* (振 – "to rise with force and spirit") to the new group in 1964, at the occasion of a *fu ji* séance that a medium called Li Ming-Jing (李明鏡) had organized in his home. This native of Chaoyang fled China in 1949, bringing with him a censer from a temple worshipping Song Chan in the present Teochew county of Huilai. Between 1949 and 1964 he organized planchette sessions which attracted more and more people because he was very successful in predicting the winning numbers of the national lottery! Due to this popularity, he was able to raise enough funds to create in 1966 the first Zhen association, Zhen Yi Ge (振儀阁), in Kuala Kurau, a small town of fishermen in the state of Perak.

The initial links of this association with De Jiao remain unclear. It is possible that members of De Jiao attended the earliest sessions of this group of mediums and exerted a religious influence on it. The fact is that most of the Zhen associations have adopted the Canon of De Jiao. The followers recite not only the *Xin Dian* but also the *Zu Shi Sheng Zhou* which praises Song Da-Feng. Let us add that early relationships between Zhen and De Jiao concerned not only doctrinal aspects but also their mutual development. At the occasion of an interview, the executive secretary of the Zhen organization shared with me the opinion of Tan Chee-Beng (1985: 50) that the spread of his movement largely benefited from the *fu ji* controversy within the Purple line. Thus, between 1969 and 1977, a period which corresponds with the ban on spirit-writing activities among the Zi and Zan Hua pavilions, seven more Zhen associations were founded through *xiang huo* ritual from Zhen Yi Ge.[10] In 2003, the Zhen group claimed a membership of 35 associations, and ranked second in Malaysia in terms of the number of its pavilions, behind the Zi group (65 units) but a long way ahead of the Ji group (14 units) and Zan Hua (10 units).

The outstanding spread of the Zhen group in Malaysia (it never succeeded in establishing roots in Singapore) can be attributed to its general objectives and to its approach to *fu ji*. Rather than focusing on the production of divine texts with moral or philosophical content, it favours the attainment of concrete and immediate goals. Following the example of its founder who devoted most of his *ji*-wielding activities to bringing good fortune, the Zhen group is known for organizing planchette sessions essentially for medical therapy, divination, delivering protective charms, and exorcising evil spirits. The logo of the organization perfectly reflects this emphasis on charity. It consists of the impression of a heart which bears the character *shan* (善 – the same that enters into the *shan tang* compound) meaning "benevolence" or "kindness". Concerning the *fu ji* technique, Zhen is unique among the De Jiao groups in Malaysia and Singapore because it combines two different features, that of the "scholars" or *wen ji* and that of the "warriors" or *wu ji*. Whereas the former consists mainly in the gentle writing of moral poetry, the latter usually assumes a rugged disposition, since the mediums fight malevolent spirits and enter into trances. Concretely, in most of the Zhen pavilions, the two styles are either realized by two teams acting together or by the same team practising them alternately. Tan Chee-Beng (1985: 50) noticed that this orientation is considered "superstitious" by leaders of the other groups who view it with contempt. Whatever their level of appreciation, the activities of the mediums in this group can be considered dynamic by any standard. For instance, in the small town of Kuala Kurau, whose total population was 15,000 in 2003, with around 9,000 inhabitants of Chinese origin (mostly Teochew), no less than 7 Zhen associations and more than 15 *fu ji* teams were operating at the time of the study. In other words, there were more mediums in this small place that among the entire range of De Jiao associations in Thailand.

Interestingly, the same spirit-writing frenzy can be observed today in the Huilai county of Chao-Shan from where most of the Teochew of Kuala Kurau came, including the founders of the Zhen group. This coastal area, mainly populated by poor agriculturalists and fishermen, not only has the highest number of *ji*-wielders in Chao-Shan but is also the main place where villages and *shan tang* organize large-scale *xiu gu gu*, the celebration of which usually goes hand in hand with the practice of martial planchette (*wu ji*). Loyal to this tradition, the Zhen followers of Kuala Kurau and the nearby town of Tanjung Piandang have adapted *xiu gu gu* to the local context, an adaptation which is unique in Malaysia. Although they do not collect "orphaned" bones, they periodically go over their town and the neighbouring countryside to capture, with the help of *wu ji*, the souls of wandering ghosts that they keep in the same kind of urn used to stock bones in Chao-Shan. These urns are stored for months in a room of a temple and once a year, at the occasion of the Universal Salvation Festival, devotees open them and send collectively the souls to the otherworld (Fig. 9).

Because the Zhen expansion challenged its hegemony and urged it to react, but also because an increasing number of followers became aware that *fu ji* was of vital importance for the development of De Jiao, the Zi group decided to resume it at the end of the probationary period of ten years. Accordingly, in 1977 the presidents of the "first" and "second nine" met at Zi Xin Ge of Singapore to request the advice of the gods. After a long silence the divine stick finally moved and the *xun luo* ("the patrol of heavenly warriors") came forward to allow all the pavilions but the mother-temple to start spirit-writing again. However, after a few months, an incident occurred that seriously questioned the advisability of the decision. A car accident killed three mediums of Zi Peng Ge, the association where Lü Dong-Bin had initially instructed the Purple associations to stop practising planchette divination. The event, which occurred when the pavilion was celebrating its birthday, was interpreted as a divine sanction and led part of the 18 associations to stop the activity again. It took years for a majority of them to surmount their fear and to revive the practice.[11] Sometimes, events they believed to be unable to manage without the intervention of the gods convinced them to take the plunge. Such was the case for Zi Yun Ge, the association of Penang.

This example is highly informative of the relations that De Jiao followers entertain with gods and is worth to be reported with details. In 1994 the late president of Zi Yun Ge made it known that he intended to build new premises expected to be the largest and most beautiful among the premises of the De Jiao associations in Malaysia. Construction began soon, but the president passed away in 1996 and with him his financial commitment. Although his successor supported the project, he faced unexpected financial problems during the Asian crisis of 1997. In order to avoid a cessation of the project, the managerial board of Zi Yun Ge decided to consult the "honourable masters". The president addressed a letter to the Jade Emperor containing four questions: Could the association hold again *fu ji* sessions to secure its future through divine support?

How much would the total cost of the building be? What would be the effective financial contribution of the committee? And what amount of money could be raised among the other followers? The entire De Jiao pavilions of Malaysia and Singapore (including Ji, Zhen, and Zan Hua groups) were invited to attend the request, and so were adherents of prominent associations in Thailand and Hong Kong. The president sent the letter to the gods by burning it, and the handling of divining blocks gave him a positive reply to his first and main question: could the association hold *fu ji* sessions again? Few days later, a meeting was organized wherein 10 of the 38 committee members volunteered for *fu ji* training. Through divining blocks the gods confirmed the vocation of four of them who were subsequently trained by experienced *ji*-wielders of Ji Yang Ge (Alor Setar), an association of the Ji group. From that time onward the spirit-writing activity developed so fast in Zi Yun Ge that in 2003 the association had nine teams of *ji*-wielders, with sometimes eight of them writing simultaneously during its weekly planchette sessions.

Although oracles from Zi Chang Ge of Melaka resulted in the creation of seven new Purple pavilions between 1967 and 1977, the resumption of *fu ji* by a majority of agencies relaunched the process vigorously. Thus, from 1977 to 2003, 36 new Zi pavilions were opened in Malaysia and Singapore. Some original features characterize this new impetus. First and foremost it is not regulated by the "principle of numbers", which was thus conducive to an uninterrupted flow of creations. Secondly, the incense powder that gives life to the new altars does not come anymore from a monopolistic centre, but from several regional poles. This latter evolution is partly due to the fact that the mother-temple of Zi Xin Ge has not revived its *fu ji* activities after 1967.

Zi Luan Ge, which is located in the town of Kluang, eastern part of the Johor State, perfectly illustrates the new role that some regional centres assumed in the movement's expansion. The association was founded in 1972, i.e., during the breaking-off period, through revelation and incense sharing from Zi Chang Ge. In the early 1980s it progressively stood out as the most dynamic De Jiao association in the southern part of the Malay Peninsula. The fact that it was chosen to organize the sixth World Moral Meeting of the De Jiao Divine Pen in 2004 should be interpreted as a reward for its contribution to the spread of the movement. Thus, between the early 1980s and 2003, its teams of mediums established ten Zi associations in peninsular Malaysia.[12]

Some members of the "first" and "second nine" seriously question the legitimacy of the pavilions founded outside the principle of numbers, considering that they have been established against the wishes of

Lü Dong-Bin and of the Jade Emperor. In their view, these newcomers threaten the movement's credibility because of their uncontrolled proliferation. To picture the threat they are supposed to embody, an informant referred to the metaphor of the liana which progressively smothers the tree it overruns. In return, members of the associations stigmatized in that way tend to consider the formers as snobs who are ossifying the movement because of their class consciousness. These prejudices hampered for a time the attempts of some leaders to surmount divisions through the creation of a general body.

To Be "in" or To Be "out"

Whereas in Thailand the idea of a national federation stood out in the late 1970s, in the Malay Peninsula it dates back to 1956. In October of that year, leaders of the Zi associations met in Zi Ming Ge at Ipoh to discuss a divine planchette revelation which prescribed the establishment of a central body. It was agreed that this organization would be called *Nan Yang De Jiao Zong Hui* (南洋德教總會 – "Southern Seas De Jiao General Society"), abbreviated as *Nan Zong*. At this occasion it was decided that the liturgy and altar for all associations would be standardized along those of the mother-temple of Zi Xin Ge. Although in 1957 the Registrar of Societies in Singapore approved the application, it was only in 1959 that the Malayan side succeeded in registering the society under the name *Malaiya Lian He Bang De Jiao Lian He Hui* (馬来亜聯合邦德教聯合會 – "National Society of the De Jiao associations of Malaya"), abbreviated as *De Lian*. After Singapore became an independent state in 1965, the links between *Nan Zong* and *De Lian* loosened progressively, and Zi Xin Ge was not invited to attend the annual meeting of *De Lian* in 1971. Finally, the two organizations broke off relations in the following year, after the promulgation of the Malaysian Societies Act of 1972 which imposed that the office-bearers of societies be citizens of Malaysia and that registered societies must not have any "affiliation or connection with any society established outside the Federation" (Tan Chee-Beng, 1985: 25). With the separation of *De Lian* and *Nan Zhong*, the latter went to rack and ruin. According to Tan Chee-Beng, in the early 1980s it had six institutional members comprising Zi Xin Ge of Singapore, Zi Qi Ge and Zi Gao Ge of Hong Kong, Zi Zhen Ge of Bangkok, Zi Ying Ge of Japan, and Zi Gen Ge of San Francisco. But in 2003, with the exception of Zi Zhen Ge, all of the affiliates had either disappeared (in the case of those in Hong Kong) or were inactive. At that time, even Zi Xin Ge had reduced its charitable activities to a very modest level.

When *Nan Zong* was founded in 1957, its membership was limited to the associations of the Purple "first nine". Although in the 1960s *De Lian* enlarged it to the "second nine", it took several years for the leaders of the organization to accept Zi pavilions outside the group of Eighteen that they considered to be the "De Jiao mainstream" (*De Jiao zhu liu*). In 1981, only half of the pavilions founded after 1964 had been incorporated into *De Lian*. Still more difficult was the integration of De Jiao associations belonging to other groups. A timid open-door attitude started in 1981 when two associations of the Zhen group were admitted, as well as an independent organization named Zi Ji Ge (紫濟閣 – "Pavilion of the Purple Ji Gong").[13] A major difficulty about the integration of the other De Jiao groups into *De Lian* was the resolution that all new participants should adopt the liturgy and basic pantheon of the existing members, as well as a common logo and an official name including the words *De Jiao hui*, usually translated as "Moral Uplifting society". In other words, the associations of other groups might join *De Lian* as long as they gave up the emblems of their own identity in order to comply with the rules and logo of the dominant Zi group. Indeed, few were ready to accept this mark of submission, or even to use both their own logo and that of the society as a compromise.[14] The renunciation of Zan Hua Ge to enter *De Lian* despite a divine recommendation to do so is a case in point of such reluctance.

As a consequence of the Zi group's hegemonic tendencies, the other groups founded rival central bodies whose official goals were obviously to promote the solidarity and to co-ordinate activities between their members. The first to do so was Zan Hua which created, after the completion of its "first nine" in 1967, the *De Jiao Lian Yi Hui* ("Federation of Moral Uplifting Societies [De Jiao]"), better known through the acronym of FOMUS. In 1968 the leaders of this new organization approached the president of *De Lian* with the intention to merge the two federations; this effort did not meet with success. At the beginning FOMUS included all the Zan Hua associations with the exception of Ji Yang Ge (Alor Setar), and Zi Yang Ge (Kangar).[15] However, its cohesiveness was rapidly undermined by conflicts related to the *fu ji* controversy, and its membership fluctuated significantly. The first upset occurred in 1972 when the instruction to cease *fu ji* within Zan Hua led a faction headed by a former president of Zan Hua Ge to leave FOMUS. At the time, the splinter group comprised Zi Han Ge (Kulim), Zi Feng Ge (Serdang), Zi Hong Ge (Betong) and Zi Tian Ge (Padang Serai), but the latter went back to the Zan Hua fold after few years. Conversely, when in 1977 a majority of Purple pavilions decided to hold the *fu ji* activity again, Zi Peng Ge

(Teluk Intan), which disagreed with the resolution, left *De Lian* to join FOMUS. Henceforth, the federation became the leader of the front that rejected spirit-writing. Although in 2003, FOMUS still officially counts nine members, they just meet for the birthday celebrations of each other and do not develop common projects otherwise.

In comparison with FOMUS, the "Ji Group Fraternity" (*Ji Xi Ren*) appears to be much more dynamic. It was established in 1981 by the then president of the Ji mother-temple of Ipoh, Wei Bang-Yan (魏邦彥). His purpose was twofold: to strengthen the links between the members of the Ji "first nine", and to revive through close co-operation two associations which were moribund at the time, namely, Ji Yung Ge (Singapore) and Ji Xian Ge (Petaling Jaya). Under his authority, the nine Ji associations adopted in 1982 a common charter stipulating that they should hold a general meeting once a year and attend their respective birthday celebrations. They also raised funds and organized a turnover of mediums to resume the activities of both Ji Yun Ge and Ji Xian Ge. More recently, the implementation of a Ji "second nine" has become the main project of the Fraternity. Finally, the last to come as an alternative to *De Lian* was the foundation in 1997 of *Zhen Luan Lian Yi Hui* ("Federation of the Luan Bird Zhen"). It unifies the whole Zhen associations around common projects. Among them, the most important in the early 2000s was the building in Parit Buntar (Perak) of a haemodialysis centre for the treatment of sick persons affected by kidney failure. In 2003, the centre was on the way to completion for a total cost of about US$270,000.

Eventually, all of these federations or fraternities, including *De Lian*, confirmed rather than reduced the divisions of De Jiao in Malaysia, with each group developing separately its own sphere of co-operation and solidarities. These shortcomings, and the fact that in Thailand a national federation had been successfully established in 1979, encouraged prominent leaders of *De Lian* to go ahead with respect to the open-door policy they had initiated in the early 1980s. The main promoter of this liberal attitude was LYB, the president of Zi Rui Ge (Kota Kinabalu, Sabah). This Teochew businessman was in the 1970–90s one of the prominent business tycoons in Southeast Asia. As the president of a Zi pavilion outside the Eighteen and, furthermore, located at the periphery of the Malaysian territory, LYB was certainly more sensitive than others with regard to the interest of the fringe groups which had blossomed around the mainstream Purple line. He consequently worked towards their integration into a common structure. In 1985, at the occasion of the *De Lian* annual meeting organized at Zi Yun Ge (Penang), an instruction from the gods strengthened his standpoint. By this planchette poetry the gods' society, writing as a whole, asked all the factions within De Jiao to stop their conflicts and to work hand in hand for the achievement of the movement's supreme goals. Concerning the resumption or not of *fu ji*, which was actually the main question debated and the main stumbling block, the deities instructed the protagonists to not interfere anymore in the affairs of the other associations.

Following this divine advice, *De Lian* opened up to associations of Ji and Zhen groups. Zan Hua, on its side, has so far refused to integrate an organization it considers too largely dominated by supporters of the *fu ji* resumption. In contrast with the earlier situation, the restrictive conditions to be met prior to membership in the society were significantly reduced. New members can now observe their specific religious ceremonies, and it became sufficient for them to adopt the *De Jiao Xin Dian* as their prayer text, as well as the logo of De Jiao beside their own emblem. The choice of a new name for the society in 1988 symbolically marked the new orientation. It was renamed *Ma Lai Xi Ya Yi Da De Jiao Lian He Zong Hui* ("United Moral Uplifting Society of Malaysia"), better known through the English acronym of UMUSOM. In May 2003 the organization had 92 members, counting for 65 per cent of the 142 De Jiao associations of Malaysia registered at the time. Among them, 62 belonged to the Zi group (i.e., 95 per cent of the Purple pavilions of the country), 21 to the Zhen group (60 per cent of the Zhen membership), and 8 to the Ji group (89 per cent of its membership in Malaysia). Confirming the statement of Zan Hua, all of these associations but five were practising *fu ji*.

With the registration of the new society, some important changes were introduced in the *De Lian* running rules. The most significant, from a symbolic point of view, concerns the chairmanship of the organization. Although the basic principle of a short-term chairmanship limited to one year was maintained, the rules governing the choice of the presiding association were modified. Whereas from 1958 to 1987 the associations of the "first" and "second nine" got each in turn a function that never eluded a Purple pavilion, from 1988 onward the principle of chairmanship rotation reproduced that of the federal constitutional monarchy of Malaysia, and sometimes Ji or Zhen associations have been chosen to hold office.[16] Just like the Malaysian sovereign is elected for a short-term mandate by and from the hereditary states' rulers of the Federation, the president of UMUSOM represents in turns one of the states of Malaysia, whatever the group it belongs to. Until 1990 the representative state was elected by gods, but after that date, the system was changed, becoming cyclical. In fact, most of the time a pool of pavilions, including Zi, Ji, and

Zhen members, is chosen to represent a state, even if executive power is embodied by the president of one of them, appointed through *fu ji*.

Also chosen by gods are the deputy-chairman and the treasurer. The other staff members (7 vice chairmen, a secretary, a deputy secretary, an assistant treasurer, 13 committee members, and 52 representatives) is elected through correspondence voting by body-electing members (three representatives for each associations). The main function of the president consists in organizing a yearly general get-together as well as presiding over bimonthly committee meetings. At these occasions, everyday matters are discussed as well as the establishment of new pavilions and relationships with other De Jiao federations. Another task of the president is to represent the organization for the celebration of many events (establishment of new pavilions, funerals of prominent adepts, and the like), including the birthday celebration of each member association. He is assisted in this heavy task by the deputy and vice-chairmen. To conclude about the activities of the UMUSOM, let us mention the half-yearly periodical, entitled *De Xun* ("Information Bulletin on *De* [*Jiao*]"), that it has continuously published since 1987. It reports recent and forthcoming events concerning members of the organization, but in contrast with the *modus operandi* of the De Jiao quarterly of Thailand, it does not spread *fu ji* texts, in order not to alienate the small minority of members who decided not to resume the activity.

Finally, a sketchy parallel between Thailand and Malaysia regarding the institutional development of De Jiao during the 1970–80s reveals interesting analogies, among which the most significant is the takeoff of the movement in those countries during the 1970s. From that time onwards, the rhythm of foundation of new agencies accelerated as an indirect consequence of both regional economic growth and important political changes such as the democratization in Thailand, and the New Economic Policy in Malaysia. As a reaction to the multiplying of new agencies, the next decade was a time of institutional strengtening in both contexts, through the establishment of national federations coordinating the activities of their members and standardizing their basic liturgy and emblems (flag, logo, and anthem).

Ji Gong and the "Asian Values"

From 1987 onwards, UMUSOM rekindled links with Singaporean associations that had loosened in the 1960s. Representatives of major De Jiao organizations in the city-state were thus invited to attend celebrations of UMUSOM and reciprocally. Although the development of De Jiao in

Singapore partly reproduced the Malaysian divisions with the competing spread of Zi and Ji groups, it is however remarkable by the role that was assumed by two institutions considered "odd men out", namely Ling Yin Si (灵隐寺) and Tai He Guan.

Ling Yin Si was named after the monastery from Hangzhou (Zhejiang) where Ji Gong started his career as a Buddhist monk. Founded in 1942 during the Japanese occupation of Singapore by a group of Teochew families worshipping Dao Ji, it called itself at the beginning He Ping She (和平社 – "Society for Peace"). Its general goals were those common to all *shan she* of the time: to rescue victims of war and to support the poor. This cult community held planchette sessions with a divine pen, believed to be a very powerful one that it had acquired together with a statue of Ji Gong from a private spirit-writing circle of Bahau (Negeri Sembilan). In view of the great magical power attributed to these items and the skill of its mediums, Ling Yin Si became the best-known Ji Gong worshipping place in Singapore after the Second World War.

Some of its members and mediums were associated with De Jiao adepts of Zi Xin Ge until the establishment of Ji Yun Ge in 1953, and Ling Yin Si absorbed the members of this first Ji association of the city-state when it stopped its activities in the early 1960s. A few years later, in 1965, the hegemony of Ling Yin Si on the local cult of Dao Ji was again demonstrated with the key role its committee played in the foundation of Ji Fang Ge. Although this Ji association had its own premises and set of charitable activities, its staff and committee remained partly in common with that of Ling Yin Si up to now. Because of this deep involvement in the affairs of the Ji group, the latter considered it as its virtual ninth member from 1959 onwards. However, it was only in 1977 that the president of Ji De Ge convinced the leaders of Ling Yin Si to assume this function officially. Although the *shan she* integrated Ji Xi with the alleged approval of Ji Gong, in 1999 a conflict with Ji De Ge led Ling Yin Si to stay itself aloof from the Ji group. The official reason for the dispute was the fact that the leaders of Ji Xi had decided to start a "second nine" without asking the advice of Ling Yin Si, but in fact the true motive was leadership rivalry with another Singaporean De Jiao leader, LJX, the president of Tai He Guan.

Whereas he was still an outsider in 1980, LJX progressively hoisted himself among the five top-ranking leaders of De Jiao. He is also first and foremost the president of Tai He Guan, one of the biggest voluntary welfare organizations of Singapore. On account of this position he is in charge of 43 health and welfare institutions such as hospitals, clinics, orphanages, disabled centres, and poorhouses, and spend yearly an amount equivalent to US$17 million in charitable activities.[17] Some aspects of the outstanding rise of this business lawyer in the field of charitable works sheds light both on the history of De Jiao in Singapore and on its notable adaptation to the theory of "Asian values" promoted by the former prime minister of the city-state, Li Guang-Yao (Lee Kuan Yew). His career is also a fascinating example of how De Jiao leaders succeed by combining opportunism and the manipulation of "gods' oracles" with a genuine interest in moral uplifting.

According to accounts I recorded in 2003, LJX was born in 1944 in a rich Teochew family involved in many kind of businesses, including banking and real estate. He graduated from the National University of Singapore in 1969, and founded a law firm while serving as public prosecutor afterwards. In 1971, he was appointed member of the Minister's Advisory Committee on Drug Abuse. His interest in charity is related to the long-standing commitment of his parents in this field; they had supported Buddhist benevolent halls as well as Taoist organizations. Among other religious occupations, they used to worship the Earth Mother Di Mu Niang-Niang in a downtown temple. But in 1978 the government regained ownership of the plot where the shrine had been built. The Earth Goddess then miraculously appeared in a dream to LJX, asking him to take care of her cult. At the time, he was already known in Singapore to be a "religious lawyer", because of his particular involvement in the defence of religious and charitable organizations. Abiding by the wishes of the goddess, he brought her statue to another temple, Tai He Guan ("Taoist Temple of the Supreme Peace"), that he was trying to save from oblivion through its management. This independent charitable association was established by Teochew migrants after the Second World War through *xiang huo* from a temple worshipping Hua Tuo and Lü Dong-Bin in the city of Chaozhou.[18] Before becoming its president, LJX had been serving as legal advisor of the association for years. Due to the help of his younger brother who was a medium, and with the support of wealthy businessmen, he succeeded to provide a strong impetus to the reinvigoration of Tai He Guan whose motto became "to serve mankind without any ambition for name, fame, and gain".

But the success of LJX resulted first and foremost from his ability to build the welfare campaigns of the association around the tenets that Prime Minister Li Guang-Yao promoted as part of his ideology of "Asian values". Among these tenets were the preservation of strong family ties and the inculcation of a selfless sense of community as basic requirements to build a harmonious and hard-working society. In perfect congruence with such ideals, the first prominent action of Tai He Guan under his management was the awarding of a Filial Piety Prize in 1978; in the following year it organized a Nationwide Essay Competition for all schools in Singapore, to promote "respect for elders". More recently, Tai He Guan established a Moral Family Service Centre offering a comprehensive range of programs and services that aim at "strengthening and building strong families". Still more instructive is the campaign that the association organized in the late 1990s to promote family virtues. It put up posters in four languages on 90 buses. The posters contained messages such as "FAMILY – where true love and warmth is", or "Treasure your spouse, love your children, respect your siblings, be filial to your parents". Because of his eagerness to be in line with the policy of Li Guang-Yao, LJX was quickly acknowledged in the highest spheres of power as a faithful ally. In response to his enthusiasm in upholding government policy, the government supports most of his projects, which therefore benefit from wide media coverage and draw in large amounts of money from a multitude of benefactors, especially those among the prominent business tycoons who are keen to increase their prestige and political credit.

The great fame that LJX enjoys among De Jiao leaders throughout the world ensues not only from the high status he has attained in Singaporean civil society, but also from his involvement in a series of miraculous events which happened in the early 1980s. These events also mark the starting point of his affiliation with the Ji group. The train of events began when the committee of Zi Xin Ge, the mother-temple of the Purple line in Singapore and Malaysia, decided to sell the plot of land where the premises of the association was built in 1958. Wealthy Indonesian investors were after this piece of land, which was ideally located in the business district of the city. However, the deal was controversial. Although committee members hoped to make a significant profit on the sale to swell the association's coffers, it was believed that De Jiao had bought the plot due to divine intervention. Lao Zi himself had reportedly appeared in a dream to the initial European owner of the land to inform him that the plot should be kept for the gods' rest. Given this background, LJX, who was a member of the board of trustees and the legal advisor of Zi Xin Ge, went against general opinion by suggesting to ask the advice of the "honourable masters" at Zi Jing Ge, the association in Hong Kong where the directive and incense powder to found Zi Xin Ge originated. LJX's attitude was all the more courageous in view of his personal circumstances: his financial status was weakened at the time by unsound investments in real estate, and the banker backing the sale was willing to push him into bankruptcy if the project to sell the land failed.

Finally, a delegation went to Hong Kong to obtain the gods' advice. There, a *ji wen* attributed to Ji Gong ordered to keep the plot, predicting that things will sort themselves out. When the representatives of Zi Xin Ge returned home, they learned that the transaction was going to fall through, since the group of potential buyers turned out to be members of a criminal organization. Therefore, LJX emerged from adversity with greater prestige. He was considered to be a wise, selfless, and honest man, blessed by the gods. Committee members of Zi Xin Ge, as a mark of gratitude, stood as guarantor to the banks in order to allow him to recover from his financial problems.

The Zi Xin Ge affair coincided with the attempt by Wei Bang-Yan to revive Ji Yun Ge, the second Ji association to have been established in the Malay Peninsula but which had ceased all activities in the early 1960s. The president of Ji De Ge rented premises to house the altar, and teams of *ji*-wielders were regularly coming from Malaysia to hold *fu ji* sessions, but to relieve his efforts he could hardly rely on Ling Yin Si and Ji Fang Ge, the two Singaporean associations affiliated with the Ji group. Being afraid that their hegemony on the Ji Gong local cult could be challenged by the new association, they were reluctant to get involved in its renewal. Then Wei Bang-Yan approached LJX, whom he considered to be sufficiently faithful and dynamic, and who seemingly had a strong fate affinity with Dao Ji. This fate affinity found new evidence in 1984 when a *ji wen* attributed to Ji Gong instructed the Singaporean lawyer to become president of Ji Yun Ge. That same year, another oracle stated that Tai He Guan was in fact a De Jiao association. LJX was all the more ready to accept these oracles because the moral aims of De Jiao were congruent with the Confucian values he intended to promote steadily through his charitable activities. By joining De Jiao, he could reach a wider audience and tap an international forum with regard to his lyrical and inspired sermons.

After a few years under his management, Ji Yun Ge became very prosperous. A piece of land was bought on Bedok Road for his prayer hall in 1985, and ten years later new premises were built to host the World Moral Divine Pen Third Meeting organized by De Jiao in 1995–6. The building includes a large prayer hall and a "moral home for the aged sick" which can accommodate 112 patients and has a health staff of 39. Year after year, the association steadily developed its welfare services, so that Tai He Guan became the unchallenged leader, with respect to welfare services, among the De Jiao associations in Malaysia and Singapore. In 2004, in addition to the home for the aged sick, it managed also a child care centre, two senior activity centres, a replacement home for destitute mentally burnt-out residents, and a family service centre.[19]

These achievements made LJX a "big man" among De Jiao adherents in Singapore and Malaysia. In 2002 he backed the establishment of a Ji association of the "second nine" in the city-state, so he now controls, more or less directly, three local pavilions. He has also woven close personal links with Zi Jing Ge (紫經閣), an independent De Jiao association, which was set up originally for collecting and publishing religious documents and scriptures.[20] For years this pavilion relied on the occasional visits of mediums from Hong Kong, and more precisely from Zi Jing Ge (紫靖閣), but in the early 2000s Tai He Guan accepted for training its first generation of *ji*-wielders. The pool of pavilions that it forms with the associations led by LJX was in the Singaporean De Jiao limelight at the time of the study. In 1994–5 it succeeded in tapping the energies of the De Jiao pavilions in the city-state (with the exception of Zi Xin Ge[21]) to prepare the third three-yearly meeting of the World Moral Divine Pen Conference. Moreover, at the occasion of the last installment of the event (Kluang, Malaysia, 2004), LJX was chosen for the second time to organize the next conference in 2007. This de facto honour, granted by other prominent De Jiao leaders, will inevitably reinforce his local position.

Reflexive Charity

The welfare services that Tai He Guan and Ji Yun Ge provide to a large extent bring us to the more general question of the charitable and moral activities that De Jiao conducts in Singapore and Malaysia, and of the population that these activities target. Concerning such aspects, the difference of orientation with the agencies of Thailand is especially salient. Whereas in the latter country charity is mainly directed toward the native populace and an important part of it consists in making up for an insufficient level of public rescue services, in Malaysia and Singapore, where these services are provided at a high level of efficiency, De Jiao has developed other kind of activities.

A small part of such activities consists in regular or occasional donations either to prominent charitable organizations (Salvation Army, Red Crescent) or to public hospitals, orphanages, poorhouses, and homes for disabled. Moreover, blood donation campaigns are often organized to fulfill the needs of local hospitals when they face blood shortages (especially during Ramadan). Occasional or regular supplies of food to the needy are also widespread.[22]Although the assistance provided in such circumstances is given to needy individuals whatever their race or origin, an overall view of De Jiao charitable activities in Malaysia and Singapore reveals nevertheless that a significant portion of such assistance benefits the ethnic Chinese. Such an orientation may be interpreted with reference to the demographic preponderance of the Chinese in Singapore and in reaction to the government policy favouring *Bumiputra* in Malaysia, as well as a consequence of the cultural and religious barriers demarcating the Chinese and the Malay Muslims. For example, the need for access to *halal* food prevents Malay Muslims from benefiting from Chinese charity in these countries.

The main contribution of the De Jiao associations in Malaysia to the welfare of their own folk concerns costly medical care excluded from public health cover. Such support may concerns either a surgical operation which could not be carried out without such assistance, or intensive therapeutic regimens. Among the latter, Zi, Ji and Zhen agencies provided haemodialysis services at the time of my investigation. They supported low-income patients affected by end-stage kidney failure. In most cases, compliance with established medical standards was guaranteed by the National Kidney Foundation of Malaysia (NKF), a non-governmental authority established in 1969. Although the support of many De Jiao associations was limited to the raising of funds for NKF, they sometimes provided both building and equipment, while NKF paid the medical staff and maintained the machines. The dialysis centre built in Ipoh and inaugurated in 1996 is a good example of the latter case. The donations to establish the centre came from a pool of 18 Zi and Ji pavilions in Perak state. The pool offered the building and 29 haemodialysis machines for a total cost of 2 million ringgit (about US$533,000). It even pays the salaries of the administrative staff and covers part of the treatment cost for the 60 patients the centre looks after. The dialysis centre that four Zi and Ji associations of Taiping (Perak) manage in co-operation with NKF operates exactly on the same basis. It is equipped with 13 machines and looks after an average number of 30 patients. Another example already mentioned is the Zhen Federation's dialysis centre located in Parit Buntar (north of Perak State), which was being completed in 2003. It will be fitted out with 10 machines and could provide treatment to 20 patients. At the time of the study, some very rich associations were even able to manage a centre without any help from NKF. Such was the case for Zi Luan Ge (Kluang, Johor) and Zi Ying Ge (Batu Pahat, Johor). It emerged from inquiries that two-thirds of the patients in these centres were ethnic Chinese, a quarter was citizens of Indian origin, and Malay counted for less than 10 per cent of the total.

Such figures should be partly interpreted with reference to the reluctance of most Malay to be treated by Chinese medical staff. This because of the segregation that Islam establishes between "pure" and "true" Muslims and non-believers, and as a result of the prejudices that decades of inter-ethnic tensions have rooted in the people's mentality. The same factor and also the analogous services that Muslim charitable organizations offer help explain the fact that very few Malay attend the free surgeries in western medicine that several De Jiao pavilions offer to sick individual whatever their level of income.[23] In return, the Malaysian policy of positive discrimination favouring *Bumiputra* prompts the ethnic Chinese to give precedence to the interests of their own community and to develop all activities preserving their culture. The fact that almost every De Jiao association in Malaysia supports financially the Chinese schools and colleges in its neighbourhood is also illustrative of this attitude. Some pavilions go as far as to have a school of their own. Zi Ping Ge thus manages since 1976 the biggest private kindergarten in the city of Taiping. It can accommodate 500 children, amongst whom 90 per cent are ethnic Chinese. A majority of parents are not adepts of De Jiao, but take advantage of the small tuition the association asks for. Zi Peng Ge of Teluk Intan, Zan Hua Ge of Bukit Mertajam, and Zhen Shan Ge of Began Serai also manage the same kind of establishment at a smaller scale.

Another aspect of this involvement in education lies in the bursary awards that most associations in Malaysia offer to meritorious students. Usually the contest is restricted to children of followers. Several agencies also manage a Chinese library, a service unknown to the pavilions of Thailand. For example, Ji Cheng Ge of Taiping and Li Shan Ge of Sungai Petani have opened in the 1980s libraries which accommodate between 30 and 60 students daily and had in 2003 collections of about 15,000 Chinese books each. Ji Cheng Ge also manages a publishing house which prints Buddhist and Taoist classics as well as De Jiao *fu ji* texts. For its part, Zi Luan Ge of Kluang established in 2001 a library which had gathered a collection of more than 5,000 Chinese books in 2003.

A wide range of teachings and training programs which would interest both adults and teenagers are also proposed. Some associations such as Ji De Ge (Ipoh), Zhen Nan Ge (Johor Bahru), and Zhen Wen Ge (Parit Buntar) organize classes and contests in calligraphy; others do the same for Chinese poetry or Buddhist meditation. In some places, youngsters are also taught in Confucian and Buddhist morals through regular lessons, and several pavilions invite occasionally theosophists and representatives of the "five great religions" to do conferences. Chinese music is not neglected as well: Ji Yang Ge and Zi Ji Ge have set up renowned Teochew orchestras, three other pavilions have a choral, and karaoke has not spared De Jiao in Malaysia and Singapore, as groups of seniors spend nights singing with gusto Chinese popular tunes in the reception halls of their associations. Training in *tai ji quan*, *qi gong*, and *wai tan gong* is also popular among the Malaysian adepts. About ten pavilions organized in 2003 sessions to teach one of these techniques aimed at health, longevity, and spiritual harmony.

With respect to health care, the most recurring service remains the supply of free Chinese medicine. Most associations manage a pharmacy stocked with traditional and modern Chinese drugs. The medicine is either bought from Malaysian wholesalers or imported from China. In many agencies the service is part of *fu ji* curing: patients receive a divine instruction and the pharmacy supplies the prescribed drugs. Otherwise, doctors of Chinese medicine, either remunerated or volunteers, issue free prescriptions that the association honours. Sometimes, the De Jiao association is locally in the vanguard for this service and therefore allocates to it large amounts of money. Such is the case for Zi Chang Ge (Melaka), which is also the most dynamic in this field. It manages a stock of drugs mainly imported from China whose approximate value is 500,000 ringgit (about US$130,000). In 2003 it had a staff of four doctors, and provided treatment to an average of 7,000 patients yearly. Ji Yang Ge (Alor Setar) is another case in point. It employs a Chinese doctor who graduated from a famous university in China and another one who works for the association as a volunteer. Together they conduct about 1,000 surgeries a month. Zi Peng Ge (Teluk Intan) offers surgeries and medical prescriptions as well as acupuncture treatments to an average number of 150 patients a week.

To provide a complete picture on the activities of the Malaysian and Singaporean pavilions, let us briefly mention their involvement in these key moments of family life: weddings and funerals. Concerning the first aspect, many agencies use to rent their reception halls for Chinese wedding ceremonies and festivities. In the north of peninsular Malaysia (Kedah, Penang, Perak), where strong interethnic tensions exist, they also act as a proxy for the Malaysian Bureau of Civil Affairs in the registration of marriages between ethnic Chinese. With regard to activities pertaining to funerals and ancestor worship, although very few associations have Chinese cemeteries because of the traditional primacy of lineage and dialect associations in this sector, a large number of them manage a funeral parlour and a tablets' hall. Following a recent trend, they also build columbaria to lodge funeral urns, as the Malaysian authorities urge the Chinese to cremate their dead. These services represent an important source of income, since the families who want their tablets and urns patronized by the "honourable masters" have to pay an initial accommodation fee as well as an annual fee to cover the cost of incense. For example, Ji Fang Ge of Singapore manages both a tablets' hall and a columbarium. Concerning the former, it has a total capacity of 16,000 spaces, of which 5,000 were already occupied in 2003. At that time, depending on the position of the tablet, the accommodation fee ranged from S$3,000 to S$5,000 (US$1,800–US$3,000). The columbarium for its part has a capacity of 5,000 spaces, of which 2,000 were already occupied, with the fee ranging from S$2,000 to S$6,000. Zi Luan Ge of Kluang (Johor) is another good example of an association having made significant inroads in this sector. It manages the main funeral parlour in the city, offers free funerals and tablet accommodation to poor families, and has built in 1997 a hall of 5,000 spaces which accommodated 2,000 tablets in 2003, the fee ranging at the time from 2,000 to 3,800 ringgit (US$520–US$988). Interestingly, though the De Jiao associations have few connections with the *shan tang* of Malaysia and Singapore, they have reproduced for their own ends and at a lesser extent the funeral services for ethnic Chinese which characterize the latter in these national contexts.

* * *

Finally, the accounts in this chapter and the previous section provide new evidences concerning the close links that De Jiao has maintained, all along history, with the Teochew "halls for good deeds". As was already the case in China, the movement's spread into Southeast Asia was carried out in occupational affinity and sometimes in co-operation with the network of these benevolent halls. Of course, the range of activities of the latter never coincided exactly with that of the former, so that each institution maintained its own identity. For instance, the practice of *fu ji* spirit-writing is of minor importance among the "halls for good deeds", while in return De Jiao hardly challenge the *shan tang* for services aiming at "good" management of death. At first glance, De Jiao and *shan tang* also differ concerning their overt objectives, the former theoretically placing greater stress on moral uplifting than the latter. But in practice, very few De Jiao associations develop a missionary zeal, most of them falling in consonance with the immediate charitable goals of the *shan tang* such as the relief of the poor and victims of disasters, the distribution of free medical care and medicine, and the "rescue" of orphaned dead. These links and the fact that the *shan tang* were already long established when De Jiao emerged in Southeast Asia explain that the former significantly helped the latter to take root locally by providing it with a proven model of adaptation, and by serving as a front to its activities in the Thai context. In Malaysia, the *shan tang* tradition also brought its cult font to a Zhen group resolutely turned toward immediate goals. In return, De Jiao contributed to enlarge the institutional basis of the Teochew religious identity overseas, notably by incorporating to its pantheon emblematic figures of this identity such as Song Da-Feng and He Ye-Yun.

The comparison between Thailand, Malaysia and Singapore regarding the spread of De Jiao confirm this movement as an excellent indicator of the Hua Qiao situation in those countries. First, this comparison makes appear the spatial distribution of De Jiao and that of the Chinese immigrants as closely correlating. De Jiao settled in countries and places where ethnic Chinese, and notably Teochew, were numerous (the West coast of Peninsular Malaysia, and the Central Plain of Thailand). Its political economy also changed in close connection with that of the Chinese of Malaysia and Thailand. For example, the impetus given to the spread of De Jiao in the 1970s ensues from both the regional economic boom of that time, which favoured Chinese entrepreneurship, and from important political changes (democratization in Thailand, political stabilization in Malaysia and Singapore after years of unrest due to decolonization). Furthermore, in full reflection of the relationships between natives and Chinese, De Jiao developed outward-oriented charity in Thailand, whereas in Malaysia the New Economic Policy favouring *Bumiputra* encouraged welfare activities benefiting first and foremost the Chinese community. In the specific case of Thailand, the patronage of De Jiao congregations by figures of the native elite also reflect the high degree of social integration of the Hua Qiao in this national context, while the lack of mediums that the movement locally faces, results of restraints on Chinese education imposed by the Thai state from 1932 onwards. More generally, the analysis proposed in Chapter II suggests that the main issue for the Chinese of Thailand is to resist the assimilationist policy they are subjected to, by the means of philanthropic redistribution and political connections. Although in comparison with those of Malaysia, the Chinese of Thailand enjoy an unchallenged control over the national economy, they are in return more assimilated, and religious practice, either private or collective, is the main domain where they can cultivate their cultural specificity. In this context, De Jiao perfectly exemplifies a common strategy used by local Chinese businessmen looking for community leadership, which consists of improving his social status by closely linking wealth, morality, and the defence of the in-group traditions, this behind the screen provided by outward-oriented charity. As M. Weber (1968: 242) rightly put it, “Chinese believe in the value of wealth as a universal means of moral perfection"; a statement that J. DeBernardi relays when she writes about the Chinese of Penang: "wealth indicates that a person has moral merit, but it also enables individuals to perform acts of charity that further confirm their moral status" (2006: 59). Because of its emphasis on moral uplifting and spirit-writing, De Jiao offered an ideal platform to manify, through signs of divine election, the high status to which could pretend the men in prospect of good deeds. In the particular case of Thailand, however, the prestige that the wealthy may gain from De Jiao active membership is enhanced by the fact that the free services they sponsors benefit, alternately and sometimes simultaneously, to adepts and to outsiders. As a consequence, their outlay for visibility and respectability is rewarded by both sides. On the ground of Buddhist values shared by both groups, they are unanimously acknowledged for their good morality, but they are also respected by their ethnic fellows for supporting the endangered Chinese sub-culture, and appreciated by the Thai for their welfare activities benefiting the host society. At the same time they give evidence of material detachment, a value that the Thai Buddhists particularly praise, they increase their credibility, a quality favourable to the development of political connections and businesses. In such conditions, philanthropic commitment may be viewed as a 100 per cent profit investment. It is certainly why the directorial boards of the main De Jiao pavilions incorporate prominent Teochew figures of Malaysia, Singapore, and Thailand. Through these community leaders, De Jiao has so far succeeded in reaching an audience much larger than its official membership could let suppose.

Headed by influent tycoons, De Jiao also recruits a majority of its members among entrepreneurs and traders, in congruence with the dominant occupational status of the Chinese immigrants. This sociological feature is part of the movement's identity, and although the two main instigators of De Jiao, Ma Gui-De and Li Huai-De, were respectively headmaster and civil servant in China, the movement eventually turned to merchants' management overseas. Significant of this evolution is the fact that Ma Gui-De became retailer of Chinese medicine after his move to Hong Kong, while Li Huai-De worked as an import-export broker when he settled in Singapore. It is certainly because its membership was patterned on the socio-economic profile of the overseas Chinese communities that De Jiao so intimately reflects their situation and strategies of adaptation. Reciprocally, it is in close connection with the structure of its membership overseas, that the most typical features of De Jiao took form. The early history of the movement, related in Chapter I, reveal that the migration of its adepts to Nanyang constituted a decisive step for its institutionalization. Accordingly, the ethos and praxis of the Chinese merchant communities living overseas permeated the patterns of its organization and expansion. In this new environment, business activities often constituted a useful framework to the spread of De Jiao. Such was the case when Zi Xin Ge took advantage of the frequent business trips of Ma Gui-De between Hong Kong and Singapore to devise important symbols of the De Jiao identity (logo, anthem ...), or when the main medium of Zi Zhen Ge extended the movement to several provinces of Thailand, thanks to his occupation of commercial traveller. Noteworthy too, is the fact that in this movement, like in business circles, formal links between institutions give precedence to interindividual and more flexible deals, as the Zi Piao Tan case illustrates it. Moreover, the correlated values of trust (*xin ren*) and interpersonal understanding (*kan qing*), which cement business relationships among Chinese, prove to be criteria of crucial importance in the "divine choice" of pavilions leaders. Lastly, pragmatism as key factor of adaptability and success in business, expecially in challenging environments, is also an important characteristic of De Jiao. Such pragmatism finds a good expression in the progressive integration of locally born temples or lines of cult. Whatever the country considered herein, the process was of significant extent and largely explains the quick spread of the movement overseas. The above descriptions have shown that the requirements to become a member of the organization were very few. In most cases, the mutual acknowledgement of divine oracles as well as the commitment of the applicant community to adopt the "Canon of De Jiao" and certain emblems sufficed. The motivations of the De Jiao leaders to admit so easily new members were manifold: to enlarge at a lesser cost the social basis of the movement, to increase the number of their mediums in a context of shortage, or to surpass rival organizations. In return, the applicants could hope to benefit from the logistics and solidarity of an extensive international organization officially approved at the national level. In the case of overseas-born groups such as Ji, Zhen, and Zan Hua, they could also strengthen their legitimacy by joining with a religious movement whose origins could be traced back to China.

The consequence of such a propensity is a noteworthy variability concerning strategies and local adjustments. In such a process of adjustment, the minority can hardly pretend to a complete mastery of the local conditions, though the opportunistic manipulation of cultural otherness and of the government's political agenda may occur. Let us be reminded here that acculturation partly rests on unconscious borrowings resulting from the possibly combined effects of ideological inculcation, empathy, and routine. It is with reference to these sociological factors that one should interpret the spontaneous reproduction by UMUSOM of the short-term rotating chairmanship model which applies to the Federation of Malaysia, as well as the adaptation by the De Jiao Federation of Thailand of the so-called galactic polity which characterized Thai society for centuries. In these cases De Jiao leaders reproduced the patterns of organization and legitimacy which were the most recognizable within their limited political horizons. To take another example, LJX, the president of Tai He Guan and Ji Yun Ge, was certainly clever enough to take conscious advantage of Li Guang-Yao's ideology of "Asian values", but he did it especially as he had grown in a Singaporean political context where the inculcation of such values was a priority, and their promotion was part of "the nature of things".

Indeed, the result of such a pragmatism and correlative open-door policy is that De Jiao may appear as a real mess for those sociologists and anthropologists who study either very localized and non-stratified religious complexes or conversely universalistic religions based on a dogma, a clerical hierarchy, and a sharp distinction between true believers and infidels. Antithetic to these features, De Jiao should prompt us to question how religious movements conveyed by minorities scattered over wide social spaces may maintain a minimal ground of common meaning, basic identity, and shared interests despite a broad geographical footprint and diversity in practices.

Local variation being the common lot of the religion in practice (and practice of religion) as soon as it extends over the village micro-level, the analysis of how De Jiao manages it on a large scale may be all the more useful to qualify the monolithic and oversimplified view of religious activity that so many monographs convey. In the next chapter, by carrying out this analysis through the comparison of various congregations I shall make mine the observation of F. Barth (1993: 4) that: "Local variation (…) is not a surface disturbance to be covered over by generalization or tidied away by a typology. It is a ubiquitous feature (…) and we should make it a major component of our description and characterization (…) rather than a difficulty to be overcome."

CHAPTER IV

De Jiao's Unity and Diversity

The previous chapters have shown that since its early beginnings De Jiao developed by progressively amalgamating small-scale cult communities, and that the phenomenon gained in importance when the organization began to spread to Southeast Asia. Although enlargement, splitting, segmentation, and internal diversification are part of the usual dynamics of religions in complex societies, observable variations were rendered more pronounced with respect to De Jiao by the fact that this religious movement was neither strongly institutionalized nor dogmatic. Also contributing to its striking diversity is the wide geographical scattering of its congregations and their necessary adjustments to various national and socio-cultural contexts. Because of this international expansion, the seemingly endless local variations that D. Johnson (1995: VIII) rightly identifies as a leading characteristic of popular religion in premodern China were significantly increased in the present case.

These features make De Jiao a case study remarkable enough for one to reconsider the relation between unity and diversity in Chinese religion that M. Freedman and A. Wolf debated about in the mid-1970s. Let us recall that for Freedman (1974), and before him for L. Dumont (1966), religious diversity in the Asiatic holistic societies stems from various transformations of a basic structural unity, the identification of which being the main task of the anthropologist. To take a musical metaphor, they are minor variations on a common theme. A. Wolf (1974), on the contrary, is sceptical about the existence of such a theme. Emphasizing diversity over unity, he argues that between the religion of the elite and that of the peasantry the gulf is so vast that whether a common set of ideas or symbols was shared by the whole society it would be relatively insignificant or easily invested with different meanings. Consequently, the task he assigns to the scientist is to reconstruct the beliefs of people who view the Chinese landscape from different perspectives. More recently, R.P. Weller tried to get over the shortcomings of this simplistic debate, which consists of envisaging Chinese religion as unified if one focuses on the entire society, and diverse if one focuses on the groups within it. He instead invites us to adopt a more comprehensive and less deterministic view of religion "which does not automatically associate a predetermined set of beliefs with a particular, bounded group" (1987: 5).

Weller's approach greatly benefited from reassessments of the concept of culture that previous authors have proposed. He himself refers to R. Williams (1977), who views culture and ideology as a kind of work, and to E. Sapir (1934), who was the first to denounce the dominant trend which depicts culture as a sum of picturesque traits and patterns of behaviour (1934: 200). Another pioneering contribution, though not mentioned by Weller, is that of A.F. Wallace (1952: 747–8), who stresses individual variations and opposes the classical standardizing view of culture as a quasi-statistical one, based on regularities in behaviour and cognition.

In this chorus of reappraisals, the point of view of F. Barth should not be omitted, since he radically breaks with the idea of society as a structure or a closed system, considering it instead as a set of combined processes. Barth suggests that each person constructs his own reality by making choices between the ranges of options and notably the ideational possibilities that a person's cultural context offers. The variations he identifies at the micro-social level concern received traditions, local history, experiences, and expertises, as well as the pragmatics of purposes and interests. Finally, he suggests that we should "give up the pipe dream of coherence and concentrate on developing theory and concepts for analyzing disordered systems" (1993: 5).

The focus of Barth on works of social construction of reality rightly counterbalances decades of emphasis on how cultural knowledge is patterned and instantiated. Nevertheless, my own experience of Southeast Asia inspires me to consider societies and cultures as mixed realities, partly systemic and partly resulting from a multitude of individual and collective processes of adjustment to changing conditions and environments. Although F. Barth does not deny the existence of shared conventions and ethical commitments, he follows Wolf by thinking that they are too numerous to be put together into one cohering structure, and too many to be universally and equally shared (1993: 5). Against this view which ignores the systemic, though pragmatic, aspects of education,[1] we should be reminded that each society depends for its perpetuation on a minimal set of ideas, values, and institutions transmitted from generation to generation, if not identically, at least in continuity of meaning. As L. de Heusch (1997: 190) notes: "It is precisely because they are convinced to be the heirs of a pre-existing socio-cultural system that people usually live with the delusion that they share the same ancestors."

In the present chapter, without neglecting the ways information and knowledge are produced and transmitted, I wish to explore, through the case study of De Jiao, these concrete processes, neither necessarily coherent nor essentially contradictory, which maintain a feeling of unity among members of religious groups whatever the variations they produce. To what specific set of practices, institutions, ideas, and values do these processes refer? How do they create links between people and communities? What are the properties and scope of these connections? How, in such a context, may local and global identities hang together? Finally, how can the combination of disparate worshipping activities result in a self-conscious religious organization? The fact that De Jiao was never centrally governed and that its tenets were never standardized through the agency of a papacy-like centre of power enhances the relevancy of such questions. It also leads us to think about the organisational features of this movement. Does it correspond to the "a-centred" systems that J. Petitot and P. Rosenstiehl (1974: 48–51) define as a network "in nebula", where communication takes place between neighbours, and where local operations are coordinated so that their achievements can be synchronized apart from any central authority? The two authors contrast these organizations with "directory structures", which are holistic in ideology and regulated both by leaders and subordinates, the latter adjusting their behaviour step by step with regard to the norms that their position in the arborescence requires. The fact that local segments of De Jiao sub-groups are historically ordered according to the *xiang huo* ritual and that some pavilions exert great influence over the others due to their prosperity and political connections suggests that the movement could possibly present hybrid forms between a-centred and directory structures. I shall verify here whether this hypothesis holds through a comparative review of the pantheons, liturgies, and ideologies they promote.

Resorting to the concept of *rhizome*, as defined by G. Deleuze and F. Guattari (1980: 30–6), may also be useful in characterizing De Jiao relational patterns and in discussing the main aspects of the movement's dynamics. These authors draw a distinction, which largely tallies with that of Petitot and Rosenstiehl, between two models of organization and spread: one defined with reference to the *tree*, and the other to the *rhizome*. Whereas the relational logic of the former is *descent*, that of the latter is *alliance* (in the case of De Jiao, headed and shaped since its early beginnings by traders and businessmen, the similar notion of *contract* would be more appropriate). Any point or element of the rhizome can be connected to any other one. This property, which perfectly corresponds to De Jiao, endows it with an outstanding adaptability and durability. When the rhizome is broken in one of its parts, it can grow back through any of its stems or start a new one. The question is indeed to know if these properties apply to the De Jiao social and cultural "metabolism". The concept of rhizome is also interesting for our purposes since segmentation is one of its basic features, and it is compatible with the idea of hierarchy. According to Deleuze and Guattari (1980: 30), there are nodes of arborescence within the rhizome and sometimes even despotic formations.

Architecture and the Pavilions' Ornamentation

The architecture and adornment of the shrines are certainly the most immediately perceptible aspects with regard to the "formal" diversity that De Jiao espouses. Although in most religions throughout the world, uniformity in these domains is the exception rather than the rule, and although there is no Chinese temple whose building and ornamentation are similar to those of the others, in the case of De Jiao the variations are increased by the wide range of economic and political constraints that the movement faces. For example, because of the scarcity of land in Hong Kong, two out of the three local De Jiao associations occupy flats at the top floors of skyscrapers; such associations chose to occupy the topmost floors because adherents believe that the gods will not take kindly to the knowledge that people can actually reside in dwellings that allow mere mortals to stay above the gods. Also, the associations are ostensibly aware that condominium residents, if they live in units which are located above the storey or level where the shrines are situated, will find the constant smoke and smell of incense emanating from the shrines to be intolerable. In addition to such constraints, De Jiao is not allowed to display outer marks of religiosity in its establishments because of restrictive joint-ownership rules in Hong Kong's condominiums.

The land pressure characterizing the New Territories gives way to political and legal restrictions concerning Malaysia and Singapore. In these countries, according to informants, several legal restrictions hamper the founding of religious shrines (especially in the case of the non-Muslims in Malaysia); thus, it is more profitable from a political viewpoint for the De Jiao congregations to be registered as "moral societies". But, in exchange for attaining such status, the terms and conditions stipulate that moral societies should steer clear of the external display of religious symbols. With the exception of the logo or flag of the movement, whose display is authorized, nothing distinguishes the frontages of the premises of De Jiao associations from the features of buildings dedicated to housing secular services and commerce. Indeed, many De Jiao pavilions in these countries occupy nondescript ordinary shop houses located along streets in business districts. Concealment of the movement's overt symbols is most manifest in the PRC, where De Jiao is officially banned. Thus, De Jiao activities in the PRC are necessarily conducted in secret in private flats and houses. Conversely, in a country such as Thailand, which is known for its religious openness, De Jiao associations can openly display their religious inclinations by adorning more or less ostentatiously the frontages and roofs of their establishments with dragons and other traditional symbols of Chinese identity.

Whatever the level of regulatory restrictions which inevitably affects the structural design and ornamentation of the individual pavilions, the conditions imposed by local authorities are secondary in comparison with the architectural and aesthetic choices enforced by *ji wen*. Whenever I asked devotees about how the general framework of their pavilion or its decoration was arrived at, their usual answer was that "it had been done according to the tastes and wishes of the honourable masters". According to this view, the shrine is a place devoted to the gods' rest and enjoyment; thus, it is all the more important to make the place appealing, in order for the gods to be enticed to visit it regularly. Another idea is to rely on "divine" calculations to strengthen the geomantic power of the pavilion and to make it a truly effective place of exchange and interaction between humans and deities.

In some associations, the argument is pushed to the point that gods are consulted for every detail. Such was, for example, the case for Zi Luang Ge of the Malaysian town of Kluang. In 1997, its influential leaders decided to construct new premises which they envisioned to become the biggest and most richly decorated religious establishment in the country. To this end and to make the pavilion a very auspicious place, spirit-writing was used at every stage of the construction. The blueprint of the building, its orientation, and its precise placement in the yard were all determined through *fu ji*, as well as the height of the edifice, the extent of the surface area and other dimensions of its halls and rooms, the size of its gates, doors, and windows, the colour of its walls, the size of the main gods' statues, and even the number of steps and the height of each step of its staircases, with no step having the same height as the others. In fact, Zi Luang Ge represents these few pavilions built without any architectural and financial restrictions. When devotees convert premises originally allocated for commercial purposes into pavilions and have little money to do so, the gods' whims and expectations are reduced accordingly. In other words, "divine choices" in practice are often the outcome of a set of compromises between human capabilities and *ji wen* instructions.

In June 2003, I attended by hazard the planchette sessions and meetings preparatory to the building of the premises of the National Federation of Thailand. SZM, the president of the said Federation, hired the services of a firm of architects to prepare the building's design. As the main sponsor of the project, he was anxious not to exceed his budget and instructed the architects accordingly. Planchette writings suggested, however, the implementation of costly "improvements" which the project committee finally agreed to consider. In this particular case, the decision-making process unfolded as follows: the president of the Federation, the project committee members, and the architects would submit their plans to the gods during a *fu ji* session. This would be followed by a debriefing in order to ascertain how to best implement the alleged divine instructions and how the association could finance the additional expenditure. The mediums involved in the oracles would not be participating in the meetings, although they would be informed of their outcomes. Interestingly, in this particular case the gods proved to be flexible: they "chose" to acquiesce to the "counsel" of their adherents regarding the unsuitability of further changes. Against the followers' claim, such an example suggests that the divine orders legitimate, in practice, human choices and capabilities.

This process of inducement applies not only to the building of shrines, but also to the selection of the shrines' adornments, which are constantly augmented by offerings from worshippers. These offerings may consist of mural paintings, banners, statues, and other religious items, and in certain cases the generosity of devotees can go as far as to contribute funds to expand the premises of the association. In each case, the gods' approval is requested through *fu ji*. Ji De Ge, the mother-temple of the Ji group, offers a good example of this process. The magic painting and the calligraphy which now serve as emblems of the group and whose copies are hanged on the altars of every Ji associations were initially a present from a founder of the association, You Ming-Qi. He claimed to have received them, through *fu ji*, as a personal gift from Bai Yun and He Ye-Yun. The painting and the calligraphy were interpreted as a tribute of the two Immortals to Ji Gong. They were stored in a sacred room devoted to Crazy Ji, together with other precious items. In 2003, these *sacra* consisted of: (1) an ancient head of Guan Yin carved from an elephant tusk, that You Ming-Qi bought in China and offered to the association; (2) a old statue of Ji Gong brought from Hangzhou by a group of devotees; (3) another precious statue of Ji Gong that LJX, the president of Ji Yun Ge (Singapore) offered to the president of Ji De Ge; and (4) old willow sticks that members of the Ji group discovered miraculously in the ruins of Zi He Ge, one of the earliest De Jiao pavilions founded in Chao-Shan.

The devotees who contribute to the enrichment of their respective pavilions are motivated not only by issues of parochial identity but also by the desire to make the pavilions a very attractive place for the gods to visit. Believed to be promoters of the glory of ancient Chinese civilization, the "honourable masters" cannot but be pleased by the overt display of their own culture's refinement and strength. It explains in part why the aesthetic choices of the adepts try to conform as much as possible with Chinese standards of splendour and sophistication. For the same reason, but also in order to encapsulate the major principles of the universe into the microcosm of the temple, the mural paintings and other elements of iconography derive without exception their themes and symbols from Chinese cosmology and mythology. The precious objects that I described above as the *sacra* of Ji De Ge perfectly illustrate this cultural introversion. Most of the *sacra* are deemed ancient relics closely associated with the gods and are thus sufficiently holy to be brought from the country of origin. These relics therefore contribute to the strengthening of the association's sense of identity and spiritual links with the motherland that the temples and other shrines embody.

The Gods' Society

In previous chapters I mentioned several times the compound *de de she* ("association of the great virtue"). By this concept, which is specific to De Jiao, the devotees refer to the community of gods who use spirit-writing as a medium for teaching virtue. In Chapter I, I provided a definition of it which a Malaysian pavilion published as part of its exegesis on the *De Jiao Xin Dian* (Ji Cheng Ge, 1998: 18). According to this definition, *de de she* is a divine association established by the Jade Emperor, together with the founders of the five great religious doctrines and other heavenly gods. Although in Thailand and in the PRC the divine "teachings" are reduced from five to three because of the lesser relevance of Christianity and Islam in those national contexts, the basic ideas remain: that the *de de she* brings together the gods of heaven under the leadership of the Jade Emperor, who is also considered as the main founder of the association and is assisted by Guan Ping as master-in-charge.

From the above statements it may be inferred that, although the *de de she* may be expanded to cover so-called western gods, it remains under the authority of Chinese rulers. The fact that the deities who straddle the flying *luan*-bird are invariably of Chinese origin and that the Malaysian adepts respect Jesus Christ and the Prophet Muhammad but do not worship them confirm the China-centrism underlying the concept. The association is not clearly delineated for all that. Even if some gods are more active and popular than others, the *de de she* encompasses potentially all the Taoist Immortals and Buddhist saints who are supposed to inhabit the heavenly empyrean. In so doing, it theoretically leaves room for an infinite number of local combinations.

I personally observed the variability that such openness implies while doing fieldwork. Among the 80 or so pavilions visited between 1993 and 2004, none had its shrine exactly laid out as another one, and the same observation applies to the portfolio of deities they venerated. Tables 1 and 2 provide insight on these local variations concerning the gods being venerated for a sample group of 50 associations distributed throughout five countries or territories (Thailand, Malaysia, Singapore, Hong Kong, and the PRC). This sample reflects the ratio that each national branch denotes with regard to the total number of De Jiao associations in 2004. In the case of Malaysia and Singapore, I also tried to take into account the relative proportion of the different sub-groups (Zi, Ji, Zhen, and Zan Hua). The census only takes into account the gods whose presence in the shrine was permanently marked both by a specific incense burner and a painting or a statue.[2] It does not cover those deities who were invited to rally the temple occasionally, either at the occasion of *xiu gu gu*, calendar festivals (Spring Festival, *Pu Du*), or birthday celebrations. Moreover, the scope of the inquiry being limited to the heavenly gods entering the *de de she*, Tu Di Gong, Di Mu Niang-Niang, San Shan Guo-Wang,[3] and other earth gods were excluded.

A brief analysis of the two tables reveals that the De Jiao local cults are based on specific clusters of gods selected within an array of about 40 divine entities. The largest combination, that of Zi Feng Ge of Chonburi (Thailand), does not exceed 20 gods, whereas the smallest is composed of a pair (such was the case of most of the Ji associations in Malaysia). In fact, the cults of a majority of associations (62 per cent) are based on clusters ranging from five to nine deities. In Thailand, the congregations worship the largest number of gods (from 8 to 20); this can be attributed to the influence of a local environment which is teeming with popular Buddhist cults and gods. The proportion of Buddhist saints being worshipped in the pavilions of Thailand is higher than in the other countries,

Table 1 Local De Jiao Cults, An Outline (Part I)

	Taoist Deities																			Buddhist Gods																Others				
Asso-ciations / *Gods*	*1*	*2*	*3*	*4*	*5*	*6*	*7*	*8*	*9*	*10*	*11*	*12*	*13*	*14*	*15*	*16*	*17*	*18*	*19*	*20*	*21*	*22*	*23*	*24*	*25*	*26*	*27*	*28*	*29*	*30*	*31*	*32*	*33*	*34*	*35*	*36*	*37*	*38*	*39*	*40*
1. Malaysia																																								
Zi Group																																								
Zi Fang Ge Kuala Lumpur	x		x	x	x						x	x																												
Zi Seng Ge Seremban	x		x	x	x						x										x																			
Zi Chang Ge Malacca	x		x	x							x	x								x	x																			
Zi Luang Ge Kluang	x		x	x		x					x	x								x	x				x	x								x						
Zi Peng Ge Teluk Intan			x	x	x						x	x																												
Zi Ping Ge Taiping	x		x	x	x						x	x																												
Zi Xiao Ge Ipoh			x	x	x						x	x									x															x				
Zi Yun Ge Penang	x				x	x					x	x	x																											x
Zi Kang Ge Bahau	x		x	x	x						x	x																												
Zi Liang Ge Kuala Lumpur	x		x		x						x	x																						x						x
Zi Jia Ge Kuala Lumpur	x		x	x	x						x	x									x																			x
Zi Ying Ge Batu Pahat	x		x	x	x						x	x																												
Zi Shu Ge Johor Bahru	x		x	x	x						x	x										x																		
Zi Ming Ge Ipoh	x	x	x	x	x						x	x																						x						
Zi Feng Ge Serdang			x	x			x													x																				

Table 1 continued

Gods / Associations	*Taoist Deities*																			*Buddhist Gods*																*Others*				
	1	*2*	*3*	*4*	*5*	*6*	*7*	*8*	*9*	*10*	*11*	*12*	*13*	*14*	*15*	*16*	*17*	*13*	*19*	*20*	*21*	*22*	*23*	*24*	*25*	*26*	*27*	*28*	*29*	*30*	*31*	*32*	*33*	*34*	*35*	*36*	*37*	*38*	*39*	*40*
2. Thailand																																								
Zi Group																																								
Zi Wei Ge Bangkok	x		x		x						x	x	x	x						x	x									x			x	x	x					x
Zi Tong Ge Bangkok		x	x		x						x	x	x	x			x				x		x												x			x		x
Zi Ming Ge Bangkok			x		x						x	x	x	x						x	x	x																		
Zi Lan Ge Rangsit		x	x		x						x	x	x	x					x	x	x	x												x	x		x		x	
Zi Zhen Ge Bangkok	x	x	x	x	x			x			x	x	x	x				x	x	x	x	x												x	x		x			
Zi Chen Ge Bangkok			x		x						x	x	x	x		x				x	x													x						
Xuan Chen Bangkok	x	x									x	x								x	x	x												x						
Zi Feng Ge Chonburi	x		x		x						x	x	x	x			x			x	x	x	x	x	x	x		x			x	x							x	x
Zi Piao Tan Siracha	x		x	x	x	x					x	x	x	x		x				x	x				x	x				x					x					
Zi Nan Ge Hat Yai					x						x	x	x	x							x													x	x					
Zi Ming Ge Ranong					x						x	x	x	x						x	x														x					
Zi Yi Ge Roeit					x						x	x	x	x						x	x	x																		
Zi Qing Ge Chumpae					x						x	x	x	x						x		x												x	x					

Table 2 Local De Jiao Cults, An Outline (Part II)

	Taoist Deities																			*Buddhist Gods*																*Others*				
Gods / *Asso-ciations*	*1*	*2*	*3*	*4*	*5*	*6*	*7*	*8*	*9*	*10*	*11*	*12*	*13*	*14*	*15*	*16*	*17*	*18*	*19*	*20*	*21*	*22*	*23*	*24*	*25*	*26*	*27*	*28*	*29*	*30*	*31*	*32*	*33*	*34*	*35*	*36*	*37*	*38*	*39*	*40*
3. Hong Kong																																								
Zi Group																																								
Zi Xiang Ge	x		x		x			x				x								x								x	x		x			x	x					x
4. Singapore																																								
Tai He Guan	x		x	x	x							x							x															x					x	x
Zi Xin Ge	x		x	x	x						x	x																						x						
5. P.R. of China																																								
Zi Group																																								
Zi Ying Ge Guangzhou	x				x							x								x	x		x											x						
Zi Xiang Ge Heping											x	x								x	x													x						
6. Malaysia																																								
Ji Group																																								
Ji De Ge Ipoh																					x													x						
Ji Xian Ge Petaling Jaya																					x													x						
Ji Yang Ge Alor Setar					x						x		x			x					x													x	x					
Ji Cheng Ge Taiping																					x													x						

Table 2 continued

	Taoist Deities																			Buddhist Gods																Others				
Associations / Gods	1	2	3	4	5	6	7	8	9	10	11	12	13	14	15	16	17	18	19	20	21	22	23	24	25	26	27	28	29	30	31	32	33	34	35	36	37	38	39	40
Zhen Group																																								
Zhen Zhong Ge Malacca	x					x									x																									
Zhen Wen Ge Parit Buntar				x		x			x	x					x						x													x	x					
Zhen An Ge Tanjung Piandang				x		x	x								x				x	x	x													x	x					
Zhen Yi Ge Kuala Kurau				x		x			x						x																				x					
Zhen Shan Ge Began Serai	x			x											x															x				x	x					
Zhen Nan Ge Johor Bahru													x		x																			x						
Zhen Guan Ge Tanjung Piandang						x									x																			x	x					
Zhen Xing Ge Sitiawan	x					x									x																			x						
Zan Hua Group																																								
Zi Tian Ge Padang Serai				x			x																																	
Zan Hua Ge Bukit Mertajam	x		x		x		x													x														x						
Li Shan Ge Sungai Pettani						x	x														x											x		x						
Others																																								
Ji Huo Gong Ji Johor Bahru			x			x			x						x						x						x							x	x					
Zi Ji Ge Bukit Mertajams	x		x								x									x	x													x						

(continued overleaf)

Notes:

List of Gods

Taoist Gods

(1) *Guan Yu* enthroned as the Jade Emperor
(2) *Guan Ping Shao-Di*
(3) *Lao Zi*
(4) *Ba Xian* (as a group – The Eight Immortals)
(5) *Lü Dong-Bin* (one of the *Ba Xian*)
(6) *Li Dao-Ming* (one of the *Ba Xian*)
(7) *He Xian-Gu* (one of the *Ba Xian*)
(8) *Zhong Li-Quan* (one of the *Ba Xian*)
(9) *Nan Xiang-Zi* (one of the *Ba Xian*)
(10) *Zhang Guo-Lo* (one of the *Ba Xian*)
(11) *Liu Chun-Fang*
(12) *Yang Jun-Song*
(13) *Bai Yun*
(14) *Wu Meng-Wu*
(15) *Song Chan*
(16) *He Ye-Yun*
(17) *Sun Si-Miao* (Famous Physician of the Tang Dynasty)
(18) *San Quing* (the Three Perfects or Heavenly Venerable)
(19) *Xuan Tian Shang-Di* (The Supreme Lord of the Dark Sky [North])

Buddhist Saints and Bodhisattva

(20) *Śakyamuni* (Buddha)
(21) *Guan Yin* (*Avalokitesvara*)
(22) *Mi-Le Fo* (*Maitreya*)
(23) *Di Zang-Wang* (*Ksitigarbha* – Lord of the Kingdom of the Dead)
(24) *Wei Tuo Pu-Sa* (the "warrior" Buddha of the Chinese Buddhist mythology)
(25) *Pu Xian* (*Samantabhadra*, a promoter of Tantric Buddhism, pictured as straddling a white elephant)
(26) *Wen Shu* (*Manjusri*, symbol of the wisdom, who controls the forces of Death and Life, pictured as straddling a golden mane's lion)
(27) *Shi Ba Luo-Han* (the Eighteen Arahants)
(28) *Yao-Shi Fo* (*Bhaishajyaguru*, Buddhist deity of medicine)
(29) *A-Mi-Tuo Fo* (*Adhibuddha* of the West)
(30) *Cai Shen* (*Kuvera* or *Vaishravana*, head of the Yaksha and Guhyaka who protect wealth)
(31) *Ru-Lai Fo* (Tathâgata. A classifier for Gautama and his six forebears)
(32) *Da Mo* (a famous monk of Shao Lin)
(33) *Bu Kong* (Amoghavajra)
(34) *Ji Gong*
(35) *Song Da-Feng*

Others

(36) *Ri/Yue* (Sun/Moon)
(37) *Ma Zu* (Goddess of Heaven and of the Southern Sea)
(38) *Sun Wu-Kong* (the fabulous monkey, hero of the *Journey to the West*)
(39) *Hua Tuo* (famous physician of the Eastern and Three Kingdoms Era)
(40) *Liu Bei-Gong/Guang Di Fu-Gong/Zhang Fu-Gong* (deified generals of the Three Kingdoms Era)

so that the imbalance in favour of Taoist deities, which is salient for most pavilions (those of the Ji group apart), is reduced in this national context.

A careful analysis of the clusters reveals that most associations of the same group share a minimal core of gods as a hallmark of collective identity, without claiming however any monopoly of worship redounding to the benefit of their respective cults. Thus, the 30 Zi pavilions of the sample but three worship the Taoist masters Liu Chun-Fang and Yang Jun-Song, while the Ji associations venerate Ji Gong and Guan Yin, the Zhen associations venerate the Taoist master Song Chan, and the Zan Hua agencies revere the Immortal He Xian-Gu. The pattern takes on a new dimension for the national branches of the Zi group, the cult core being enlarged in this case to encompass a new set of gods. For instance, all of the Zi associations of Thailand but one share the basic Taoist scheme: Lü Dong-Bin + Liu Chun-Fang + Yang Jun-Song + Bai Yun + Wu Meng-Wu; whereas most of their Malaysian counterparts have in common the following amalgamation: Guan Yu enthroned as the Jade Emperor + Lao Zi + The Eight Immortals + Liu Chun-Fang + Yan Jun-Song.

These cult cores of variable extent, which help define the religious identity of each group and of their national branches, illustrate what G. Deleuze and F. Guattari (1980: 19–21) call a *calque*. According to them, this pattern is based on the principles of *deep structure* and of *genetic axis*. Whereas the deep structure is defined as the basic series, decomposable in discrete components, the genetic axis is conceived as a "swivelling objective unit" which is paradigmatic of successive stages. By working in close combination, these two principles produce duplicates. Deleuze and Guattari oppose this model to that of the *map* which characterizes the rhizome-like processes. They describe the latter as a fluctuating structure, open to endless and continual variations, connectable through all its dimensions, which can be dismantled or inverted. Such features define the germane aspects of the De Jiao pantheons which are left to the discretion of local initiatives, thus suggesting that these pantheons are hybrid structures, partly *calque* and partly *map*, retaining properties both of the tree and of the rhizome, of the genealogy and of the anti-genealogy, of the hierarchy, and of a-centred systems.

An analysis of the De Jiao "supernatural maps" shows that the choices which shape the specific identity of the local cult communities may refer indistinctly to prominent deities of the Taoist and Buddhist pantheons (such as the Eight Immortals, Sun Si-Miao, Maitreya, Adhibuddha), or to minor gods, whose popularity does not extend beyond the frontiers of the Teochew area (such as He Ye-Yun, Song Chan, or Song Da-Feng). Even within the first category, the devotees often select the figures to worship according to the cult traditions of their respective hometowns in China. For instance, the high number of Chinese shrines in Thailand, including some De Jiao associations, which worship Xuan Tian Shang-Di, The supreme Lord of the Dark Sky, results in the great popularity of his cult in Chao-Shan, especially in the areas of Chaoyang, Jieyang, Huilai and Lufeng.

The gods of Chao-Shan and the gods popular in Chao-Shan are logically familiar to a majority of Teochew followers of De Jiao who usually know folktales about their legendary lives and main attributes. Although the followers' knowledge of the features and properties of the "great gods" may be fragmented, these deities are among the most popular and, put together, form a religious idiom whose basic meanings are known to almost every Chinese. Even in the context of post-Mao China, few are indeed those who are unaware, for instance, that Hua Tuo and Sun Si-Miao are divine physicians, that Guan Yin is the Buddhist Goddess of Mercy, or that Guan Yu was a famous general during the Three Kingdoms' period.

Finally, by combining through its localized segments the main popular gods of China with those of Chao-Shan, the *de de she* expresses the embedding of two major levels of identification: the motherland and the place of origin within it. The "imagined community" of the heavenly gods thus symbolizes the "imagined community" of China as it is perceived through the prism of the Teochew worshippers. It also mirrors the political order of late imperial China, with the Jade Emperor at its apex and below him his heavenly appointees, literati, soldiers, or both. As rightly noticed by M. Shahar and R.P. Weller (1996: 5), the bureaucratic image applies not only to the structure of the Chinese heavens but also to the rules and means by which they operate. These two authors identify written documents as one of these primary means, and interpret the sealed charms (*fu*) as bureaucratic writs, which subdue ghosts by the superior authority of the gods. The divine instructions that the De Jiao followers receive through *wen ji*, result from the same logic. Accordingly, *de de she* not only features an imperial China that the overseas followers of De Jiao view with more or less nostalgia; it is first and foremost conceived as the quintessence of the potential energy and powers radiating from the empyrean. The virtue that De Jiao puts forward covers in fact a series of more concrete and immediate goals. Among them are concerns for individual health, longevity, wealth through supernatural mediations, and indeed the reinforcement of elders' authority through the promotion of "good morality" within Chinese families and local communities. The last prospect is logically emphasized overseas in response to acculturation and the threat of assimilation.

The metaphor of the "purple *qi* coming from the East" perfectly summarizes the idea, widely spread among followers, that the gods of the *de de she* are the true initiators of Chinese civilization, and that they reward the faithful worshippers by instilling in them spiritual energy, life force, subtle knowledge, and high moral standards. Their cult is therefore an act of culture. By directly connecting the devotees to the heart of Chinese civilization, it perpetuates a spiritual link with a community of putative forefathers, thus offsetting the decline overseas of ancestors' worship. It also reduces the cultural distance separating the Hua Qiao from the motherland. In this context, the importance that De Jiao confers to Guan Yu as the enthroned Jade Emperor is meaningful. This figure, whose icon occupies the seat of honour on the altars of more than half of the associations in the sample described above, embodies the centre of power as well as the power of the centre, i.e., China. Because he wields overwhelming power on the great mythical China of the past, he is perceived by worshippers as the most able to satisfy their eager quest for identity, meaning, power, and ethics.

One question remains, however: how do the pavilions select the divine symbols of their own identity? Among followers the idea is often expressed that they "only carry out the divine instructions". They therefore limit their role to that of faithful subordinates of heavenly officials. At the same time, they reassert the belief that the gods and their human followers are united together by bureaucratic links, as members of an encompassing socio-cosmic order. The relation thus phrased is not only hierarchical; it is first and foremost elective. If the deities are believed to choose their worshippers rather than the reverse, they are also supposed to do it by appraisal of the applicants' moral uprightness and purity of faith. This is the reason why the incorporation of new followers into the movement is systematically submitted to *ji wen* approval. Besides morality, another criterion applies more specifically to leaders and mediums. They are appointed to their functions as a mark of their *yuan fen*, or "fate affinity" with the patron gods of their respective congregations. Informants are evasive about the criteria on which the selection rests. However, the idea of astrological adequacy and of spiritual harmony is sometimes expressed. Thus, the board of the pavilions is composed of "sons of affinity" (*yuan zi*), while a good medium is supposed to transcribe so easily and accurately divine thoughts that he is viewed as a hypostasis of a god's hand, a "heaven's hand" (*tian shou*). The fact that good moral and spiritual "affinity" with the gods is a leading principle in the founding of De Jiao pavilions is also evident from the compound *jie yuan* ("node of affinity") which is used to designate to such congregations.

The presence of persons of good morality who also share a strong affinity with deities is a necessary but not sufficient condition to establish a new pavilion. Another important prerequisite is the alleged determination of a god to use an incipient group of followers to uplift virtue locally. The foundation of Ji De Ge, the oldest Ji association, perfectly highlights this aspect. In the previous chapter, I reported that Ji Gong was said to have ordered its establishment after he observed that there was a pressing need to enhance the level of morality in Ipoh. Logically, after the completion of the temple there, Ji Gong held the divine office of the new moral and religious jurisdiction. The establishment of Zi Ji Ge in 1973 is another good example involving Ji Gong. The order to institute it came as early as 1964, through oracles issued in both Li Shan Ge, a Zan Hua association in Sungai Pettani, and Zi Tong Ge, a Zi association in Bangkok. The oracle at Li Shan Ge was proclaimed by the Immortal He Xian-Gu. It predicted that Zi Ji Ge would play a key role in reconciling the Zi and Ji groups which consequently would strengthen the whole De Jiao movement in Malaysia. As for the oracle of Zi Tong Ge, it was allegedly delivered by Ji Gong who suggested that the forthcoming association would be instrumental in restoring fruitful communication links with the gods. For almost eight years these edicts remained unfulfilled. But in 1972 a clash between the leaders of Zan Hua Ge and the former president of this association, Wen Yu-Tang, initiated the launching of the project. One of the reasons for the conflict was the decision of Zan Hua Ge to cease spirit-writing activities. Wen Yu-Tang then referred to Ji Gong's oracle of 1964 to legitimate his project to found an alternative association in Bukit Mertajam, and resolutely turned toward the practice of *fu ji* as a means "to restore fruitful communication with the gods". Significantly, the hierarchical structure of the altar of Zi Ji Ge reflects the nature of divine involvement. Both Ji Gong and He Xian-Gu are considered "great" in terms of their placement on the stage. The tablet symbolizing the former is placed at the centre of the highest level, and is surrounded by the tablets of the Eight Immortals, with that of He Xian-Gu holding the position of honour, on the left extremity of the row.

More generally, the way the altars of the De Jiao associations are laid out refers both to the circumstances of their founding and to further events, which sometimes correspond to the commitment of new gods, and entail a reorganization of the cult accordingly. Zi Ming Ge offers a good example of these readjustments. The association, located in Ranong, a town of the Isthmus of Kra, on the border with Myanmar, was inaugurated in 2003. The initial command to found it allegedly came in 2002 from Lü Dong-Bin, during a *fu ji* séance organized at the headquarters of the national De Jiao Federation of Thailand. Because Ranong was located in the South, under the jurisdiction of Zi Nan Ge (see Chapter II), the association of Hat Yai organized a few weeks later a second spirit-writing session in the premises of the local Teochew dialectal association. Then, a *ji wen* attributed to Ji Gong appointed president of the forthcoming pavilion an 'unknown' Teochew who attended the séance by hazard. On the same day, a small committee was designated to assist this newcomer. Furthermore, by calling it Zi Ming Ge ("Pavilion of the Purple Tablet"), the *ji wen* suggested a close co-operation with the private Chinese school of Ranong, whose name was Ming Xing (銘幸 – "Inscription [bringing] good fortune").

The oracle reportedly proved its accuracy when the headmaster of this school, who was also in charge of the shrine to the Chinese god of the city, offered premises in the shrine's compound to host the De Jiao deities. On the altar of this small hall, the icon of Lü Dong-Bin sits prominently on the highest row, and below him we find a statue of Ji Gong flanked on its both sides by the four Taoist masters whose combination is typical of the Zi branch of Thailand. The central position of Ji Gong on the same row with those Taoist deities is part of the specific *map* of Zi Ming Ge. Another particularity is the presence of a picture of the city god on the altar's left side, and of a statue of Guan Yin straddling a sea-dragon on its right side. Whereas the local god's icon was set as a token of gratitude for his hospitality, the presence of the statue of Guan Yin subduing the ferocious forces of the sea can be attributed to one of the instructions of Ji Gong proclaimed in 2003. During that year, a *ji wen* appointed the president of Zi Ming Ge as the head of a committee whose charge was to build a 33 feet-high statue of the Goddess of Mercy. The aim of such a project was to provide supernatural protection to fishermen and sailors, as the area where the statue was to be erected is well known for shipwrecks. The spot where the statue, envisioned to be facing the open sea, was planned to be built is an islet located ten miles away from the seashore. At the time of the study, the monument was under construction.

Other examples could be mentioned to illustrate the processes of these "god-driven cults", which are supposed to rely on divine oracles for their founding and setting up. The narratives about these processes constitute aspects of a vernacular theory, whose dogma of "divine determinism" possibly gives way in practice to the strategies and self-interests of leaders and mediums. The difficulty for the anthropologist lies in the fact that most of the devotees' real states of mind remain unfathomable, either because the informants are unwilling to be part of a retrospective heart-to-heart confession or as a consequence of their inability to reconstruct via an intellectual framework the "true" process of their intersubjective decision-making. Indeed, the social scientist may interpret the choice of an "unknown" as president for Zi Ming Ge as the likely result of his good reputation in the South as a wealthy and trustworthy entrepreneur. He may also consider that the "appointment" of such a person by Ji Gong correlates with the fact that Dao Ji was already patronizing Zi Nang Ge, in the orbit of which the new pavilion should evolve. However, between plausible correlations and real causations there is a gulf that can be hardly overcome in the present case.

Multivocal Ways of Worshipping

"Divine determinism", as a leading factor of diversification, not only characterizes the setting up of the De Jiao local pantheons, but also its ritual procedures. The initiatives of the national branches in standardizing the activities of their members, as well as the peculiarities of each group, are ruled by the compelling principle that it is both the duty and the honour of the devotees to satisfy the gods' wishes, whims, and commands. In such a context, an overview of a large number of congregations claiming the label "De Jiao" reveals that they are not united by a common or even minimal liturgy, but by a religious idiom which, in perfect analogy with language, produces continually new sentences on the basis of a shared vocabulary, syntax, and grammar, thus entertaining the belief among its users that they belong to the same community.

P. Ebrey (1995: 134) rightly notices that the cognitive and ideological power in Chinese ancestral rites comes "not from specific ceremonies, no matter how important, but from the cumulative effect of the larger patterns of rites". In other words, popular religious ideas, symbols, and patterns of action in the Chinese context are held by their continuous rearrangement in related forms, rather than through the formal duplicating of complex and stable sequences. They are *maps* rather than *calques*, in accordance with the typology of Deleuze and Guattari.

The invocation prayers make a good case for this statement. Because they usually start off the ceremonies and are the means for initiating communication with gods, they can be considered as a major ritual sequence. In 2003, five invocation texts were concurrently in use within De Jiao. The main one, called *Qi Zan* ("The Invocation"), is part of the *De Jiao Xin Dian*. As a consequence of the policy of standardization adopted by the national federations, the *Qi Zan* is now adopted by about 90 per cent of associations throughout the world. The mediums of all the Zi pavilions but one strike it up when inviting the flying *luan*-bird to come down. The only exception is Zi Xiang Ge, the mother association of the Purple line in China. Due to questions of precedence, Zi Xiang Ge never deigned to replace its prayer text with new wording that was promulgated in a "younger sister" association. When, in 1997, Zi Xiang Ge was reinstated, its members started chanting once more the invocation attributed to Liu Chun-Fang and Yang Jun-Song (see appendix, document 2). Although the Ji and Zhen denominational groups had also created chants of address of their own, they gave them up when they joined the UMUSOM in the 1980s. In the case of the handful of Zhen associations which remained out of the federation, the mediums refer to close variations of the "Sacred Text from the Quiet Garden" (*Dian Sheng Jue Yuan You*). This text, reproduced and translated in the appendix (document 3), was initially proclaimed in 1955, at Zhen Shan Ge (Began Serai), the first Zhen association to have been created. Zan Hua has its own invocation too, which is actually an adaptation of the *Qi Zan*, with minor changes (appendix, document 4). Although the associations of this group ceased spirit-writing after 1977, they still chant their old invocation as part of the *De Jiao Xin Dian* during their ceremonies. Finally, Zi Piao Tan, the association of Siracha in Thailand, whose leaders are composed of defectors from Ming Tan, remained loyal to the invocation typical of the latter group (see appendix, document 5).

A brief comparison of the five invocation texts shows that despite differences in content, they share common features. First, they are short psalms of 53 to 81 characters, whose metric structure is of 4-, 5- or 7-foot lines, and which are chanted in chorus by the assistants of the mediums to start the spirit-writing. Second, the concepts or compounds they use to make the gods straddle the *luan*-bird are either the same or very close. Thus, *feng qing* ("to invite in reverence") is used both in the *Qi Zan*, the Sacred Text from the Quiet Garden, the invocation text of Zan Hua Ge, and that of Zi Piao Tan. The alternative compound, used in the psalm of Zi Xiang Ge, is *gan qing* ("to dare to invite"). Third, the invitation is explicitly addressed to the Immortals in four texts and to the gods of the five directions in three of them. The *Qi Zan* and the invocation text of Zan Hua Ge concur by adding to this group the Buddhist saints, whereas Zi Xiang Ge, as a mark of difference, implore the Lord of the Fourth Heavenly Stem in addition to the Immortals. The Heavenly Stems (*Tian Gan*) are an ancient cyclic numeral system associated with the concepts of *yin* and *yang*, and the five elements. The *Qi Zan* and its adaptation by Zan Hua Ge refer to these basic components of the Chinese cosmology too. Finally, the five prayer texts make implicit reference to the circulation of *qi* energy from heaven to hearth, through various metaphors and allegorical evocations of nature. For instance, the *Qi Zan* and the Zan Hua Ge's text mention *yin/yang* dynamics through the fecund alliance of sun and moon; the invocation prayer of Zi Xiang Ge refers to the motion of the clouds as contributive to beneficial effects or to that of a purple cart making its way from the East (an implicit allusion to the purple *qi* coming from the East). For its part, the Sacred Text from the Quiet Garden calls to mind the treasures of nature as a source of wealth, and the Ming prayer mentions alternately the blow of the wind and the thunderbolt sound as symbols of cosmic forces. It also invokes the cinnabar heart as an energetic endowment from heaven, cinnabar being the colour of life and eternity in Taoist thought.

The unity of meaning that these shared features convey is both confirmed and reinforced by the "adoption with slight variation" of others' liturgical items, as a mark of acculturation between the De Jiao groups. We note that Zan Hua made the *Qi Zan* its own by introducing a few changes to the original version promulgated in China. These minor changes consist in the addition of a stanza, and the positioning of the compound *feng qing* at the end of certain verses rather than at their beginning. Other ritual aspects enter into this logic of "margin derivation". The way the members of most of the Ji associations pray is a case in point.

During worship, the adepts of this group stand before the altar and raise their right hand to the chest level with fingers pointing upwards, and the palm facing the left side of the body.[4] This style slightly differs from *he shi*, the usual Chinese way of worship that the other De Jiao adepts follow and whose characteristic is to raise both hands with palms placed together vertically. Tan Chee-Beng (1984: 37) reports cautiously the testimony of a leader, according to whom the custom started unintentionally in Ji Qing Ge (Seremban) at the initiative of a *ji*-wielder. The medium had to use one hand to hold the planchette stick and so raised only his other hand. Later on, other worshippers followed his style of raising only one hand, thinking that it was the proper way. Such an explanation based on a sequence of fortuitous events and misunderstandings may appear flimsy. I myself recorded another interpretation from Ji followers. They explained that this style of worship was a distinct feature of Ji Gong himself, and a mark of his legendary laziness and eccentricities. When he was praying, they said, he used his left hand either to feel his beads or to wave about a fan which is one of his emblems. Although the iconography of Crazy Ji rarely depict him in prayer, the mother-temple of the Ji group has taken to distributing to devotees amulets and small statues of the master raising his right hand to the chest, thus legitimizing the practice among the followers.

The logic of "margin variation" may lead to the elision of elements from an existing sequence, like in the previous example (to raise one hand rather than both), or conversely to the merging of two distinct practices resulting in a new one. The various kinds of incense used by De Jiao highlight the phenomenon. Whereas the Zi associations use joss sticks, the Ji and Zan Hua groups prefer *xiang mu*, which is a scented powder made of sandal wood poured with a small spoon on embers. As for the Zhen associations, they either use joss sticks or combine joss sticks and scented wood. Unfortunately, no one could explain to me the origins and basis of this combination. It could be attributed to the desire to preserve some liturgical links with the Ming Shan She movement whose previous members were the founders of Zhen and which exclusively uses scented wood. Within the context of this hypothesis, the Zhen mother-temple has two incense burners on its altar, one to receive sandal powder and the other to receive joss sticks, the latter being perhaps a concession to the Zi group's requirements.

Interestingly, the groups which use scented wood as a unique or a complementary way to establish communication with the gods are all born overseas. Although the followers of Ji, Zan Hua, and Zhen that I questioned about the topic put forward practical reasons to justify the custom (compared to joss sticks, the sandal powder would emit more fragrance for less smoke), the leader of the Ji group, HMK, gave me a more controversial explanation. According to him, his group, as well as Zan Hua and Zhen, had no legitimacy to use "true incense", since their incense burners had not been activated by ashes coming through the *xiang huo* ritual from a temple of the motherland. In other words, they could not lay claim to having any religious roots in China.

Multifarious *Luan*-Bird Writings

Spirit-writing, which is actually the core activity of the De Jiao groups whatever their attitude toward its continuation, does not escape the principle of unity-in-diversity. We have already described the various invocation prayers which introduce the De Jiao ceremonies and also serve to initiate spirit-writing sessions. In the introduction, I argued that the De Jiao associations share basic features concerning communication with the gods. All of them practice spirit-writing through the handling of a forked branch by a pair of wielders. These two mediums write divine poems on a tray, whose content is orally interpreted and literarily transcribed by clerks. However, within this general framework, which entertains a feeling of unity, the door is open to significant variations, and an overall view of *fu ji* activities reveals several patterns. If *wen ji*, the "spirit-writing of the literati", is the dominant way, in some associations it is combined, depending on the circumstances, with *wu ji*, "spirit-writing of the warriors", whereas in few cases a third style, called *jiu ji* ("spirit-writing with alcohol"), is practised.

In the Chinese systems of beliefs, *wen* and *wu* are the basic and complementary attributes of imperial power which exerts its rule by using either military force (*wu*) or enactments enforced by the mandarins (*wen*). Because politics and religion are inextricably embedded together in China and other Asian societies, the *wen/wu* binomial is logically projected on the celestial bureaucracy in its relations with the human world; hence the two styles of spirit-writing. The purpose of *wu ji* is mainly to chase away ghosts and other malevolent influences from individuals, buildings, and other spaces. In this function, the divine stick is used as a sword or a spear, rather than as a pencil. Another difference from *wen ji* lies in the more conspicuous state of possession that *wu ji* entails. In this case, the mediums frequently display overt signs of entering into a trance such as eructations, brutal and helter-skelter movements, faces and eyes seemingly contorted with pain, or foam emanating from the mouth. Interestingly, the *wen/wu ji* distinction overlaps the boundaries between the various De Jiao groups. Although Ji and Zan Hua claim to perform only *wen ji*, the Zi associations, depending on the context, practice *wen ji* exclusively, or combine it with *wu ji*, and so it is for the pavilions of the Zhen group. The difference between the Zhen and Zi groups in this respect is that the former systematically pairs up *wen* and *wu* styles, whereas the latter alternates them. During the spirit-writing sessions organized in the Zhen associations, either two teams of mediums carry out side by side the two methods, or the same team divides the séance into two periods, one aimed at the deliverance of divine edicts and protective devices, and the other restricted to exorcisms and other procedures to expel illness or bad influences. A third alternative, observed in a few cases, requires the Zhen team of mediums to handle two stacked willow sticks: one set below, named *bi ji* ("the pen of the *ji*") is then used to draw characters and represents the *wen* function, while one set at the top, named *liu ji* ("the willow *ji*"), symbolizes the *wu* aspect.

The combination of the two styles is more limited in scope with respect to the Purple line. The only Zi associations to practice *wu ji* are those in Thailand, when they organize or take part in a *xiu gu gu*. In such a case, the mediums use it to rescue the souls of the orphaned dead whose bones are buried in deep forests. With the willow stick in one hand and a sword in the other the mediums run into the bushes, waving their weapon to chase out devils. Finally, among the Zi associations of Thailand and Malaysia, Zi Zhen Ge (Bangkok) and Zi He Ge (Penampang – Sabah) are known to be frequently visited by Ji Gong. Under such circumstances, the "Crazy Monk" imposes on the mediums he possesses his immoderate liking for wine, and the spirit-writing consequently shifts from *wen* to *jiu ji*.

The items that the mediums use to communicate with the gods constitute another aspect of spirit-writing where formal variations are important. Even between closely related agencies of the same group, the shape of the tray, the material put on it to draw the characters, or the position of the *ji*-wielders may change significantly, depending on local divine instructions. For example, Tai He Guan and Ji Yun Ge of Singapore, though managed by the same team, display contrasting habits. Whereas the former use a *ba gua*-shaped tray containing a blend made of sand, incense ashes, and water, Ji Yun Ge observes the custom of the Ji group by using a square-shaped tray containing white sand. Table 3 gives a general outline of these variations for a sample of 25 associations chosen at random among the 80 and more visited between 1993 and 2004. The practices of this sample group reveal 13 different combinations, depending on the criteria selected (i.e., one on two associations). The uniformity that Ji Xi had demonstrated concerning its pantheon is confirmed here, since all its agencies share a common combination: a square-shaped tray containing white sand, as mentioned above. In contrast, the Zhen group is the most heterogeneous: there are as many combinations as associations in the sample.

D. Johnson, A.S. Nathan, and E. Rawski (1985: XI–XVIII) note that diversity is an obvious function of China's immense geographic mass. In this wide social space, there are evidently many varieties of elite and non-elite subcultures reflecting differences in power, prestige, education, wealth, occupation, region, and dialect. For the authors, these diverse elements are nevertheless integrated into a complex cultural system, the intellectual and spiritual worlds of the scholar or official being not utterly alien to the peasant or labourer. In view of the De Jiao materials, it is possible to conclude with them, at variance with A. Wolf or F. Barth, that there are common elements in the mental worlds of all Chinese, and that finally Chinese religion is "both extremely diverse and highly integrated".

* * *

Although the diversity that De Jiao displays may appear striking at first glance, a careful analysis reveals that it is mainly based on the continuous

Table 3 Items Used for Spirit-writing in a Sample Group of 25 De Jiao Associations

	Shape of the Tray			*Material Used to Draw Characters*					*Position of the ji Wielders*	
Features *Associations*	*Square*	*Ba gua*	*Round*	*Sand*	*Incense ashes*	*Tea*	*Lustral water*	*Red ink*	*Standing*	*Sitting*
Malaysia										
Zi Seng Ge Seremban		x		x	x				x	
Zi Chang Ge Malacca		x		x	x				x	
Zi Luang Ge Kluang		x		x					x	
Zi Xiao Ge Ipoh		x		x		x			x	
Zi Yun Ge Penang		x		x					x	
Zi Liang Ge Kuala Lumpur		x		x					x	
Thailand										
Zi Tong Ge Bangkok		x		x	x	x	x		x	
Zi Zhen Ge Bangkok	x					x	x			x
Zi Piao Tan Siracha			x				x	x	x	
Zi Yi Ge Roeit	x					x	x			x
Singapore										
Tai He Guan		x		x	x		x		x	
Ji Yun Ge	x			x					x	
Hong Kong										
Zi Jing Ge		x		x	x				x	
P.R. of China										
Zi Ying Ge Guangzhou		x		x	x				x	
Zi Xiang Ge Heping	x	x		x	x				x	
Malaysia										
Ji De Ge Ipoh	x			x					x	
Ji Yang Ge Alor Setar	x			x					x	

Table 3 continued

	Shape of the Tray			*Material Used to Draw Characters*					*Position of the ji Wielders*	
Features Associations	*Square*	*Ba gua*	*Round*	*Sand*	*Incense ashes*	*Tea*	*Lustral water*	*Red ink*	*Standing*	*Sitting*
Ji Cheng Ge Taiping	x			x					x	
Zhen Zhong Ge Malacca		x		x					x	
Zhen Wen Ge Parit Buntar		x			x	x			x	
Zhen Yi Ge Kuala Kurau		x		x	x	x			x	
Zhen Nan Ge Johor Bahru		x			x		x		x	
Zhen Guan Ge Tanjung Piandang	x					x			x	
Zi Ji Ge Bukit Mertajam		x			x	x	x		x	
Zi He Ge Penampang	x					x	x			x

rearrangement of ideas, symbols, and characters which are among the most popular and therefore the most integrative of the Chinese religious complex. In Southeast Asia, the combined effects of distance and of acculturation accentuate this trend by limiting in scope the knowledge that the Hua Qiao have of the motherland culture. Thus, the total numbers of gods the De Jiao followers worship hardly reach the figure of 50 among the hundreds that the popular pantheon incorporates, while the cult core of a majority of associations does not exceed a handful of well-known deities. The prayer texts they use to make the *luan*-bird fly down to earth share the same themes, allegories, and cosmological references, whatever their formal differences may be. Furthermore, their *fu ji* procedures use common tools and technology despite variations concerning the shape of the mediums' tables, their position while writing divine messages, or the materials on which the latter are written.

The consequences of the uprooting apart, the institutional integration of the De Jiao groups is made easier by the common goals and the core of activities they share. For instance, they all make communication with the gods through *fu ji* the keystone of their religious practice; they also emphasize charitable works, and promote Confucian virtues such as filial piety, brotherly respect, loyalty, sincerity, and righteousness. Another factor of integration lies in a basic set of common beliefs. The adepts think that there is an overriding necessity to implement "divine instructions"; all of them consider the *de de she* as the metaphorical expression of imperial China's greatness as well as the quintessence of the potential energy and power radiating from the motherland.

In some ways, the De Jiao materials confirm the proposal of F. Barth that everybody constructs their own reality by making choices between the ranges of options and ideational possibilities that the cultural context offers. With respect to De Jiao and other similar groups (Peng Lai, Ming Tan), this set of possibilities and options are however limited in scope. The congregations construct their liturgies by applying a few rules of transformation such as "margin derivation" or subtraction or aggregation of basic elements, these procedures being implemented without disruption in meaning. Accordingly, the adepts of each congregation remain familiar with the rituals of the others, even when they attend the ceremonies of a different denominational group. The organization of national federations as well as the creation of a World Moral Meeting of the Divine Pen in the mid-1990s increased the level of awareness among the De Jiao adepts that their congregation is somehow unique but also related to the others.

P. Ebrey's observation pointing out that the cognitive and ideological power of Chinese rituals rests mainly on the cumulative effects of common patterns, rather than on the reiteration of the same formal procedures, is indeed of special relevance concerning De Jiao. It is mainly through the involvement of devotees into the celebrations of close "brothers in virtue", within the same branch or group, that the abovementioned religious idiom is transmitted. This step by step logic of transmission corresponds to the model of the rhizome. It appears nevertheless that the cognitive processes within De Jiao are partly *calque* and partly *map*, and that this hybrid character is extended to the movement's institutional and organizational aspects, with the latter retaining properties both of the tree and of the rhizome, of the genealogy and of the anti-genealogy, of the hierarchy and of the a-centred systems.

CHAPTER V

The Flying Vermilion Bird

In previous chapters, spirit-writing appeared progressively to be the keystone of De Jiao. Almost everything in this religious movement, from the few "canonical" texts it has so far produced to the architecture of shrines, are issued by mediums. Even those among the Malaysian associations which suspended the activity in the late 1970s still rely on texts and rituals "revealed" by the gods straddling the flying vermilion bird. The main reason that the informants invoked in order to justify their interest and "faith" in De Jiao is the close and personalized interaction with the gods that spirit-writing offers, a pattern that sharply contrasts with the faith in divine words proclaimed to hold for all eternity by universalistic religions and which are propagated through the production of sacred books. In some respects, the followers conceive of their transactions with the gods as *performative* (Austin, 1962), in the sense that the faith in the oracles' truth compels those to whom the *ji wen* are intended to act accordingly. As a consequence, divine oracles often have a significant impact on the followers' decisions and way of life, thus permitting the mediums to exert a significant influence on personal destinies as well as on the initiatives, projects, and overall development of the congregations where they officiate.

In the following pages, the focus of attention will be upon those who assume this very important duty. How do they become mediums in the first place? What are their perspective and the viewpoint of the other followers about their vocation, training, and states of mind before, during, and after spirit-writing? What are their relationships with the association leaders who hold economic power and are therefore in a position to implement the gods' instructions? I shall also report, and analyze with reference to the proceedings of previous conferences, the sixth World Moral Meeting of the Divine Pen that De Jiao organized in Kluang, Malaysia. This event, which assembled in 2004 more than 40 De Jiao and non-De Jiao teams of *ji*-wielders, constituted an excellent opportunity to observe the various methods and styles of *fu ji* practised today. It was also a suitable occasion to record a wide range of points of view about the experience of spirit-writing, as well as to verify the claim of De Jiao that it plays a federative role concerning this particular activity. Finally, I shall consider the attempt by a minority of Malaysian followers to make De Jiao a universalistic religion by anchoring it in a "divinely revealed" holy book, and to distance it simultaneously from *fu ji*, which in their opinion has been corrupted by "human affairs". Such an effort is noteworthy because its rejection of spirit-writing is all the more relative, as the "bible" of the said adepts is an anthology of famous *fu ji* texts. But before dealing with these matters, the kind of communication that the *ji*-wielders establish with the "honourable masters" must be described in greater detail.

What Kind of Possession is *fu ji*?

The most comprehensive taxonomic study about possession so far published is undoubtedly *Music and Trance* by G. Rouget (1985). According to this author, a basic distinction should be established between *ecstasy* and *trance*. Whereas the former is defined as "the action of moving through space, displacement, deviation" and involves "disturbance, agitation, wandering as applied to the mind", the latter signifies a different kind of interaction. It entails a convulsive stage and, in numerous cases, is linked to symbolic death through depersonalization, as though the visiting spirit had taken over the medium (1985: 7). G. Rouget suggests that ecstasy should apply to the states of immobility, silence, hallucination, and isolation, whereas states of trance apply "solely to those that are obtained by means of noise, agitation and in the presence of others", without hallucination (1985: 8). Concerning the latter, he makes a distinction between what he calls the conscious or "reprobate" possession and the "cultivated" type of trance which is always followed by amnesia. The De Jiao *fu ji* is frequently consistent with the latter type. However — and Rouget is the first to admit that the features he describes with respect to trances are not necessarily always directly observable — it should be noted that most De Jiao séances do not involve the generation of noise, with mediums trembling, shuddering, dashing off, falling to the ground, or having convulsions. These symptoms are rather typical of *wu ji* that only a minority of De Jiao adepts practise. Under those circumstances, other, more spectacular demonstrations of spiritual possession may be displayed. These may consist of piercing one's own flesh without bleeding, self-flagellation with hobnailed spherical sledgehammers, or "chewing" fine porcelain cups without any outward signs of pain and with the blood pouring of the medium's mouth being put on talismans to empower them.

Concerning the "spirit-writing of the literati" (*wen ji*), which is the dominant way of communication with the gods, the mediums may also sometimes show obvious signs of possession, through convulsive motions, tics, noisy breathing, or fixed gazing when the god who possesses them expresses discontent or anger (Fig. 10). Nevertheless, most of the time, the mediums give the impression that they have lost all consciousness of their surroundings, but in an unobtrusive and quiet way. Spiritual possession then becomes so internalized as to go almost unperceived by an inexperienced spectator. The hands of the mediums holding the forked branch seem to be taken over by an unseen external force; the mediums' eyes usually remain closed during the trance, thus showing that they have been completely taken over. The feeling of calm radiating from the mediums when doing *wen ji* is enhanced by the fact that they do not shout and even speak. *Fu ji* is certainly one of the few trance forms to be mainly based on writing.

In keeping with the previous features, music does not play a central role. It is limited to an invocation that the assistants of the mediums strike up in polyphony without any instrumental accompaniment. Similar to the other types of possession, this chant goes *accelerando* and *crescendo*, and its function is to trigger the possession of the mediums, or to restart the session after a break. In observance of a division of tasks between the musical assistants and the persons possessed, the latter do not take part in the incantation and reciprocally the former never enter into a state of trance (Rouget, 1985: 113). In fact, the only words one can discern during the séances are those of the assistants, whose role is to interpret the ideograms that the divine pen stealthily draws on the plate, and to convey in loud voices their interpretations to the gathered adherents. Dance is totally absent during the performance, and consequently the theatrical aspect of entrancements which characterizes many other forms of possession in Asia, such as the cult of *nats* in Burma, of the *Ba Dong* in Vietnam, or of the Hokkien mediums studied by J. DeBernardi (2006), is of minor importance in the case of *fu ji*. This theatrical aspect however can be observed when a medium impersonates a specific deity whose habits and mannerisms he reproduces. For instance, *ji*-wielders possessed by Ji Gong usually drink great quantities of wine or brandy while entranced and generally exhibit a state of drunkenness while writing the master's poetry; this particular behaviour derives from the monk's reputation of being an inebriate.

Even when the mediums do not overtly impersonate the gods' temperaments, the idea prevails among the adepts that the subject of the possession is pervaded by deities, and as such may switch from one personality to another. The relationship between divinity and medium is never seen as an encounter which could be experienced as a communion, a revelation, or an illumination. It is instead perceived as the visit of one or more deities who then invest the *ji*-wielder and use him as a tool to convey their power and knowledge. Thus, followers have no problem accepting those *ji*-wielders who present themselves as illiterate or having a low level of Chinese education but who can easily draw ideograms and sentences of a high level of erudition while in trance. It appears, however, that most of them have a good knowledge of the Chinese classics when questioned. Furthermore, in Thailand where education in Chinese language was severely restricted for decades, there are very few mediums able to impersonate the gods.

How to Become a Medium?

In a recent paper, P. Clart (2003) qualifies the model of the Chinese medium as a passive and reluctant mouthpiece of the gods. For their part, the accounts of J.J.M. de Groot (1910: 1270), A.J.A. Elliott (1955: 47), and D.K. Jordan (1972: 73, 84–6) convey the idea that prospective mediums usually suffer seizures or ailments. According to Clart, even if latent mediums resist the eventuality of becoming a conduit of the gods' messages and initially repudiate the idea of lending their bodies to the practice of divination, the "anointed ones" "ultimately succumb and restructure their lives to accommodate the possession experiences". Although oral accounts confirm that the career of certain De Jiao *ji*-wielders can be explained with reference to this pattern,[1] they are however of relatively little significance compared to other constructs which make the mediums' calling the result of a more balanced relationship between gods and men.

These processes correspond more or less to an alternative model that P. Clart (2003: 156) calls "moral-cultivational mediumship", which he considers to be of particular relevance concerning *wen ji*. In this particular case, possession is seen as a form of partnership between a deity and a human being of great moral purity whom the former initially appointed as a messenger because of his ability to achieve such a moral state. The involuntary and sometimes violent character of mediumship is then replaced by a voluntary and cultivational effort on the part of the candidates. The way De Jiao appeared as a religious movement in 1939 perfectly illustrates this men-to-gods interaction, since the channel of communication that Yang Rui-De and his friends succeeded in establishing at the time with Liu Chun-Fang and Yang Jun-Song was the result of an initiative from "men of good morals", whose aim was to cultivate and spread virtue. In fact, most of the De Jiao *ji*-wielders I met claimed to have been selected by the gods among applicants who longed to perform the function. In some respect, their selection had something to do with the mandarin examinations for entry into the imperial bureaucracy.

Overseas, wherein those who have the cultural background and the requisite motivation are few, the process by which gods are believed to make a choice within a group of prospective mediums is evidently of particular importance in strengthening the vocations, and somewhat counterbalances the shortage of callings. Because this process is based on the idea of a "fate affinity", it institutes in the medium's perspective a "life pact" with the "honourable master". Personally, I have never heard among the De Jiao worshippers the folk theory that J.J.M. de Groot reports about involuntary possession in Xiamen. According to this theory, the mediumship vocation should be due to defects in the practitioner's "eight characters" (*ba zi*), thus predestining such an individual to a short lifespan (1910: 1269). However, informants were keen to interpret the mediums' careers with reference to the principle of *yuan fen* (fate affinity). This special affinity with gods and the pact it underlies are reinforced by the idea that the "honourable masters" take an active part in the training of the people they choose as mediums, and that it would be a dreadful betrayal not to honour this divine involvement. Outside of mainland China, training as a prerequisite to efficient communication with the gods is overemphasized. Such training has two dimensions: one coming allegedly from the gods, and the other from a "human teacher" (*ren shi*), usually an older medium from the same congregation or from an affiliated one. In the former case, the instructor is called either *xian shi* ("Immortal teacher") or "honourable master" (*shi zun*). More than 80 per cent of the De Jiao *ji*-wielders I interviewed during my investigations were either under training or had completed such a regimen after months and frequently years of learning. Interestingly, the students of *fu ji*, whatever their age, are called "children of the *ji*" (*ji tong*), thus underlining the intellectual virginity and flexibility, two properties associated with childhood, that such students should embody.

The "divine" and human dimensions of training are inextricably linked in and by practice, since the students are from the beginning invited to hold the stylus under the supervision of experienced mediums. This is done during special sessions and, if a student has sufficiently advanced in the course of his training, during ordinary séances. In the last instance, *ji tong* sometimes operate as pairs of beginners, but frequently an inexperienced medium serves as *fu ji zhang*, or "left hand", to an experienced one. When they do not operate directly as *ji*-wielders, the students assume the various functions of an assistant. For instance, when sand is used on the tray, they may be in charge of levelling it after a divine sentence has been written. Otherwise they act as oral interpreter (*bao yu*), or as clerk (*ji yu*) by writing the messages on a register. They thus carry out the various functions of spirit-writing and therefore incorporate the techniques.

Informants identified five aspects to the training of a medium which can in no way be considered as successive steps, since they are usually taught concurrently. The first aspect consists in learning how to chant properly the prayer of invocation. The exact phrase used to express the appropriateness of the performance is *zheng cheng* ("correct and sincere"). The idea that underlies such formula is that, while chanting, the medium must be motivated by a great purity of feeling and intention. He or she must have exclusively in mind the sincere, eager wish to invite the masters to uplift morality on earth. The second aspect consists in the production of protective and healing written charms (*fu*) on various materials, such as rice paper, pieces of cloth, or wood. Because the training on this subject is mainly based on observation of the way more experienced mediums act, it is closely related to the third aspect, that is, the study of famous *fu ji* texts of the past. Apprentices spend many hours and days in deciphering and translating into intelligible and literary forms the elliptic moral poems delivered by the "honourable masters". The tens of morality books (*shan shu*) published by the De Jiao congregations offer a rich corpus of oracles to these exercises. Moreover, most books or magazines propose one or several exegesis of the main *ji wen*, thus giving the students the opportunity to compare their own interpretations with those of more experienced mediums. Although the stated goal of these exercises is to make understand the "profound reason" of spirit-writing (*xuan ji*, literally "deep key link"), their implicit function is to familiarize the apprentices with the moral patterns, key concepts, and the typical expressive style of *fu ji*. In other words, the ultimate aim is to standardize the writings of the new cohort of mediums in accordance with the tenets of a pre-existing spirit-writing tradition. In a lecture given at the occasion of the

Fifth World Moral Divine Pen Meeting, CWB, a well-known De Jiao medium from Malaysia and at the time president of Zi Gui Ge (Sabah) clearly expresses this goal when he says that:

> Undoubtedly, the "palm of the *ji*" (*ji shou*) who does not know enough characters will be unable to render faithfully the marvellous nature of the divine messages. He will fail to express the true meaning of the "imperial sayings" (*sheng yu*), and many secrets will remain in the hands of the honourable masters (…). Consequently, although *ji*-wielders simply write on behalf of the gods, they must study the *xuan ji* of spirit-writing as well as the profound theory of Taoism. (CWB, 2001: 82–3)

The interpretation of *fu ji* texts remains a part of the careers of the De Jiao mediums well after their period of training, and it is actually one of their favourite occupations. They not only form the main readership of the De Jiao divine messages printed in books and magazines; they also get to interact with their colleagues during regular séances or special events. Such interaction then becomes an opportunity to comment on the performances of the various *ji*-wielders and to compare translations of divine edicts. In this respect, the opening ceremonies and anniversaries of pavilions, or other significant celebrations involving several teams of mediums, are high points in the ongoing exchange of views and knowledge, contributing in large part to a relative homogenization of spirit-writing within this religious movement. Such circumstances are also of crucial importance in drawing common criteria of evaluation used to assess whether the *fu ji* performance is coming from a "human" or a "divine" planchette.

The fourth aspect of the mediums' training is to make the new recruits rely entirely and faithfully on the gods. This part of the training agenda then consists of inculcating in the students a steadfast trust in divine instructions. Doubt, fear, and other ambiguous states of mind must disappear in favour of the unfailing conviction that the gods are omnipotent, omniscient, and basically benevolent, as long as one respects their edicts. Among these instructions are the taboos and prescriptions that the mediums should observe before or after the possession. They are enunciated as the training séances go by, and vary in detail from one medium to another, thus contributing to the reinforcement of the pact between the divine enactors and the practitioner. It is believed that these rules vary according to the *ba zi*, the "eight characters of birth", which define the basic astrological identity of the medium. The aim of such a set of dispositions is to get rid of the obstacles, linked to specific signs of destiny, which could prevent the medium from becoming a genuine channel of communication. In addition to the observance of certain personal directives (such as a permanent prohibition to eat certain kinds of meat, vegetables, and fruits), most De Jiao *ji*-wielders share a common set of transitory prescriptions, adherence to which is expected to facilitate the attainment of spiritual purity before possession. They thus restrict their diet to vegetarian fare and refrain from sexual intercourse during the days preceding the séance. The strict observance of the rules enacted by the masters is, among other prescriptions, a mark of respect and obedience. More generally, the *ji*-wielders are taught not to discuss or even to think about the messages and orders they convey during their trance. This is one of the reasons why obtaining the mediums' opinions and attitudes about their practices is often a problematic undertaking. Too great an understanding by the practitioner of the processes at work during performances is believed to be a major obstacle to the attainment of the "truth" and "profound reason" of the *ji*. The following account that Mr. Z., a prominent member of Zi He Ge (Hong Kong), related to me is all the more indicative of such kinds of obstacles.

According to him, in the early 1990s his congregation had trained a young couple of mediums. The man, who acted as "celestial hand", was a student in philosophy at the University of Hong Kong. He was well-versed in Taoist teachings but was ill-tempered. As for his girlfriend and assistant, she received a good Confucian education and had a good background in classic Chinese literature, a quality that was not readily apparent however. After six months of training, their *fu ji* was lively, accurate, and smart. The man eventually became a petty official in the New Territory's administration system. But to improve his family's income he started to work as a taxi driver by night. During one stormy evening, he was wielding the willow tree when suddenly the storm outside intensified and the divine pen stopped. After a long while without any motion, the *ji*-stick suddenly stood up and struck the main medium's head. He then rushed to the altar, while his assistant let go of the willow stick, screaming in apparent fright. It became clear that he was actually delivering, at the top of his voice, a gods' message in a language that nobody could understand. The audience was panic-stricken. Then, the president of the congregation, after recovering from the surprise dealt by the unprecedented performance, knelt down before the altar and implored the "honourable masters" to put things in order. He then threw water from the altar's flowerpots at the face of the medium, who subsequently fainted. An older, more experienced medium then took the willow stick, and through him Lü Dong-Bin allegedly blamed the young man for having perfected his intelligence to the detriment of the control of the "diabolical fire of the heart". The *ji wen* concluded by ordering him to go home and copy *fu ji* poems in order to calm and train his mind.

This anecdote leads us logically to the fifth and perhaps main principle which is inculcated in the minds of *ji*-wielders, that is self-forgetting. It is only by training himself to attain a level of concentration that adepts call alternately *ru ding* ("calm"), *kong xu* ("empty void"), or *ji ran* ("silence") that a medium can reach the extinguishment of desires (*yu nian*), thus allowing the gods' spirit (*shen ling*) to become manifest. The spontaneous account that LYT, one of the earliest De Jiao adepts and mediums of Hong Kong, published in 1998 is a good *emic* depiction of this state of non-being as well as of the difficulties in reaching it. He writes:

> When I started to do *fu ji* the first time, my heart was beating hard and my stylus remained motionless for a long while. Suddenly, the willow stick moved very fast and began drawing circles in the air. Though I was at the time very calm (*ru ding*), the divine pen was too fast and at the beginning I was unable to write any characters. My arm had gone completely numb. Then, I thought that such a block was the consequence of my inability to make my heart sincere (*cheng*), and that I was swamped by my subconscious. It was better to calm down and to try to make my mind go blank. Then a message came to me: *If the heart is sincere, the mind will be right.* It was followed by another one that I wrote without restraint and that the "honourable master" Bai Yun was sending to me. Its content was: *to be doubtful of the miracles makes the communication mistaken. Only the appeased heart can receive the spirit of the "honourable masters".* Liu Chun-Fang and Yang Jun-Song came down too. Finally, they were followed by Lü Dong-Bin who wrote that: *when the mind is magnificent and solemn the willow stick cannot stop anymore.* This message was actually delivering the profound truth of *fu ji*. After fifty minutes of spirit-writing, I felt that my head was becoming heavy and my feet very light. The upper part of my body suddenly toppled on the left side of the planchette. In my heart of hearts, I was willing to ask the *shi zun* to stop. The wish was almost immediately fulfilled. Other worshippers came to hold me up, and to make me sit down. They poured perfumed water on my whole body. However, I still felt sleepy for a long time. My fingers that held the stick were frothing; their skin was burnt out...." (LYT, 1998: 65)

Despite the pain and difficulties he experienced, LYT was lucky enough to enter into communication with the gods at his first attempt. Such ease in taking up the mantle of mediumship appears to be quite uncommon. In most cases, the willow stick can remain motionless for hours, and even when it begins moving, it is usually unable to deliver coherent messages over a period covering several sessions. However, to "fine-tune" (*wei tiao*) the medium's mind so as to produce clear transmissions is not an easy undertaking. LYT admits (1998: 66) that:

> Up to now, I am unable to deepen the philosophy of the *dao*. I am not tenacious enough to uplift my mind! I finally think that the "honourable masters" are content with using my weak abilities to bring to the surface small drops of information. I should confess that after several months of practice, I became aware that I was not calmed down sufficiently. It is why it is difficult for me to hold the willow stick, and the transmission is interrupted from time to time. It is like an old radio not tuned properly: sometimes the reception is clear, sometimes it is jammed. In that case, if I have to complete a sentence, I must do it by myself. It is why the messages I transmit become *yi ji* ("the *ji* of the [human] mind"), and I consequently asked the "honourable masters" not to hold the willow stick anymore. The first condition to do *fu ji* is to be calm (*ji ran*) and to switch oneself off (*xu kong*). Otherwise one cannot host the heaven's spirits and our consciousness can even prove to be harmful (LYT, 1998: 66).

The analogy of radio transmission to which LYT refers is frequently used among *ji*-wielders. P. Clart (2003: 167) quotes for instance a worshipper of the Taiwanese Ming Zheng Tang Phoenix hall who believed that "a good medium is a person whose mind can work on the same frequency as that of the communicating deity; he is like a radio set whose transmissions become clearer the more finely it is able to tune in to the signal-emitting station". Another medium among my De Jiao informants compared the "palm of the *ji*" (*ji shou*, a metaphor for the medium) to a dish aerial receiving Hertzian waves from the *de de she* acting as a moral broadcasting centre. P. Clart (2003: 167) is certainly right to suggest that such analogies are not drawn arbitrarily, that they are "grounded in a worldview that does not recognize a discontinuity between the natural universe and the moral cosmos".

To come back to LYT, his account shows that he remained partly conscious during his first trance, not only because he was feeling the physical effects of possession, but also because he was able to link the meaning of messages he was writing with changes in his level of receptiveness to the divine inflows. Although interesting, this account is nonetheless unrepresentative, and it is perhaps why LYT admits that he is not sufficiently blessed with the requisite level of abilities to practice *fu ji*.

In most cases, the mediums claim to be able to switch themselves off completely at the time of possession. Absolute self-obliviousness, including insensitivity to pain, is the state of mind being put forward. The most extreme example of this utter self-forgetting state is FSM, the main *ji*-wielder of Zi Zhen Ge, who is specifically known to be a favourite "stylus" of Ji Gong. This young man (he was in his late 30s in 2003) radically changes behaviour during possession. While in the normal course of life he is rather shy, gentle, and abstemious, when in a trance he belches and generally exhibits rough manners, ingesting bottles of cognac or other strong brandy without restraint. After hours of being in a trance and heavy drinking he never displays any manifest signs of exhaustion, and even declares afterwards that he feels alleviated (*jian qing*), although physically drained. These aspects of his mediumship contribute to the popular perception that he is a pure channel of transmission.

Finally, the emphasis that folk theory places on self-obliviousness during possession raises the question of the locus of the mediating function. Is the stylus moved directly by the gods or is it moved by the medium as an agent of the god? According to P. Clart (2003: 164–5), the mediating function is clearly located in the human medium, despite the believers' theorizing which localizes it simultaneously in the latter and in the forked branch. The main argument he puts forward to support his thesis is the great concern for the medium's purity of mind. The training of the *ji*-wielders within De Jiao also insists on this purity, which is in no way limited to the mind. It equally applies to the physical as well as spiritual aspects of the person, hence the dietary and sexual restraints imposed before the séances. The Ming Zheng Tang worshippers and their De Jiao counterparts also are of one mind with regard to the mediating function, which they believe to be assumed both by the divine pen and the *ji*-wielders. It is precisely on this second point that my interpretation diverges from that of Clart. From the very moment we take into account both folk representations and practices, there is no reason to give precedence to the human agent in the chain of causation. On the contrary, the worshippers make the efficacy of material, human, and divine mediums (the *luan*-bird as gods' mount) depend on the same steps. Thus, while the accomplished medium need to make his mind go blank and his body pure so as not to interfere with the inflow of divine thoughts and matter-energy (*qi*), the *luan*-bird is believed to be *sui generis* a paragon of virtue. Furthermore, the willow or peach tree from which divine pens are taken is usually chosen, following divine instructions, in a "clean" (*chun jing*) natural area, and should have neither knots nor malformations. I also mentioned in a previous section that the willow tree's central node was believed to be *ba gua* shaped, thus acting as an efficient symbol of the cosmos and of the positive combination of its basic components. Finally, the divine pens are kept in a sacred place, usually a corner of the central altar of the congregation's prayer hall, near the divine icons. Stored that way, they are protected from the influence of malevolent spirits and of profanes' stain (usually their handling is restricted to the mediums). They are also kept in closer contact with the gods and are therefore in an ideal place to absorb their radiating magical power.

That the efficiency of the human medium, of the divine pen, and of the *luan*-bird be considered closely interdependent and of equal importance is suggested by the equivalence and interchangeability of the terms applied to them. The emphasis is sometimes placed on the *ji*, the divine pen, through compounds such as *fu ji* ("to support the *ji* with hand"), *ji shou* ("hand of the *ji*"), or *ji tong* ("children of the *ji*") to designate the planchette divination and the mediums engaged in such divination. In other illocutionary contexts, the emphasis is placed on the *luan*-bird through compounds such as *luan bi* ("*luan*-bird's pen"), *luan yu* ("*luan*-bird's command") and *luan wen* ("*luan*-bird's writing") to identify the divine pen and the messages it draws. In yet other contexts, compounds refer directly to the human medium. The main term is *shen ren he yi* ("deity and human become one") that the Ming Zheng Tang worshippers and their De Jiao counterparts use to express the interaction between mediums and deities during trances. Let us note however that the references to the human mediums in the terminology are few in comparison with the mentions of the planchette or of the fabulous bird. We can conjecture that the long training process and harsh discipline involved in establishing mediumship makes *a priori* the *ji*-wielders less reliable and less easily identifiable to the gods than the two other mediums. The fact that the De Jiao comments about *fu ji* focus on *ji*-wielders and their experiences is essentially symptomatic of the problems they raise.

Although the degree of reliability of a medium may not be fully ascertained, he nonetheless can receive "divine recognition" when, in due course, the gods confer on him a "heavenly degree" (*tian wen ping*). This "degree", which takes the form of *fu ji* poetic allegories conveying the idea of completion, is delivered at the occasion of a *fu ji* séance during which the medium thus singled out is excluded. Because it is considered similar to an imperial diploma, opening the way to an official appointment, it is another piece of evidence that gods and devotees are thought to operate along the lines of a "heavenly bureaucracy". Significantly, the *ji*-wielder, upon receipt of such a level of recognition, may use the "seals of authority" (*yin ba zi*) of his congregation. Such an appointment does not suggest, however, that the human medium takes over the mediating process. According to folk theory, he remains a "driving belt" in the process of communication. Moreover, the "heavenly degree" can hardly be considered as the final stage of an initiating process. *Ji*-wielders without divine accreditation can also be efficient "receivers" and be renowned for their capabilities, whereas the recognition conferred by the gods may be invalidated in the event of infringement of taboos. Although some mediums report that the gods had put to the test, through dreamlike visions, their resoluteness and other virtues before the awarding of accreditation,[2] these experiences, which are strictly personal, seem to be reproduced all along the medium's career. Accordingly, they do not correspond to levels of training, and the medium's divine appointment is not acknowledged through a *rite de passage*. In contrast with the custom of the Taiwanese organization studied by P. Clart (2003: 168), attainment of the above-described status is not marked by the granting of a "pen name" or other signs of public recognition.

What Status and Power for the *ji*-wielders?

That some mediums are officially appointed by the gods raises the question of their status within the religious community they belong to. In the view of P. Clart (2003: 170), a medium is not a particularly gifted individual, and "spirit-mediumship is the practical application of ability attainable by anyone at a fairly high level of cultivation"; this remark perfectly applies to De Jiao. On the other hand, the observation of J.J.M. De Groot that the *tong ji* (*tang ki*) of Xiamen belong to the lower social stratum does not apply to De Jiao mediums, since the people who take up the function come from every stratum in the social scale. There is a small number of business tycoons who hold the forked branch, but members of the middle and working classes are equally represented: truck or taxi drivers mix with shopkeepers, school teachers, students, engineers, accountants, and salesmen. In Malaysia, where there is a plethora of *ji*-wielders, women are admitted in mediums' circles which are largely dominated by men. They either form two-female teams or male-female pairs. In the latter case, the usual combination is a man in the position of heaven's hand with his wife or girlfriend assisting him. A brief survey I conducted in 2003 among 50 De Jiao mediums revealed that their average age was over 57 and that nearly 85 per cent of them had received formal education in Chinese schools. As for the remaining 15 per cent, most of them were residing in Thailand, and, because of severe restrictions imposed for decades on Chinese schools in this country, they were usually self-taught in written Chinese.

Only a minority of mediums are members of the directorial board of their congregation, and very few are those who, following the example of WZG of Zi Lian Ge (Kuala Lumpur) or of JCD of Zi Ying Ge (Guangzhou), act both as leader and "celestial hand". Usually, they work unobtrusively in the shadow of wealthy and influential businessmen who represent the political and financial "task force" of the cult community. This does not mean, however, that the mediums do not involve themselves in the community's current affairs. On the contrary, whereas most directors, who are usually deeply involved in the management of their own businesses and are also active in the board of several philanthropic organizations, have little time to spare for the administration of each of them, the mediums are often very active in the daily affairs of their respective pavilions. This is particularly true when they are past middle age and have retired from their professions. Otherwise, young, devoted mediums are frequently recruited by directorial boards as permanent staff. Such is the case of FSM, the main *ji*-wielder of Zi Zhen Ge, who manages the publishing house of the association, and who also oversees its administration on behalf of the directorial board. Another good example is JTX, the main medium of Zi Piao Tan (Siracha – Thailand), who is also its executive manager.

Indeed, the more the mediums involve themselves in the activities of their congregation, the more they develop their knowledge of its members, of their aspirations and concerns. Even if it is well-nigh impossible to establish a causal connection between such knowledge and the alleged accuracy of oracles, we can however surmise that they somehow correlate. Here we touch on the main point. How large is the extent of personal manipulation on the mediums' performance? And what is the effect of this possible bias on their fame? Evidently, the vast majority of De Jiao worshippers would deny the possibility that those they consider to be true "heavenly hands" may introduce human opinion and expectation in their *fu ji*, even with regard to meeting the general goals of the organization or to offering people some degree of relief. We have seen previously that the main criterion they use to decide of the reliability of the oracle is precisely the ability of the medium to create an intellectual void within himself. However, indisputable signs lack to identifying whether the practitioner has reached this state of mind. Consequently, the difference between *ren ji* (human planchette) and *shen ji* (divine planchette) is primarily a matter of personal assessment.

The more or less good reputation of the mediums apart, the "human" or "divine" character of the oracle is usually assessed with reference to its possible effect on the movement's unity, and to its effectiveness in the treatment of individual problems. Whereas the divine origin of spirit-writings whose contents fit the general purposes of the movement is rarely discussed, those which intend to restrict the *fu ji* activity or favour certain associations at the expense of others inevitably raise misgivings. Such was the case of an oracle attributed to Lü Dong-Bin which proclaimed in 1958 that Zan Hua will play the key role of uniting the Zi and Ji groups of Malaysia under its own authority. Another example is the command, attributed to Lü Zu, to suspend *sine die* all *fu ji* activities. Those who were averse to the implementation of this command promptly interpreted it as a human planchette.

With respect to the achievements of the mediums in replying to individual requests, it unambiguously appears that the more their oracles and healing prescriptions prove to be effective, the more their performances will be regarded as divine planchette and the greater their fame will be. Within De Jiao, like in other religious contexts, people who are not convinced of the outcome of an oracle often visit another spirit medium to check the validity of the diagnosis (DeBernardi, 2006: 105). Moreover, the collective memory is prompt to forget or downplay failures and to conversely retain and magnify miracles or noteworthy events, especially those which strengthen the *raison d'être* of the devotees' faith. In the case of De Jiao this trend is reinforced by two sociological phenomena. First, the fame of the medium as a true "heaven's hand" tends to be function of his degree of involvement in the life of the congregation. This may be partly due to the better accuracy of his predictions linked to his familiarity with devotees, but it may also be attributable to the influence and power he has accumulated as an active member of the association's staff. It is indeed more difficult to question the authenticity of the oracles delivered by a core member of the organization than by a near-outsider. When such a challenge occurs, it inevitably leads to a clash and to the departure of one of the conflicting factions. As for the second phenomenon, it is correlated to the number of mediums operating concurrently in a given national context. The fewer the *ji*-wielders, the more the devotees depend on them, and the fewer are those who dare to challenge their oracles. Thus, whereas the human/divine planchette controversy has always been a crucial element of the De Jiao history in Malaysia and Singapore where *ji*-wielders are numerous, it is of little significance in Thailand, Hong Kong, and the PRC, where, for various reasons, they are fewer in number. As a consequence, the status of the mediums in the latter set of countries is often considered to be higher compared to that of their Malaysian and Singaporean colleagues.

Even among the mediums who are unanimously considered to be pure channels of communication with the gods, the pending question remains whether their power and prestige is related to their state of possession or to their ability to be possessed. In other words, and to reconsider an issue addressed by D.K. Jordan (1972: 73, 84), D. Sutton (1989: 113), P. Clart (2003: 155), and others, do the worshippers respect the possessing deity or the possessed individual? When we take into account the point of view and attitudes of the De Jiao devotees, such lines of inquiry appear to be meaningless, since the adherents do not separate the status of the medium *in* and *by* practice, during the trance and after. According to them, the man who proved in the past to have an outstanding propensity for receiving high-tune transmissions from the gods should logically maintain or reinforce such power, except if he infringes the taboos associated with the function. This is the reason why renowned mediums who leave their congregation after a clash usually bring with them a large number of followers. Such was the case when LLZ, a founder of Zan Hua Ge, joined Ji Yang Ge after a falling-out with other Zan Hua leaders concerning the conduct of *fu ji*, or when JTX left the mother-temple of the Ming religious movement to found Zi Piao Tan in Siracha (Thailand). In both examples, these influential figures brought with them tens of followers enthralled by their effectiveness as mediums. In certain instances, these powerful *ji*-wielders may even become the objects of a cult founded after their demise. So it was for LLZ, a small altar devoted to him having been erected at the fifth floor of a pagoda built in 1970 in the courtyard of Ji Yang Ge. It should be noted however that these mediums are not worshipped as deified humans, but as privileged tools of communication with the gods, whose capacity remains intact after death. In other words, they are not considered as subject but as object of the miraculous powers radiating from heaven. Significantly, the worship of LLZ is restricted to occasions when *fu ji* proves to be inefficient, and devotees would be searching for a special means of mediation.

I have so far focused the analysis on the *ji*-wielders. However, the role that their assistants play in the production of oracles should not be neglected. Whereas the mediums are supposed to be in a state of self-obliviousness during the trance, the *bao yu* who report the oracles in a loud voice, and the *ji yu* who write them, ought to be particularly clear-sighted. This faculty is all the more needed for the *bao yu* who should quickly decipher series of cabalistic ideograms scrawled on the tray and must render them into legible human writing. Although usually ignored by the literature, these assistants play a key role in shaping the divine instructions and in presenting believers' requests to the gods, either individually or collectively. With regard to the latter aspect, the assistants usually "adjust" the content of the divine reply to reflect the nature of the request, and are expected to do so by those who are anxiously looking for a personalized answer. Such bespoke interpretation is validated by its collective character (several *bao yu* working together), and also by the fact that it is read to the *ji*-wielders and thus submitted to divine checking at the end of each sequence of the ongoing session. Freer and more controversial are the exegesis provided after the séance by the mediums or other literati who attend it as observers. They assume an important function by providing the devotees with a digest of the heavenly instructions. Finally, the interpretative process relies on several agents, organized in concentric circles around the divine pen: from the mediums in charge to the *bao yu*, and from them to the literati who are well-versed in divine poetry. Although ethnographers commonly follow the devotees by focusing their attention on the *ji*-wielders, who assume paradoxically the main responsibility of "good" or "wrong" oracles in the native view, the issue of the interpretative process ultimately proves to be in the hands of individuals who are not only in a state of perfect consciousness, but are also located at the outpost of human expectations.

Finally, the De Jiao materials partly confirm the statement by P. Clart (2003: 174–5) pertaining to a bipolar hierarchy between *ji shi* (濟世 – "to be of help") and *zhu shu* (著書 – "to compile scholarly works"); in other words, between *wu* and *wen*, "warrior" and "literati". If, according to the author, the first pole, characterized by violent behaviour and bloody sacrifice (including self-mortification) is at the bottom, the second, characterized by refined conduct and vegetarianism, is at the top. P. Clart adds that "this bipolar hierarchy is not limited to the group-specific value system of phoenix halls, but resonates with basic categories of Chinese culture concerning purity and impurity, the civil and the martial". Although the De Jiao practitioners stand out from the mediums studied by A.J. Elliott (1955) or P. Clart by considering *wen* and *wu ji* as two aspects of the same practice, they however establish a clear distinction between those well-versed in *wen ji*, who practice *wu ji* exceptionally, and others who emphasize relief of the needy as a supreme goal (the *ji shi* aspect). These contrasting trends are reflected at the institutional level as well, since Zan Hua emphasizes the production of moral teachings while Zhen gives precedence to divination, healing, and exorcism, with the Zi and Ji groups assuming a more balanced attitude. Such a continuum, together with the conflicting appraisals underlying it, helps to qualify the hierarchical structure put forward by P. Clart. Because the various De Jiao Malaysian groups do not share a common scale of values concerning these aspects, the leaders of Zhen tend to characterize the members of Zan Hua as arrogant and pretentious, whereas the latter are prompt to antagonize the former by accusing them of charlatanism. These prejudices are cultivated whatever their common assessment concerning the authenticity of the *wen ji* texts, which refer to their degree of literary refinement. For example, in both groups the lack of rhymes or their reduplication in versified parts of the oracles casts doubt on their divine origin, just as do logical inconsistencies and prosodic flaws.

The Sixth World Moral Divine Pen Meeting

In 1986, at the occasion of the 25th anniversary of Zi Nan Ge (Hat Yai), top representatives of major De Jiao associations from Singapore, Hong Kong, Thailand, and Malaysia were present at the proceedings when a *ji wen* attributed to Guan Ping came, advising them to strengthen their links by organizing regular meetings. A few months later, the De Jiao leaders met again to discuss the matter. They then submitted to the gods a proposal for an international conference organized periodically, whose main purpose would be to bring the divine and human communities together for a full day of collective *fu ji* séances. The main goal was for the adherents to receive the very essence of the honourable masters' teaching. Thus was devised the principle of the *Jie Huan Qiu De Jiao Da Hui Luan Te Kan* (届环球德教大会鸾特刊 – "World Ring Periodical Session of the De Jiao Great Vermilion Bird Meeting", later termed the World Moral Divine Pen Meeting). The logo of the event, allegedly created by the gods through *fu ji*, perfectly outlines the idea of communion between the forces of the universe. It consists of three circles fit into each other and whose pattern symbolizes unity. Into the inner one, three new adjacent circles, put together so as to form a small pyramid, represent the *san cai*, the "three abilities", an allegory expressing the fundamental combination of heaven, earth, and man. Finally, the entire drawing is crossed by a Y-shaped pattern that suggests the transcendent communication links established through the agency of the divine stylus (Fig. 12).

The first session of the World Moral Divine Pen Meeting was arranged in 1989 by the pavilion where the oracle had been delivered: Zi Nan Ge. Two years later, the second meeting, organized by the United Moral Uplifting Society of Malaysia, forbade *fu ji* sessions from being held. The reason was that the society had been founded only three years earlier (in 1988), and within it the differences between partisans and opponents of spirit-writing remained simmering. In fact, the second "*luan*-bird meeting" took place in 1993, at the Bangkok headquarters of the Federation of the Moral Uplifting Societies of Thailand. After this assembly, other meetings were organized with increasing regularity — gatherings were held once every two or three years — and a growing number of *fu ji* teams began taking part in the event. There were 20 pairs in 1996, at Ji Yun Ge (Singapore), 31 in 1998, at Zi Rui Ge (Kota Kinabalu, Sabah, Malaysia), and 34 in 2001, at Zi Zhen Ge (Bangkok). More recently, in August 2004, I attended the sixth meeting at Zi Luan Ge (Kluang, Johor Bahru, Malaysia), wherein no fewer than 45 spirit-writing teams coming from six countries took part.

Because the gathering assembled for three days practitioners and aficionados coming from all over the Chinese world, these meetings yield valuable insight into the practice of contemporary *fu ji*. Thus, during the last event in Kluang, a wide range of spirit-writing techniques were used concurrently: from the classical *wen ji*, eventually alternating with short sequences of *wu ji*, to the *jin zhi miao fa fu luan* ("marvellous method of the golden *luan*-bird indicator"), a technique mostly in use in Taiwan, consisting of writing oracles on a sheet of paper with a brush or a felt-tip pen.[3] Another Taiwanese device demonstrated during the occasion was the use of a small forked divine pen by a single medium. Although most oracles were delivered in Chinese, some were written in Thai or English. Finally, this event is an excellent occasion to examine the structural properties of the *field* through which spirit-writing is produced in the Chinese world. The concept of *field* I refer to here is borrowed from the theory of practice of Pierre Bourdieu. According to Bourdieu, *fields* are spaces of structured social positions. The persons who occupy such positions share the same *habitus*,[4] implying both knowledge and acknowledgement of common rules and stakes. Bourdieu contends that "all the peoples involved into the same field share basic concerns about the true existence of the field, so that even their harsher antagonisms are underlain by an objective deep bond" (1980: 113–5). Exploring this notion in the context of De Jiao, I assume that the participants in the World Moral Divine Pen Meetings, whatever their country and institutional affiliation may be, share basic values, rules, and stakes which offer a platform for the common appraisal of mediums' performances and "gods' enactments". Evidence of this shared idiom can be discerned from the great fame that De Jiao "heaven's hands" have attained among adepts of other Chinese religious movements. Thus, when I interviewed *ji*-wielders from the Ming Tan or Peng Lai organizations in Thailand as well as peers from sectarian groups of Taiwan, Hong Kong, or Malaysia, it appeared that WMY of Zi Jing Ge (Hong Kong) and FSM of Zi Zhen Ge (Bangkok) were considered as very accurate mediums by many individuals, majority of whom had never found the occasion to meet them personally. They had just heard that prominent overseas Chinese had travelled hundreds of miles in the hope of obtaining an oracle from them. Another evidence of this shared idiom lies in the fact that the mediums of other religious movements who take part in the international meetings of De Jiao readily accept its program and requirements.

Beside the introductory and conclusive speeches whose obvious functions are to welcome the attendants and to thank them for their participation, the main event consists of two complementary parts: a series of lectures about the experience and virtues of *fu ji*, and the collective practice of *fu ji*, with the participants devoting an entire day to this practice. The gathering therefore combines spirit-writing and its exegesis, two aspects which are inextricably linked. Traditionally, the first day of the World Meeting is devoted to sermons and comments from top-ranking leaders about the deep meaning of spirit-writing. In fact, the moral, philosophical, and even metaphysical aspects of *fu ji* cannot be dissociated in these speeches, whose current generic title, which is all the more suggestive, is *luan li yu xuan ji zhe xue* (鸾理与玄机哲学 – "the reason of the *luan*-bird, the very true theory of Dao, and the education of virtue"). An overview of the previous meetings reveals that those who deliver such speeches are chosen either within the remaining handful of the earliest De Jiao adepts still alive, or among the respected leaders of the second generation. In both cases, most orators have been *ji*-wielders for a time, and when they provide accounts about this activity they readily combine the recounting of personal experiences with demonstrations of varying degrees of erudition emanating from the study of the classics. To take few examples, when CLJ, the sole surviving member of the group who spread De Jiao in Singapore in the 1950s, made his lecture at the occasion of the Fifth World Moral Meeting (held in Bangkok, 2001), he enriched his narrative with a discussion of the developments concerning the symbolism of the *luan*-bird and the metrics of *fu ji* poetry with reference to treatises going back to the Han Dynasty. As for CWB, the then president of Zi Rui Ge, the association which organized the fourth World Meeting (Kota Kinabalu, 1998), he augmented his comments on the "reason of the *luan*-bird" by questioning the privileged use of willow trees to make divine pens and by referring to the *Liu Ren*, one of the three divinatory Magics of ancient China.

Bearing in mind that true mediums must be self-forgetting while in trance, how should one interpret the retrospective comments by some of them regarding this particular experience? Can such remarks be conceived as a betrayal of their fate affinity with the gods and of their accruing obligations? How could one reconcile exegesis turned toward open-minded quest of meaning and a faith that presupposes wholehearted adherence? To answer these questions let us recall that the individuals invited to give these lectures are retired mediums who for the most part have ceased engaging in *fu ji* because they believed to have lost their ability to serve as high-tune channels of communication. Unlike active practitioners, they are no longer compelled to demonstrate self-forgetting as a mark of mediumship authenticity. More importantly, the purpose of their retrospective comments is not to question the merits of spirit-writing, but to clarify the criteria regarding its "right" practice and to illustrate aspects of its symbolism. In other words, their goals are more didactic and apologetic than analytic.

The lectures they give, which serve to link the De Jiao philosophy to the Chinese literary tradition, attract a wide audience (more than 400 people attended the last conference in 2004). Nevertheless, the apex of the gathering occurs its second day, when the mediums of the different delegations perform simultaneously in the large hall that the organizers have fitted out for the occasion. Spirit-writing is then rigorously regulated. An *ad hoc* committee composed of well-known leaders and retired *ji*-wielders establish a protocol and oversee its implementation. They also arbitrate possible disputes and judge the degree of human or divine nature of the oracles delivered during this day. The protocol gives precedence to the associations who have organized the event; next in the hierarchy are the most influential pavilions of the De Jiao nebula. For instance, at the occasion of the sixth World Moral Meeting in 2004, 36 mediums' plates had been arranged in the hall. Among them, six had been placed to form a hexagon in front of the temporary altar devoted to Guan Yin and a wide range of De Jiao gods. Two of the six tables were to be occupied by the mediums of the host associations of Kluang (Zi Luan Ge) and Mersing (Zi Lin Ge); the remaining four were reserved for guests of honour. These distinguished associations had been carefully chosen to accommodate concurrently the most dynamic pavilions, the De Jiao groups still practising *fu ji*, and the main countries where the religious movement had been established. Thus, the leading De Jiao organization in Thailand, Zi Zhen Ge, was positioned next to Ji Yang Ge and Ji Yun Ge, the biggest pavilions in Malaysia and Singapore respectively and representatives of the Ji group, while the deputy association for the Zhen group was Zhen Luan Ge of Tampin (Melaka). As for the 30 other tables, they were set along three parallel lines and were allocated to the other delegations, depending on their order of registration. Interestingly, the organizers arranged these tables in such as to present a zigzag pattern reproducing a dragon's body, with the head of the fantastic animal being symbolized by the hexagon that the top associations formed.

The dragon metaphor applied to the assembly of mediums cannot be dissociated from the *luan*-bird that the gods ride to earth to possess them. Put together, the dragon and the vermilion bird express complementary properties: the male connotation of the former balances the feminine nature of the latter, just like the *yang* balances the *yin* and heaven pairs with earth. Moreover, both animals are icons of imperial authority, and the dragon is well known as a major symbol of Chinese geomancy. Still on the symbolic aspects of the conference, let us mention the recurrent choice of the number 6. It is illustrated by the hexagonal head of the dragon as well as by the 36 spirit-writing plates (i.e., 6 × 6), whose number below that of the *fu ji* teams attending the event, forced some of them to use the same table in turn. The organizers explained that the gods had chosen this figure as a fitting numerological emblem to mark the occasion of the sixth gathering of the World Moral Meeting.

With regard to the composition of the mediums' assembly, it was largely dominated by men, as only two teams were composed of women, and two other teams were made up of male-female pairings. From an institutional point of view, De Jiao, with 42 teams, was over-represented, the three other pairs belonging to a Ming Tan association from Surat Thani (Thailand) and to two Taiwanese religious organizations, namely Chong Xin Tang (崇心堂) from Taoyuan, and Wen Hua (文化) from Gaoxiong. The host country, Malaysia, where there are numerous mediums for reasons cited above, was logically the most represented with 29 teams (among them, the Zi group dominated, with 24 teams against three Zhen and two Ji associations). Thailand was second with seven delegations, then Singapore and Taiwan with two each, and the People's Republic of China and Hong Kong with each territory presenting one team.

However, these figures do not completely reflect the structure of the audience. Although followers from the different parts of Malaysia, including the insular states of Sabah and Sarawak, accounted for 75 per cent of the 1,500 participants, adepts from Taiwan, Hong Kong, Australia, and the PRC numbered more than a hundred. This turnout is significant when one considers the geographical distances involved and the expenses required to attend the event. In the case of the nearly 20 "brothers of virtue" coming from the PRC, their airfare had been paid for by business tycoons in Malaysia and Thailand who had contributed funds to facilitate the reintroduction of De Jiao in mainland China. Moreover, the accommodations and meals of guests coming "from far away" (including insular Malaysia) were paid for by the pool of 15 De Jiao associations of Johor state which organized the meeting, under the leadership of the most influential of them: Zi Luang Ge. More than three hundred rooms in the hotels in Kluang and its environs were thus booked for the three-day gathering.

At the morning of the collective spirit-writing session, before the start of the performance each team put its implements in the place allocated to it. If *pa gua*-shaped tables were provided by the organizers, some *ji*-wielders preferred to use their own tray. All of them had brought for the meeting the divine pens, seals, printed charms, and sand they were accustomed to using at home; entire sets of spirit-writing paraphernalia had been brought to the gathering in suitcases and sometimes in attaché cases which are so much in vogue among businessmen and officials. The spirit-writing session began at 11:00 a.m. on 4 August 2004, after the offering of incense and food to the gods was completed. According to pre-established convention, top-ranking leaders and honoured guests lifted the lid of the *fu ji* tables simultaneously, and purified the trays containing sand with water blessed by the gods. Afterwards, the whole assembly intoned the *Qi Zan*, the De Jiao invocation, and the "heaven's hands" began writing characters on the sand. From that time onwards, a tightly packed crowd of onlookers massed around the tables, eager for divine messages. Although this crowd was in no way static and groups of strollers moved from one spot to another, their uneven distribution between the tables had to do either with the relative fame of the *ji*-wielders or with the exotic character of their practice. For instance, the Taiwanese who were writing oracles very fast with a felt-tip pen were assailed with questions from a pack of Southeast Asian Chinese unaccustomed to seeing this technique, while a very famous pair of *ji*-wielders from Zi He Ge (Penampang, Sabah), who performed a seated trance with the "heaven's hand" embodying Ji Gong, attracted tens of onlookers. Evidently, some séances were as much performance as exhibition, with assistants spending a lot of time convincing bystanders about the efficiency and accuracy of the technique they were using. Thus, to some extent, the meeting had taken the appearance of a fair, with each organization trying to promote its champions and *savoir-faire*. The members of the various teams were wearing sweatshirts sporting the colours, logos, and the names of their association. The lively atmosphere brought about by the simultaneous presentation of competing abilities and the inclination of onlookers to congregate around the most spectacular trays lent to the conference an air of contest, without however any award at stake. The reference to the concept of social *field* is particularly relevant with regard to this aspect since the event is the occasion *par excellence* for intense exchanges of views, the homogenization of knowledge, and the comparative appraisal of the various spirit-writing methods among adepts. It is also of prime importance in establishing the reputations of the next generation of mediums and in celebrating the outstanding abilities of the most renowned mediums.

Following a current pattern, about half of the spirit-writing performances at the sixth World Moral Meeting were composed of two parts: a *wen ji* sequence made of moral poems and instructions benefiting the whole assembly, and a *wu ji* stage aimed at addressing individual problems. The duration of the first phase could be anything between 30 minutes and two hours, depending on the tables. The messages it yielded were gathered for further appraisal by the supervising committee. Only the most noteworthy of them, undoubtedly acknowledged as edicts of the gods because of their outstanding literary value, would be selected for publication in the book commemorating the event, together with the inaugural speeches and the lectures of the first day. As another evidence of the greater value attributed to *wen ji* in comparison with the "warrior" way, the oracles delivered for individual divination and healing were not taken into account by the committee and were not even mentioned in the book.

Despite their seeming relegation to second-class status, the *wu ji* performances met with great success among the onlookers, with devotees crowding around the *ji*-wielders to ask the gods about their future or to seek solutions to various difficulties (health, business, etc.). Ironically, leaders of De Jiao or of other religious movements were among the first to seek divine advice for existential matters. Such was the case of CLJ, one of those who introduced De Jiao in Malaya and who was over 80 years old in 2004. He sought answers regarding his frail health and the time he has left to live, spending more than 15 minutes posting questions to Ji Gong. The mediums concluded the consultation by applying the divine pen on the head and belly of CLJ, in order to expel CLJ's afflictions. Another significant example is LD, a citizen of Hong Kong who claims to be a living Ji Gong. As one of the main sponsors of the gathering he was entertained as a guest of honour. He came to Kluang with a group of adepts who distributed to other participants a miraculous image of "Crazy Ji", which suggests that LD's countenance has a striking resemblance to the monk's face, as well as copies of *fu ji* oracles alleging his divine identity. In other words, he had made the trip first and foremost to promote himself and to elevate his position in the *fu ji* social field. In the same vein, he made the rounds of the most famous *fu ji* tables at the meeting in the hopes of obtaining new evidence regarding his exceptional fate. A message from Zi Zhen Ge, the association in Bangkok with which he is closely connected, effectively met his expectations.[5]

Because they were very much in demand, the renowned mediums had to diagnose and cure up to the point of exhaustion. At 6:00 p.m., two tables were still open after hours of performance: that of Ming Tan (Surat Thani, Thailand) and a second one merging the main mediums of Zi Zhen Ge (Bangkok) and of Ji Yang Ge (Alor Setar, Malaysia), i.e., the two pavilions which combined their efforts in reintroducing De Jiao to the motherland. This last table was at that time the locus of an incident which occurred when the medium of Ji Yang Ge acting as "heaven's hand" suddenly felt dizzy and collapsed, almost certainly because of fatigue. He was immediately replaced by another *ji*-wielder from the same institution, while assistants succeeded in reviving him through massages and by making him drink strong tea. The fact that this table should remain active as late as possible was due to several factors. Its mediums were known as the best and their prestige was at stake. The World Moral Meeting was also a special occasion for Zi Zhen Ge and Ji Yang Ge to receive oracles about China. Finally, the directorial board of the World Moral Meetings relied on this table to appoint officially the association which would be in charge of the next Divine Pen Conference.

This directorial board brings together the chairmen of the pavilions which have already organized one or several conferences. In Kluang, the arbitration of the gods was all the more needed because the leaders of Zi Nan Ge and of Tai He Guan-Ji Yun Ge were involved in a keen competition to organize the gathering for the second time. Finally, after several rounds of discussions and a *ji wen* attributed to the Jade Emperor, LJX, the charismatic manager of Tai He Guan (Singapore) secured the decision. Interestingly, with respect to this decision as well as others concerning the management in the long run of an institution, the adepts prefer to rely on human choices rather than divine instructions. The managerial and financial stakes are so important that the dominant trend is to over-engineer the results of the divine arbitration by restricting the number of options.

Although there are stories about the miraculous selection by the gods of absolute strangers to become the head of De Jiao associations, a careful analysis reveals that these "miracles" concern pavilions on the wane, those whose cult community is inactive, or congregations that are to be established in remote areas where De Jiao has so far remained unknown.[6] In the first case, to call on an outsider seems to be a final attempt to reinvigorate the pavilion. In such a situation, there could be two outcomes: either the newcomer fails to stem the pavilion's collapse, or the "fresh blood" strategy works and the new leader manages to provide a new impetus to the cult community. Opportune *ji wen* usually reduces the risks of failure by appointing men who are locally known to be both dynamic and superstitious.

That, contrary to such situation, leaders contend for organizing the World Moral Meeting results from both the prestige and the important incomes that the event brings. To increase their fame, many wealthy individuals sponsor the event, at the image of LD. It goes without saying that the tycoons who are serving as leaders of the association finally chosen must be included in the list of the main donors. The funding thus gathered are to be used in order to host with splendour hundreds of guests, but also, to carry out renovation or construction works that could hardly be done otherwise. Significantly, the first arguments that the two competing pavilions put forward to carry the day in 2004 were the need to rebuild obsolete premises and the desire to develop facilities for charitable purposes. Other criteria contribute to the final decision. Among them, the manpower that can be mobilized for the event is crucial. The fact that Zi Zhen Ge (Thailand), Ji Yung Ge – Tai He Guan (Singapore), and Zi Luan Ge (Malaysia) are among the few De Jiao associations to claim more than five hundred members certainly contributed to their selection as host associations. Finally, another criterion is political. The De Jiao leaders favour the associations which maintain close relationships with the local governments. Accordingly, in Thailand they give precedence to Zi Zhen Ge which is, alone among the De Jiao pavilions in this country, under royal patronage; with regard to the World Moral Meeting of 2007, the selection of Tai He Guan partly resulted from its leader's connections with the political elite of Singapore.

To conclude these remarks on the World Moral Meeting, the festivities that accompany it bear mentioning. Sumptuous banquets, which attracted between one to two thousand guests, took place during the evenings of the three days in Kluang. In each case, the meal was supplemented with official speeches and various forms of entertainment (folkloric dances, performances of Chinese opera, or gymnastics). The grand finale was a beautiful fireworks display; on the same day, the lunch menu included more than one hundred Malay and Chinese specialties from Malaysia. These moments were a rare occasion for the devotees to meet "brothers in virtue" from other countries, to increase the number of their acquaintances, and indeed to exchange views about De Jiao and spirit-writing. Thus, new adepts from Kunming who had just founded a pavilion had the opportunity to sit down with fellow adepts from Taiwan,

Malaysia, and Thailand, while the president of the De Jiao association in Melbourne had his closing dinner with leaders of the Zhen and Ji groups and members of the Hong Kong delegation. If the World Moral Meeting contributes so significantly to the self-consciousness of De Jiao as a religious community, it is largely because it brings together a wide range of devotees who hail from different places and backgrounds, but are united by common goals and interests.

The "Bible" of Bukit Mertajam

In Chapter III, by relating the blossoming of several groups in Malaysia around the Second World War, I related the story of Zan Hua, whose incipient form appeared in 1918, when a recent immigrant from Chao-Shan named Tang Zi-Huan established a domestic shrine devoted to Lü Dong-Bin in Bukit Mertajam. Twenty years later, in 1939, an oracle attributed to Lü Zu was proclaimed in this mediums' circle forecasting the imminent rise of De Jiao in China. It also entrusted these Teochew with the task of spreading the new body of religious teaching into Malaya. Further oracles passed through Tang Xi-Ru, a relative of Tang Zi-Huan, confirmed such an assignment. This group later became known as Zan Hua, which now claims to serve as the "roof", and thus implicitly stakes its claim as leader, of the whole De Jiao movement in the Malay Peninsula.

Interestingly, as early as 1943, messages imputed to Lü Dong-Bin urged Tang Xi-Ru and his colleagues to compile a "holy canon" (*sheng dian*). The earliest of these oracles was a poem claimed to have been addressed on the tenth day of the ninth Lunar month in 1943, whose content was: "There is only one way to virtue. If the doctrine is not recorded in a holy book, depraved persons may be lead astray by it. It is only when gods issue a book that we can speak of a true religion [*zong jiao*]." It was followed one month later by: "The holy Canon must put together the gist of the five doctrines [Christianity, Islam, Buddhism, Taoism, and Confucianism]. Its aim is to make explicit their teachings, and to dissipate the misunderstandings and prejudices which opposed their adepts for centuries" (*Sheng Dian*, 1986: 39). If the date of the event is correct, this second message is the oldest one that takes into account Islam and Christianity which was received by an association later affiliated with De Jiao. Such a sign of openness to encompass the so-called western systems of beliefs is confirmed by the use of the modern concept of *zong jiao* for "religion", and by the fact that the compound *sheng dian* is sometimes replaced by *sheng jing* in oracles from Bukit Mertajam. Since the latter compound commonly refers in Chinese to the Christian Bible, adepts of other Malaysian De Jiao groups have ironically dubbed the "holy book" published by Zan Hua Ge as the "Bible of Bukit Mertajam", and taxed this organization with the desire to "ape" the western religions.

Another obvious stamp of the Abrahamic religions on the founders of Zan Hua was their claim that the "true" De Jiao faith is monotheistic. Although the great variety of gods being worshipped by the adepts contradicts this assertion, they argue that all of these deities are comparable to the Christian saints, as divine projections of a supreme being of transcendent consciousness. In the introduction to their "holy book" it is said that "everything [on earth] goes back to a unique ruler" whose will is absolute (*Sheng Dian*, 1986: 2). The Jade Emperor embodies this omnipotent and omniscient "true Lord" (*zhen zhu*), while Guan Ping is believed to be his main assistant. and Lü Dong-Bin his spokesman. Altogether, they form a holy trinity (*san wei yi ti* – "Three positions, one body"), whose prophets are Buddha, Lao Zi, Confucius, Jesus Christ, and Mahomet.

We know little about the religious background and the specific considerations which motivated the founders of Zan Hua to adopt such an approach. It should be said, however, that the cosmopolitan city of Penang served during the first half of the twentieth century as a hub for the westernization of Malaya. Because the Penang's elite was directly subjected to this influence, in the early twentieth century some of its members actively participated in movements of revival of Buddhism, Taoism, or Confucianism, which advocated the adoption of forms of rationality from the West (DeBernardi, 2006: 21). Later on, in the 1970s and 1980s, the Penang's Chinese vividly reacted to the Malaysian NEP by turning to their popular religious organizations to fortify their community, in the name of cultural revival and nationalism. According to J. DeBernardi (2004, 2006: 170), Taoist priests, Buddhist monks, the leaders of moral uplifting societies and sectarian groups then presented "their lay followers with catechism-like formulations of religious precepts and moral guidelines". It is likely that these reactive movements and the ideas they conveyed influenced the founders of Zan Hua, whose certain reportedly had acquaintances among Catholic priests of Butterworth. The attitude of Tang Xi-Ru and his colleagues may also be interpreted, more prosaically, with reference to the "*fu ji* controversy". Indeed, the *ji wen* instructing the Zi associations of Malaysia to cease doing spirit-writing arrived just when it was needed for Zan Hua. The other De Jiao groups had steadily rejected its claim to leadership, so that, after having completed its "first nine", Zan Hua was looking for an alternative strategy to the *fu ji* way, in order to sustain its messianic aspirations. The fact that Lü Dong-Bin was a prominent figure of the Zi pantheon in Malaysia, that he had given the name of its last hermitage to the association of Bukit Mertajam, and that he regularly referred to it in important messages, generated ambivalent feelings toward Zan Hua Ge. On the one hand, the Zi group tried to marginalize it by preventing its incorporation into the Nan Yang Moral Uplifting General Society, but on the other hand, it took Zan Hua Ge's oracles seriously and was concerned with their impact on followers.

When in 1967, the Zi pavilions ceased spirit-writing until further notice, Zan Hua took advantage of the situation by becoming the unique channel through which Lü Dong-Bin could send his instructions in Malaysia. Because the Ji group received its messages almost exclusively from Ji Gong, and the Zhen group was still in its initial stages of development, Zan Hua was then in a position to strengthen its image of being the gods' "chosen one". This period of privileged communication with the main figure of the Eight Immortals lasted for four years. In 1971, Lü Zu instructed Zan Hua to burn its divine pens and to stop practising spirit-writing indefinitely. Opportunely, this date coincided with the completion by Tang Xi-Ru of the holy book which was supposed to make De Jiao one of the great religions of the world, so the leaders of Zan Hua were prompt to interpret the order as a divine acknowledgement of their efforts, consecrating the definitive character of the teachings thus compiled. For its promoters and partisans, the book offered a digest which incorporated in its entirety all of the wisdom taught by the major gods of the various civilizations; therefore, further practice of *fu ji* was useless, and even dangerous. To justify this, they referred to the last message attributed to Lü Dong-Bin wherein he expressed the unhappiness of the gods who were being perpetually disturbed in their heavenly rest by personal requests from humans; Lü Zu even predicted that misfortune would befall anyone who would try to carry on with spirit-writing.

The *Sheng Dian* ("Holy Book") that Tang Xi-Ru compiled between 1967 and 1971 is a 919-page volume divided into eight "books" by analogy with the framework of the Christian Bible, and notably with the "books of wisdom" of the Old Testament. The first book (composed of 37 pages) comprises a foreword which relates the reasons for the digest's writing and a biography of the main gods that contributed to it. These gods are respectively: the Jade Emperor, Lao Zi, Śakyamuni, Confucius, Jesus Christ, Prophet Muhammad, and Lü Dong-Bin, the biography of the latter being more detailed than that of the others. The second book (42 pages) is entitled *Qian Dian* ("Earlier Canon") and is an anthology of 20 moral poems that Lü Dong-Bin sent to the Tang family between 1938 and 1943. Among them are the two texts which urged Tang Xi-Ru and his fellows to write a holy book. The third volume (162 pages) is entitled *Hou Dian* ("Later Canon"). It complements the earlier canon by way of presenting the two anthologies in a manner similar to the Old Testament-New Testament dichotomy, since the *Qian Dian* and the *Hou Dian* correspond to two critical moments in the establishment of the alliance between gods and men: an initial stage when a chosen family receives a divine revelation, in the manner of Moses receiving messages from Yahweh, and a subsequent stage, when the revelation is transmitted under a new form by different testator institutions. In actuality, the 50 chapters that compose the *Hou Dian* are instructions that Lü Dong-Bin proclaimed on behalf of Guan Yu as the enthroned Jade Emperor, between 1957 and 1971, in Zan Hua Ge (48 chapters) and secondarily in Zi Peng Ge (2 chapters).

It is possible to extend the parallel with the Bible, since the classic formula of Saint Augustine which explains that "the New Testament is hidden into the Old one, which is in turn unveiled in the New" perfectly expresses the complementarities between the *Qian Dian* and the *Hou Dian*. They echo each others' principles by the moral values they teach, the religious goals they set, and the role they confer on De Jiao for achieving the concord of the five great religions. The *Qian Dian* emphasizes the teaching of virtue, whereas the *Hou Dian* gives precedence to other aspects. Finally, just like the Christian Bible is the unification of the Old and New Testaments, the core part of the *Sheng Dian*, known as *De Dian* ("Book of Virtue"), unifies the *Qian Dian* and the *Hou Dian*.

The other sections of the "Bukit Mertajam Bible" are selections of scriptures from the "great religions". Thus, the fourth book reproduces the *Dao De Jing*, the "Book of the way and its virtue", assorted with comments from Taoist masters of different periods, while the fifth one is a choice of 31 sutras commented from the *Prajñā Paramitā*, the Mahayana Buddhist scriptures dealing with perfect wisdom. The sixth book is an anthology, also infused with commentaries, of three well-known Confucian texts: the *Da Xue* ("the Great Learning"), the *Zhong Yong* ("The Doctrine of the Mean"), and the *Lun Yu* ("Analects"). Finally, the seventh and eighth books are extracts from chapters of the Bible and suras of the Qur'ān.[7] The western and Chinese scriptures to be incorporated into the *Sheng Dian* are said to have been selected by Lü Dong-Bin on behalf of the Jade Emperor. The fact that the *Sheng Dian* provides exegesis of the Chinese texts to the exclusion of the western ones reveals the ethnocentrism of its writers. The contents of the Qur'ān and the Bible seem to be too foreign to the concerns of the De Jiao adepts for them to decipher the real goals and meanings of such scriptures. Furthermore, the intense focus on Lü Dong-Bin is singularly indicative of a Taoist bias.

That the revealed scriptures making up the *Sheng Dian* have been either devised or chosen through *fu ji* seems to conflict with the open goals of the book, which is precisely to serve as a substitute for spirit-writing. However, the contradiction becomes irrelevant if we consider that the promoters of the "Bible of Bukit Mertajam" do not intend to question the Chinese popular conception which makes *fu ji* the most literate and sophisticated way to enter into communication with the gods. What they contest is the subservience of this medium to political intrigues and personal ambitions. *Fu ji* is, moreover, presented as a divine creation and consequently the instruction to interrupt it which came from the pinnacle of the gods' hierarchy should not be discussed. Chapter 14 of the *Qian Dian* readily expresses such conceptions. In this chapter, Lü Dong-Bin proclaims that the gods had given De Jiao the right to use *fu ji* temporarily to increase the number of its believers, but this practice was too easily subverted by extremists who sowed discord and doubt, thus damaging the reputation of the deities. This is the reason why, later on, the burning of the *luan*-bird became imperative in restoring the majesty of the heavenly rulers and in order to avert the exodus of adherents from De Jiao.

The reasons given in this oracle to justify the cessation of *fu ji* require a few comments. First, the reference to a possible loss of interest in the movement was not surprising in the Malaysian context of the late 1960s. Conflicting *ji wen* which limited the conferment of religious legitimacy to a group or to a limited number of congregations to the exclusion of the others were corroding De Jiao from within, with predictable dire consequences for its continued growth. Thus, between 1967 and 1971 no new congregations were established in Malaysia and the number of adherents was not growing. To counter this stagnation, some De Jiao followers reacted by creating the Zhen group. Second, the causes of the decline and the solution to counter it, attributed to Lü Zu, correspond to the usual narrative structure of the myths of origin. According to this structure, humans, because of their cupidity and foolishness, corrupted the Edenic relationship that existed with the gods, thus urging the latter to cut off the umbilical cord (through *fu ji* communication) that linked earth to heaven, men to gods. The next sequence of the narrative, which is more western in pattern, is provided by Chapter 15 of the *Qian Dian*, wherein Lü Dong-Bin allegedly adds that the divine teachings, whose observance by mankind should ideally restore harmony, peace, and order on earth, would be henceforward conveyed by scriptures of "unique and perfect sacredness" (*jue dui shen sheng*). The compound *shen sheng* ("sacredness") as used here has a meaning very close to that of *sacer* in classical Latin, i.e., what is set apart from the secular, is reserved for the exclusive use of the gods and will be dreadful for the men who try to use it for ill-conceived reasons. The resort to such a concept suggests that the purpose of the Zan Hua leaders was, at the time, to substitute in exchange for a dialogical relationship between men and gods, a wholehearted belief in the Holy Scriptures, escaping to human thumb. The emphasis was no more on a ritual orthopraxis addressed to a divine assembly, but on a dogma whose permanence was an essential factor of truth and efficacy. Significantly, a *fu ji* message attributed to the Jade Emperor and reproduced in full in Chapter 11 of the *Hou Dian* proclaims that: "without any sacred book, belief is 'blind' (*mang mu*) and remains without proper goals to achieve. The religion then holds contradictions and is unauthentic" (*Sheng Dian*, 1986: 28–30). For his part, a *ji wen* from Lü Dong-Bin concludes Chapter 15 of the *Qian Dian* by revealing that those who will choose not to believe in the *Sheng Dian* can in no way be considered as true adepts of De Jiao.

The compulsion to comply with the gods' moral requirements to achieve salvation is also closely associated in the *Sheng Dian* with the theme of final chaos. One of the first oracles the Jade Emperor allegedly sent to Zan Hua Ge in 1958, and whose content has been reproduced in the *Hou Dian* (Chapter 18), predicts the apocalypse in a Confucian way, though by reference to the Christian Bible. According to this oracle: "The final chaos is inevitable when the sons do not obey their fathers anymore, the elder and younger brothers, husband and wife, kin and neighbours do not get on, and the country is not ruled, thus entailing a proliferation of wars. It is the autumn of a disastrous year, when nature and the whole mankind is going to die. According to the Christian Bible it is the time of the Last Judgment, at the occasion of which the criminals cannot be redeemed. In the present age, a nuclear war can be its possible expression. The virtuous alone will survive. They are eternal ..." (*Sheng Dian*, 1986: 53–4). In another passage, the sacred book is presented as a temporary solution, before the visit of divine saviours whose mission is to restore peace and harmony in the world. The messianic character of the book appears clearly here.

The excerpts illustrate a typical feature of the Bukit Mertajam Bible, which is the great number of divine oracles whose only purpose is to justify the writing of the said text and the cessation of *fu ji*. Thus, 18 of the 70 chapters which comprise the *De Dian* deal with one of these topics, or both. Such an emphasis on self-legitimization should indeed be interpreted with reference to the controversy provoked by the attempt to substitute canonical scriptures for spirit-writing. The dates of the oracles promulgating the *De Dian* serve also as a factor of self-legitimization, especially in the case of the *Qian Dian*, whose content was allegedly issued between 1938 and 1943, at a time when De Jiao was still incipient in China and had not yet spread to Southeast Asia. The claim of Zan Hua to be the "roof" of De Jiao as well as the unifier of the world's greatest religious doctrines is also a recurrent theme in the *De Dian*, since ten chapters of it develop this supreme goal. Furthermore, if we consider that five among the eight "books" of the Bukit Mertajam Bible are devoted to the Buddhist, Taoist, Confucian, Christian, and Muslim teachings, we can conclude that this collection of *fu ji* represents the apotheosis of the *wu jiao* doctrine.

* * *

In a *ji wen* addressed to Zan Hua Ge on 5 January 1971, the alleged aim of Lü Dong-Bin in ordering the writing of a holy book was to standardize the teachings and cults among De Jiao followers. The idea was indeed to counterbalance the centrifugal forces — particularly strong in Malaysia due to the profusion of mediums — which led to the founding of several competing groups, each of them developing specific cults and promoting its own interests. However, this attempt failed for several reasons. First, Zan Hua was a group born overseas, and its claim to be the De Jiao "roof" referred mostly to private spirit-writings. The suspicion that this claim was based on "human planchette" was indeed all the more entertained by Zi members that they wanted to preserve the leading position of their group. Another reason was the strong western influence that the project of Zan Hua revealed. Going far beyond the formal reference to Christianity and Islam which characterized the *wu jiao* theory, the holy book of Bukit Mertajam borrowed many concepts from the Christian Bible, such as the Holy Trinity, the Prophets, and a Lord conceived as a supreme being of transcendent consciousness. The basic framework of the Christian Bible was also adopted and, more importantly, the instigators of the Zan Hua book endorsed basic aspects of the Abrahamic system of beliefs, such as the idea that monotheism is a basic requirement for the "true" faith, whose cultivation rests mainly on the study of a unique sacred book. These conceptions and the correlative stigmatization of the further practice of spirit-writing introduced a sharp distinction between Zan Hua adherents and those who remained involved in *fu ji* activities, the latter being considered as heretics. The idea of excommunication which thus far was being ignored by the De Jiao followers became a recurrent theme in the speeches of the Bukit Mertajam leaders. Because of this orientation, Zan

Hua is certainly the group among the De Jiao organizations that comes close to the Weberian ideal of the sect. Making it similar to sects is its protest-like attitude against the development of the religious body from which it split, and its claim to offer a more authentic version of the De Jiao faith. The "epistemological authoritarianism" that Roy Wallis (1977: 14–5) considers to be characteristic of sectarian groups is also present in this case. According to this pattern, the adherents of the community regard all outsiders as "in error", therefore delineating clear boundaries between the cultic milieu and its surroundings. However, with regard to its seeming western orientation, Zan Hua defends a position all the more paradoxical. This group reinterprets the cosmology in reference to Christian categories, but the universal order it depicts remain under the control of Chinese rulers, namely the Jade Emperor, assisted by Guan Ping and Lü Zu. In the same vein, its holy book reproduces the Christian Bible framework, but its content is an anthology of *fu ji* texts and of scriptures selected through *fu ji*. Ironically, at the same time it severely condemns spirit-writing, Zan Hua cannot imagine a more accurate channel than *fu ji* in reaching the supreme divine revelations. Finally, whatever its claim to universality, it remains profoundly China-centric. From this point of view, a parallel can be tempted with the Confucian Revival, a nationalistic social movement which, according to J. DeBernardi (2006: 21), flourished among Penang's elite in the early twentieth century. Although it advocated the adaptation of Chinese thought to ideas coming from the West, it militated for maintaining Chinese identity through the practice of Confucianism.

In some respects, the Zan Hua holy book concurs with the organization of regular World Moral Meetings, since both projects are in response to the cult diversification that the increasing number of congregations entails. But whereas Zan Hua presents *fu ji* as a major obstacle to religious standardization, the promoters of the World Moral Meetings use its great popularity as an implement for unity. The intention in the latter case is less to standardize the spirit-writing practices, although the gatherings may have this effect, than to create a periodic forum wherein *fu ji* aficionados throughout the Chinese world can share experiences about an activity which is perceived as the paramount way to communicate with the gods.[8] The multifunctional kind of *fu ji* that most congregations perform explains the keen interest that this way of transacting with the gods arouses among a majority of followers. By usually combining *wen* and *wu ji*, the catch-all spirit-writing pattern in use within De Jiao combines elevated but distant ends with mundane and immediate goals. The moral uplifting, if not salvation, of mankind thus coexists, in the oracles, with the divine treatment of individual requests about good fortune, magical protection, or healing. In this context, the celebration of philanthropic and altruistic values is compatible with the open expression of ego-centred needs without any doctrinal tensions, except for these few puritans who, inspired by the example of the Zan Hua members, have been influenced by the western beliefs systems. Under such conditions, the difference between orthodox and heterodox practices is of little significance, and, with regard to the regulation of spirit-writing, few are the institutional resources devoted to this end. The World Moral Meeting, through its organizing committee, is one such body, although it supervises the planchettes of only a minority of De Jiao congregations, and furthermore it is held only once every three years! Another resource is the publication of divine messages in various books and periodicals. Two De Jiao national federations, those in Malaysia and Thailand, and among them two prominent congregations, Zi Zhen Ge and Ji Yang Ge, contribute to the dissemination of "authoritative" *wen ji* texts. Interestingly enough, the two leading associations in this field are also the most active in sowing the seeds for the resurgence of De Jiao in mainland China.

The pragmatic approach of spirit-mediumship which characterizes De Jiao partly explains why the World Moral Meetings of the Divine Pen have great appeal. The gathering for one day of various *fu ji* styles under one roof arouses the curiosity of a wide audience coming from within or outside the De Jiao nebula. Because this forum is unique in the Chinese world, it makes of De Jiao a spirit-writing hub. Taking into account that *fu ji* is both a salient feature of Chinese religious identity and a valuable tool for linking those who believe in its utterances to an apotheosized form of Chinese civilization, we can assume that De Jiao is in the forefront of the overseas religious attempts aimed at building new projective forms of identification with the homeland.

In the case of this religious movement, mediums are logically central to construct utterances adapted to the requirements of projective identity. Analysis of the present chapter shed light on their power in this domain, whose extent varies in accordance with their renown. This power mainly lies in what I call a *basic structuring antinomy*. On the one hand, the mediums' efficiency and fame rest on their ability to display a deep state of self-obliviousness at the time of possession, and henceforth to temporarily suspend interpersonal inferences. But on the other hand, their accuracy and power correlate directly with their involvement in the daily life of the congregation they belong to, and implicitly with their responsiveness to the expectations of their "brothers in virtue". In other words, their real hold rests on this fictional disconnection, which is more or less consciously cultivated by them and other followers, between the *divine devolvement* characterizing *fu ji* and their otherwise *mundane involvement.* In any event, it is by stealthily making use of information derived from social, political, and religious contexts that they can sometimes meet the expectations of their coreligionists, in the guise of divine intervention.

To be effective, such manipulations need to be assumed collectively. Against the common focus of ethnographical accounts on the medium's function, a more comprehensive analysis, proposed in this chapter, reveals that gods' utterances are construed through the cooperation and tacit complicity of several agents organized in concentric circles around the divine pen. Significantly, legible oracles result from an interpretative process which is entirely in the hand of individuals, either oral interpreters or literati, who are not only in a state of perfect consciousness, but are also expected to adjust divine utterances to human requests and concerns. A close examination of the criteria and mechanisms leading to the public acknowledgement of divine prophecy confirm fulfilment of individual or collective goals as an important requirement. We thus observed that the oracles unambiguously interpreted as divine planchettes were those which echoed the moral and unitarian objectives pursued by a majority of adepts. Sociological factors are also to be taken into account; the human versus divine planchette's controversy being a central issue in Malaysia, whereas it is of little significance in the other countries where mediums are in need. Finally, divine oracles prove to act in close reflection of human abilities, goals, and expectations. In the next chapter, by reporting on the successive stages of the reintroduction of De Jiao in post-Mao China, I shall provide new evidences of this mirror's game.

CHAPTER VI

Back to the Motherland and Towards the Global World

In 1994, a divine message delivered at Zi Zhen Ge referred allusively to the reintroduction of De Jiao in mainland China. However, the decisive event which motivated some leaders to the attainment of this objective occurred in 1996, when an instruction came from Xie Tian Ge, the "Heavenly Pavilion for Mutual Aid" that the "honourable masters" had allegedly created in heaven to propagate virtue on earth. The message was: "De Jiao spread from the North to the South. Today, it goes back from the South to the North." Few days later, it was followed by an oracle attributed to Ji Gong, whose content was: "Look for the origin, move forward and do promote De Jiao! The origin of Ji is distant (…). Where is actually the place of origin? To look for the early traces of De Jiao finally amounts to identify Zi and Ji." The *ji wen* also appointed eight well-known leaders to launch the project, who together represented "eight pavilions" (*ba ge*), the figure eight being that of the perfect ritual order in Chinese thought. Among these leaders were LYB, then president of Zi Rui Ge (Kota Kinabalu); SZM, the president of Zi Zhen Ge (Bangkok); LGZ, the president of Zi Yun Ge (Penang); HMK, the president of Ji De Ge (Ipoh); CGQ, the president of Zi Shu Ge (Johor Bahru); and LYT, the honorary chairman of Zi He Ge (Hong Kong).

This *ji wen* reciprocated, after an interval of 40 years, the order to spread De Jiao to Southeast Asia which had been issued in 1945. The fact that Crazy Ji reportedly replied to the initial instruction from Taoist masters is in itself significant of the cult and institutional diversification experienced overseas. Whereas the movement's expansion to the Southern

Seas originated from the Purple line as a unique source, the "boomerang" process of its reintroduction to the motherland was conversely a two-headed initiative, with top Ji and Zi associations acting together. The implication of Crazy Ji in the process should be interpreted with reference to his increasing popularity in the Southeast Asian and Chinese contexts. Following Lü Zu's ban on *fu ji*, Ji Gong appeared to be the most active, authoritative, and federative provider of oracles within De Jiao. Transcending the inner segmentation of the movement, he is said to have sent in the 1990s and early 2000s frequent oracles not only to Ji associations but also to Zi and Zhen pavilions. Zi Zhen Ge, which received his enactment, is thus known to be one of his privileged "aerial dishes", although it belongs to the Purple line.

Interestingly, the eight leaders chosen in 1996 to constitute the Research Committee on the Origins of De Jiao (RCODJ)[1] claimed to be his *yuan zi* ("sons of affinity"), in reference either to important appointments, to successful businesses or to miraculous healings. Moreover, the political, economic, and religious criteria underlying the "divine" choice of these leaders reveal a rationality that most western capitalist managers should emulate. LYB, LGZ, and SZM were, for instance, the most efficient financial backers that the movement could have imagined. LYB was a self-made man who had become after the Second World War one of the main tycoons of Malaysia; LGZ had founded Pensonic, the main Malaysian manufacturer of household electrical appliances; and SZM controlled in Thailand more than six companies supplying engineering services as well as mechanical and electrical products for infrastructure, waterworks, and construction projects.[2] Meanwhile, LYT, one of the earliest De Jiao members now based in Hong Kong, could use the New Territories as a bridgehead to resume contacts with ancient "friends of virtue" still living in Chao-Shan.

A few months after the *ji wen* of Dao Ji, the Research Committee was officially established at the occasion of the 25th anniversary of Zi Nan Ge. This pavilion, founded in Hat Yai (Thailand) by the Ji group and which mainly worships Ji Gong under the Zi group's label, served once more as a privileged link between the two main national branches and groups of De Jiao. Because most of the leaders chosen to be members of the RCODJ attended the event, a meeting to ascertain their roles was organized. The group's biggest tycoon, LYB, was logically appointed chairman of the committee, a position which required him to be the committee's main sponsor. He pledged to give HK$100,000 (about US$12,900), but resigned immediately in favour of SZM, citing poor health as his reason for stepping down. SZM offered HK$50,000 in support of the project. Finally, LYT, LGZ, and CGQ received divine appointments to conduct research in the PRC and to serve as executive managers of the whole project.

The Hat Yai event was the starting point of a very unique "boomerang" process, whose steps will be described in the following pages. I shall also investigate its features and motives, the overseas practitioners' response, and the reasons of the ban on De Jiao by the PRC government. The project to reintroduce the movement in mainland China was couched as a "research on the origins". Such a wording could appear illogical in view of the clearly identified origins of De Jiao. It appears, however, that during its exploratory trips to China the "origin" the committee was looking for was the ultimate one. In fact, its "research" was aimed at obtaining a new claim to legitimacy by demonstrating that the origin of De Jiao coincided with that of Taoism, and finally with the founding of Chinese civilization. This quest for legitimacy apart, the research trips were also conducted with more immediate goals in mind. I refer here to LYB, CGQ, and SZM who were at the time developing their own businesses in China. LYB, who had extended his shipping activities to the mainland in the 1980s, was making frequent trips to Chaozhou for philanthropic purposes. In the 1990s, he gave about RMB8 million to be used to build in his native county of Chao'an a college named "mind and love", a water-reprocessing plant, and a road. SZM, for his part, was trying to open markets in China for his mechanical and electrical products, while CGQ, whose main business in Malaysia was tourism-related, was establishing at the time joint ventures with office supplies companies in Guangdong and Zhejiang provinces, and had signed contracts with other firms to become their exclusive agent abroad. Although reestablishing their roots in mainland China was, for economic or existential reasons, a priority for these business leaders, the pervasive process of economic globalization should not be neglected. It was seemingly adapted into the religious field by the "honourable masters" and their "sons of affinity". They then "ordered" the founding of pavilions on a worldwide basis, in developed or developing countries where the Teochew community was large enough to provide basic support. Interestingly, the alleged gods' invitation to a bi-directional impulse, one directed to the global world and the other to the homeland, conflated the recurrent tensions within this religious movement between openness-to-the-West and China-centric attitudes, albeit with a clear imbalance in favour of the latter. The use of the Internet served to facilitate this bi-directional expansion, although modestly. In the last part of the present chapter, I shall deal with these recent developments.

The Restoration of Zi Xiang Ge

In the months following the Zi Nang Ge's oracle, LYT and CGQ visited Shantou several times to re-establish contacts with early followers. As a mark of the importance the Chinese confer on ancestry and descent, their first task was to approach the family of Yang Rui-De, the founder of Zi Xiang Ge, the oldest De Jiao pavilion. With the help of his sons, still living in Heping, they tried to buy the family house of Yingxi Gang where Zi Xiang Ge had been established in 1939. The premises were confiscated in 1951 and allocated to another family. Although LYB and SZM offered a good price for the old house, their highly symbolic project to revive Zi Xiang Ge in its original birthplace was rejected by the local Bureau of Religious Affairs on the grounds of the non registration of De Jiao with the central government.

Despite this rebuff, the eight leaders went to the main gate of the Yingxi Gang village, where a poetic stanza of Liu Chun-Fang and Yang Jun-Song had been carved in 1942, which called to mind the affinity linking the village to Nanchang, the heartland of Taoism. There, they presented the incense burner of the new Zi Xiang Ge that the descendants of Yang Rui-De accepted to revive privately. Into this incense burner were poured bags of incense powder coming from the "eight directions", in fact from the eight overseas Ji and Zi pavilions constituting the RCODJ. Hence, for the purpose in hand, the logic of the *xiang huo* ritual was reversed. Whereas, traditionally, the gift of ashes from a mother shrine to a new one initiates both the divine radiant energy in the new place and a descent relationship, in the present case, the influx was provided to the mother shrine from its descendants, from the expanded religious universe to its centre and source, from the South to the North.

About 90 followers from Thailand, Malaysia, the PRC, and Hong Kong attended the pavilion's inauguration which took place in the eighth lunar month of 1997. The mediums officiating during the occasion were those from Zi Zhen Ge. Interestingly, though the revived pavilion received incense from its "descendants", its statues or other icons did not come from tributaries. The sons of Yang Rui-De, mainly with their own funds, ordered a local artist to make a new copy of the portraits of Liu Chun-Fang and Yang Jun-Song that another artist, inspired by dreams, had initially painted in 1939. Small statues of the two Taoist masters, reproducing the main paintings' features, were also cast and set on the altar, together with icons of Guan Yin and of Ji Gong.

Between 1997 and 2003, the mediums of Zi Zhen Ge performed *fu ji* sessions three or four times at Zi Xiang Ge, mainly when they visited

Chao-Shan to open new pavilions. Delegations from the Ji group also visited it several times, and so did members of Zi He Ge and Zi Jing Ge, two of the three De Jiao pavilions of Hong Kong. Meanwhile, the third pavilion, Zi Xiang Ge, never made any attempt to worship the icons of the association whose identity it had assumed for decades. Its leaders certainly feared the troubles that could ensue in the wake of the name confusion. In fact, an awkward and unprecedented situation had been created by the resumption of Zi Xiang Ge in Heping. Henceforth, which one should be considered as the mother-temple of the movement? Should it be the Hong Kong association, whose incense powder had been brought from the original Zi Xiang Ge, and which claimed to have been allowed by the gods to take up its name? Or should it be the new Zi Xiang Ge, restored through initiatives from overseas, but located in the primitive hearth of the movement, Yingxi Gang, and managed by the sons of Yang Rui-De? The RCODJ promptly indicated that it favoured the second choice, probably under the influence of LYT, who was a defector from the Zi Xiang Ge in Hong Kong. Thus, the committee not only omitted to inform the latter association of its initiatives, but also took ashes from the incense-burner of the Yingxi Gang pavilion to open several shrines in China. This legitimization was also reinforced by the fact that, soon afterwards, the eldest son of Yang Rui-De proved to be one of the few accurate De Jiao mediums based locally.

Researches on the Origin

At the invitation of LYT, a De Jiao practitioner of the earliest times, named LLZ, attended the opening ceremony of the new Zi Xiang Ge. In Chapter I, I briefly narrated the tragic fate of this late president of Zi Hao Ge (Da Hao). From 1951 to 1979 he had either been imprisoned or interned in re-education camps. Just after his liberation, he was approached by former members of a local *shan tang* who intended to restart it, but he discovered that the committee had been infiltrated by Communists, and thus rebuffed their approaches.

During the *fu ji* session of this opening ceremony, LLZ reportedly received a personal address from Dao Ji instructing him to find a book concealed into a wall. Following the oracle, LYT asked LLZ to uncover the Ji Gong's self-portrait delivered at Zi Hao Ge in 1946. The old man thus visited the previous members of his congregation and finally found the miraculous painting in the attic of an adherent's house. Copies of it were made and distributed in varying sizes among devotees in China and abroad. But, actually, the hidden book mentioned in the oracle was another document, known as the *Bamboo Bridge Original Collection* (*Zhu qiao chu ji*). LLZ had fortuitously found the original script three years ago, in a cache that one of his late comrades had made in a wall of his house. Because the original one was damaged, he quickly made a handwritten copy. Although Li Huai-De had already printed a digest of the manuscript in 1955, LYB published the whole document in 1998, under the title *Luan wen ji cui* ("An Anthology of the Essential *Luan*-Bird Writings"). Its original parts consist mainly of a collection of *fu ji* messages from Song Da-Feng. This morality book aimed at universal salvation is entitled *Jiu sheng du* ("Rescue"). It dates back to the reign of Tong Zhi (1862–74), and is attributed to a benevolent hall of Anbu named Guang Ji Shan Tang. Other fragments concern the biography of Taoist saints such as Liu Yuan-Yang (柳元杨) and Xing Ti (兴替), from Shanxi province.

The original anthology, including the Song Da-Feng teachings, was probably compiled by Li Huai-De and Ma Gui-De between 1940 and 1947. It begins with a section composed of biographies of the main gods worshipped by De Jiao, namely Buddha, Lao Zi, Confucius, Guan Yin, Guan Yu, Guan Ping, Lü Dong-Bin, Yang Jun-Song, Liu Chun-Fang, Song Da-Feng, Hua Tuo, Ji Gong, Bai Yun, and the Eight Immortals. In the editions of 1955 and 1998, Jesus Christ and the Prophet Muhammad were added. The next section is a chronicle of the "De Jiao revival in modern times" written by both Ma Gui-De and Li Huai-De. It mainly relates the spread of the movement in Chao-Shan from 1939 to 1947, and sheds light on the circumstances which led to the opening of an increasing number of pavilions during that period. In the 1955 edition, Li Huai-De extends the chronicle to cover the first congregations founded overseas: in Thailand, Singapore, and Malaysia. Finally, the teachings of Song Da-Feng apart, the last and main part of the collection consists of the *fu ji* texts proclaimed between 1939 and 1947, accompanied with comments from Li Huai-De or Ma Gui-De. Interestingly, these comments put less emphasis on morality than on affinities and miraculous events involving the "honourable masters".

This *fu ji* anthology and the chronicle preceding it are full of valuable information concerning the first steps of De Jiao. Although the authors' comments do not take into account the sociological context, they nevertheless interpret the divine enactments with reference to economic and political events. They also provide key elements to understand the adherence of prominent figures to the movement. Their interpretation of one of the earliest oracles proclaimed at Zi Xiang Ge, in 1939, illustrates the first aspect. In it, allusion is made to a forthcoming "year of great warmth", which corresponds to 1943, when Japan completed its conquest of China.

Another passage suggests, through the metaphor of the "westward sunset", that in 1945, the empire of the "rising sun" will lose the war. As for the second aspect, another oracle from 1939 explains the interest of Ma Gui-De in the mediums' circle headed by Yang Rui-De, with reference to his vision of "nine purple lights" illuminating the sky when he was very ill in 1936.

Part of the original manuscript was composed of poems attributed to Song Da-Feng, but the title of the anthology also refers implicitly to the Teochew bodhisattva and to his charitable works. A message thus refers to the first Sino-Japanese war (1894–5), which resulted in China ceding Manchuria to Japan. China's defeat is then allegorically presented as the destruction of the bridge of "peace and happiness" (*he ping*). Interestingly, Heping is the township where Song Da-Feng built a stone bridge through miraculous means during the twelfth century. It is also the place where his hermitage and the first De Jiao pavilion in history were established. The oracle suggests that the greatness of Chinese civilization may be restored: "the bridge can be rebuilt with stones from the Peak of the West (the Western paradise), and, failing that, the use of bamboo trunks will suffice to rescue the virtuous people by making them cross the river safely" (Li Huai-De, 1955: 248–9). The allusion here to the theme of "rescue" echoes the title of the Song Da-Feng morality book included in the Bamboo Bridge collection. Finally, these references and inclusions provide another evidence of the strong social and philosophical affinities as well as common charitable goals that De Jiao shares with the benevolent halls of the Song Da-Feng tradition.

Concerning now the symbolic reference to bamboo, in the Teochew language its pronunciation is homophonous with that of virtue (*tek*). It is hollow too and bends with the wind without breaking, which can be taken as a mark of perseverance. According to LLZ, it is also a symbol of tolerance (*jian ren*). Furthermore, the bamboo is known in Chinese thought, together with the plum, the orchid, and the chrysanthemum, as one of the "Four Noble Ones" (*Si Jun Zi*), representing the four seasons. As for the bridge, LLZ mentioned it as a metaphor used in Buddhist sutras to link the worlds of the gods and the humans. Beyond these symbols, the whole anthology is a manifesto for De Jiao to serve as a moral though unofficial link (the difference between bamboo and stone certainly can be discerned here), between the great but dominated Chinese culture of contemporary times and its divine forefathers. In other words, the implicit intention is to maintain, whatever the circumstances, a bridge of unity and continuity between the teachings of the divine forefathers and the demand of the distraught masses. The fact that two successive editions of the Bamboo Bridge anthology were published — one directed toward Southeast Asian followers, released in 1955, and a second one mainly aimed at post-communist China, in 1998 — could be interpreted as a sign that the mission allegedly assigned to De Jiao by the *de de she* remains intact, i.e., to revive morality among the Chinese people whose spiritual education suffered because of geographical and ideological hindrances.

Pictures or texts from the gods apart, the research trips carried out in the late 1990s led to the discovery of other precious items. Independently of the trips organized by Zi leaders, Ji members also received revelations to conduct their own researches. In 1997, HMK and 30 other adepts went to Shantou and visited the ancient premises of Zi He Ge, where the *De Jiao Xin Dian* had been promulgated. The prospectors discovered hanging on a high beam of the house's structure a blackened forked branch used in bygone days as a divine pen. They immediately used it, and an oracle attributed to Ji Gong came forth. It mentioned a place in Anhui which was devastated by floods and was instructively called Zi Yang Shan ("Mountain of the Purple Yang"). The Malaysian group raised funds to contribute to the relief efforts, thus gaining the trust of the local authorities. There, another *ji wen*, but from Lü Dong-Bin, asked them to go to his hermitage in Jiu Hua Shan (九华山), and more precisely to a place named Hui Xiang Ge (回香閣), whose appellation was reminiscent of Zi Xiang Ge. Finally, they performed a spirit-writing séance, at the occasion of which Lü Zu is said to have ordered them to rebuild his hermitage. This oracle, which was attributed to a master who had not sent any messages to the Purple line for years, was considered as an affront; accordingly, HMK's membership in the RCODJ was not renewed. A few weeks after the visit of the Ji delegation to Anhui, the Purple line organized a research trip to Nanchang (Jiangxi), which was allegedly commissioned by Ji Gong. It involved the grandson of Yang Rui-De and CGQ. During this expedition, the "explorers" opportunely found traces of a palace named Wan Shou Gong ("Palace of the Ten Thousand Year's Longevity"). They also discovered in this heartland of Taoism the spiritual trace of a shrine devoted to the cult of Lü Dong-Bin, whose name was Zi Jin Ge ("Pavilion of the Purple Gold"). On the summit of a neighbouring mountain, a small stone house was located, on the walls of which was written Zi Yang Gong ("Palace of the Purple Yang"). According to a subsequent oracle, Lü Dong-Bin had slept three nights on a stone bed within this house, which was later considered as the oldest De Jiao pavilion to have ever existed. Due to this discovery, the pre-eminence of the Zi group was deemed to be safe, and to show that the Ji and Zi lines were still working hand in hand, a delegation of 120 people, including Zi and Ji leaders, prayed together a few months later at Lü Zu's hermitage, in Nanchang. At this occasion, they received the order to establish locally a new pavilion, named Zi Hua Ge.

In 1998, at the occasion of its second biennial meeting, the RCODJ revised its membership roster to form a group of thirteen. The new grouping only retained the main sponsors of the first committee (LYB, SZM, CGQ, LYT). Nine new figures were appointed, namely: LYW and YWD, respectively chairman and vice-chairman of Zi He Ge (Hong Kong); ZJB, the chairman of Zi Ying Ge (Batu Pahat); CWB, the honorary chair of Zi Rui Ge (Kota Kinabalu); CYB, the leader of Ji Yang Ge; ZLX, the honorary president of Zi Chang Ge (Malacca); HGH and LXD from Zi Zhen Ge (Bangkok); and PJ, a businessman from Nanchang (Jiangxi).[3] The top priority of the new committee was the registration of De Jiao with the Beijing government. Its members also put together HK$580,000 to finance the foundation of new pavilions.

The Beijing's Ban

Between 1996 and 1998, the RCODJ had tried to reinstate the movement in China through a semi-official approach turned toward territorial jurisdictions. It relied on freshly incorporated adherents, preferably influent local businessmen, and used their personal know-how and connections to deal the foundation of shrines with municipality, district or county officials. In return of the supply of much-needed infrastructures and social services (roads, schools, dispensaries ...), the RCODJ expected a tolerant attitude from the local authorities toward De Jiao cults. In so doing, the committee transposed to the religious sphere the local-agent system its members commonly used for the development of their businesses in China, while its locally oriented approach of the administration was motivated by the statement that the degree of religious restrictions varied significantly from jurisdiction to jurisdiction and that, traditionally, in Chao-Shan, government supervision of religious activity was minimal. However, the fairness of local agents proved to be sometimes unpredictable, while the political context soon appeared unfavourable to the kind of local deals that the RCODJ had initially contemplated.

The foundation of Zi Hua Ge in Nanchang is a case in point of the difficulty to find reliable correspondents that De Jiao faced. The school teacher chosen through *ji wen* to be its president was unknown to De Jiao. This man, actually, served as a screen for another one named PJ. The RCODJ had accepted this local entrepreneur for membership on the strength of a recommendation of CGQ, who considered him as his "adoptive son" (*yang zi*), due to a close business partnership. At first, the shrine was located in rented premises. The RCODJ then commissioned PJ to apply for local registration, but the attempt failed for about the same reasons than Zi Xiang Ge, and PJ put forward a rental rate which was deemed excessive to move the shrine to his warehouse. Later, the RCODJ discovered that, despite the HK$79,000 he had received, PJ had neglected his duties by placing the statues and incense burners in an untidy heap within a dusty room. He was therefore expelled from the committee.

As for the restrictions that De Jiao experienced while dealing with the local authorities, they find a good illustration with the Fengshun case. The township of Fengshun is located about 50 kilometers northwest of Shantou. In the 1990s the local government built an imposing administrative headquarters and around it a new town named Tangkeng, which was planned to serve as a tourism hub due to its proximity to hot springs and to a famous geomantic place known as Hu Tou Shan (虎头山 – "Mountain of the King of Tigers"). A Teochew woman from Thailand, ZQD, who was a member of Zi Zhen Ge, bought, through local business connections, a piece of land on the slope of this mountain in 1997, and the president of Zi Zhen Ge managed to obtain an official letter from the Fengshun government allowing the construction of a temple worshipping Ji Gong. In the view of the De Jiao leaders, it could serve as a platform to attract new followers, while for the local authorities a shrine devoted to the very popular Dao Ji could attract cohorts of tourists. During the Spring Festival of 1999 a delegation from Zi Zhen Ge went to Fengshun to choose the exact location of the shrine and to draw the divine blueprint of the building. According to a witness, at the moment when the delegation was alighting from their vans to walk to the spot, Ji Gong "pulled" the hands of the mediums in a harsh manner for an unexpected *ji wen*; meanwhile, it started to rain heavily. The rain was interpreted as a good omen, and the divine oracle delivered for the occasion confirmed the place as very auspicious.

Putting forward this miracle, the promoters of the project started raising funds. As usual in such circumstances, they opportunely received divine support and a *ji wen* attributed to Dao Ji appointed the president of Li Shan Ge (a Zan Hua association located in Sungai Pettani) as the main sponsor of the project. He and his pavilion consequently absorbed more than 40 per cent of the total construction cost (US$294,000). Among other prominent contributors were the president of Zi Zhen Ge (US$23,333) and leaders of pavilions from Thailand, Malaysia, Singapore, and Hong Kong. Finally, the shrine, registered as a Buddhist pagoda, was inaugurated in 2001. It is located on the top of a hill. At its feet, the local government has built a rest pavilion and a monumental gate. A road connects this gate to the temple. More than one hundred philosophical maxims, some of them coming from western writers such as Emerson, have been carved on the initiative of De Jiao on marble tablets along the path. When I visited the shrine in 2003, I saw hundreds of people paying their respects to the gods. However, a tacit requirement in the deal between Zi Zhen Ge and the Fengshun township government was not satisfied, leading the De Jiao leaders to think that they had been duped. The dispute concerned the discreet posting of the movement's identity onto the shrine. Although on the day of the opening ceremony the authorities allowed the overseas followers to display the De Jiao flag and a tablet containing the ten De Jiao virtues and eight rules, they were prompted after the event to remove these items. Moreover, the local government, by taking advantage of the shrine's registered status, housed in the temple's outbuilding a group of monks, sent on secondment from a local Buddhist monastery; their implicit function was to control the devotional activities in the place.

This unsuccessful attempt to open a semi-official De Jiao pavilion had been preceded by a similar failure a few years ago, when Zi He Ge (Hong Kong) had raised HK$9 million to build a temple also devoted to Ji Gong on a hill near the city of Chaozhou. The man who served as a go-between with the local authorities for this project, FSY, was a relative of LYT, the president of Zi He Ge. This influential entrepreneur of Chaozhou, the owner of a pharmaceutical factory, had joined De Jiao in 1989 due to oracles from Zi He Ge. His faith was later confirmed by messages delivered at Zi Zhen Ge (Bangkok), the spirit-writing sessions of which he attended several times. After a long period of private worship in a room of his factory, the divine instruction came to establish a pavilion named Zi Xuan Ge and to combine it with a shrine which would be opened to a wider audience. The permit from the local government to build this shrine was obtained in return for the De Jiao leaders' commitment to finance the construction of a primary school. LYB and the other members of the RCODJ collected RMB3 million to satisfy this prerequisite. The building of the temple was finally completed in 1999. It consists of a large hall with a big statue of Dao Ji occupying the central stage and icons of Guan Yin and Ma Zu on lateral altars. Although individual devotions are allowed, the authorities have so far prevented collective celebrations as well as all public marks of the temple's affiliation with De Jiao. Local adepts have no other option but to meet at Zi Xuan Ge, the pavilion founded by FSY, whenever they want to worship the "honourable masters", or to attend one of the very occasional *fu ji* séances organized locally. Inaugurated in 1998, this pavilion was secretly put up in a house that FSY has built, by following the geomantic instructions of He Ye-Yun. It is located near the Ji Gong shrine. In the followers' view, this proximity sufficiently overcomes the restrictions imposed by the government, given the magic and radiating aura of Crazy Ji.

Several arguments may be put forward to explain the reluctance of the local Religious Affairs Bureaus (RAB) to tolerate the activities of De Jiao in the late 1990s. Firstly, by adapting to the post-Mao context a strategy that had proved to be effective in Thailand during the ultra-nationalist period, the Committee used the *shan tang* label as a screen. In its applications to the RABs and latter to the State Administration for Religious Activities (SARA), De Jiao thus presented itself as the *De De Ci Shan She* ("Benevolent Society for Love and Great Virtue"); a compound which merged the reference to the halls for good deeds (*shan she*) with that of the De Jiao typical gods' society, the *de de she*. However, this stratagem proved to be a wrong choice. In the late 1990s, the religious landscape was already saturated in the Teochew area by more than three hundred *shan tang* operating concurrently, thus leading some districts to impose restraints. On the other hand, the affiliation to the halls for good deeds that De Jiao claimed was hardly credible in the view of the local authorities. Compared to the traditional *shan tang*, the movement displayed specifities which raised suspicion. It was controlled from overseas and its scope was transnational; just like banned Taiwanese sectarian groups it stressed the importance of spirit-writing, whereas this activity was marginal amid the Teochew *shan tang*. Moreover, by analogy with Yi Guan-Dao, Ji Gong was its main oracles bearer, and it could be considered as a syncretic group that blend tenets from a number of religious beliefs. With regard to these features and to the official classification, De Jiao was more accurately falling into the stigmatized category of "cults". Although the movement did not deified core leaders, and was not reportedly confusing and deceiving people, it nonetheless fitted the three other criteria retained by the Ministry of Public Security to define cultish groups. It was seemingly setting up illegal organizations in the name of religion; was initiating and spreading superstitions and "evil teachings" by means of spirit-writing, and because of that could potentially engage in disturbing the social order. In 1995, the State Council and the CCP's Central Committee had issued a circular labelling several religious organizations "cults" along these criteria and making them illegal. Here certainly lies the main reason for the local authorities' reluctance to allow De Jiao to operate in their jurisdictions.

The same assessment also explains why the State Administration for Religious Activities rebuffed the official request for registration that the RCODJ presented in 1999. Moreover, the application was considered at a time when the authority of the China's leaders was directly threatened by the silent mass demonstrations of Falun Gong. In those circumstances, the central government's response was to harden its religious policy, thus precluding the registration of movements that the Beijing's paranoia was prompt to equate with Falun Gong. Kept informed of the official grounds for rejection, the De Jiao leaders found the amalgam with Falun Gong particularly unfair, so striking are the differences between the two movements. Whereas Falun Gong is a homegrown spirituality expressing dissatisfaction with larger societal problems, and whose philosophical aim is to reconnect the physical exercises of *qi gong* with their historical spiritual base (Schechter, 2001: 47), De Jiao may be interpreted as a conservative and nostalgic reaction of uprooted overseas Chinese who intend to build new spiritual links with the homeland, but whose adepts avoid to involve themselves into current political affairs. Moreover, the threat that Falun Gong constituted by recruiting among China's elite was not transposable to De Jiao, whose sociological impact was at the time and still remains insignificant in the PRC. Although we have no reliable information concerning the arguments of the SARA's officials for rebuffing the De Jiao's application, we can speculate that they were conscious of the differences between this movement and Falun Gong, but that, beyond this incidental and opportunistic parallel, they intended to sanction the non appropriatness of De Jiao with most of the six official requirements for the registration of "venues for religious activity". Thus, De Jiao could claim neither an organized governing board clearly located, nor a set of operating rules and a legal source of incomes, these requirements being adapted to church-type organizations and to the control framework set by the PCC and the state.

Although disappointed by this official rejection, the members of the RCODJ decided to circumvent the ban, either by establishing unregistered pavilions in private flats and houses, or by setting up De Jiao altars into registered temples, this in return of financial support. Another one-off strategy, akin to marketing, consisted of inviting SARA's officials and specialists in religion of the Beijing University to attend, in 2001, the opening ceremony of the Chinese style pagoda that Zi Zhen Ge had built to commemorate the 50th anniversary of the association, and the 72nd birthday of King Bhumibol. Because Zi Zhen Ge was registered as a Buddhist association and operated under royal patronage, it offered an ideal showcase of the De Jiao political integration and charitable works.

Major figures of the Thailand's gotha, such as the Supreme Buddhist Patriarch of Thailand and Princess Sirindhorn attended the event, thus suggesting to the PRC officials that De Jiao was not a subversive but, on the contrary, a perfectly well-established movement. Following the visit, a member of the delegation, Huang Xia-Nan, published an article in the broadly distributed magazine *Shi Jie Zong Jiao Wen Hua* ("Cultures of Religions of the World"), where he provided a sketchy description of the doctrine, organization and history of De Jiao. His conclusion was that "the syncretic nature of this religious movement reflects both the situation of the Hua Qiao and their attachment to the traditional culture" (2003: 61). The lights that the visit to Zi Zhen Ge and this article shed on the nature and goals of De Jiao did not, however, curve the attitude of Beijing.

The Importance of Personal Links

The impossibility for De Jiao to exist openly in China led the RCODJ to rely on a handful of trustworthy correspondents to promote the movement locally. Although PJ, the businessman in charge of the pavilion of Nanchang, did not properly fulfill this mission, he had maintained personal relations with a member of the RCODJ for years, and such was the case of some of the leaders of the other congregations created in China. A good example is Zi Ying Ge, the second congregation of the new generation which was established in the motherland, in the suburbs of Guangzhou. The chairman, whose religious name is JCD, was an officer in an ocean freight company of LYB; through his personal links with the Malaysian tycoon, he started attending De Jiao *fu ji* sessions in Sabah, and eventually received the revelation to become a follower. Other employees of the same company, together with local businessmen, school teachers, private sector employees, and shopkeepers belong to this congregation. In 2003, its membership was over 30 in a city where the Teochew community is economically important. The pavilion is located in the personal flat of JCD, and no signs of religious activity are visible from the outside. Although this man started in 1997 to worship privately Guan Yin, Ji Gong, and Lü Dong-Bin, the order to institutionalize the cult came from Ji Yang Ge (Alor Setar), and mediums of this pavilion officiated in 1998 to establish it officially. In 2003, Zi Ying Ge was the most dynamic De Jiao pavilion of China, because of the accreditation it reportedly received in 2000 from Ji Gong to perform *fu ji* by itself and of the periodic séances it organises.

Sometimes, kinship relations replace business connections. The establishment of Zi Ning Ge ("Pavilion of Purple [Pu]ning") in the town of Guangtai in Puning district is a case in point. In 1998, Dao Ji is said to have proclaimed at Zi Zhen Ge that this pavilion should be opened as soon as possible and asked LXD, the prosperous owner of a textile factory, to take charge of the project. The choice of this man proved to be a shrewd one: he still had siblings living in Puning. He therefore asked them to find suitable premises, and made the trip with mediums from Zi Zhen Ge to choose the best place. He thus bought a shophouse to settle his parents, with a room being devoted to the shrine. At the time, the windows of these premises were shuttered to allow the performance of *fu ji* and other religious offices in secret. In 2000, however, perhaps because of this blockage, a *ji wen* attributed to Ji Gong instructed that the shrine be moved to another place. Consequently, LXD purchased a second building. Although he passed away a few months later, his heirs have so far respected his vow to send a pension to his siblings in return for their maintenance of the new shrine.

As another good example of the importance of personal links for the creation of new pavilions in China, we should mention Ji Yuan Ge (济沅閣), whose local promoter owns a chain of supermarkets. This man has maintained for years business connections with prominent members of Zi He Ge (Hong Kong), and of Zi Zhen Ge (Bangkok). In 1999, he opened a pavilion in a popular district of a Shenzhen satellite town, following an instruction from Dao Ji during a spirit-writing session at Ji Yang Ge. For his part, SZM, the president of Zi Zhen Ge received a divine message asking him to buy the house whose first floor serves as a place for worship. Although this association belongs to the Ji group and is regularly visited by the president of its Malaysian mother-temple, it was sponsored by a Zi association, which highlights the joint efforts of both De Jiao lines to resettle the movement in China. The identity and layout of the "overseers" on the altars illustrates this Ji/Zi partnership. The icon of Dao Ji is at the center on the highest level of the stage, with Guan Yin on its left and Lü Dong-Bin on its right. In the next stage, the icons of Ji Gong and Guan Yin are placed, with He Ye-Yun on the right side. Finally, a set of statues of the four "honourable masters" being worshipped by De Jiao in Thailand occupies the third and lowest stage. Another mark of this close cooperation is the fact that mediums from Ji Yang Ge, Zi He Ge, Zi Zhen Ge, and Zi Ying Ge (Guangzhou) have agreed to a rotating schedule to perform, once every two months, a *fu ji* séance within the premises of the association.[4] Ji Yuan Ge has a membership of about 20 Teochew businessmen, both local and Hua Qiao from Southeast Asia working in Shenzhen.

With regard to size, membership, distance from Chaozhou, and the gods worshipped, the association in Shenzhen is very close to its homonym of Shanghai, Ji Yuan Ge (济愿阁 – "Pavilion [to redeem] the wish of Ji [Gong]"). The latter was set up in 2001 by XXY, an entrepreneur in Shanghai, who listed among his acquaintances HWZ, a De Jiao follower working as the local agent of a Singaporean confectionery company. The father of HWZ had joined Ji Yang Ge in 1963, and later became one of its mediums. HWZ, for his part, was a member of Zi Shan Ge, the association of Klang. When he moved to Shanghai, he got in touch with XXY, thanks to good neighbourliness. One day, this wealthy businessman told him his wish to open a private shrine to Buddha. HWZ then convinced him to follow De Jiao and to open a pavilion dedicated to Ji Gong. The name of the new shrine was proclaimed at Zi Zhen Ge. Other important oracles were delivered at Hat Yai, with mediums of Zi Zhen Ge and Ji Yang Ge acting together. Accordingly, its *xiang huo* ritual combined incense powders from Ji Yang Ge and Zi Zhen Ge. Similar to the arrangement in Shenzhen, the statue of Ji Gong was set on the highest level of the stage, with the four Taoist teachers typical of the Thailand's Purple line occupying a lower degree. According to HWZ, the name of the association is a divine acknowledgement of his efforts to repay Dao Ji, who is believed to have granted his wish of finding a good job in China.

The Trojan Horse Strategy

Because of the De Jiao illegality in China, which obviously sowed fear and hesitation among potential followers, and because of its limited personal and business connections outside Chao-Shan, the RCODJ quickly realized that alternate means should be found to spread the movement. Having in mind the experience of Zi Zhen Ge, which had been initially hosted by a Buddhist monastery of Bangkok, it took advantage of the luxuriant and open-ended character of Chinese religiosity as well as of the local demand for financial support to establish shrines within existing temples. This "Trojan horse strategy" was often combined with the miraculous appointment of top members of these institutions as chairs of the new pavilions. Although in some cases the local Religious Affairs Bureaus heard about such infiltrations, they did not interfere from the moment De Jiao was not displaying overt signs of religious identity, and avoided to proselityze openly. This tolerant attitude suggests that in the view of the authorities De Jiao was not considered as a real threat.

Due to the key role conferred to Ji Gong in resettling the movement in China, the leaders of RCODJ logically turned first toward the city of Hangzhou and the Buddhist monasteries where Crazy Ji had lived as a monk, to apply this Trojan horse strategy. According to a reliable source, between 1999 and 2001, members of the RCODJ attended the annual festivities marking the death of Dao Ji at Jing Ci Si (净慈寺), the monastery where the master spent his last years and died. During the series of commemorations, a joint team of mediums from Zi Zhen Ge and Ji Yang Ge performed *fu ji* séances. The oracles asked the De Jiao leaders to open a pavilion named Zi Hang Ge ("Pavilion of the Purple Hang[zou]") within the pagoda premises. At the time the lay committee in charge of Jing Ci Si planned to rebuild part of the monastery for a total cost of RMB160 million. The RCODJ offered to sponsor the project and to donate RMB22 million towards the building of a hall containing a gigantic statue of Dao Ji. The temple committee and the local government accepted the donation, but refused to name this hall Zi Hang Ge. Finally, the RCODJ gave up this claim; the hall is due for completion in 2008, the year celebrating the 800th anniversary of the Dao Ji's ascension to heaven.

Few years later, in 2003, the RCODJ tried the same strategy in relation to Bai Yun Guan (白雲观), the main temple of the Quan Zhen Taoist sect, in Beijing. On the twelfth day of the twelfth lunar month of that year, a pavilion secretly known as Zi Xin Ge was, just like in Hangzhou, established without any outward display of its own identity, through the presentation and the placement of statues of Lü Dong-Bin and Ji Gong in a specific hall. Two years before this event, De Jiao had penetrated another Taoist temple in northeastern China. An oracle had been proclaimed at Ji Yang Ge describing in great detail a place in the port of Qingdao (Shandong), where a shrine was to be placed named Zi Cang Ge. The divine instructions, set out in a medieval map of Qingdao, led the De Jiao prospectors to a famous Taoist temple and to its chairman. It is said that the latter was waiting them under a tree in the temple courtyard. This man, who was identified in the oracle as the future leader of Zi Cang Ge, had received during the previous night an oneiric message from Lü Dong-Bin ordering him to meet his messengers there. Just like in the preceding cases, the opening of the new pavilion was limited to the gift of a statue to the temple (one of Lü Zu in Qingdao), and further activities in the pavilion consisted only of daily incense offerings by members of the host association's staff in return for payment by De Jiao of the "incense cost". A similar process, characterized by dreamlike visions of a "perfect" outsider, led to the creation of another *jie yuan* ("node of affinity") in Tianjin (Hebei). The man was the owner of a tea house and a pious Buddhist, who had been elected committee member of a prominent monastery of the city. A statue of Ji Gong was offered in 2001, at the occasion of the inauguration of this new hidden pavilion, named Zi Hang Ge.

Slightly different, because of a better taking into account of De Jiao basic liturgy and values, is the case of Zi Qin Ge, which Zi Zhen Ge inaugurated in Kunming (Yunnan), in 2004. In this example, the initiative did not come from the Bangkok association, but from a group of natives of Kunming, SCC and his sister-in-law, YYZ. The former, a doctor, had worked in the early 2000s as a volunteer for a Chinese NGO in Laos, more specifically in the Phakse area. There, a De Jiao pavilion was in the course of being set up and, through professional connections, SCC attended its spirit-writing sessions. He was then approached by members of Zi Zhen Ge to convince him to found a pavilion in his hometown. The project was made possible due to his sister-in-law who received in 1999 a revelation from Guan Yin to open a shrine for the veneration of Ji Gong and other Buddhist saints. By making her privileged relationship with the Goddess of Virtue widely known, thus enabling her to raise funds accordingly, this woman, a renowned fortune teller, succeeded in establishing an important Buddhist centre near Kunming. This centre, which contains, among others, a monumental statue of Ji Gong, houses a clinic employing three doctors and providing free medical care to the poor. A few weeks after her brother-in-law was approached by De Jiao, a *ji wen* from Zi Zhen Ge opportunely appointed YYZ president of a new pavilion named Zi Qin Ge. Due to the financial backing of SZM, a hall was quickly built, and in 2004 the shrine was inaugurated. In contrast with the Beijing, Tianjin, and Qingdao cases, a true opening ceremony took place, which involved more than one hundred people, including De Jiao leaders from Thailand, Malaysia, Singapore, Hong Kong, and Chaozhou. The powder placed into the incense burner during the *xiang huo* ritual came from both Zi Zhen Ge and Ji Yang Ge. The former offered a set of its typical statues, and the latter an icon of Ji Gong. Furthermore, a joint team of mediums from the two associations performed *fu ji*. After the event, Ms. YYZ, because of her faith and charisma, succeeded in establishing a local community of followers who learned the *De Jiao Xin Dian* and met for regular religious services. A delegation from Zi Qin Ge attended the sixth World Moral Divine Pen Meeting organized in Kluang.

The example of Zi Qin Ge can be compared to that of another pavilion, Zi Yu Ge, founded at the same time in the suburb of Shantou. Fortunately, I was present during the preparations for the pavilion's opening ceremony in November 2003. This pavilion is housed in a Buddhist monastery founded under the Southern Song dynasty. It is through her sister-in-law that the manager of this temple, CWY, got in touch with leaders of De Jiao. The former had attended a *fu ji* session of

Zi Zhen Ge at the occasion of a sightseeing trip to Thailand. Impressed by the performance and the reputation of the mediums, she put SZM in touch with CWY. Another important promoter of the project, who was appointed by the gods as the first president of Zi Yu Ge, is a businessman, LMJ, who owns a civil engineering firm, a restaurant, and a tourist agency. He joined De Jiao through connections with the *shan tang* of Jinping he supported and charitable organizations of Thailand, such as Peng Lai. During a *fu ji* séance in a Peng Lai temple, he met representatives of De Jiao and was invited to attend a *ji wen* at Zi Zhen Ge. At this occasion he received the revelation and the instruction to found Zi Yu Ge.

When I visited the Buddhist temple in 2003, SZM and other leaders of Zi Zhen Ge had already given RMB500,000 as a contribution to the fitting out of a room dedicated to the cult, while LMJ and other local businessmen, approached to serve as committee members, had donated RMB400,000. A few months earlier, a team of mediums from Zi Zhen Ge visited the temple to select a room within the existing premises and to place statues on the altar. The hall had been previously allotted to Di Zang-Wang and the Eighteen Arahants. The transfer of the latter to an upper floor was allegedly made with their assent. In addition to the central figure of Ji Gong whose statue was provided by the host institution, the two other deities who flanked him on the stage at the time of the study were Song Da-Feng (due to the affiliation of LMJ with a local *shan tang*) and He Ye-Yun, the Taoist master and geomancer who patronizes the Peng Lai chain of temples in Thailand, and who reportedly proclaimed during a *fu ji* session that, 800 years ago, he had stayed for a short time in this place. At the occasion of a *wen ji* performed by the mediums of Zi Zhen Ge, He Ye-Yun opportunely "revealed" that CWY, the manager of the temple, had come down from heaven to relieve the plight of the needy and thus could be considered as a living bodhisattva. Such an oracle indeed contributed to reinforcing the faith of this woman, whose participation was crucial. Asked about her involvement in the propagation of an unlawful movement, she answered that De Jiao generously contributed to the charitable activities of the monastery and that such an involvement could only become a source of difficulties whether the temple was becoming a tourist spot. Residents of the neighbourhood that CWY considered to be faithful Buddhists and reliable persons were subject to the proselytization of preachers. Meeting groups consisting of five to ten persons were organized in the temple courtyard for the purpose of recruiting new followers. Volunteers then explained the movement's goals and divine achievements as well as the content of the *De Jiao Xin Dian*. Particularly involved in these activities was a Teochew, XHR, a native of Jieyang and member of Zi Ying Ge (Guangzhou). Owner of a joinery business in Shantou, he became a "son of affinity" in the early 1990s, when De Jiao mediums from Hong Kong performed *fu ji* séances in secret in the *shan tang* of Jieyang where he used to worship Song Da-Feng. A few years later, he supported LYT in reestablishing the movement in Chaozhou. At the time of the study, this proselytizing activism was marginal with respect to the creation of new pavilions in China. Zi Yu Ge apart, such activities applied only to Zi Ying Ge, Ji Yuan Ge (Shenzhen), and Zi Guang Ge (Guangzhou).[5]

The foundation of Zi Yu Ge confirms once again the strong ties linking De Jiao to the *shan tang* of the Song Da-Feng tradition. All throughout their history, these benevolent halls offered an ideal ground for the recruitment of followers eager to combine, at a more intense level than in most *shan tang*, charity and spirit-writing, altruistic goals and the self-centred quest of good fortune. The circumstances which led the local promoters of Zi Yu Ge to join De Jiao also reveal the role of the go-between assumed by closely related organizations such as Peng Lai. The setting up in 2002 of Zi Pu Ge ("Pavilion of the Purple Pu[ning]"), which involved former core members of Ming Tan, is another case in point illustrating the utility of connections and of the Trojan horse strategy.

In Chapter II, I briefly mentioned these defectors of the oldest Ming Tan congregation of Thailand who joined De Jiao in 1993 to found Zi Piao Tan. In fact, the Ming Tan chain of temples emerged in Thailand in 1925 as an offshoot of a *shan tang* of Puning, created in 1911 and called Piao Ran Tai. As explained in Chapter II, during the opening ceremony of the Fengshun pavilion, the gods appointed its president, CJW, as leader of the forthcoming Zi Pu Ge. Although the new pavilion was not part of the Piao Ran Tai temple, but had been laid out in distinct premises bought by Zi Zhen Ge, the mediums who performed spirit-writing on the day of the opening ceremony were from Zi Piao Tan. Moreover, the central figure being worshipped in this pavilion, the Immortal Li Tie-Guai, is also prominent in Siracha. After the inauguration, JTX, the main medium of Zi Piao Tan, visited Zi Pu Ge on several occasions, both to perform spirit-writing and to train to conduct this activity on one of CJW's sons. In 2003, Zi Pu Ge had a membership of about 30 individuals, with most of them relatives of CJW. Interestingly, during the religious services they usually chant the *De Jiao Xin Dian*, whereas they systematically strike up the Ming Tan invocation prayer when they invite the gods to do *fu ji*.

The establishment of Zi Pu Ge was made through the Trojan horse strategy because it shares with Piao Ran Tai the same manager and relies on his personal network for its religious activities; also, Piao Ran Tai possesses a double identity in the view of De Jiao. It is the Ming Tan mother-temple and it is also a pavilion belonging to the *de de she*. The latter claim refers to a *ji wen* by Li Tie-Guai, when the Iron-Crutch Immortal reportedly renamed the shrine Zi Xia Tan (紫霞坛). After the event, the new name was carved on a marble tablet placed above the altar. This episode may be interpreted as an attempt by defectors to take over the institutional and spiritual source of a cult they still support. It is also indicative of an opportunistic philosophy of action whose aim is to make its own shrines be housed by legally recognized and, whenever as possible, prestigious temples, without necessarily working toward its sustainability as a cult community. In this respect, the effort is directed less toward the spread of the faith through all-out proselytism (an attitude which could court disaster in a context of political repression) than toward the coverage of the entire territory of China by potential, if not immediately effective, *jie yuan*, or "nodes of affinity". Among members of the RCODJ, a common idea was that the pavilions opened in China were just like seeds sown in a vast field. Some of them will grow fast and yield "beautiful flowers of virtue" (*hua de*); others will not flourish. Their fates depend on the geomancy of the place, and on the *yuan fen*, the "fate affinity" between local men and the "honourable masters". This teleology, which is based on a partnership between the gods and men, is also proposed to interpret the varying degrees of involvement of the RCODJ members in the project. Thus, during a meeting of the committee, LYW, in response to accusations that he and his uncle, LYB, made contributions which were not in line with their financial capabilities, asserted that they had no *yuan fen* with the enterprise and were therefore not in a position to contribute more (RCODJ, 2001: 126).

Outside China

Despite the abovementioned criticism, LYB and his cousin contributed significantly to the funds of the RCODJ. Between 1997 and 2004, the committee members have raised, or put together more than RMB50 million (about US$8 million), to establish 16 pavilions in the PRC. This amount is all the more important, when we consider that in 1997 a severe financial crash weakened for years the economies of Thailand, Malaysia, and other Southeast Asian countries, with negative effects on the personal fortunes of these De Jiao businessmen.

Although they logically privileged the reestablishment of the movement in China, these entrepreneurs never neglected another mission that recurrent spirit-writings ascribed to them: to extend the De Jiao network worldwide. Business connections and kinship relations were the main levers of this effort which began in 1994, two years before the founding of the RCODJ, with the creation in Savannakhet of a pavilion named Zi Su Ge. Its promoters were members of a De Jiao association in northeast Thailand who moved to this town in southern Laos to open a factory. To set up the new shrine, they obtained gods' icons and incense powder from the headquarters of the De Jiao Federation of Thailand. Representatives of pavilions in the northeast (Mukdahan, Chumpae, Roeit) attended the event. Indicative of the patronizing attitude that Thai citizens often display toward their Laotian "younger brothers", Zi Su Ge, despite its extra-territoriality, is considered as a full-fledged member of the National Federation of Thailand. The same applies to Zi Yao Ge, the shrine established in Phakse in 2000. Although these pavilions regularly received leaders and mediums of Zi Zhen Ge during the first few years of their existence, the *fu ji* sessions organized in their premises (which are discreetly arranged rooms within storehouses) were too occasional to arouse the interest of local people. Consequently, the size of these congregations remained embryonic and their activities have so far stagnated.

The same statement applies to the five pavilions opened either in the United States or in Australia between 1996 and 2003.[6] For want of mediums, their cult and charitable activities are reduced to a minimum. Moreover, to arouse the interest of the Teochew immigrants living in western countries for a little-known religious movement like De Jiao proved to be more difficult than expected. In most cases, curiosity gave way to suspicion in the minds of the individuals that the proselytes of De Jiao approached, especially when the former had no previous experience of *fu ji*. The *ex nihilo* founding of Zi Cheng Ge in Melbourne is all the more indicative of such difficulties. HL, the president of this pavilion which was inaugurated in 2002, is a Cantonese, born in Brunei. In 1974, he migrated to Australia, where he got a job as bank accountant. He was enjoying a western way of life and his involvement in religious affairs had been so far insignificant, when he was visited in 2001 by one of his nephews, a rich contractor based in Thailand. This relative had made the trip to Melbourne with six other businessmen who were, like him, members of Zi Zhen Ge, and had acquaintances or relatives in Australia. Following an oracle of Ji Gong, they were looking for someone who could help them provide further impetus for De Jiao in Australia after the decline of pavilions opened in Canberra and Sydney. At first, HL was sceptical regarding his nephew's claims that he could become this providential man. The De Jiao representatives insisted, however, and they offered to take up the cost of the flight tickets of a round trip which would take the group from Zi Yun Ge (Penang) to Ji Yang Ge (Alor Setar), and from there to Zi Zhen Ge (Bangkok). This trip was arranged in order for HL and his relatives to ascertain the power of *fu ji*.

HL and the persons he had chosen made the trip in November 2001, and attended spirit-writing sessions in these three associations. If the oracles delivered at Zi Yun Ge and Ji Yang Ge were insufficient to allay their scepticism, at Zi Zhen Ge, HL received a *ji wen* attributed to Ji Gong asking him whether his faith was sincere. Puzzled but flattered to be thus addressed by Dao Ji, and certainly also concerned about the possibility of being publicly disavowed in case of non-commitment, he proclaimed his faith, and then received a divine instruction to open a pavilion in Melbourne. His nephew promised to be in charge of every material aspect of the project, and raised US$275,000. One hundred individuals, including guests from Southeast Asia, attended the opening ceremony in May 2002. More than US$650,000 were gathered for the occasion through individual donations. This amount of money was spent on embellishments to the shrine and charity work.Thus, the association supported Australian research on cancer and rare diseases. During the following years, however, it failed to raise significant funds for charitable works or for inviting mediums to perform occasional spirit-writing. As a consequence, in 2004 the association had only 40 members, who were mostly relatives or acquaintances of HL. They meet together for worship twice a month. Although HL and some of his friends received basic training in liturgy from Zi Zhen Ge, they sometimes make international calls to consult Ji Yang Ge, Zi Zhen Ge, or Ji De Ge, especially with regard to the gods' anniversaries. It should be noted that the Melbourne association has few links with the pavilions in Canberra and Sydney. This lack of connections between cult communities within the same country was also the trend in mainland China. In the latter case, compartmentalization as a care against political repression could be invoked. But this argument must be put in perspective if one considers that the only local congregation open to partnership in China, namely Zi Ying Ge, is also the only one to have well-trained mediums and to be therefore under constant threat of police persecution. Let us be reminded that Zi Ying Ge regularly sends staff to train members of Zi Yu Ge (Shantou) and Zi Guang Ge (Guangzhou), and regularly performs *fu ji* in these pavilions as well as in Ji Yuan Ge (Shenzhen). The lack of interaction between pavilions in China and western countries mainly ensues from their geographical dispersal, and from the virtual character or lethargic state of some of them. After the surge of interest in these pavilions following the opening ceremonies, most of them are unable to remain active due to lack of mediums and motivated followers. More generally, the Melbourne example is confirmatory of the crucial function of oracles in the spread of De Jiao, either within Southeast Asia or outside the region. But, while *fu ji* serves as the main tool for the propagation of the movement, through the founding of new "nodes of affinity", it also mortgages the future of these "seeds of devotion". The physical distance between the "broadcasting station", mainly Zi Zhen Ge, and the "relays" to be reached is so great, and the speaker's voice (the gods flying down the *luan*-bird) is so broken up (occasional), that in most instances the channel fails to build up an audience.

Interestingly, the Trojan horse strategy being employed in China also marginally applies to other countries outside Southeast Asia. The only case reported at the time of the study concerned Zi Xiong Ge ("Pavilion of the Purple [Gao]Xiong"), which was opened in the city of Gaoxiong, in the southwest of Taiwan, in 2001. CW, the adherent who established it, is the manager of both a cultural and religious body called Wen Hua Yuan (文化院), "Office for [the promotion of] Culture". This man, who has written several academic books, conducted in 1973 a survey on the religions of the world. In the course of this undertaking, he met Li Huai-De and other members of Zi Xin Ge (Singapore). It was the starting point of a long-lasting collaboration, marked by mutual visits and exchanges of magazines or other publications. Occasionally, the leaders of Zi Xin Ge would consult Wen Hua Yuan concerning religious or cultural matters, as it is considered as an authoritative reference institution on Chinese customs (in Gaoxiong, it manages a museum and a theme park on the topic). Such levels of cooperation can be attributed to the pursuit of common goals. Wen Hua Yuan is a charitable organization providing relief to the poor and disaster victims under several forms. Its membership roster also includes several teams of well-skilled mediums who frequently organize spirit-writing sessions by using either a forked branch on a plate or a brush on a sheet of paper. The *ji wen* produced that way are published in a *shan shu*-style magazine entitled *Chong Xin* ("Sublime Heart") which is widely distributed within the network of *shan tang* and *shan tang*-like organizations in Taiwan and abroad. Because of its enthusiasm for the practice of *fu ji* and its institutional ties with Zi Xin Ge, Wen Hua Yuan has been sending delegations to successive World Moral Meetings of the Divine Pen. Opportunely, at the occasion of the fifth gathering (in Bangkok, 2001), a *ji wen* attributed to Ji Gong came, instructing the Taiwanese association to open a shrine in its Gaoxiong premises. Finally, the association of Bangkok, "head of the dragon" in Thailand, absorbed the cost of establishing the new shrine.

The case of CW, who combines research goals (directed toward the preservation of Chinese heritage) and religiousness, is comparable to that of KY, a Japanese scholar who studied De Jiao in the 1970s, both in Chao-Shan and Thailand. A few months before the sixth World Moral Meeting of the Divine Pen in Kluang (2004), he received a revelation through a *ji wen* from Ji Gong to found a pavilion in Nagoya. Once again, SZM, the president of Zi Zhen Ge, where the message had been delivered, supported the establishment of the shrine within specific premises.

Moral Uplifting Websites

Recent studies[7] have shown how quickly and skilfully indigenous peoples and diasporas could adapt the tools and resources offered by the Internet to reach new levels of communication and community. To explore the way De Jiao uses these new technologies seems *a priori* of great relevancy, especially when we consider the nebulous character of this religious movement and its recent efforts to spread worldwide. Because of such features and trends, the Internet could appear as an ideal instrument to introduce the Canon, virtues, and rules of De Jiao to a wider audience, and eventually to rally new followers. It could also help promote charitable works and raise funds, or to render the interactions between pavilions easier, especially for those located in different countries. But paradoxically, this movement has so far underused the opportunities offered by being online. In 2005, only a handful of the movement's 250 pavilions had built their own website, and among them very few were using such a platform to present De Jiao, its general goals, ideals, and history, or to report miracles, individual experiences of the faith, and other accounts likely to expand membership.

The most all-round of these websites, which I found particularly useful in obtaining general information about De Jiao, is certainly <http://aooi.tripod.com>. It was created in the early 2000s by HWZ, a businessman in his forties, who is the co-founder of Ji Yuan Ge (Shanghai). Although most of its content is in Chinese, the website gives, in most cases, the name and addresses of the pavilions both in Chinese and English. The architecture of the site is very simple: no main page and subordinates, no bookmarks and window tabs to click, and the whole content can be read as a linear text. It begins with the creed, virtues, and rules of the movement, followed successively by a brief historical sketch, the *De Jiao Xin Dian*, and the logo of the organization. The main part consists of a directory of about 170 associations scattered throughout the world with understandably more data about Malaysia, Singapore, and

Thailand where De Jiao is well established. Addresses, telephone numbers, and website details are then provided, except for the pavilions opened in the PRC in order to prevent their detection by the police. Accordingly, HWZ does not mention the existence of two congregations in Laos, another Communist country wherein the movement has no legal existence. The directory incorporates some pictures about *fu ji* or shrines. In a few cases, *ji wen*, either about the origin of the pavilion or about those which played an important role in its history, are reproduced. With regard to the shrines founded or to be founded in China, the gods' instructions are the most frequently mentioned in the website, certainly because their main function here is to legitimate institutions whose existence is threatened by a hostile political order. If, at its launch, this website had a section dedicated to new pavilions, it was later taken out, and it seems that in recent years HWZ has only sporadically updated the contents of the site. As a consequence, some data are now obsolete and the directory does not take into account a large number of pavilions founded during the past few years.

Although the management of websites of their own could allow the De Jiao federations of Thailand and Malaysia to give more fluidity and density to their inner exchanges of information, while offering a glimpse of their activities to the outside world, they have so far favoured the production and distribution of magazines, periodicals, and books. In Thailand, a platform <www.ThaiTekka.com>, was under construction at the time of the study; three years later the project had come to nothing, which can be taken as indicative of a manifest lack of interest by the De Jiao leaders regarding this kind of initiative. In the same vein, major events or institutions such as the RCODJ and the World Moral Meetings of the Divine Pen are not publicized on the net, and most of the prominent pavilions (Ji De Ge, Ji Yang Ge, Zi He Ge, Zi Nan Ge, Zi Luang Ge) have no websites of their own. Although Zi Zhen Ge has built a homepage (<http://www.chinnawit.com>), its content is limited to three lines in Thai language indicating its date of foundation and its general goals. Finally, the few websites accessible concern a handful of associations which are either very active in the fields of charity or social welfare or intend to present themselves as attractive tourist places.

The website of the association of Penang, Zi Yun Ge (<http://www.dejiaohui.com>) certainly is representative of the first type. Just like <http://aooi.tripod.com>, it starts with the Canon of De Jiao, the "eight precepts and ten rules", and a brief historical sketch. Its architecture is however more sophisticated, with a main page and links to sections describing its organizational chart and reporting its charitable or teaching activities for the last two years. A selection of recent noteworthy oracles enacted through the *ji*-wielders of the association is also available online. Another website which mainly focuses on charitable works and moral teaching is the one built by Tai He Guan, the Singaporean philanthropic organization affiliated with De Jiao (see Chapter II). Unlike the Zi Yun Ge platform which is entirely in Chinese, Tai He Guan (<http://www.thkms.org.sg>), uses English as its exclusive medium. This choice may be explained by the association's claim to universality. Its moral, welfare, and charitable works are emphatically said to be directed towards the whole of mankind, and more concretely, toward the people of Singapore, irrespective of colour, creed, language, culture, and religion. The partnerships it mentions in its website reflects such openness. Such partnerships involve, for instance, the Inter-Religious Organisation, the Singapore Indian Development Association, a Malay charitable body named Yayasan Mendaki, and the Eurasian Association. Certainly because of this orientation, the text of presentation of Tai He Guan places emphasis on Confucian and humanist values, but never makes explicit reference to De Jiao and its doctrine. The main part of the website is devoted to descriptions of moral promotion projects and welfare services (free clinics, hospitals, homes for the disabled) that Tai He Guan has developed since its foundation in 1978. Detailed accounts on recent charity galas are also provided to give evidence of the association's dynamism in this field and to attract new donations. Such was the case for the first televised charity show that Tai He Guan organized on 16 April 2006. According to the website's report on the event, the three-hour show that Media Corp TV, the main Singaporean media group, presented that day was a great success. A wide range of showbiz stars participated in the gala, while the speeches of the charismatic LJX led to 53,000 calls, allowing Tai He Guan to achieve its target of S$4 million (about 2 millions euros). To prove that its finances are in good order and indeed to increase the number of its supporters, the organization posts its updated financial statements online, specifying income receipts, expenses, balances, and assets. But in contrast to the website of Zi Yun Ge, which presents outstanding *ji wen*, spirit-writing is totally absent in the Singaporean site. The same characteristics apply to <http://www.ckmps.org.sg>, the website of Ji Yun Ge, the Ji group association that the lawyer LJX manages in addition to Tai He Guan. The website shows no sign of its affiliation with De Jiao: there is no mention of the *De Jiao Xin Dian* and of the "eight precepts and ten rules". Moreover, the logo of De Jiao in its homepage takes over for that, more specific, of Ji Yun Ge. The site is entirely written in English, and its overall profile is very close to that of Tai He Guan, with similar objectives.

With regard to the De Jiao websites which are tourism-oriented, the most representative case is <http://chankongkok.tripod.com>. This platform, in Chinese and English, introduces the Internet user to Zhen Guang Ge, a pavilion of the Zhen group which was initially founded on October 1971 in Tanjung Rambutan (Perak), but was relocated in a cave in Ulu Kinta ten years later, following a *ji wen*. In its homepage, the association stresses that, "apart from moral uplifting activities, Chan Kong Khor [the translation of Zhen Guang Ge in Teochew] is also a famous tourist attraction, known for its natural untouched limestone caves, flora and fauna". Among the goals it puts forward, the promotion of tourism comes first, followed by moral uplifting lectures, herbal medicine studies, and the provision of free medical services. Although under the section "About us", Zhen Guang Ge presents the De Jiao "eight precepts and ten rules" as the guiding principles of its activities, the achievements mentioned in the historical outline consist only of the shrines and other features the association constructed to enhance the attractiveness of the place. Further evidence of the emphasis on sightseeing in this website are the photo gallery and the map of the cave, which shows how tourists can reach the said attraction. Net users who visited Zhen Guang Ge may also sign the association's virtual guestbook.

Zi Zhen Ge, the leading association of Thailand, has no real website save for a minimalist homepage which contains a few lines; but it is mentioned by more than 50 online travel guides or tourist blogs as a "must-see" religious attraction. It is thus comparable to Zhen Guan Ge, in terms of the image of itself that it intends to project. A brief survey of the websites which mention it, such as <http://www.thailandforvisitors.com>, <http://www.thaipro.com>, <http://chiengfa.com>, or <http://www.travelblog.org>, reveals that its fame as a sightseeing place is attributable mainly to the towering Chinese style pagoda it opened in 2001 to commemorate both the fiftieth anniversary of the association and the seventy-second birthday of King Bhumibol. Located on the west bank of the Chaophraya River, this nine-storey tower attracts the attention of tourists who go boating down the river. Adjoining it is one of the oldest and nicest Chinese-themed houses in Bangkok, the Wang Lee Mansion. This structure, which is a private property, is not open to visitors, but tourists have access to the top of the Zi Zhen Ge pagoda and from there can get the best view both of the mansion and the very Chinese-styled temple of the association.

Finally, this outline of the use of Internet by De Jiao reveals that most congregations are indifferent to the possibilities that such a technology offers. The websites built by its members can be counted on the fingers of one hand; furthermore, those containing references to the movement are minimalist in their presentation of its ideals, goals, and achievements. Spirit-writing is either not mentioned or allusively quoted through *ji wen* snatches, without any explanation or comments, and the same holds true for the *De Jiao Xin Dian* and the "eight precepts and ten rules". Although most websites provide an e-mail address for those seeking more information, in general, the queries addressed through this way receive no answer. If the website of Tai He Guan, which had more than 50,000 visitors in 2006, enjoys great popularity, its success can hardly redound to the benefit of De Jiao, since the website never makes a single reference to the movement. The exchanges of information within this embryonic network that the De Jiao websites could form are also hindered by the multiple languages they use as medium of communication. Because most adepts of Thailand are unable to speak and to read English, they can hardly have access to the information that Tai He Guan or Ji Yun Ge provide online; reciprocally, Singaporean or Malaysian adepts would not have an inkling about the content of Zi Zhen Ge's homepage, which is presented in Thai.

The age of the majority of adepts may explain their lack of interest toward the functionalities of the Internet. At least two-thirds of the devotees are more than 60 years old. They belong to a generation which grew up unfamiliar with information technology. Significantly, the few De Jiao websites accessible so far were built in the most westernized and cosmopolitan countries of Southeast Asia — namely, Singapore and Malaysia — at the initiative of devotees who were in their 40s or 50s. An analysis of their profiles reveals that not only were they experienced Internet users, but they are also businessmen perfectly integrated into the networks of the global economy. The best example is certainly the abovementioned HWZ, the instigator of <http://aooi.tripod.com>, a Chinese native of Malaysia who works in Shanghai as the agent of a Singaporean confectionery company. Another case in point is ZRJ, the president of Zi Yun Ge and executive chairman of Pensonic, who has extended the activities of his business group to several countries in Asia. These managers have been profiting personally and professionally from their international partnerships, are ardent supporters of globalization, and have accordingly adapted the credo of global openness to the religious sphere.

Against this view, a large number of adepts I interviewed between 2000 and 2004 were rather local-oriented in their motivations and interests. For the elder generation, becoming a member of a dynamic De Jiao association offering spirit-writing, access to Chinese medicine, and cultural or recreational activities was a cure for idleness, loneliness, and uprooting. It was also a way to offer some semblance of resistance against what they perceive as the decline of Chinese values, which follows the weakening of patrilineal and dialectal solidarities in the context of their urban lives overseas. The Buddhist ideal of improving one's destiny through good deeds and the use of *fu ji* for solving immediate problems apart, they were interested in De Jiao because its cult communities operated as Teochew clubs. There is therefore nothing exceptional in their lack of concern for a cyberspace community of virtue or a religious adaptation of the concept of "global village" that the Internet is supposed to help build.

The content and distribution of the periodicals that the leading pavilions or national federations publish reflect this state of mind. The reproduction of outstanding *ji wen* apart, an important part of these magazines consists of holding a review of the various events organized by local congregations during the period covered by a particular issue. These events concern the building and inauguration of new pavilions, important meetings, charitable works, welfare services or campaigns of *xiu gu gu* in the case of Thailand; they thus contribute to these "unbound serialities" and, beyond, to this shared grammar of representations which is the precondition of the "imagined communities", according to B. Anderson.[8] In the present case, the scope of these serialities and related representations is limited to the country where the devotees live. If the magazines that the federations of Malaysia and Thailand publish separately, although under the same title (*De Xun*, "Messages on Virtue"), sometimes refer to the works of the RCODJ and to the inauguration of new pavilions in foreign countries (including China), these initiatives are of little interest to the grassroots adepts. Even if they may appear to them as praiseworthy acts contributing to the worldwide spread of the movement, they are commonly interpreted as "hobbies" of very wealthy businessmen, the only individuals capable of backing these costly projects. Rather than reading about these distant and "elitist" achievements, they prefer accounts pertaining to events that they actually attended or projects involving some of their relatives and friends, as such events logically arouse curiosity, empathy, and self-identification. In accordance with such preferences, the charity solidarity and works of the grassroot followers are mainly directed toward the local population; the same applies to those who are affiliated with the few associations involved in the RCODJ projects. The primacy conferred to events within a familiar environment partly explains why the magazine published by the Federation of Thailand is not distributed outside the country and why the Malaysian *De Xun* has no readership in Thailand.

* * *

The priority that a majority of practitioners attributes to local preoccupations and interests underscores the Achilles heel of the worldwide ambition harboured by a small minority of leaders. The project to re-seed De Jiao in China is in fact driven by three associations, namely Zi Zhen Ge of Thailand, Ji Yang Ge of Malaysia, and Zi He Ge of Hong Kong, assisted by the leaders of ten other pavilions at most. The whole group does not represent more than 5 per cent of the total number of De Jiao associations. In practice, the promoters of the project are less than 20 wealthy businessmen, who claim for the most part the status of Ji Gong's "sons of affinity", and rely on two or three pairs of mediums to receive divine commands. If having such a small group of people driving the process may minimize the risk of personal disagreements and mismanagement (although these problems nevertheless occurred), it in turn increases the possibility that the whole undertaking would collapse in the event of the loss of a key figure such as SZM, whose donations have so far covered more than half of the expenses of the RCODJ, or FSM, the main medium of his association, who was instrumental in delivering about two-thirds of the oracles linked to the opening of new pavilions abroad.

These problems apart, to make Crazy Ji the supreme instigator and flag-bearer of the whole process was very opportune. Due to the ambiguous and catch-all image of Crazy Ji that Chinese vernacular fiction had been propagating since the seventeenth century, he progressively appeared either as a symbol of nonconformism or a mouthpiece for conservative values, but above all he is perceived as an all-powerful miracle worker, with his popularity gaining ground in view of such perceptions in contemporary China, Taiwan, and Southeast Asia (Shahar, 1998). However, there is a lack of local mediums which could be in a position to take over from those of Nanyang, and to display the master's magical powers at a sustained pace, an essential precondition to the expansion of the membership base of the new congregations. This is indeed a major hindrance to the movement's expansion out of its Southeast Asian base. How could De Jiao gain new followers and foster their faith in socio-cultural environments where the practice of *fu ji*, conceived as the true and almost exclusive channel of communication with the gods, is either meaningless or non-sustainable? For want of local experienced *ji*-wielders, the efforts of the RCODJ have so far consisted in sowing seeds, or potential "nodes of affinity", the implicit hope being that only a small part of them will finally germinate through the development of local cult communities. An overview of the "nodes of affinity" so far founded in mainland China reveals that the rooting of new offshoots succeeded only in the Guangzhou area, due to the fast and efficient training of a pair of local mediums which was conducted in conjunction with recruitment campaigns aimed at the Teochew community.

In view of the significant sums of money and the energy that the RCODJ expended in the pursuit of its aims, the project could be considered a failure at this point. But the businessmen involved in it would certainly disagree with such an assessment. An analysis of their strategies shows that, in spreading De Jiao back in China, their purpose is to make the "honourable masters" reconquer the motherland for the sake of virtue rather than to attract large numbers of new adepts, an objective which was totally out of bounds in the context of the post-Mao China of the late 1990s. At that time, Ji Gong or Lü Dong-Bin were, of course, already being worshipped in a multitude of shrines in the motherland, but not as members of the *de de she*, this heavenly congregation of gods coming from all horizons, specifically founded to uplift morality. Because devotees conceive the pavilions they establish as somewhat similar to radio relays tuned to receive supreme moral teachings from the heavenly pavilion, Xie Tian Ge, their leaders believe it is of prime importance to permeate China's territory with these pavilions. Although not sufficient in themselves, they are however necessary to connect a large number of potential users to the divine operator, the other condition being indeed the regular activity of *ji*-wielders able to attain high-tune communication and thus to conduct transactions with the gods.

The radio broadcasting metaphor may apply to the geographical distribution of the new shrines as well. The sites which have so far been chosen in China are located in very potent places deemed likely to provide good "signal reception" and able to tap into a wide audience. The Teochew area apart, which was the original place of De Jiao and remains its stronghold, Nanchang is known in China to be one of the historical heartlands of Taoism; Beijing and Hangzhou served as imperial capitals and, for this reason, are emblematic of political power, while Tianjin, Shanghai, and Guangzhou are major hubs of economic development along the Pacific coast. Everything is going as though the De Jiao "nodes of affinity" should be located — for geomantic purposes and consequently for control of the *qi* — on the religious, political, and economic "veins of the dragon" of past and present China.

The process of institutional expansion investigated in this chapter reveals that business initiatives and connections constituted a crucial support for the creation of a majority of De Jiao pavilions in the PRC. Moreover, *compradore* relationships, dealing methods, and marketing strategies proved to be adapted to this end, thus confirming that De jiao's ways of action are largely modeled on managerial habits. The structure of leadership of this religious movement, dominated by tycoons, also explains

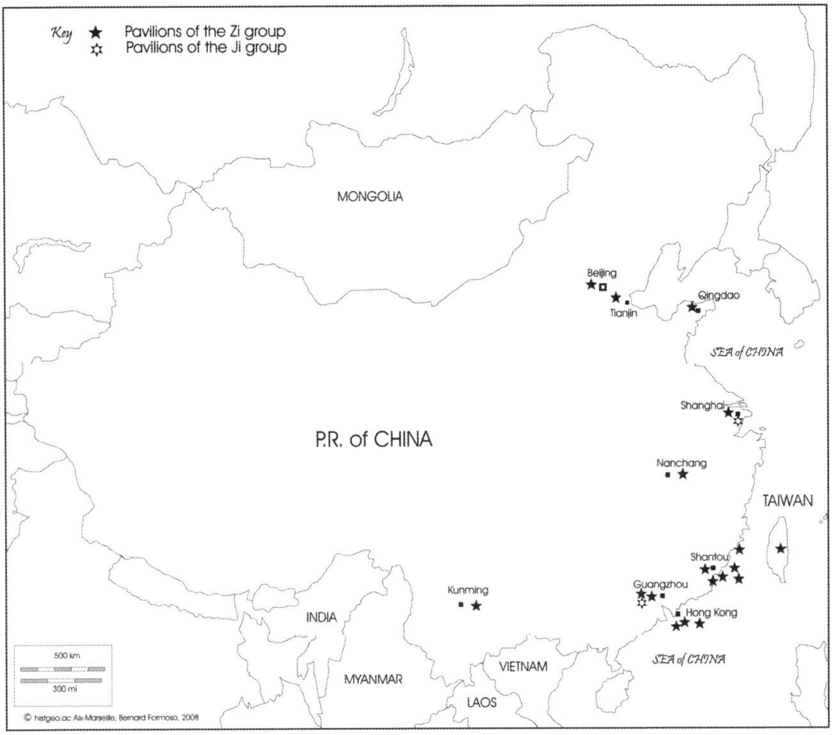

Map 4 Distribution of the De Jiao Pavilions in the People's Republic of China (2004)

that the divine wills underlying the RCODJ's projects reflect current business concerns and orientations. It must be remembered that the gods' instructions to spread De Jiao worldwide came at a time when the tensions of the Cold War had come to an end, and most Asian countries were speeding up the process of their integration with the regional and global economy. As previously suggested, the *de de she* community accordingly rode on the globalization wave to delocalize its "nodes of affinity", and to symbolically take over the "veins" of the Chinese dragon. This ambition remained, however, in the scope of *projective identity*, since neither the businessmen who are carrying out the project nor the mediums have any intention of settling in the mainland or even to have their mortal remains repatriated to China. Perfectly integrated in their overseas environments, they are well-entrenched in the local economies, consider themselves as citizens in their adopted countries, and remain wary about the possible political evolution of China. Hence, inconstant support and poor monitoring of the newly-created pavilions should not come as a surprise.

CONCLUSION

De Jiao is one of the Asian new religious movements (NRMs) which formed part of the escalation in religious innovation following the Second World War. Although it was originally a local reaction by Teochew mediums to the occupation of China by Japan, De Jiao rapidly took another dimension, the turning point being the Communist takeover of China in 1949, and the subsequent repression of cults which compelled some of its instigators and adherents to flee to Hong Kong and to migrate to Southeast Asia. Although through the impetus of Ma Gui-De an embryonic doctrine had been promulgated in 1942, it is overseas, into the cosmopolitan contexts of Hong Kong and Singapore, that De Jiao definitively transformed from its humble status of "Society for the recitation of sutra" or of an association named after the minor Taoist gods it worshipped to become a syncretistic religious movement uniting tens of congregations through a common set of values and emblems. After 1949, Ma Gui-De, Li Huai-De, and their fellows added to the *De Jiao Xin Dian* a basic creed of five tenets, a corpus of ten virtues, and eight rules which the followers should observe. A flag and an anthem, symbols of collective identity, were also devised, and at that time they tried to make their religious movement accessible to a larger audience through the publication of its earliest miraculous achievements (cf. the *Bamboo Bridge Collection*) or through articles which traced its beginnings to the origins of Chinese civilization.

The inevitable culture shock resulting from the emigration overseas of Ma Gui-De and his associates, and the necessity for them to adapt to the host societies, partly explain such a change of orientation and scope. In this new environment, their early motivations against the spread of secular materialism in post-imperial China became reinforced. Their attitude in the face of westernization then took two forms: a conservative reaction advocating more radically than before the return to a society dominated by Confucian ethics; and an attempt to appropriate, at least symbolically, the major religions of the west. By incorporating Jesus Christ and Prophet Muhammad into the *de de she*, but under the supreme authority of the Jade Emperor, they tried to compensate for the immersion of a majority of followers into ideological universes dominated by Christian or Muslim values. The fact that their experience of social uprooting and cultural shock was shared by most of the Teochew immigrants in Southeast Asia, channelled to the movement thousands of people of different age groups and social conditions who were searching for meaningful and efficient links with an idealized Chinese civilization that the divine "society of virtue" apotheosized.

After its resettling in Southeast Asia, De Jiao became a movement of uprooted Chinese whose projective quest for identity was exacerbated accordingly. Spirit-writing as a core activity of the movement responded to this sharpened quest by reconnecting the adepts' identity to multisecular symbols of authority and centrality. Thus, against acculturation and endangered family structures, the divine teachings profess moral revival as a basic requirement for individual salvation, social order, and cultural unity. Moreover, by resorting to the notion of "son [daughter] of affinity", *fu ji* oracles substitute metaphorical kinship with gods for loosened genealogic links. More precisely, the notion of "fate affinity" between certain followers and the "honourable masters" anchors their personal identities into a spiritual line of descent incorporating the forefathers and preceptors of Chinese civilization. In this respect, it overcomes the weakening, overseas, of lineage membership and ancestor worship. The fact that the *de de she* incorporates Teochew Buddhist saints or Taoist masters such as Song Da-Feng, Song Chan, or He Ye-Yun also substantiates the thesis that, overseas, one of the implicit functions of De Jiao spirit-writing is to entertain meaningful and effective links between practitioners and these two major levels of identification that are the homeland and within it the dialectal place of origin.

With regard to the reformulation of individual identity, another important function of spirit-writing consists in incorporating, through divine appointments, the followers into the celestial bureaucracy whose Jade Emperor is the supreme ruler. The outcomes of this symbolical incorporation are threefold. Migrants living on the fringe of the Chinese world are thus directly connected to its mythical centre of power. Although most overseas practitioners are poorly educated in Chinese, thanks to proficient mediums they believe to be acknowledged by gods as literati, worthy to receive and to propagate the fine poetry and litterary tradition that spirit-writing conveys. Last but not least, the prestigious mandarinal function ritually attributed to them overcomes the low status traditionally conferred to merchants in Chinese society. Together with mediumship, morality as a supreme goal of De Jiao links the two statuses: it legitimates personal fortune as far as it leads to charity and justifies the divine appointment of the meritious capitalist. A new ideal-typic hero emerges accordingly, who embodies both the perfect self-made man, and the honorific status and inculturative power traditionally associated to official positions. The binomial military and literary forms of power (*wu/wen*) that De Jiao spirit-writing still performs is replaced in the human sphere and overseas context by a new binomial, combining the power of money and the authoritative power of the litterati. I wager that this modern variant of the traditional levers of imperial authority is promised to a bright future in mainland China, due to the rise of a powerful entrepreneurial class and the disruptive effects of the fast economic growth experienced by the PRC.

Finally, the assumption that De Jiao is good to think regarding the problematic of overseas Chinese identity finds confirmation in the new self-images it produces by conflating moral charter and spirit-writing channel. By these means, it builds new meaningful and rewarding links with unanimously acknowledged emblems of Chineseness, and symbolically reinstates the centrality and authority of its practitioners for the sake of "virtue". In so doing, it fulfills most of their existential expectations, though in the realm of fancy. However, its contribution to Chineseness is not only limited to self-representations and projective identity. It also supports the religious and cultural specifity of the Chinese minority in the countries where it settled in. Thanks to its institutional features and ability to work in close connection with Singaporean and Thai elites it succeded to champion Chinese distinctiveness under the appearance of selfless philanthropy in those countries, while in Malaysia it actively participated to the welfare and cultural specificity of the Chinese minority despite a state policy favouring ethnic Malays.

With regard to the impact of the religious environment on the spread of De Jiao, it emerged from Chapter I that its Canon comes from within the tradition of the morality books (*shan shu*), with a possible influence in that matter of a *shan tang* of Haimen. More generally, De Jiao grew all along its history in close cooperation with the Teochew *shan tang* of the Song Da-Feng tradition, whose charitable works and strategies of adaptation it reproduced at a lesser extent. Facing political adversity in Thailand and the PRC, it also more or less successfully used the flag of the halls for good deeds to develop its own activities. Finally, my characterization of De Jiao as *a shan-tang*-like movement is justified, regarding its institutional connections as well as its philosophy and ways of action.

Although no clear link exists between De Jiao and Yi Guan-Dao, and significant differences separate the two movements, they both blossomed in the 1930s as a reaction to what was perceived as a decline of Chinese civilization, and they share some common features. They thus incorporate much older elements from Confucianism, Buddhism, and Taoism (the *san jiao*) and recognize, though formally, the validity of Christianity and Islam. Both emphasize the observance in daily life of the five tenets and eight virtues from Confucianism. They are also based on the practice of what P. Clart calls *moral-cultivational mediumship*, and share most of their main gods, with in both cases a special focus on the cult of Dao Ji. But, in contrast to Yi Guan-Dao and other Chinese sectarian groups such as Guan Yin Fa-Men ("Way of the Goddess of Mercy"), De Jiao has no supreme living teachers, or patriarchs, who claim a divine ancestry. Its founders have not been deified after their passing, and their memory is not honoured through monuments, cults, and pilgrimages. Its temporal and temporary leaders draw their legitimacy not from hereditary hand-over but from the personal fortune they have amassed and from the economic power they consequently control. Furthermore, contrary to the sectarian ideology of Yi Guan-Dao and other Chinese NRMs, De Jiao neither expects membership commitments nor makes clear demands. For its followers, morality practices are an ideal to reach rather than a set of strictly enforced rules of conduct whose non-observance places the offender in danger of exclusion. Vegetarianism is, for instance, recommended but not enforced, and few are the adepts who follow such a diet, out of the few ritual contexts where the consumption of meat is strictly forbidden. Another sign of the relatively few requirements of membership is the fact that the devotees have no training to undergo and tests to pass to enter the movement. In contrast with the followers of Yi Guan-Dao who must go through an initiation ceremony at the occasion of which they receive the "three treasures" (*san bao*) allowing them to ascend directly to heaven upon their demise, those of De Jiao, including the mediums, are not subjected to rites of passage and have no esoteric knowledge to keep secret. Although the incorporation of new members must obtain the approval of the "honourable masters" to be effective, and a special relationship with the gods confers to certain devotees the status of "sons [or daughters] of affinity", this status has more to do with "fate" and astrological coordinates rather than with the acquisition of special knowledge or with the observance of an ascetic way of life. It is conceived as the outcome of a personalized and evolving spiritual exchange with the divine masters rather than the final achievement of a moral unfolding under the direction of human instructors. In other words, the master/disciple pattern, so typical of didactic methods in Asia, is projected onto the relationship with the gods through the mediation of *fu ji*, thus limiting the weight of hierarchical ordering within the religious organization.

If a degree of hierarchy exists within De Jiao, it depends rather on the power of wealth as well as the elective nature of the relationship with the gods, and it fluctuates accordingly. Instead of being integrated into a pyramidal framework, the groups and their local branches benefit from a large degree of autonomy concerning both the identity of the gods they worship, the content of the rituals they perform, and the charitable activities they develop. Basically, the division of work within each local cult community includes at most three kinds of agents: (1) a board of wealthy philanthropists who assume its leadership and form its economic task force, but rely on subordinates for its daily management; (2) one or several teams of mediums, whose performances are decisive in establishing the reputation of the association and to enlarge its membership; and (3) a group of volunteers whose services and skills are needed to carry out at the lowest possible cost its charitable works (doctors, nurses, acupuncturists, accountants). These three categories overlap in many cases, and the differences of status within or between the pavilions mainly depend on their achievements in the corresponding spheres (financial sponsorship, mediumship, and services offered for relief, medical, and social welfare works). From this point of view, De Jiao sharply contrasts with other contemporary Asian NRMs such as Yi Guan-Dao and Cao Đài which have developed a more or less complex hierarchy of titles and functions reproducing at a lesser scale the bureaucracy of an idealized Confucian state whose restoration they desire. Such a contrast certainly results from the sociological characteristics of these movements. In the case of Cao Đài, for example, its founders were high-ranking Indochinese officials working under French colonial rule. They tried to counterbalance their status of being upper-class subordinates by organizing a religious movement with a sophisticated directory and a clerical bureaucracy. By contrast, the instigators and leaders of De Jiao have made their living as entrepreneurs and merchants, and their loosely structured movement significantly reflects the adaptable and close-knit business networks in which they are involved. While studying the re-seeding of De Jiao throughout mainland China, I have shown that the RCODJ has consistently chosen local business partners of the committee members to manage the newly created pavilions. More generally, a high proportion of leaders of local congregations appointed by the gods are entrepreneurs who have proven themselves to be efficient, fair, reliable, and trustworthy in business. In other words, their appointment correlates with their aptitude to embody the managerial ethos shared by the Hua Chiao upper class. The opportunistic and catch-all strategies they develop in their businesses pervade their religious way of action, and, *per mimesis*, are transposed onto the gods' expectations and instructions.

The De Jiao organizational pattern has to do with the *a-centred systems* that J. Petitot and P. Rosenstiehl define as networks in nebula, where cooperation works gradually from neighbour to neighbour, and local operations coordinate themselves so that their achievements can be synchronized apart from any central authority. The role that the pavilion of the border-city of Hat Yai assumed in coordinating the branches of Thailand and Malaysia, after more than thirty years of parallel development and mutual ignorance, is illustrative of the primacy conferred to the relations of nearness in such a religious movement. The fact that no overarching international federation of the "moral uplifting society" has been established thus far, and that attempts to spread the movement worldwide has found little support among the grassroots followers, confirm this trend.

De Jiao is a very opportunistic, nondogmatic, and adaptable religious group whose deployment to Southeast Asia was made possible, at parity, by ramification or by the aggregation of disparate elements. The spread overseas of the mainstream Purple line through two ways, one from Shantou to Thailand and another from Hong Kong to Malaya, illustrates the first process. From the start, the two branches displayed significant differences with regard to their respective pantheons and their political economies, with important consequences for their charitable activities. As for the aggregation of disparate elements, it finds several illustrations, such as the extension to overseas-born groups (Ji, Zan Hua, and Zhen) in the case of Malaysia, or the incorporation of charitable bodies and defectors from other *shan tang*-like organizations, for Thailand. Such an extension resulted in the heterogeneous content of the movement, the common feature shared by the De Jiao associations being restricted to a concept — the "teaching of virtue" — but under various modalities, and led to the emphasis on spirit-writing as a privileged way to receive instructions from the divine tutors. The proteiform character of De Jiao partly results from the multiple national contexts in which it flourished. The movement proved sufficiently nimble in adjusting its activities in response to the local restrictions imposed on overseas Chinese. Whatever the setting or milieu may be, De Jiao's spirit-writings do not deal with current political affairs and, in contrast with the endeavours of other NRMs (such as Falun Gong, Cao Đài, Yi Guan-Dao), its activities can hardly be considered subversive. The Chinese government's ban on the movement was evidently based on a misinterpretation of its purpose. Far from pretending to challenge any contemporary political rule or social order, De Jiao instead aims to connect devotees, mostly uprooted Hua Qiao, to the Golden Age of Chinese civilization whose *de de she* constitutes both the heavenly matrix and the ultimate sanctuary. This Edenic society is believed to have ended with the Three Kingdoms period, i.e., long before the important, traumatic changes experienced by China during the twentieth century. Although the encroachment of materialistic values on the societal fabric is perceived as a threat, followers usually interpret this evolution by referring to the advent of modernity rather than construing such change within a specific political context. Even if De Jiao has adopted as its own the millenarian theme of Guan Yu as the enthroned Jade Emperor, the relationship that the practice of *fu ji* establishes with the *de de she* has no messianic character, except in the specific and marginal case of Zan Hua. In other words, the flying *luan*-bird does not link the heavenly rulers to a community of "chosen" bestowed with the supreme mission to set up a New Age, or an ideal society, after a redemptive phase of apocalypse. The supreme goal which consists of uplifting morality for the benefit of mankind is a distant issue when related to De Jiao's socio-cultural basis and to the few demands on its members. Epistemological individualism as a dominant feature of membership corresponds in practice to more immediate and self-centred goals (good fortune, health, longevity, improvement of karma). Thus, the "honourable masters" deliver sermons, but their instructions emphasize the building of new shrines in potent places. Eventually, they appear less as moral preceptors than as investors and entrepreneurs, thus reflecting the professional background and orientation of their most active worshippers.

As can be observed in the precepts of any other religious movement, some of the various objectives that De Jiao is pursuing seem to conflict with each other. Thus, while some members claim that De Jiao is the forthcoming "great religion" of the twenty-first century, De Jiao is too China-centric and Teochew-oriented to be able to attract recruits on a large scale out of this dialectal group. The practice of *fu ji*, as a quasi-exclusive channel of divine revelation, also constitutes a major impediment: it is too culturally idiosyncratic to make sense outside the Chinese world, and too open-ended to sustain the production of a holy book, which in turn could be used a common dogmatic basis for large-scale conversion. Such a gap between the ambition proclaimed and the means at disposal for its attainment is easy to interpret, if we admit that, less than other religious formation, De Jiao can be portrayed as a monolith whose every element would share exactly the same views and ideals. That a handful of leaders, taking after the example of Ma Gui-De, Li Huai-De or Tang Xi-Ru, seek to make De Jiao an encompassing synthesis of several mainstream religions does not mean that a majority of followers adhere to such an ambition. In the same vein, the attempt by the RCODJ to give the movement a worldwide dimension was met by most grassroot devotees with apathy, as they are mainly concerned by local, more concrete achievements.

The Zan Hua leaders' ill-fated attempt to replace the open-endedness of *fu ji* with a holy book, whose truths are expected to hold for all eternity, highlights the difficulties met by any attempt to dogmatize De Jiao. The promoters of this "bible" were blamed for threatening the Chineseness of the movement. Such a charge reveals that, whatever the genuineness of the intentions of Ma Gui-De and others to make De Jiao one of the "greatest religions" of the world, this movement is for the most part culturally introspective. The fact that the committee constituted to reinstate De Jiao in China was named "Research Committee on the Origin of De Jiao" perfectly reflects this introverted nature. The inability of Zan Hua to "envisage" a revealed text outside of the context of the *fu ji* channel is also indicative of this introversion.

Although this study ought to deepen the analysis of *fu ji*, especially in the context of a diasporic, nonsectarian group, many aspects of the way oracles may "fit" adepts' expectations remain hidden in the black box. We touch here one of the limits of ethnographic inquiry, i.e., the difficulty to record, on the spot, the exchanges of information and ideas conditioning unequivocally the process of decision-making. Under these conditions, the only way is to approach the processes at work by providing a set of reasonable hypothesis. The ethnography of De Jiao concerning among others the *fu ji* controversy in Malaysia and the reseeding of the movement in China suggested a strong correlation, which the followers would certainly deny, between the acknowledged "accuracy" of the oracles a medium conveys and his degree of involvement in the affairs of his congregation. A medium's fame depends on his ability to compile psychological, sociological, and financial information, gleaned from his day-to-day interaction with his local community and from his dealings with the network of other associations, which would be later utilized to "provide" realistic projects and believable predictions. Finally, the prestige associated with this "pure channel of communication" with the gods emanates in large part from his capacity to act as a grassroots-oriented, eclectic social scientist.

In an interval of about 50 years, De Jiao experienced several changes. Born in Chao-Shan, it was eradicated from the area by the Communist regime, and then found the resources to spread throughout several countries in Southeast Asia. Outside the mainland, despite its arduous adaptation with respect to contrasting political and socio-cultural contexts, De Jiao blossomed by founding hundreds of local congregations. More recently, the gods' invitation to a bi-directional impetus, one directed to the global world and the other to the homeland, reopened the recurrent tensions within this religious movement between openness-to-the-west and China-centric attitudes, with however a clear imbalance in favour of the latter. Accordingly, it was reseeded in China while extending its settlements in an increasing number of new countries. The RCODJ will certainly carry on its plan of worldwide expansion, with the pending question being its attitude toward the pavilions created during the past decade, as most of them are in need of strong support and are struggling against extinction. Another recent trend, which further confirms the introspective character of the movement, is the rise of a reflection from within on the essence of *fu ji*, the nature of De Jiao, its origins, and its links with other Chinese religious traditions. The research on the origin of the movement, which was implemented by the RCODJ in China, constituted an initial step in this sense. Another step is the creation of a De Jiao Research Centre as part of the new headquarters of the National Federation of Thailand. This phenomenon is not specific to De Jiao, as other Asiatic NRMs such as Cao Đài have recently started the same kind of reflection. It expresses a desire toward patrimonialization and the appropriation of Cartesian features. The latter effort is still finding traction, with *fu ji* remaining the basic and only legitimate method for existential prospects and the attainment of "truth". Although the present work did not employ the same means, could the insights it provides contribute to the general knowledge of this religious movement, as a valuable expression of contemporary forms of Chinese religiosity and ethnicity.

APPENDIX

The Invocation Texts

III. The *Qi Zan* (Invocation Text of the *De Jiao Xin Dian*) (China – 1942)

阴阳分晓日月尊 / 浑浑五行合乹坤 / 帝德玄黄参化育 / 订立慧緣修真根 / 奉请东方木德星君 / 奉请南方火德星君 / 奉请中央土德星君 / 奉请西方金德星君 / 奉请北方水德星君 / 奉请德德社诸佛仙尊

Literary translation*: "Since the creation of the world with the separation of *yin* and *yang*, the sun and the moon have become supreme, and *De Jiao Xin Dian* can be likened to the sun and moon which give us light. The immense force of the five elements operates in coordination in the universe. The virtue of the Jade Emperor fills the whole world and gives life to all living things. Let us cultivate the purity of our natural self in order to establish our close relation of wisdom with the deities. We are respectfully inviting Mu De Xing-Jun of the east and the deities of the eastern region, Huo De Xing-Jun of the south and the deities of the southern region, Tu De Xing-Jun of the middle and the deities of the central region, Jin De Xing-Jun of the west and the deities of the western region, Shui De Xing-Jun of the north and the deities of the northern region, and finally all the Buddhas, Immortals and other masters of the *de de she*."

* The non-literal translation is excerpted from *De Dian Ying Yi* (Ji Cheng Ge, 1998).

II. The Invocation Prayer of Zi Xiang Ge (China – 1939)

敢请師符真需 / 雲遍下坡 / 兵肌玉符 / 草車於處 / 紫車東途 / 願排并悟 / 瞻仰雲途 / 聰明銳智 / 歌賦詩詞 / 天上人間 / 雲水超超 / 敢请仙照 / 獨然行邀 / 議論府界雪裹雲霄 / 我奉太上老君丁 / 急急如律令

Literary translation: "In the grip of pressing needs, we dare to implore the magic powers of the Taoist masters. Clouds from everywhere are moving over the mountain slope with upon them heavenly soldiers' forces, carrying jade and magic powers. The purple chariot carrying fresh grass makes its way on the road from the East. In the hope to improve both the harmony and the understanding in this world, we are gazing the clouds to look up the path through which gods will spread down verses of Chinese classical poetry. Their chanting will convey an acute transcending wisdom and knowledge from the higher heaven to the men cross clouds and rivers. We dare to solicit the Immortals from their mansion and kingdom about the right way to comment the Analects of Confucius. In the heaven are clouds loaded with snow. I address this chant to the Supreme Lord of the 4th Heavenly Stem. Let's hurry to conform to his highest command to rule ourselves!"

III. *Dian Sheng Jue Yuan You* (幽箢阙圣典 – The Sacred Text from the Quiet Garden), Zhen Shan Ge (Malaysia – 1955)

福泽长春德业永存 / 正统山河神功乾坤 / 奉请诸福德帝君 / 善积宝质山川 / 通天下之财源 / 掌万民的福泽握四方之循环 / 奉请五方财神 **(repeated three times)**

Literary translation: "The beneficence and good fortune brought by the study of virtue exists as perpetual spring for the whole life. At the occasion of the New Year Festival we invite the gods and ghosts of the earth, male and female, to share with us the various achievements of the virtue taught by the Jade Emperor. Good communication with heaven allows us to accumulate the treasures of the nature as a source of wealth. The palm hands of the *ji*-wielders draw loops in the four directions to grasp good deeds and good fortune in favour of the multitude. We implore the gods of the five directions to endow us with wealth."

IV. The Invocation Prayer of Zan Hua Ge (Malaysia, 1957)

阴阳分晓日月尊 / 浑浑五行合乹坤 / 帝德玄黄参化育 / 订立慧緣修真根 / 請德社藷真辭 / 东方木德星君奉请 / 南方火德星君奉请 / 中央土德星君奉请 / 西方金德星君奉请 / 北方水德星君奉请 / 德德社诸佛仙尊

Literary translation: "Since the creation of the world with the separation of *yin* and *yang*, the sun and the moon have become supreme, and *De Jiao Xin Dian* can be likened to the sun and moon which give us light. The immense force of the five elements operates in coordination in the universe. The virtue of the Jade Emperor fills the whole world and gives life to all living things. Let us cultivate the purity of our natural self in order to establish our close relation of wisdom with the deities. Let us invite the *de de she* to deliver various true poems. We are respectfully inviting Mu De Xing-Jun of the east and the deities of the eastern region, Huo De Xing-Jun of the south and the deities of the southern region, Tu De Xing-Jun of the middle and the deities of the central region, Jin De Xing-Jun of the west and the deities of the western region, Shui De Xing-Jun of the north and the deities of the northern region, and finally all the Buddhas, Immortals and other masters of the *de de she*."

V. *Qing Luan Yu* (請鸞語 – Invitation for the Flying Phoenix to Speak). Invocation Prayer of Zi Piao Tan and of the Ming Tan Group (Thailand, 1925)

奉請蓬莱仙 / 獻符達儿天 / 丹心通文語 / 符使能稟上 / 誠心誠念節 / 火急風雷嚮 / 誠驅速妖離 / 翘首祈誨仰 / 風清月白到 / 蓬莱請衷仙 / 急急如律令常

Literary translation: "We invite the Immortals of the Peng Lai Islands to direct us written charms of protection through the nine levels of heaven. The vermilion heart is an energetic endowment from heaven coming down through literary spirit-writing, *wen ji*). Pure heart, sincere worshipping! The wind blows and the thunderbolt sounds! We are sincere in our prayer to receive instructions from the head of the gods to expel quickly the devils. A light blow is going under the bright moon to the Peng Lai Islands to invite a multitude of Immortals to come down. Let's hurry to conform to their highest command to rule ourselves!"

NOTES

Introduction

1 My personal account of the number of subscribers claimed by De Jiao associations approximates to the figure of 75,000 (about 50,000 in Malaysia, 20,000 in Thailand, 2,500 in Singapore, 1,000 in Hong Kong, 1,000 in PRC, and 500 in other countries). However, each subscriber represents a household whose several members are informally but actively involved in the life of the congregation, so that a total membership of 230,000 is a reasonable figure.

2 Shantou became in 1981 one of the first five Special Economic Zones (SEZ) in China. Together with the Jieyang, Chaozhou, and Lufeng municipalities (*shi* – 市), they form the Teochew heartland. The SEZ and adjacent municipalities divide either into districts (*qu* – 区) or counties (*xian* – 县), which comprise in turn several townships (*zhen* – 镇). For example, the Shantou SEZ is divided into the districts of Chenghai, Longhu, Jinping, Haojiang, Chaoyang and Chaonan, and the county of Nan'ao, while the Jieyang municipality comprises the districts of Rongcheng, Puning, and Dananshan, and the counties of Jiedong, Jiexi, and Huilai.

3 In Malay it mainly appears as *Persatuan Pendidikan Akhlak* ("Union for the Teaching of Morality") or *Persatuan Memperbaiki Akhlak* ("Union for the Promotion of Morality"). In Thai the most frequent designations are either *munithi kan kuson* ("Foundation for Charity"), *munithi khunatham songkrô* ("Virtuous Foundation for Assistance"), or *munithi songsoem khunatham* ("Foundation to Promote Virtue").

4 For instance, Lin Wu-Shu (2002: 1) mentions that the Teochew *shan tang* corporately and successfully resisted the attempt by Guomingdang to destroy the Song Da-Feng shrines in 1924, as part of its policy to eradicate superstitions in Guangdong province.

5 In Thailand, I surveyed 26 congregations out of a total of 74 (35%), in Malaysia 41 among 142 (28%), in Singapore, 6 out of a total of 11, in Hong Kong the 3 locally established congregations, and in the PRC 10 out of a total figure of 13.

6 Among these messages, one involved both Lü Dong-Bin and Ji Gong, at the occasion of the opening ceremony of a congregation in Bahau (Malaysia); two allegedly came from Ji Gong, writing alone (at Ji Yun Ge in Singapore, and

Zi Zhen Ge in Thailand), and one from Hua Tuo, the God of Medicine, at Tai He Guan (Singapore).

7 I prefer the term "complex" to that of "system" for the true reason given by M. Freedman (1974: 20). He rightly remarks that: "To use the word 'system' systematically would be to run the constant risk of appearing to impute to Chinese religion a thoroughgoing unity and tightness that manifestly it does not have."

8 De Groot (1910: 1296) relates the basic rules which govern the choice of a good fork among the potential Y-shaped branches to cut off. Some of these principles are akin to those that my own informants put forward, others are not. With regard to the crosschecks, we can mention the carving of powerful charms on the bark of the tree, the pronunciation of efficient spells during the cutting, and the choice of a universal *yang* auspicious day and hour. Although the forked branch can be quite often painted red to increase its ghost-expelling capacity, it is not a general rule. Moreover, there are few De Jiao congregations which use a stick whose end is nicely carved with a dragon head. Those which have such a fork in their arsenal mainly use it when Jade Emperor manifests itself.

Chapter I

1 According to his hagiography, Liu Chun-Fang became palace councillor during the De Zhong reign (780–805), and later on was appointed private tutor of princes. When he was 72 years old, Lü Dong-Bin invited him to retreat on the *Zi Yang* ("Purple Yang") Mountain (Sichuan). He thus explored the *dao* for years, just surrounded in his hermitage by white swans. He was said to have finally reached the condition of Immortal (Zi Xin Ge, 2002).

2 The reference to the south may be explained by the fact that the new congregation was opened in Nanxun, the native village of Ma Gui-De, which is located south of Yingxi Gang, the locality where Zi Xiang Ge was established. Liu Chun-Fang added that: "a flower [*hua*, metaphor for China] of brightness had spread over ruins, that the pavilion had been established in Chaoyang and had reinstated the Virtue" (Li Huai-De, 1955: 251–2).

3 The Japanese occupied Chaoyang in 1941, according to historical records (*A Brief History of Chaoshan*, 1993: 186).

4 This information contradicts the report of Li Huai-De (1955: 1), according to which they used a willow stick that had been kept by the Yang family for generations, suggesting that this family had *ji*-wielders among its ancestors.

5 According to hagiographies published by Zi Xin Ge of Singapore (2002), Yang Jun-Song was a Taoist master skilled in the art of geomancy, who lived during the Tang dynasty. He was appointed geomancer at the court of Jing Zong (824–26) when he was only 17 years old. During the Huang Chao peasants' revolt (875–84), he took refuge into the Kun Lun Range (at the southern part of Xinjiang province), where he practised meditation. Later on,

he chose a remote area of the Jiangxi province to increase his magical powers through ascetism, and became very popular among the folk for his use of geomancy to bring fortune to the poor. Yang Jun-Song passed away when he was 72 years old. He is considered to be the founder of the Luan Tou Pai school of geomancy which emphasizes topography.

6 Taking place during the 7th lunar month, it is known in English as the Universal Salvation Festival, since its aim is to make offerings to gods, ghosts, dead, and poor who are invited to rally at the ceremony's spot.

7 When they rebuilt the wall, the inhabitants wrote at the main village's gate the poetic stanza by which the two Taoist masters had assigned to them the supreme mission to spread *dao de*. The content of this stanza, which still adorns the gate, is the following: «南昌流传, 浮莲再开» (*Nanchang liu chuan, fu lian zai kai* – From Nanchang, the lotus flower is blossoming again on the lake). According to legend, Lao Zi, and the Immortal Lü Dong-Bin had hermitage in Nanchang, as well as Liu Chun-Fang and Yang Jun-Song. Accordingly, the stanza suggests that initially born in Jiangxi, the virtue of Dao (symbolized by the lotus flower) is now arising (blossoming) again in a new place bordering a lake (the house of Yang Rui-De was nearby a large pond).

8 Today, about 60% of the total population of the Heping township are members of this lineage.

9 More precisely, in the family house in his native village, Nanxun Xiang (南薰乡).

10 This article was revised several times, and was reprinted under the title *De Jiao Gai Zhuo* (德教概説 – *Introduction to De Jiao*). The version that I have consulted was edited in 1997 by Zi Zhen Ge (Bangkok).

11 The specific compound he uses is *zu zong de jing yan* (祖宗的经验 – «ancestors' experience»).

12 Such as the *Great Study* (*Da Xue* – 大学), the *Canon of Documents* (*Shu Jing*, 书经), or the *Li Lou* (离婁) attributed to Mencius.

13 *Guan gong zuo tian gong* (关公作天公). Li Huai-De (1955: 258) reveals that, on the 26th day of the first lunar month of 1942, a *fu ji* oracle delivered at Zi He Ge (Shantou) correlated the enthronement of Guan Yu as the Jade Emperor with the birth of the *De De She*, the De Jiao community of gods. A majority of adepts in Hong Kong and Southeast Asia believe that the De Jiao of modern times began in 1924, the supposed date of Guan Yu's enthronement.

14 According to Wang Jian-Chuan and Li Shi-Wei (2000: 215), this text was first published in 1923 by the Taoist *shan tang* Xian Tian Dao Wan Quan Tang (先天道万全堂) located in Sichuan and because of its success was reprinted in 1930.

15 According to the chronological order of their foundation, these associations were: Zi Yang Ge in Long Qi (Chao'an), Zi Xiong Ge in Shantou, Zi Mei Ge (紫美阁) in Mianyi, Zi Hao Ge in Da Hao, Zi Yuan Ge in Gezhou, Zi Ying Ge (紫英阁) and Zi Zong Ge (紫宗阁) in Shantou, Zi Dao Ge (紫道阁),

Zi Yi Ge (紫仪阁), Zi Yuan Ge (紫元阁), Zi Huan Ge (紫环阁), Zi Hua Ge (紫华阁) and Zi Rong Ge (紫容阁) in Mianyi, Zi Xing Ge (紫星阁), Zi Zhen Ge (紫真阁), Zi Wu Ge (紫悟阁) and Zi Ming Ge (紫明阁) in Chenghai, Zi Yuan Ge (紫原阁), Zi Xi Ge (紫溪阁), Zi Fang Ge (紫芳阁), Zi Xing Ge (紫兴阁), and Zi Xiang Ge (紫湘阁) in Chaozhou (Li Huai De, 1955: 3).

16 *Hao* refers to the name of the town, Da Hao, where the association was established.

17 More precisely, the gods' message equated his age, 29, to 2 × 9. Later on, this strange equation was interpreted with reference to the role that Zi Xin Ge, the pavilion he founded in Singapore, played to establish 18 pavilions which constitute the "mainstream" of De Jiao in Singapore and Malaysia.

18 The original treatise of Lao Zi numbers 81 chapters, corresponding to the 81 years (9 × 9) he spent gestating in his mother's womb. According to the legend, Li Huai-De and Ma Gui-De hold the willow stick for seven days, and seven hours each day, i.e. 49 hours, to complete the new version of the *Dao De Jing*.

19 This is the point of view of CLJ, a former secretary of the 4th association to have been created in China and who is now a physician in Singapore. To illustrate that the event was a bad omen, he indicates that two days after the spirit-writing session, the building where it had been conducted was totally destroyed by a Japanese bombing raid.

20 This revelation coincided with a prophecy about the end of the war with Japan. When the adepts asked to the "honourable masters" when Ma Gui-De and Li Huai-De could leave China to spread the movement overseas, the latter answered indirectly by suggesting the twenty-third day of the eighth lunar month, which effectively corresponded to 15 August 1945.

21 According to legend, Wu Meng-Wu was born in 1430. At the age of 22 he started a brilliant career as a military officer and when he was 34 the Ming Emperor Cheng Hua appointed him chief commander protecting the western border. At the age of 59, he became minister at the imperial court, but resigned soon to start a Taoist ascetic life in Jixian (薊縣), where he received the revelation of the Huang Ting Zhi Jing (黄庭之經 – "Canon of the Yellow Palace"). He became a famous geomancer and the Emperor used to get his advice. Finally, at the age of 70 he was ordained a Buddhist monk and trained himself in Chan meditation up to his death at 88. As for Bai Yun, his original name was Shang Xuan-Tong, and he was born in the town of Xiangbin (province of Hubei) during the Jia Jing reign (1522–66) of the Ming Dynasty. With reference to his hometown and perhaps some aspects of his physiognomy and personality, one of his nicknames was *Bin Yan* ("Wild goose of [Xiang] Bin"). He was 23 years old when he was appointed governor of a district in Sichuan. Afterwards, he moved from a position to another into the imperial bureaucracy up to his encounter with a famous Taoist master of his time. Then he withdrew from administration to live an ascetic life and to practice meditation in a retreat of the Mount Bai Yun ("White Cloud").

In 1566 he received the divine command to leave this world and to become an Immortal under the name of Bai Yun.

22 The content of this address was: "Purple *qi* is coming from the East, the blossoming goodness moves ahead to the fresh South in order to stand virtue" (Zi Xin Ge, 2002: 100).

23 The lyrics are: "Three very large rivers and five majestic mountains make China prosperous. Benevolence, righteousness, propriety and wisdom as well as the support for the weak and for the common aspirations of the people are the *raison d'être* of De Jiao. Our power can change the universe by uplifting morality among the people, and by contributing to the respect of the old masters. Brotherhood, peace and the prosperity of each country are the Universe's foundations. One heart, one moral, it is the glory of our doctrine."

24 I agree with G. Deleuze and F. Guattari (1980: 255–7) when, against a majority of anthropologists, they consider it nonsense to oppose segmentary and state societies. They pertinently notice that the state not only perpetuates social, religious, or ethnic segments, but also creates and imposes its own segmentarity. The two philosophers make a difference between a non-dual and non-centred, *flexible* segmentarity which should characterize the primitive societies, and a *hard* one, concentric and bearer of a higher institutional resonance which should be typical of the Moderns. Indeed, I hardly follow this evolutionist point of view. Furthermore, De Jiao materials prove that a flexible segmentarity whose diacritics are those of the authors may apply to modern contexts as well.

25 M. Castells (2004: 7) distinguishes among the three forms of identity building: (1) *legitimizing identity*, which is "introduced by the dominant institutions of society to extend and rationalize their domination *vis-à-vis* social actors"; (2) *resistance identity*, "generated by those actors who are in position/condition devalued and/or stigmatized by the logic of domination, thus building trenches of resistance and survival on the basis of principles different from, or opposed to, those permeating the institution of society"; (3) *project identity*, "when social actors, on the basis of whatever cultural materials are available to them, build a new identity that redefines their position in society and, by so doing, seek the transformation of overall social structure".

Chapter II

1 V. Purcell (1965: 224) gives for 1957 the figure of 12.1% of Teochew in Malaysia. According to Li Wei and Al. (1997: 366), in Singapore the Teochew (22.1%) form the second largest sub-group within the Chinese community.

2 A. Reid (1993: 133) observed that: "the most intense period of both Islamization and Christianization coincided with the high tide of the age of commerce" in the Malay world.

3 Whereas 10,000 immigrants were allowed to enter annually the country up to 1948, from 1949 onwards their number fell to 200.

4 The family founded the fish cans' trademark Haichi, and so was the name of its main shop in Bangkok. It was located on Krongwat Street.

5 In 2003, 200,000 people were buried in the cemetery, and 10,000 ancestors' tablets were stored in a funeral hall. The graveyard received an average of 1,750 bodies annually, and has a storage capacity for 20 more years.

6 In 1947, only 11 per cent of the Chinese lived in the central plain, the north, and the northeast, although these three regions cover four-fifths of the country. In contrast, at about the same time (1952), more than half of Bangkok's population was of Chinese origin (Skinner, 1954: 246–8).

7 This influential member of the Thai aristocracy later became rector of the Thammasat University (1971–3).

8 In fact, *Charity Foundation for the Promotion of Culture* is the literal translation of the Thai compound. The Chinese one might be translated as *Benevolent Hall for the World Awareness.*

9 The outstanding development of Bao De Shan Tang owes a lot to Zheng Wu-Lou (郑午楼). His father, a pawnbroker and distillery owner, was among the founders of this benevolent hall in 1910, together with other influential leaders of the Chinese community. For his part, Zheng Wu-Lou managed the main brewery and liquor company in the country as well as the Bangkok Metropolis Bank. He also contributed to the construction of an important industrial plant on the seaboard in the 1970s, and to build the Bangkok World Trade Center in the 1980s. He accumulated one of the largest fortunes in the country, and was honoured several times by the Crown. A fervent admirer of the famous Singaporean businessman and philanthropist Chen Jia-Geng (陈嘉庚 – Tan Kah Kee), Zheng Wu-Lou quickly stood out as the main sponsor of Bao De Shan Tang. In 1937 he was chosen as vice president and became its undisputed leader in 1972. He is assisted by a committee of about 20 prominent Chinese patrons (including bankers, rice exporters, Japanese cars' distributors, owners of chains of tourist hotels, and so forth). Zheng Wu-Lou made Bao De Shan Tang the biggest enterprise in Thailand in the field of humanitarian action. In the 1970s, Bao De Shan Tang constructed the Hua Qiao Hospital in Bangkok, which was inaugurated by the king in 1976. This high-technology, 750-bed hospital receives an average of 500 patients a day. It was followed by the establishment of a college for training nurses and emergency relievers, and more recently (1996) by the setting up of the private Hua Qiao Chalem Prakiat University ("University of the Hua Qiao Excellent Honour" in Thai), which was inaugurated by the king in 2003. In the 2000s, the foundation owned a fleet of 20 emergency rescue vehicles, some of which are very technogically sophisticated, and it employed two teams of 50 well-trained rescuers working on a 24-hour basis.

10 Song Da-Feng was born around 1039. He was appointed governor of a district in Zhejiang, but gave up the position to become a monk in the neighbouring

province of Fujian. Afterwards, he settled in the ruins of an old monastery located on a hill of the present-day district of Chaoyang. He rebuilt the monastery and became famous by assisting the needy. He offered free medical treatment for the masses, donated coffins, and sponsored funerals. He also raised funds to build a stone bridge at the mouth of a local river whose floods were devastating. According to legend, Song Da-Feng wrote to notify the Gods of the Water to bless the project. As a mark of acknowledgement, they interrupted the tide flood for seven days, thus allowing the completion of the bridge. Song Da-Feng is said to have passed away when he was 88 years old (1127?), but nobody found his remains. A few years after his death, the people of Chaoyang began to worship him, and in the late Ming Dynasty pursued his charitable works by making his hermitage the first *shan tang* in the Teochew area.

11 Jip Tan ("Altar for Unity") is a dissident branch of Ming Tan ("Altar of Brightness"). It arose in 1969 because of a dispute concerning the ownership of a statue. The organization is until now limited to two temples located in the northeast (Formoso, 2003a: 838).

12 According to his hagiography, He Ye-Yun (1325–93) was born in Jiangxi. Because of his early and outstanding skills in divination and geomancy, he became a councillor of Chen You-Liang, a leader of the Red Turbans rebellion against the Mongols. After the rebellion was subjugated by Zhu Yuan-Zhang, the founder of the Ming Dynasty, He Ye-Yun chose an ascetic way of life, wandering southwards from place to place through Fujian and northern Guangdong. His grave is located near Xiancheng, in the present Teochew district of Chaonan. For more details about his legendary life, see Formoso (2004).

13 Ming Deng Tan (明灯壇) is the name of this mother-temple, founded in 1925.

14 Piao Ran Tai was founded around 1911 and is located in the suburb of the town of Puning.

15 Another significant example of this strategy concerns Zi Ming Ge (紫明阁), located in Taradnoi, nearby the central railway station of Bangkok. This Buddhist funeral association (*gong de fo jiao she* – 公德佛教社), was integrated with authority to De Jiao in the 1970s by its then president and main sponsor. It received a full set of De Jiao statues, and its regular *ji*-wielder was sometimes asked to officiate for "true" De Jiao associations.

16 See M. Freedman (1971: 118–23) for details about second burials in Guangdong province.

17 Among these changes is the fact that after the gathering of the bones, the skeletons are not put in urns, as is the case in China, but are collectively cremated, thus following the Thai tradition. Another major difference is that in China, *shan tang* organize small-scale *xiu gu gu* almost every year, whereas in Thailand, they are performed by the congregations once every 7 to 10 years.

[18] There is evidence that De Jiao associations never organized *xiu gu gu* while in China. In Thailand, they learned how to conduct such events from Ming Tan temples.

[19] In 2003, each issue had a print run of 3,000. A number of copies are distributed among the Zi Zhen Ge members, others are sent free of charge to every De Jiao association in the country. Copies are also sent abroad to *shan tang* and De Jiao pavilions in Malaysia, Singapore, Hong Kong, China, Taiwan, Australia, and the United States.

[20] Heavy rains fell down on the day of the opening ceremony. The event was interpreted with reference to the gods' wish to purify the place, and notably to chase out forever a multitude of dangerous yellow-green snakes which lived on a tall tree in the compound. Later on, it was observed that the place also proved to be unaffected by flooding, despite the regular occurrence of floods in the area.

[21] Among the main charitable activities of Zi Zhen Ge in the early 2000s, we can mention the regular donation of rice to more than ten primary schools in Bangkok, the gift of 60 tons of rice to villages in remote areas at the occasion of the Universal Salvation Festival, and the supplying of 5,000 blankets every year to the needy. The allotment of these blankets is very significant to the patron-client relationships in which Zi Zhen Ge is involved. Thus, it has to allot 1,000 blankets to the charitable organization of Princess Sirindhorn (in view of royal patronage and all that such patronage entails), it distributes by itself 1,000 more items to hill tribal families in the north, and the remaining 3,000 blankets are distributed to the poor through the mediation of other De Jiao associations.

[22] Although the Federation's full name is *Thai Guo De Jiao Ci Shan Cong Hui* (Federation of the Moral Uplifting Societies of Thailand), it is better known as *De Cong*.

[23] W.T. Rowe (1984: 248) considers *shan tang* as the key institutions in China's urban communities during the late nineteenth century. Among their main activities were the provision of refuge to the homeless and meals to victims of war, starvation, and floods, as well as providing free medical care to the poor, the establishment of orphanages and schools, and the setting up of teams of firefighters. More recently, S. Naquin (2000: 653–69) has noted that in the Beijing of the 1860s–70s *shan tang* took in the old and sick each winter, fed, clothed, and when necessary buried them. They were also very active in organizing relief activities for the victims of cholera epidemics and floods which affected the capital in the mid-nineteenth century.

[24] These two associations are, namely: Zi Nan Ge of Hat Yai which teaches the Chinese language to 30–40 children during weekend sessions; and Zi Ming Ge (紫铭閣) of Ranong which supports the Chinese school in the town. Both are located in the south and have certainly been influenced in the promotion of such activities by the brother associations in Malaysia.

Chapter III

1 Lü Dong-Bing is reputed to have lived during the Tang Dynasty. Hagiographical accounts agree that he was born in 798 C.E. in the town of Yongle (Shanxi Province). He is said to have been the grandson of a vice-minister of rites and the son of a guard's officer at the Imperial court. One day, he was taking a walk when he met the hermit Zhong Li Quan (鍾籬權), who perceived that Lü was of uncommon make, and enticed him to study the way of the Immortals. He transmitted to Lü secret instructions for internal alchemy, together with magical sword techniques. Lü Dong-Bin then used the Taoist name Chun-Yang, which means "purified *yang*", and broke off all ties with mundane affairs, building a hut of grass on the Lu Shan Mountain. Later he attained a position among the Immortals and even became the leading figure of the Ba Xian. He is considered as one of the five founding fathers of Quan Zhen ("Perfect Realization") sect of Taoism. He is worshipped as a healer and wonder-worker, a patron god of various tradespeople, a powerful spirit of *fu ji*, and as the best known of the Eight Immortals (Katz, 1996: 70–1).

2 Among these eight pavilions, four were created in 1954, successively in Malacca, Batu Pahat, Penang, and Ipoh. In 1955 a branch was opened in Kuala Lumpur, and another in Teluk Intan, followed in 1956 by one in Muar, and in 1957 by one in Johor Bahru.

3 I have reported in detail elsewhere the contents of the poem that Ji Gong delivered in September 1999, at Ji Yun Ge of Singapore (Formoso, 2003: 103). Only two Ji pavilions of the new generation have been founded so far: one in Mentakap, the other in Singapore.

4 The other associations of the "second nine" were created in Penang, Pangkor Island, Seremban, Sungai Bakap, Taiping, and Klang.

5 The eight Zan Hua pavilions which together with Zan Hua Ge form the "first nine" were successively founded in Sungai Petani (1962), Kulim (1964), Pulau Langkawi (1965), Baling (1965), Serdang (1965), Gurun (1966), Balik Pulau (1966), and Padang Serai (1967).

6 According to a witness, the true reason of the split was that Zi Xin Ge and Ji Yun Ge were both, but separately, instructed by the gods to set up a pavilion in Muar. The followers from Muar consulted the president of Ji Yun Ge about the name for their future pavilion. Tan Chee-Beng (1985: 38–9) relates the next events as follows: "The president suggested the name Ji Xin Ge since it was being established through the joint efforts of Ji Yun Ge and Zi Xin Ge. But the leaders of Zi Xin Ge received this news too late and so the name Ji Xin Ge was adopted. In retaliation, the leaders of Zi Xin Ge established Zi Chang Ge in Malacca and informed Ji Yun Ge later."

7 Tan Chee-Beng (1985: 28) reports the details of the event: "The first pair of planchette mediums dropped divining blocks to see if the deities would allow them to hold the planchette stick for the divination. The two were prominent

leaders who were in favour of planchette divination. They failed to receive the divine blessing to hold the stick. The second pair was leaders who wanted the cessation of planchette divination. They received the divine blessing to begin the planchette session. It was after a long while that a divine messenger revealed a message in four verses of four characters each; that is *De Jiao qian qiu, zi luan yuan zhou, jing cheng tui zhan, ren shi shan mou* [德教千秋紫鸞圓週精誠推展人事善謀 – "De Jiao is going to last for thousand years if the purple *luan*-bird comes full circle (comes to an end), the sincere choice will be rewarded and the human affairs will be sorted out]. The planchette stick came to a stop after the characters were written."

8 The businessman named Lian Yuan-Da (连远達), who founded Ming Shan She, was a native of Huilai county in Chao-Shan. He migrated to Malaysia in 1944, and settled in Began Serai where he founded a factory of umbrellas. Before leaving China he had kept incense ashes from a temple devoted to Song Chan in the town of Da Bu (大埔). Lian first established a small shrine in his house, and later got in touch with Huang Song-Hua (黄松华), a famous medium who later received the revelation from Song Chan to become his local messenger. In 1958, the Taoist master gave them instructions to establish a *shan she* in the town, named Ming Yue Shan She (明月善社). From this temple other "benevolent altars" were progressively established through *xian guo* ritual in Sungai Petani, Sungai Siput, Teluk Intan, and Tasik Lukut.

9 According to legend, Song Chan was born in Huilai during the Jia Jing Reign of the Ming Dynasty (1522–66). He very soon devoted himself to the Taoist ascetic lifestyle and lived for years in a cave near Huilai named Long Cang-Dong (龙藏洞 – "The Hidden Dragon Cave"). Huang Da-Xian (黄大仙), another Taoist master native of Guangdong Province, joined him in his hermitage. In 1994, a Taoist *shan tang* based on their cult was built in this place. Song Chan was a skilful geomancer, while Huang Da-Xian was a renowned physician. Because they used their magical powers to relieve the masses' ills they became very popular in Huilai and are revered as Immortals. Song Chan is supposed to have reached nirvana as well. During his old age, he was ordained as a Buddhist monk and lived in a monastery of the town of Huilai where he made charitable works. After his death, due to his status as Immortal, his body became mummified and was preciously kept as a relic. At the time of the Cultural Revolution, the mummified corpse was concealed by a devotee in a secret place, but it disappeared afterwards.

10 They were successively founded in Tasek Glugor (1969), Tanjong Rambutan (1970), Tanjong Piandang (1970), Pulau Pangkor (1972), Tanjung Piandang (1974), Parit Buntar (1975), and Sitiawan (1975).

11 In 2003, only 7 among the 18 Zi associations of the "first" and "second" nine had not yet resumed the spirit-writing activity. They were, namely: Zi Xin Ge, the mother-temple of Singapore; Zi Fang Ge of Kuala Lumpur; Zi Peng Ge of Teluk Intan; Zi Wei Ge of Butterworth; Zi Yi Ge of Sungai Bakap; Zi Pheng Ge of Taiping; and Zi Sheng Ge of Selangor.

12 These associations were founded in Tanjung Malim (Perak), Kuala Kangsar (Perak), Klang (Selangor), Kuantan (Pahang), Segamat (Johor), Yong Peng (Johor), Kulai (Johor), Pontian (Johor), Pengkalan (Johor), and Masai (Johor).

13 The two Zhen associations were namely Zhen Guang Ge of Tanjong Rambutan and Zheng Xing Ge of Sitiawan. As for Zi Ji Ge, it occupies a specific position. Its founder, Wen Yu-Tang (温毓堂), a rich businessman, owner of an important pharmaceutical factory, had been the first President of Zan Hua Ge, but left it in 1972, because of its involvement with the faction which was in favour of the continuation of *fu ji* within Zan Hua. A few months after the latter stopped its spirit-writing activities, he formed Zi Ji Ge (紫济閣). The name Zi Ji Ge, which combines the characters symbolizing the two main groups of De Jiao, was given by He Xian-Gu, one of the Eight Immortals, during a *fu ji* séance organized in 1964 at Li Shan Ge of Sungai Petani. In the 1970s, Zi Ji Ge was the leader of a splinter group favourable to the continuation of *fu ji* within Zan Hua.

14 As was the case for Zi Ji Ge and the two Zhen associations incorporated in 1981.

15 Ji Yang Ge was established jointly by Zan Hua Ge and the Ji group. However, after few years of close partnership with Bukit Mertajam, their opinions diverged and it then rallied the Ji group. This association and Zi Yang Ge are closely related, not only because Alor Setar and Kangar are nearby, but also because Ji Yang Ge participated in the establishment of Zi Yang Ge and for several years provided logistical assistance for the training of its mediums. The two associations also co-operated to develop De Jiao in the south of Thailand.

16 During the *De Lian* era, the associations of the "first" and "second" nine held the office 25 times (from 1958 to 1975 and from 1981 to 1987). The rotation order reproduced strictly the chronology of their establishment. Zi Xin Ge of Singapore (number 1) held office the first time (1958), Zi Chiang Ge (number 2) assumed power the second time (1959), and so on. The only period when that pattern did not work was between 1976 and 1980. During this interval, newly integrated Zi pavilions assumed the function in an untidy turn. Concerning the associations of other groups chosen for the chairmanship, let us mention in 1990 the Selangor state pool that incorporated a Ji association; in the following year the Perak state pool was headed by Ji De Ge. In 2003, for the first time, a pool consisting only of Zhen associations of Perak state held office.

17 The organization employed a staff of 700 in 2003. An important proportion of the donations it gathered comes from nationwide advertising campaigns and from charity galas.

18 The full name of this temple was *Feng Cheng Tai He Guan Hua Xian Miao* (鳳城太和觀華仙廟 – "Taoist Temple of the Fengcheng Supreme Peace and Buddhist Temple of the Immortal Hua [Tuo]"). Although the shrine was

partly destroyed during the Cultural Revolution, it was rebuilt and it restarted its activities in 1986.

19 It also provided bursary for needy students, funding for poor families, and free funeral rites services.

20 This pavilion was founded in 1981 by a former committee member of Zi Xin Ge. As mentioned by Tan Chee-Beng (1985: 58), the legitimacy for its establishment can be traced to the planchette revelations of Ji Gong in Zi Jing Ge and Zi He Ge (Hong Kong), and Ji Fang Ge (Singapore).

21 Zi Xin Ge, though not very dynamic at the time, was offended by the fact that its status of being the oldest De Jiao association in the Malay Peninsula, defining it as *primus inter pares*, had been flouted by the choice of Ji Yun Ge.

22 Usually, this kind of distribution goes with Chinese calendar festivals (Spring Festival, *Pu Du*) or with the birthday celebrations of the associations. Ji Yang Ge of Alor Setar is exceptional by organizing its main yearly distribution of food at the occasion of Sultan Day. It thus expresses its gratitude to the sultan of Kedah for the gift he made of the plot of land where the temple was built. On that day it distributes rice and other essential commodities to more than 600 old people. Red envelopes containing small amounts of money are also distributed in the orphanages and old people's homes in Alor Setar. In some cases the distribution occurs on a more regular basis. For instance, since its very beginning Zi Ping Ge of Taiping uses to give bags of husked rice with milk and sugar to an average number of 200 poor people who present themselves at the gate of the temple on the first day of each lunar month.

23 More than 20 Zi, Ji or Zhan Hua pavilions were offering that service in Malaysia at the time of the study. The doctors were either remunerated or volunteers. They were giving free surgeries from one to seven days a week depending on local conditions. For example, Li Shan Ge manages a clinic which treats about 250 patients a week. Its medical staff includes four doctors who work here as volunteers. Two of them are specialists in Chinese medicine, while the other two can prescribe western treatments. The clinic is opened four days a week.

Chapter IV

1 These systemic aspects can be phrased as follows: "I transmit through experience what I like to who I like, who, in turn, adopts it because of empathy with those he likes, all the more that their shared experience proved to be effective in social situations."

2 Here we should recall with K. Schipper (1982: 36) that the offering of joss-stick is not only an act of opening a communication link with the gods by showing formal deference. It is, first and foremost, the main aspect of the Chinese ritual. If the presence of images of the deities is of secondary importance, an incense burner devoted to their cult is nevertheless essential. The same author adds that the incense burner is a major emblem of the social unity of the cult community.

3 San Shan Guo-Wang (the "sovereigns of the Three Mountains Country") is a cluster of three spirits (*shen* – 神) issued from warriors who were deified under the Ming. Their cult, as gods of the territory, is very popular in the Jieyang County, the eastern part of Chao-Shan as well as in the Huizhou and Jiayingzhou prefectures.

4 The members of Ji Cheng Ge (Taiping) and of Ji Yang Ge (Alor Setar) do not observe this custom, placing both palms together instead.

Chapter V

1 Such was the case of Mr. Tan, a truck driver, who was 50 years old at the time of the study. For years, he attended the spirit-writing séances of Zi Xiao Ge (Ipoh). Although he faithfully believed in the efficacy of *fu ji*, he was unwilling to become a "messenger" himself. However, in 1983 a planchette instructed him to accept the charge. Because of his reluctance, he was unable to find rest for several nights; he thus finally accepted the assignment. The first time he held the willow stick, he wrote divine sentences continuously for more than an hour, depleting the energies of a more experienced medium who was assisting him at the time. As another example, we can mention the experience of Zhen Yi-Shuan, a former famous medium of Zi Yi Ge, the association of Roeit (Thailand). He became a *ji*-wielder after promising the gods that he would become one if they would restore to health a cousin, who was afflicted with cancer.

2 For example, a medium of a De Jiao congregation in Penang state informed me in 2003 that he regularly receives dreamlike visions from Ji Gong. A few weeks before the interview, the "crazy monk" had asked him to find the best way to cross a deep-water lake.

3 Representatives of a sectarian group from Taiwan named Chong Xin Tang (崇心堂 – "The Hall of the Sublime Heart") were displaying this technique at the occasion of the sixth World Meeting of De Jiao. They considered it to be faster than other forms of spirit-writing, with a possible delivery of over 200 characters a minute. According to them, on the hundreds of religious associations doing *fu ji* in Taiwan, only ten were performing *jin zhi miao fa fu luan* in the early 2000s. Zi He Ge, one of the three De Jiao associations of Hong Kong, learned a variation of it from a Confucian organization headquartered in Taipei, and uses it regularly in addition to *wen ji*. This variation, called *chai bi fei luan* ("send calligraphy by a flying *luan*-bird as messenger") consists of the writing of messages with a brush on white or yellow paper by a medium sitting at a table in front of the altar. The medium may heal patients by applying on the afflicted part of their bodies the handle of his brush, and by drawing characters in the air or on fruits that they can then eat.

4 In the same book (1980: 119), Bourdieu defines the *habitus* as a "system of dispositions, acquired through implicit or explicit learning, that works as a

system of generating schemas, and actually generates strategies which can be objectively in accordance with the objective concerns of the agents without having been expressly devised to this end".

5 In the first chapter, I briefly mentioned the story of this figure. In 2002 a *fu ji* message issued at Zi Zhen Ge had already identified him as an embodiment of Ji Gong. Two years later, at the occasion of the sixth World Moral Meeting, Ji Gong is said to have sent a similar oracle and to have given more details about the mission he assigned to him. The oracle was: "Ji Gong is LD and LD is Ji Gong, Master and disciple share the same way of thinking to relieve society. Ji Gong teaches very good precepts (hen jiao – 很教). In order to promote his doctrine, Ji Gong needs LD. Since LD is Ji Gong, the task is easy and will be achieved successfully. To rely on the organization of LD to spread this doctrine will make its propagation easier. Should LD accept the mission to spread it?"

6 Concerning the case where a stranger is selected to be the head of an association in decline, we should mention the case of LLH, a rich Teochew businessman of Ipoh (Perak) who was born in Chaozhou in 1939 and immigrated to Malaysia in 1957. In 2000, he was already known as a capable businessman but not as a De Jiao adept when he was chosen to become the president of Zi Xiao Ge by Li Tai-Bai, the famous poet of the Tang Dynasty.

7 Extracted from the Old Testament is the Book of the Genesis; from the New Testament are: the Gospel of Saint Matthew (chapters 1–6, 13, 18, 20); the Gospel of Saint Mark (chapters 14–16); the Gospel of Saint John (chapters 1, 10, 14–15); the Epistles of Saint Paul to the Romans (1, 2, 11, 13); to the Corinthians 1 (chapter 13); Corinthians 2 (chapters 8–9); to the Ephesians (chapters 4–5); Second to Timothy (chapter 3); Final Chaos (chapter 4); to the Hebrews (chapters 1, 2, 11); Epistle of Saint James (chapters 1–2); First Epistle of Saint Peter (chapter 3); Second Epistle of Saint Peter (chapter 1); First Epistle of Saint John (chapter 3); Apocalypse (chapter 1). Extracted from the Koran are the Suras 1, 5, 7, 9, 11, 14, 16, 18, 23, 25, 28–30, 32, 34, 39, 40, 43, 47–48, 55–57, 59, 62–64, 69–70, 76, 78, 81–83, 87, 92–95, 99, 97, 100–104, 110, 111, 113, 114.

8 Although oneiric messages may represent an alternate gods-to-men channel, they interest a small group of "elected" ones — mostly mediums — and usually lack this public acknowledgement which is the condition for oracles to become authoritative. Dreams may be sometimes interpreted as calls for mediumship, but a divine appointment promulgated at the occasion of a spirit-writing session is required to initiate a career as a medium in the De Jiao case.

Chapter VI

1 *De Jiao Xun Yuan Zhong Xin Wei Yuan Hui Chu Ban*, 德教尋源中心委員會出版.

2 Born in 1917 in the Teochew county of Chao'an, LYB migrated to the insular part of Malaysia in 1936. According to one of his hagiographies published in the daily *Yang Guan Xi* (5 September 2001), between 1936 and 1941 he managed to save enough money to buy a grocery store. His business was starting to flourish when war began. Taken prisoner by the Japanese, he escaped and took refuge in the Borneo jungle where he is said to have survived for years by living as a "primitive" (*orang asli*). After the war, he opened a shop selling various goods. In the early 1950s, LYB extended his business interests by becoming a timber contractor for a British company. He then bought a forest concession and managed a saw mill. His enterprises thrived so well that he founded a shipping company conveying timber to Japan, South Korea, Taiwan, and Australia. In the 1960s he was earning a considerable amount of income from his sawmill and wood shipping business, and other businessmen started calling him the "king of timber". At that time, he acquired control of the British company and became the "king of cocoa beans" by converting thousands of hectares of land in Sabah into cocoa plantations, the output of which he exported worldwide. He also started rubber plantations. In the 1970s and 1980s, he expanded his business empire throughout Southeast Asia. In the early 2000s his range of activities included logging, shipping, crop plantations (cocoa bean, rubber, oil palm), car dealerships, real estate, steel manufacture, and even Chinese theatre. He owned thousands of hectares of deep forest, a fleet of 2,000 vehicles, and employed more than 10,000 persons. Like the other prominent tycoons of Southeast Asia, he is actively involved in charitable works, thus converting a minor part of his huge fortune into prestige. In the early 1980s he was appointed chairman of the Teochew Permanent Committee for Malaysia. He was also chosen to manage Malaysia's Teochew pension funds, and used part of these funds to modernize firms in Chaozhou in the 1990s. LYB was certainly at that time the leader of the whole Teochew community of Malaysia. Accordingly, he headed national delegations of Teochew when they visited several countries in the region (Thailand, Hong Kong, Singapore); he also organized the third Teochew International Convention which took place in Kuala Lumpur in 1985.

SZM became in the 1980s a leading manufacturer in Thailand of pipes and valves to be used in waterworks. In the early 2000s he owned several companies in this sector, including Siam Cast Iron Works Co. Ltd., Siam Syndicate Trading Co. Ltd., Siam Steel Works Co. Ltd., and Siam Navaco Co. Ltd. He acted also as a major concrete contractor through companies such as Thai Universal Engineering Co. Ltd. and Thai Engineering and Construction Co. Ltd.; he also owns a holding company. At the time he employed more than one thousand personnel.

3 Most of them were wealthy businessmen. Such was, for instance, the case of ZJB, the president of the pavilion of Batu Pahat, who had built a great fortune in real-estate and rubber plantations. CWB was also a capable entrepreneur who owned important oil-palm tree and rubber plantations in Sabah. ZLX was a lawyer who could advise the committee in case controversial questions

arose. In 2000, the membership roster was again enlarged, this time to accommodate 18 members. The participation of Zi Zhen Ge was then strengthened with two additional members, and a representative of the new pavilions founded in China was incorporated.

4 Also very significant was the invitation to the opening ceremony of the president of Zi Ji Ge, an association which occupies an intermediate position between the Zi and Ji groups.

5 Zi Guang Ge was established near the industrial estate of Guangzhou in 2003. Its president, LZQ, a blue-collar employee in a smelting works, and his two assistants were introduced to De Jiao by XHR, the abovementioned zealous preacher from Zi Yu Ge. Their conversion was certainly made easier by the fact that LQZ, his two comrades, and XHR all originated from Jieyang. The order of Ji Gong and the incense powder to found Zi Guang Ge came from another association in Guangzhou, Zi Ying Ge, wherein XHR is an active member. Only forty De Jiao members attended the opening ceremony because of the SARS epidemic which was raging at the time. Before the inauguration, a miraculous event occurred however. The whole set of statues except that of Lü Dong-Bin had been melted down in Chaozhou. The Lü Zu icon made in Malaysia was initially intended for Zi Xuan Ge of Chaozhou, but this association had ordered a locally made statue, so that the imported item was given to Zi Ying Ge, which, in turn, offered it to Zi Guang Ge. The day when this statue was set on the altar, a torrential rain suddenly came pouring down together with impressive thunderbolts. Thunderbolts and rains also marked the opening day, together with a power cut at the very moment when the mediums opened the eyes of the statue of Lü Dong-Bin. These events were interpreted as manifestations of the divine wish to purify this place, which is heavily polluted due to industrial activities.

6 In the United States, two pavilions have been founded: Zi Gen Ge in San Francisco, where Teochew are numerous; and Zi Jin Ge in Alhambra, California. According to Tan Chee-Beng (1985: 17, 20), the association in San Francisco was founded by a businessman after a revelation coming from Hong Kong. It was however inactive in the early 1980s. In Australia, the first De Jiao association, Zi Yang Ge, was inaugurated in 1996 in Canberra. It was followed in 2001 by the opening in Sydney of Zi Chen Ge, and by Zi Cheng Ge in Melbourne. In 2004, a new pavilion was set to be established in Perth.

7 Such as those by D. Miller and D. Slater (2000), and by K. Landzelius and Al. (2006).

8 B. Anderson (1998: 29–33) opposes two series of serialities: a *bound* one which has its origin in governmentality, and in institutions such as polls and census; and a *unbound* one which originates in the market of printed books and newspapers. The latter is the carrier *par excellence* of an unconscious standardization "which radically overrides any formal division in the newspaper between local and foreign news".

GLOSSARY

Note: Teo = Teochew pronunciation

A-Mi-Tuo Fo. Teo: *A-Ni-To Huk*; Amithabha – 阿彌陀佛
Ba gua. Teo: *Poi guê*; *Yi Jing* divination system – 八卦
Ba Xian. Teo: *Poi Xian*; The Eight Immortals – 八仙
ba zi. Teo: *poi ze*; the eight characters of birth – 八字
bai shi. Teo: *bê se*; "white affairs" – rituals related to death – 白事
Bai Yun. Teo: *Bê Yun*; "White Cloud", a Taoist master – 白雲
Bao De Shan Tang. Teo: *Po Tek Xiang Teng*; the oldest benevolent hall in Chaozhou – 報德善堂
Bao Ling An. Teo: *Po Lêng Am*; a temple in Heping – 保灵庵
bao yu. Teo: *po yu*; "those who report instructions" – 报諭
bi ji. Teo: *bik ki*; one of the willow sticks when two stacked branches are used – 笔乩
Bu Kong. Teo: *Bug Kong*; Amoghavajra – 不空
Cai Shen. Teo: *Cai Sing*; Kuvera – 财鉮
cha bi fei luan. Teo: *ca bik hui luang*; a technique of spirit-writing – 差笔飞鸾
Chao'an. A county of the Chaozhou municipality, Chao-Shan – 潮安
Chaonan. A district of the Shantou SEZ – 潮南
Chao-Shan. An appellation for the Teochew area – 潮汕
Chaoyang. A district of the Shantou SEZ – 潮陽
Chaozhou. A municipality of Chao-Shan – 潮州
Chenghai. A district of the Shantou SEZ – 澄海
Chen Li-Jiang. Teo: *Tan Li Kiang*; one of the earliest adepts of De Jiao – 陳立健
Cong De Shan Tang. Teo: *Cong Tek Xiang Teng*; a benevolent hall in Da Hao – 从德善堂
Da Mo. Teo: *Tak Mo*; a Famous monk of Shaolin – 達摩
Da Wu Shan Tang. Teo: *Tai Ngou Xiang Teng*; a syndicate of the five biggest benevolent halls of Bangkok – 大五善堂

Da Xue. Teo: *Dua Hak*; Confucian treatise of the Great Learning – 大学
dang. Teo: *deng*; "fair" – value – 当
dao de. Teo: *dao tek*; "the way and its virtue" – 道德
Dao De Jing. Teo: *Dao Tek Gêng*; "The Book of the way and its virtue" – 道德经
Dao De-She. Teo: *Dao Tek-Sia*; a Chinese sectarian movement – 道德社
Dao Ji. Teo: *Dao chi*; another name for Ji Gong – 道济
De De Ci Shan She. Teo: *Tek Tek Ce Xiang Zi*; Benevolent society of the great loving Virtue – 德德慈善社
de de she. Teo: *tek tek zi*; the gods' society – 德德社
De Dian. Teo: *Tek Diang*; "Book of virtue", part of the Zan Hua "bible" – 德典
De Dian Hou Dian. Teo: *Tek Diang Hou Diang*; see *Hou Dian*
De Dian Qian Dian. Teo; *Tek Diang Zong Diang*; see *Qian Dian*
de Hao. Teo: *tek ho*; "name of virtue" – adept's name – 德号
De Jiao. Teo: *Tek Ka* – 德教
De Jiao Lian Yi hui. Teo: *Tek Ka Liang Ngi Hue*; FOMUS – Federation of Moral Uplifting Societies – 德教聯誼會
De Jiao Xin Dian. Teo: *Tek Ka Sim Diang*; Canon of De Jiao – 德教心典
De Jiao Xin Tiao. Teo: *Tek Ka Sing Tiao*; The seven tenets of De Jiao – 德教信條
De Jiao Yi Shi. Teo: *Tek Ka I Sek*; "Consciousness of De Jiao" – *fu ji* text – 德教意識
De Jiao zhu liu. Teo: *Tek Ka zu uang*; the "mainstream of De Jiao" 德教主流
De Lian. Teo: *Tek Liang*; abbreviation for the Society of De Jiao associations of Malaya founded in 1959 – 德聯
de sheng. Teo: *tek sên*; "students of virtue" – adepts – 德生
de xiong. Teo: *tek hian*; "elder brothers in virtue" – adepts – 德兄
De Xun. Teo: *Tek Sing*; Bulletins published separately by the national federations of Malaysia and Thailand – 德讯
de you. Teo: *tek iu*; "friend of virtue" – adepts – 德友
dian. Teo: *doin*; "higher deities" – 殿
di de. Teo: *di tek*; "the Jade Emperor virtue" – 帝德
Di Mu Niang-Niang. Teo: *Di bho Niang-Niang*; "Earth Mother" – 地母娘娘
Di Zang-Wang. Teo: *Di Zang-Uang*; Lord of the Kingdom of the Dead – 地藏皇
Dong Kai Yuan. Teo: *Tung Cheng Yuen*; a Buddist association of Hong Kong – 東开圓
feng. Teo: *hong*; phoenix – 凤

fei luan. Teo: *bue luang*; "flying *luan*-bird" – 飞鸾
feng shui. Teo: *huang zui*; Chinese geomancy – 风水
fu. Teo: *hu*; written charm – 符
fu ji zhang. Teo: *hu ki shio*; "assistant palm of the *ji*" – 副乩掌
fu ji. Teo: *hu ki*; planchette divination – 扶乩
fu luan. Teo: *hu luang*; "to hold with *luan*-bird", another phrase for the planchette divination – 扶鸾
Fu You Da-Di. Teo: *Hu Lu Dua-Di*; another name for Lü Dong-Bin – 孚佑大帝
ge. Teo: *kor*; "pavilion" – 閣
gong. Teo: *gêng*; "palace" – 宫
gong de. Teo: *kong tek*; "acquisition of merit" ritual – 功德
Guan Di Ye. Teo: *Guang Di Ia*; another name for Guan Yu – 關帝爺
Guan Sheng Di-Jun. Teo: *Guang Sêng Di-Gung*; another name for Guan Yu – 關聖帝君
Guan Ping Shao-Di. *Guang Pêng Zio-Di*; the main assistant of the Jade Emperor – 關平少帝
Guan Yin. Teo: *Guang Im*; Avalokiteçvara, the Buddhist goddess of mercy – 槻音
Guan Yin Fa Men. "Way of the Goddess of Mercy" a Chinese sectarian movement – 槻音法门
Guan Yu. Teo: *Guang U*; a deified warrior of the Three Kingdoms – 關羽
Han Xiang-Zi. Teo: *Hang Siang Ze*; one of the Eight Immortals – 韓湘子
Heping. name of the township where De Jiao was created in China – 和平
he shi. Teo: *hah zap*; Chinese way to worship – 合十
He Ye-Yun. Teo: *Ho Hia-Yun*; a Taoist geomancer who lived in Chao-Shan – 何野雲
He Xian-Gu. Teo: *Ho Sian-Gou*; One of the Eight Immortals – 何仙姑
hong shi. Teo: *hang se*; "red affairs" – rituals related to life – 红事
Hong Wan Zi Hui. Teo: *Hang Huan Ze Hue*; World Red Swastika Society – 紅卍字會
Hou Dian. Teo: *Hou Diang*; "Later Canon" of the Zan Hua's "Bible" – 后典
Hua Qiao. Teo: *Hua Kiao*; Overseas Chinese – 华侨
Hua Tuo. Teo: *Hua To*; famous physician of the Three Kingdoms – 华陀
hui. Teo: *hue*; association – 會
Huilai. A county of the Jieyang municipality, Chao-Shan – 惠来
Ji Gong Huo-Fo. Teo: *Chi Kong Uah-Huk*; the Crazy Monk – 濟公活佛
ji ran. Teo: *sok riang*; "silent" level of concentration – 寂然
ji shou. Teo: *ki shio*; "hand of the *ji*" – medium – 乩手

Ji Tan. Teo: *Jip Tua*; a line of charitable congregations – 集壇
ji tong. Teo: *ki tong*; "children of the *ji*" – students of *fu ji* – 乩童
ji wen. Teo: *ki bhung*; "spirit-writing" – 乩文
Ji Xi. Teo: *Chi Hi*; a denominational group inside De Jiao – 済系
Ji Xi Ren. Teo: *Chi Hing Ren*; Ji group Fraternity – 済系仁
ji yu. Teo: *ki yu*; "those who write instructions" – 記諭
jian ren. Teo: *giang ring*; tolerance – 坚韧
Jiao Pai. Teo: *Ka Pai*; a sect – 教派
jie bai xiong di. Teo: *gak bai hian di*; "a *fide jure* relation uniting brothers in virtue worshipping Buddha" – 结拜兄弟
jie gui. Teo: *kiak gui*; "Confucius' self-rule" – 诘规
jie yuan. Teo: *gak uang*; "nodes of affinity" – a metaphor for the creation of new congregations – 结缘
jin zhi miao fa fu luan. Teo: *gim zi miao huak hu luang*; a spirit-writing technique spread in Taiwan – 金指妙法扶鸞
Jing Wen. Teo: *Gêng Bhung*; De Jiao Scripture – 經文
jiu er. Teo: *gao no*; "second nine" – 九二
Jiu Huang-Ye. Teo: *Gao Wong-Yê*; Nine Gods Emperors – 九皇爷
jiu ji. Teo: *ziu ki*; "the *ji* of the alcohol" – 酒乩
jiu yi. Teo: *gao zek*; "first nine" – 九一
Ji Yang Ge. Teo: *Chi Iang Khor*; a prominent Malaysian pavilion located in Alor Setar – 濟陽阁
ju ren. Teo: *ge nang* or *ge ring*; mandarinic grade; 举人
kai guang. Teo: *kui guang*; "open to light" – ritual to open the eyes of statues" – 開光
Kai Yuan. Teo: *Kai Nguang*; a famous Buddhist temple in Chaozhou – 开元
kan qing. Teo: *kam kuang* or *toin kuang*; quality of the relationship between two parties – 看傾
kong xu. Teo: *kong he*; "empty void" – level of concentration – 空虚
ling. Teo: *lêng*; the soul – 灵
Ling Yin Si. Teo: *Lêng Eng Ri*; a prominent temple worshipping Ji Gong in Singapore – 灵隐寺
Li Shi-Zhen. Teo: *Li Si-Diang*; famous physician of the Ming Dynasty – 李時珍
Liu Chun-Fang. Teo: *Liu Chun-Wong*; one of the Taoist masters worshipped by De Jiao – 柳春芳
liu ji. Teo: *liu ki*; one of the willow sticks when two are used together – 柳乩
liu ji mu. Teo: *liu ki bak*; "willow *ji*" – 柳乩木
liu ren. Teo: *lak rim*; one of the three divinatory magics – 六壬

liu zhi. Teo: *liu gi*; willow branch – 柳枝
long tou ge. Teo: *lêng tao khor*; dragon-head pavilion – 龙头阁
luan bi. Teo: *luang bik*; "*luan*-bird's pencil" – 鸾笔
luan tai. Teo: *luang tai*; "*luan*-bird's terrace" – altar – 鸾台
luan tan. Teo: *luang tua;* "*luan*-bird's chapel" – 鸾墰
luan tang. Teo: *luang teng*; "*luan*-bird's hall" – 鸾堂
luan wen. Teo: *luang bhung*; "*luan*-bird's writing" – 鸾文
luan xiang feng zhu. Teo: *luang siang wong zu*; litt. "*luan*-bird – circle in the air – wind to fly" – a metaphor for the medium endowed with *fu ji* – 鸾翔风翥
luan yu. Teo: *luang ru*; "*luan*-bird's command" – 鸾谕
luan zhang. Teo: *luang ziang*; "*luan*-bird's chapter" – 鸾章
Lun Yu. Teo: *Lung Ghe*; Analects of Confucius – 论语
Lü Chun-Yang. Teo: *Le Sung-Iang*; another name for Lü Dong-Bin – 呂蒓陽
Lü Dong-Bin. Teo: *Le Dang-Bing*; a Taoist Immortal – 呂洞賓
Lü Zu. Teo: *Le Zou*; an honourable address to Lü Dong Bin – 呂祖
Ma Gui-De. Teo: *Be Kuai-Tek*, the main founder of De Jiao – 馬貴德
Ma Han-Ru. Teo: *Be Hang-Ru*; birth name of Ma Gui-De – 馬翰如
Ma Lai Xi Ya De Jiao Lian He Zong Hui. Teo: *Ma Lai Xi Ya Tek Ka Liang Hah Zong Hue*; United Moral Uplifting Society of Malaysia – UMUSOM – 馬来西亞德教聯合總會
Ma Shi-Ying. Teo: *Be Se-Eng*; one of the founders of the Ji group in Malaysia – 馬士英
miao. Temple – 廟
Ma Mian – Niu Tou. Teo: *Pê Ming Ku Tao*; buffalo and horse headed gods – 馬面牛頭
Ma Zu. Teo: *Ma Zou*; Goddess of Heaven and the Sea – 媽祖
Mi-Le Fo. Teo: *Ni-Lêk Huk*; Maitreya – 彌勒佛
ming shi. Teo: *mêng se*; a mandarinic contest – 名士
Ming Tan. Teo: *Ming Tua*; a line of charitable congregations – 明墰
mi xin. Teo: *mi sing*; superstitions – 迷信
mo jie. Teo: *muak giab*; final chaos – 末劫
Nan Yang. Teo: *Nam Iang*; Southern Seas' countries – 南洋
Nan Zong. Teo: *Nam Zong*; Nanyang Moral Uplifting General Society – 南總
nian fo she. Teo: *niam huk sia*; society for the recitation of sutras – 念佛社
Peng Lai. Teo: *Pong Lai*; a line of charitable congregations – 蓬萊
Pi Dou. Teo: *Poi Dao*; séances of public criticism – 批斗
Po Si Jiu. Teo: *Pua Si Gu*; a Communist campaign to "break the four kinds of archaism" – 破四旧

Pu Du. Teo: *Pou Dou*; Universal Salvation Festival – 普度
Puning. Teo: Pouleng; a township of Chao-Shan – 普宁
pu tong hua. Teo: *pou tong uê*; Mandarin language – 普通話
Pu Xian. Teo: *Pu Siang*; Samantabhadra – 菩賢
qi. Teo: *ki*; vital energy – 气
Qi Dao Shang Cang. Teo: *Ki Dao Zion Cang*; one of the founding *fu ji* texts of Zan Hua – 祈祷上苍
qi gong. Teo: *ki gong*; gymnastics based on the control of *qi* – 氣功
Qi Zan. Teo: *Ki Zian*; Eulogy and Invocation – Canon of De Jiao – 起讚
Qian Dian. Teo: *Zoin Diang*; Earlier Canon of the Zan Hua "Bible" – 前典
qing niao zhi shu. Teo: *cen ziao ze suk*; a type of divination – 青鸟之术
qing zhang. Teo: *ceng zion*; "clear hand's palm" – celestial hand doing *fu ji* – 清掌
Qiu Ming-Qi. Teo: *Kiu Meng-Gi*; one of the founders of the Ji group in Malaysia – 邱鸣岐
ren ji. Teo: *nang ki*; human planchette – 人乩
ren shi wen ti. Teo; *nang se mung doi*; human affairs – 人事問题
ren yi. Teo: *nang i*; "human intention" – 人意
ru ding. Teo: *rip dian*; "to enter into calm" – level of concentration – 入定
Ru-Lai Fo. Teo: *Ru-Lai Huk*; Buddhas of the past generations – 如来佛
San bao. Teo: *Sam bo*; the "Three treasures" of Yi Guan-Dao – 三宝
San cai. Teo: *Sam cai*; "three abilities", an allegory for the fundamental combination of Heaven, Earth and Man – 三才
san jiao. Teo: *sam ka*; "three teachings" – 三教教
san qi mo jie. Teo: *sam ki muak giab*; final chaos – 三期末劫
San Qing. Teo: *Sam Zion*; the Three Perfects – 三清
San Shan Guo-Wang. Teo: *Sam Sua Gok-Uang*; a Teochew god of the territory – 三山国王
San wei yi ti. Teo: *Sam ui zeg* ti; the Zan Holy Trinity – 三位一体
san yi jiao. Teo: *sam zek ka*; doctrine of the "three into one" – 三一教
sha luan. Teo: *sua luang*; "*luan*-bird sand" – wooden platter – 沙鸾
shan liang. Teo: x*iang liang*; goodness and honesty – 善良
shan she. Teo: *xiang zi*; benevolent societies – 善社
shan shu. Teo: *xiang ze*; benevolent books – 善书
shan tan. Teo: *xiang tua*; benevolent altar – 善壇
shan tang. Teo: *xiang teng*; benevolent hall – 善堂
Shantou. Teo: *Suantao*, better known as Swatow; the main city of Chao-Shan – 汕头
shen ji. Teo: *sing ki*; divine planchette – 神乩
shen ling. Teo; *sing lêng*; the gods' soul – 神灵

shen sheng. Teo: *sing sian*; sacredness – 神圣
Sheng Dian. Teo: *Sian Diang*; holy canon – 圣典
sheng jing. Teo: *sian gên*; bible – 圣经
Shi Ba Luo Han. Teo: *Sap Poi Lo Hang*; The Eighteen Arahants – 十八羅漢
shi zun. Teo: *sai zung*; "honourable masters" gods – 師尊
shi yu. Teo: *si ru*; "instruction of imperial edicts" – 示谕
Shi Jue Shan Tang. Teo: *Si Gak Xiang Teng*; another name for Zi Wei Ge, Bangkok – 泰国世觉善堂
Shi Zhang Ba Ze. Teo: *Sap Zion Poi Zek*; "10 rules, 8 regulations" – 十章八則
Shou Jing Wen. Teo: *Siu Gêng Bhung*; Closing Prayer – 收經文
shu li. Teo: *siao li*; numbers' principle – 數理
si. Teo: *ri*; classifier for Buddhist pagoda – 寺
Si jun zi. Teo: *Si gung ze*; The "Four nobles ones" – 四君子
si shu. Teo: *se gêk;* private school – 私塾
Song Da-Feng. Teo: *Tai Hong-Kong*; a Teochew bodhisattva – 宋大峰
Song Chan. Teo: *Song Chao-Yue*; a Taoist master – 宋僤
Sun Si-Miao. Teo: *Sung Se-Miao*; the famous physician of the 3rd Century A.C. – 孫思邈
Sun Wu-Kong. Teo: *Sung Ngo-Kong*; the monkey, hero of the *Journey to the West* – 孫梧空
Tai He Guan. Teo: *Tai Hua Kuan*; an important charitable organization of Singapore affiliated to De Jiao – 太和观
tai ji. Teo: *tai cip*; Taoist symbol, Ultimate absolute – 太極
tai ji quan. Teo: *tai cip kung*; Chinese martial art – 太極拳
Tang Xi-Ru. Teo: *Tang Hi-Ru*; a founder of the Zan Hua group in Malaysia – 唐希如
Thai Guo De Jiao Ci Shan Cong Hui. Teo: *Thai Gok Tek Ka Xiang Cong Hue*; Federation of Moral Uplifting Societies of Thailand – 泰國德教慈善總會
Tian Gan. Teo: *Tiang Gang*; Heavenly Stems – 天干
Tian Ji Lao-Mu. Teo: *Tiang Cip Lao-Bho*; "Ancient Mother of the limitless Heaven". The Supreme being the Yi Guan-Dao sect – 天極老母
tian shou. Teo: *tiang ciu*; heaven's hand – 天手
tian wen ping. Teo: *tiang bhung pêng*; heavenly degree – 天文凭
tian zun. Teo: *tiang zung*; masters of Heaven – 天尊
tong de. Teo: *tong tek*; same virtue – devotees – 同德
Tou Di Gong. Teo: *Tou Di Gong*; Earth God – 土地公
wai tan gong. Teo: *ghua tang gong*; a kind of martial art – 外坍功
wei tiao. Teo: *mui tiao* ; to fine-tune [in *fu ji*] – 微調

Wei Tuo Pu-Sa. Teo: *Ngui To Pu-Sak*; the "Warrior" Bodhisattva – 韋駝菩薩

wen/wu. Scholar/warrior opposition

wen ji. Teo: *bhung ki*; "scholars' *ji*" – 文乩

Wen Ying-Cai. Teo: *Bhung Eng-Cai*; one of the founders of the Ji group in Malaysia – 文英才

Wen Shou. Teo: *Bhung Su*; Manjusri – 文殊

wu dong. Teo: *ngou tou*; five orients – 五東

wu ji. Teo: *bhu ki*; warriors' *ji* – 武乩

Wu Ji Lao-Mu. Teo: *U Cip Lao-Bho*; the Mother of non-birth – 無極老母

wu lun. Teo: *ngou lun*; the Confucian five cardinal relationships – 五伦

Wu Jiao Tong Zong. *Ngou Tek Tong Zong*; doctrine of the five teachings – 五教同宗

Wu Meng-Wu. Teo: *Bho Mang-Hu*; a Taoist master – 吳夢吾

wu pin. Teo: *ngou bing*; the five principles – 五品

Wu Shan She. Teo: *Ngo Xiang Sia*; Society for Enlightenment to Goodness – 悟善社

wu xian. Teo: *ngou hiang*; five offerings – 五献

xian sheng. Teo: *xing sê;* priests – 先生

xiang huo. Teo: *hiang huê*; "incense fire" – ritual – 香火

xiang mu. Teo: *hiang bhak*; scented wood – 香木

xiao. Teo: *hao*; filial piety – 孝

Xie Tian Ge. Teo: *Hiap Tiang Khor*; "Heavenly Pavilion for Mutual aid", a residence of the community of gods – 协天阁

xin fa. Teo: *sim hiang*; law of the heart – 心法

xin ren. Teo: *sing rim*; trust, to have confidence in – 信仟

Xiong Lu-Ceng. Teo: *Seng Lu-Se*; the first medium of De Jiao who operated in Thailand – 兄颅曾

xiu gu gu. Teo: *xiu kou ku*; ritual of refining restless ghosts – 修孤骨

Xuan. Teo: *Hiang*; The Unfathomable – 玄

Xuan Chen Shan Tang. Teo: *Hiang Sing Xian Teng*; "Benevolent Hall of the Abstruse Stars", another name for Zi Zhen Ge, Bangkok – 玄辰善堂

xuan ji. Teo: *hiang ki*; the essence of spirit-writing, serenity to reach while doing *fu ji* – 玄机

xuan jiao. Teo: *suang tek*; temple's secretary – 宣教

Xuan Min Gao Shang Di Yu Huang Da Tian Zun. Teo: *Hiang Ming Gao Zion Di Ghêk Huang Dua Tiang Zung*; the Most High God Jade Emperor, the Heavenly respected one – 玄旻高上帝玉皇大天尊

Xuan Tian Shang-Di. Teo: *Hiang Tiang Zion Di*; Heavenly Supreme God of the Black Sky – 玄天上帝

xu kong. Teo: *suk kong*; the emptiness required to do *fu ji* – 虚空
Xun Luo. Teo: *Sung Lo*; the patrol of Heaven's warriors, a group of subaltern gods – 巡逻
Yang Jun-Song. Teo: *Hia Hun-Song*; a Taoist master – 楊筠松
Yang Liu Xian. Teo: *Iang Liu Soin*; primitive name for the "purple pavilions" – 楊柳先
Yang Rui-De. Teo: *Iang Sui-Tek*; one of the founders of De Jiao – 楊瑞德
Yang Ru-Hou. Teo: *Iang Re-Hou*; one of the founders of De Jiao – 楊汝後
yang zi. Teo: *iang ze*; adoptive son – 养子
Yao-Shi Fo. Teo: *Yao-Se Huk*; Bhaisajyaguru – 藥師佛
Yi Guan-Dao. Teo: *Sek Guan-Dao*; a sectarian movement – 一贯道
Yi Jing. Teo: *Goi Gêng*; Book of Changes – 易经
yin ba zi. Teo: *ing ba ze*; seal of authority – 印把子
yin xia. Teo: *ing hak*; seal which have a jurisdiction over – 印辖
Yingxi Gang. Teo: *Êngsai Gang*; name of the village where the first De Jiao association was created – 英西港
you du sheng ling. Teo: *u dok sian lêng*; to show disrespect toward the spirits – 有渎圣灵
yuan fen. Teo: *uang hung*; fate affinity – 缘份
yuan zi. Teo: *uang ze*; sons of affinity – committee members elected by gods – 缘子
yu nian. Teo: *iok niam*; desire – 欲念
Zan Hua. Teo: *Zang Hue*; a denominational group of De Jiao – 赞化
Zhang Guo-Lao. Teo: *Dion* or *Ziang Guên-Lao*; One of the Eight Immortals – 張果老
Zhang Xuan-Tong. Teo: *Dion* or *Ziang Hiang-Tong*; a Taoist master – 张玄同
Zhen Luan Lian Yi Hui. Teo: *Zing Luan Liang Hi Hue*; Federation of the *Luan*-Bird Zhen – 振鸾聯誼會
Zhen Xi. Teo: *Zing Hi*; a denominational group of De Jiao – 振系
Zhen Zhu. Teo: *Zing Zu*; True lord – 真主
zheng cheng. Teo: *zian sêng*; correct and sincere – 正誠
zheng dang de gui ju. Teo: *zian deng dek gui ge*; right rules – 正当的规矩
zheng ji zhang. Teo: *jia ki shio*; "upright palm of the *ji*" – 正乩掌
Zhi Sheng Xian Tian Lao Shi. Teo: *Zi Sian Soin Tiang Lao Sai*; "Most Sacred Venerable patriarch of Former Heaven", the supreme god of the Dao De She Sect – 只圣先天老师
Zhong Li-Quan. Teo: *Dong Li-Kuang*; one of the Eight Immortals – 鐘离權
zhong shan zi. Teo: *zêng xiang ze*; men of virtue – 众善子
Zhong Yong. Teo: *Dong Iong*; the Doctrine of Mean – 中庸

zhu cai. Teo: *zu cai*; master-in-charge – 主裁

zhu fo xian zun. Teo: *zu huk xian zung*; Buddhas and Immortals – the gods' assembly – 主佛仙尊

zhu tan shi. Teo: *zu tua sai*; "master of the altar" – gods – 主壇师

Zhu Xiang Ci. Teo: *Zok Hiang Se*; "Incense prayer" – section of the Canon of De Jiao – 祝香祠

Zi Chen Ge. Teo: *Chi Sing Khor*, first De Jiao congregation to have been created in Thailand – 紫辰閣

zi de. Teo: *chi tek*; purple virtue – 紫德

Zi Nan Ge. Teo: *Chi Nam Khor*; the De Jiao association of Hat Yai – 紫南閣

Zi Qing Ge. Teo: *Chi Cêng Khor*; second De Jiao congregation to have been created in history – 紫清閣

Zi Xi. Teo: *Chi Hi*; purple, name of a De Jiao group – 紫系

Zi Xin Ge. Teo: *Chi Sen Khor*; the first Purple line association to have been created in Singapore and Malaysia – 紫新阁

Zi Xiang Ge. Teo: *Chi Hiang Khor*; first De Jiao congregation to have been created in history – 紫香閣

Zi Zhen Ge. Teo: *Chi Chin Khor*; the main De jiao congregation of Thailand – 紫真閣

zong jiao. Teo: *zong ka*; religion – 宗教

zun. Teo: *zung*; votive plate – 尊

Zu Shi Sheng Zhou. Teo: *Zou Se Sêng Ziu*; a prayer text praising Song Da-Feng – 祖師聖咒

zu zong de jing yan. Teo: *zu zong dek gêng ngiam*; religion as ancestors' experience – 祖宗的经验

BIBLIOGRAPHY

1. Western Sources

Alexander, Garth. *Silent Invasion, the Chinese in Southeast Asia*. London: Macdonald & Co., 1973.

Anderson, Benedict. *Imagined Communities. Reflections on the Origin and Spread of Nationalism*. London: Verso Books, 1983.

_________. *The Spectre of Comparisons. Nationalism, Southeast Asia and the World*. London: Verso Books, 1998.

Austin, John L. *How to do Things with Words*. Oxford: Clarendon Press, 1962.

Barth, Fredrik. *Balinese Worlds*. Chicago: The University of Chicago Press, 1993.

Bourdieu, Pierre. *Questions de sociologie*. Paris: Eds. De Minuit, 1980.

Castells, Manuel. *The Information Age: Economy, Society and Culture, Vol. 2. The Power of Identity*. Oxford: Basil Blackwell, 2004.

Clart, Philip. "Moral Mediums. Spirit-Writing and the Cultural Construction of Chinese Spirit-Mediumship", *Ethnologies* 25, 1 (2003): 154–89.

_________. "Chinese Tradition and Taiwanese Modernity. Morality Books as Social Commentary and Critique", in *Religion in Modern Taiwan: Traditions and Innovations in a Changing Society*, ed. Philip Clart and Charles B. Jones. Honolulu: University of Hawai'i Press, 2003, pp. 84–97.

Cohen, Abner. *Custom and Politics in Urban Africa*. London: Routledge and Kegan Paul, 1969.

Cresswell, Robert. "Le terrain anthropologique", in *Outils d'enquête et d'analyse anthropologiques*, ed. R. Cresswell and M. Godelier. Paris: Maspero, 1976.

Cushman, Jennifer W. *Family and State. The Formation of a Sino-Thai Tin-Mining Dynasty. 1797–1932*. Singapore: Oxford University Press, 1991.

DeBernardi, Jean. "Teachings of a Spirit Medium", in *Religions in Practice*, ed. D.S. Lopez Jr. Princeton: Princeton University Press, 1996, pp. 229–38.

_________. *Rites of Belonging: Memory, Modernity and Identity in a Malaysian Chinese Community*. Stanford: Stanford University Press, 2004.

_________. *The Way that Lives in the Heart. Chinese Popular Religion and Spirit Mediums in Penang, Malaysia*. Stanford: Stanford University Press, 2006.

De Groot, Jan Jakob Maria. *The religious System of China*. Vol. VI, Book II. Leiden: Brill, 1910.

De Koninck, Rodolphe. *L'Asie du Sud-Est*. Paris: Masson, 1994.

De Witt Twinem, Paul. "Modern Syncretic Religious Societies in China", *The Journal of Religion* 5, 5 (1925): 463–82.

Deleuze, Gilles and Guattari, Felix. *Capitalisme et schizophrénie 2: mille plateaux*. Paris: Eds. de Minuit, 1980.

Despeux, Catherine. *Immortelles de la Chine ancienne. Taoïsme et alchimie féminine*. Puiseaux: Pardès, 1990.

Duara, Prasenjit. "Transnationalism in the Era of Nation-States: China 1900 1945", in *Globalization and Identities*, ed. B. Meyer and P. Geschiere. Oxford: Blackwell Publishers, 2003, pp. 47–70.

Dumont, Louis. *Homo Hierarchicus*. Paris: Gallimard, "Bibliothèque des sciences humaines", 1966.

Ebrey, Patricia. "The liturgies for Sacrifices to Ancestors in Successive Versions of the family Rituals", in *Ritual Scripture in Chinese Popular Religion. Five Studies*, ed. D. Johnson. Berkeley: University of California, 1995, pp. 104–36.

Elliott, A.J.A. *Chinese Spirit-Mediums Cults in Singapore*. London: Department of Anthropology, The London School of Economics and Political Science, 1955.

Feuchtwang, Stephan. *The Imperial Metaphor. Popular Religion in China*. London and New York: Routledge, 1992.

Formoso, Bernard. "*Hsiu-Kou-Ku*: The ritual refining of restless ghosts among the Chinese of Thailand", *Journal of the Royal Anthropological Institute* 2, 2 (1996a): 217–34.

_________. "Chinese Temples and Philanthropic Associations in Thailand", *Journal of Southeast Asian Studies* 27, 2 (1996b): 245–60.

_________. *Identités en regard. Destins chinois en milieu bouddhiste thai*. Paris: Eds. de la Maison des Sciences de l'Homme/CNRS, 2000a.

_________. *Thaïlande, Bouddhisme renonçant, capitalisme triomphant*. Paris: La Documentation Française, 2000b.

_________. "Marchands et philanthropes. Les associations de bienfaisance chinoises en Thaïlande", *Annales HSS* 58, 4 (2003a): 833–56.

_________. "Les adeptes de Ji Gong, 'le bonze fou' en Malaisie et à Singapour", *Aséanie*, no. 12 (2003b): 73–104.

_________. "The Rise of a Chinese Cult in Thailand: He Yeyun and the Pong Lai Temples", Singapore, *Chinese Heritage Centre Bulletin*, no. 3 (2004): 30–2.

Freedman, Maurice. *Chinese Lineage and Society: Fukien and Kwangtung*. New York: The Athlone Press, 1971. 1st ed. 1966.

_________. "On the Sociological Study of Chinese Religion", in *Religion and Ritual in Chinese Society*, ed. A.P. Wolf. Stanford, Stanford University Press, 1974, pp. 19–42.

Girling, John, L.S. *Thailand, Society and Politics*. Ithaca: Cornell University Press, 1985.

Glazer, Nathan and Daniel P. Moynihan, eds. *Ethnicity, Theory and Experience*. Cambridge. Mass.: Harvard University Press, 1975.

Goffman, Erving. *The Presentation of Self in Everyday Life*. London, Allen Lane: Penguin Press, 1971.

Granet, Marcel. *La pensée chinoise*. Paris: Eds. Albin Michel, 1988 [1st ed. 1934].

Hall, Douglas G.E. *A History of Southeast Asia*. London: Macmillan, 1986. 1st ed. 1955.

Hargett, James M. "Playing second Fiddle: The *Luan*-Bird in early and Medieval Chinese Litterature", *T'oung Pao* 75 (1989): 235–62.

Heusch, Luc de. "L'ethnie: les vicissitudes d'un concept", *Archives européennes de sociologie* 28, 2 (1997): 185–206.

Johnson, David. "Introduction", in *Ritual and Scripture in Chinese Popular Religion. Five Studies*, ed. D. Johnson. Berkeley: University of California. Publications of the Chinese Popular Cultural Project 3, 1995, pp. vii–xv.

Johnson, David, Nathan, Andrew J. and Rawski, Evelyn S. "Preface", in *Popular Culture in Late Imperial China*, ed. D. Johnson, A.J. Nathan and E. Rawski. Berkeley, Los Angeles, London: University of California Press, 1985, pp. ix–xvii.

Jordan, David K. *Gods, Ghosts & Ancestors. Folk Religion in a Taiwanese Village*. Berkeley/Los Angeles/London: University of California Press, 1972.

Jordan, David K. and Daniel L. Overmyer. *The Flying Phoenix. Aspect of Chinese Sectarianism in Taiwan*. Princeton: Princeton University Press, 1986.

Katz, Paul, R. "Enlightened Alchemist or Immoral Immortal? The Growth of Lü Dongbin's Cult in Late Imperial China", in *Unruly Gods. Divinity and Society in China*, ed. Meir Shahar and Robert P. Weller. Honolulu: University of Hawai'i Press, 1996, pp. 70–104.

Landzelius, Kyra and Al. *Native on the Net. Indigenous and Diasporic Peoples in the Virtual Age*. London: Routledge, 2006.

Li Wei and Al. "Language Shift in the Teochew Community in Singapore: a Family Domain Analysis", *Journal of Multilingual and Multicultural Development* 18, 5 (1997): 364–84.

Maspero, Henri. *Le Taoïsme et les religions chinoises*. Paris: Gallimard, 1971.

May, Tim. "Feelings matter: Investing the Hidden Equation", in *Interpreting the Field. Accounts of Ethnography*, ed. D. Hobbs and T. May. Oxford: Clarendon Press, 1993, pp. 69–97.

Miller, Daniel and Blater, Don. *The Internet, an Ethnographic Approach*. Oxford: Berg, 2000.

Naquin, Susan. *Peking. Temples and City Life, 1400–1900*. Berkeley: University of California Press, 2000.

Nelson, Geoffrey K. "The concept of cult", *Sociological Review* 16, 3 (1968): 351–62.

Purcell, Victor. *The Chinese in Southeast Asia*. London: Oxford University Press, 1965. 1st ed. 1951.

Reid, Anthony. *Southeast Asia in the Age of Commerce, 1450–1680, Vol. 2*. New Haven/London: Yale University Press, 1993.

Rosenstiehl, Pierre and Petitot, Jean. "Automate asocial et systèmes acentrés", *Communications*, no. 22 (1974): 45–62.

Rouget, Gilbert. *Music and Trance. A Theory of the Relation between Music and Possession*. Chicago: University of Chicago Press, 1985.

Rowe, William T. *Hankow. Commerce and Society in a Chinese City, 1796–1889*. Stanford: Stanford University Press, 1984.

________. *Hankow: Conflict and Community in a Chinese City, 1796–1895*. Stanford: Stanford University Press, 1989.

Sapir, Edward. "The Emergence of the Concept of Personality in a Study of Cultures", in *Culture, Language and Personality*, ed. E. Sapir. Berkeley: University of California Press, 1934.

Schaffer, Edward H. *The Golden Peaches of Samarkand: A Study of T'ang Exotics*. Berkeley/Los Angeles: University of California Press, 1963.

Schipper, Kristofer. *Le corps taoïste*. Paris: Fayard, 1982.

Seaman, Gary. "In the Presence of Authority: Hierarchical Roles in Chinese Spirit-Medium Cults", in *Normal and Abnormal Behavior in Chinese Culture*, ed. A. Kleinman and T.Y. Lin. Dordrecht: D. Reidel, 1980, pp. 61–74.

Schechter, Danny. *Falun Gong's Challenge to China. Spiritual Practice or "Evil Cult"?* New York: Akashic Books, 2001.

Shahar, Meir. *Crazy Ji: Chinese Religion and Popular Literature*. Harvard: Harvard-Yenching Institute Monograph series no. 48, 1998.

Shahar, Meir and Weller, Robert P. "Introduction", in *Unruly Gods. Divinity and Society in China*, ed. M. Shahar and R.P. Weller. Honolulu: University of Hawai'i Press, 1996, pp. 1–35.

Skinner, William G. *Report on the Chinese in Southeast Asia*. Ithaca: Cornell University Press, 1951.

________. "A Study of Chinese Community Leadership in Bangkok, Together with an Historical Survey of Chinese Society in Thailand". PhD dissertation, Ithaca: Cornell University, 1954.

Stark, Rodney and Bainbridge, Williams S. "Of Churchs, Sects and Cults. Preliminary Concepts for a Theory of Religious Movements", *Journal of Scientific Study of Religion* 18, 2 (1979): 117–33.

Sutton, Donald S. "Ritual Trance and Social Order: The Persistence of Taiwanese Shamanism", in *Social History and Issues in Human Consciousness*, ed. A. Barnes and P.N. Stearns. New York: New York University Press, 1898, pp. 108–27.

Tambiah, Stanley J. *World Conqueror and World Renouncer. A Study of Buddhism and Polity in Thailand against a historical Background*. Cambridge: Cambridge University Press, 1976.

Tan, Chee-Beng. *The Development and Distribution of Dejiao Associations in Malaysia and Singapore*. Singapore: Institute of Southeast Asian Studies, Occasional Paper no. 79, 1985.

Thoraval, Joël. "L'identité chinoise", in *Chine, peuple et civilisation*, ed. P. Gentelle. Paris: La Découverte, 2004, pp. 67–81.

Topley, Marjorie. "Chinese Religion and Religious Institutions in Singapore", *Journal of the Malayan Branch of the Royal Asiatic Society* 29, 1 (1956): 173.

Wallace, Anthony F.C. "Individual Differences and Cultural Uniformities", *American Sociological Review* 17, 6 (1952): 747–50.

Wallis, Roy. *The Road to Total Freedom: A Sociological Analysis of Scientology*. New York: Columbia University Press, 1977.

Wang Gungwu. "The Study of Chinese Identities in Southeast Asia", in *Changing Identities of the Southeast Asian Chinese Since WWII*, ed. J. Cushman and Wang Gungwu. Hong Kong: Hong Kong University Press, 1988, pp. 1–21.

Watson, James and Rawski, Evelyn, eds. *Death Ritual in Late Imperial and Modern China*. Berkeley: University of California Press, 1988.

Weber, Max. *The Sociology of Religion*. London: Methuen and Co. Ltd., 1963. First published in 1922.

__________. *L'éthique protestante et l'esprit du capitalisme*. Paris: Plon, 1964. First published in 1947.

__________. *The Religion of China*. New York: Free Press, 1968. First published in 1951.

Weller, Robert P. *Unities and Diversities in Chinese Religion*. London: McMillan Press Ltd., 1987.

Williams, Raymond. *Marxism and Literature*. Oxford: Oxford University Press, 1977.

Wolf, Arthur P. "Introduction", in *Religion and Ritual in Chinese Society*, ed. A.P. Wolf. Stanford: Stanford University Press, 1974, pp. 1–18.

Wyatt, David K. *Thailand: a Short History*. London/Bangkok: Yale University Press/Thai Watana Panich Co., 1984.

Yang, C.K. *Religion in Chinese Society*. Berkeley: University of California Press, 1961.

Yoshihara, Kazuo. "De Jiao: A Study of an urban Chinese Religion in Thailand", *Contributions to Southeast Asian Ethnography* 6 (1987): 61–79.

__________. "Dejiao: A Chinese Religion in Southeast Asia", *Japanese Journal of Religious Studies* 15, 2–3 (1988): 199–221.

2. Chinese Sources

Chaoshan bai ke quan shu 潮汕百科全书 *Encyclopedia of Chaoshan*. Beijing: 中国大百科全书出版社 Press of the Great Encyclopedia of China, 1994.

Chen Li-Jian 陳立健. "Luan li yu xuan ji zhe xue he dao de jiao yu" 鸾理与玄机哲学和道德教育 "The Truth of Phoenix, the Profound Theory of Dao, and the Teaching of Virtue", in *Di wu jie huan qiu de jiao da hui luan* 第五届环球德教大会鸾 *The Fifth World Moral Divine Pen Meeting*, De Jiao. Bangkok: Zi Zhen Ge, 2001, pp. 58–62.

Chen Wen-Bo 陈文博. "Luan li yu xuan ji zhe xue he dao de jiao yu" 鸾理与玄机哲学和道德教育 "The Truth of Phoenix, the Profound Theory of Dao, and the Teaching of Virtue", in *Di wu jie huan qiu de jiao da hui luan* 第五届环球德教大会鸾 *The Fifth World Moral Divine Pen Meeting*, De Jiao. Bangkok: Zi Zhen Ge, 2001, pp. 78–85.

Collective. *A Brief History of Chaoshan. Chaoshan shi hua chen li ming* 潮汕史话陈历明. Guangdong: Guangdong Tourist Press, 1993.

Fan Chun-Wu 范純武. "Jin xian dai Zhong guo fo jiao yu fu ji" 近現代中国佛教與扶乩 "Buddhism and *fu ji* in Modern China". Taiwan, *Yuan Guang Journal of Buddhology* 2 (1999): 261–91.

Guo Qing-Gao 郭清高. "Pi li ji de ge – wo jian wo wen wo gong zuo" 霹雳德阁间史 - 我见我问我工作 "A Brief History of the Thunderclap of Ji De Ge – What I have seen, heard, and worked ", in *De Jiao qi yuan* 德教起源 *Origin of De Jiao*. Bangkok: Zi Zhen Ge, 1997, pp. 213–44.

Huang Xia-Nian 黄夏年. "De Jiao Xin Dian jie shao" 德教心典介绍 "Presentation of De Jiao Xin Dian", *Shi jie zong jiao wen hua* 世界宗教文化 *Cultures of Religions of the World* 2 (2003): 60–1.

Ji Cheng Ge 濟誠閣. *De Dian ying yi* 德典英译 *English Translation of De [Jiao-Xin] Dian*. Taiping: Ji Cheng Ge, 1998.

Li Huai-De 李懷德. *De Jiao Yi Shi* 德教意識 *Consciousness of De Jiao*. Hong Kong: Xiang Gang De Jiao Hui, 1948. First published in 1944 by Zi Yang Ge.

_________. *Zhu qiao ji cheng* 竹桥集成 *Bamboo Bridge Anthology*. Singapore: Zi Xin Ge, 1955.

Li Huai-De 李懷德 and Ma Gui-De 馬貴德. *De Jiao Gen Yua* 德教根原 *Roots of De Jiao*. Singapore: Zi Xin Ge, 1954.

Li Guang-Zhao 李光照. "Ru shi wo wen Ming Yang, Lü Zu, Lian Yi, Sheng Dian" 如是我闻 铭阳 – 吕祖 – 联宜 – 圣典 – "I have heard that Ming Yang, Lü Zu, Lian Yi, and Sheng Dian are like this", in *De Jiao Wen Ji*. 德教文集 *Collection of papers on De Jiao*. Bangkok: Zi Zhen Ge, 1995, pp. 86–95.

_________. "Guan Yu rou shen cheng Dao deng ji shen ji" 关羽肉身成道登极神跡 "Guan Yu who became Immortal. Dao and followed in the gods' footsteps", in *De Xun* 德讯 *News from De Jiao*, no. 33 (October 2003): 162–3.

Li Shi-Yü 李世瑜. *Xian zai hua bei bi mi zong jiao* 現在華北秘密宗教 *Contemporary secret religions of North China*. Chengdu: Studia Serica Monographs, Series B no. 4, 1948.

Lian Yi-Hui 联谊会. *Sheng Dian* 圣奠 *Sacred Book* . Bukit Mertajam: Lian Yi Hui, 1986.

Lin, Wu-Shu 林悟姝. "Tai guo chao ren De Jiao xin yang kao cha" 泰国潮人德教信仰考察 "Research on the beliefs of the De Jiao Adepts in Thailand", *Xing xian ri bao* 星暹日报 *Thailand's Star Daily*, 25–29 June 2002, p. 16.

Lü Yi-Tan 吕一潭. " Luan li yu xuan ji zhe xue he dao de jiao yu" 鸾理与玄机哲学和道德教育 "The Truth of Phoenix, the Profound Theory of Dao, and the Teaching of Virtue", in *Di wu jie huan qiu de jiao da hui luan* 第五届环球德教大会鸾 *The Fifth World Moral Divine Pen Meeting*, De Jiao. Bangkok: Zi Zhen Ge, 2001, pp. 65–7.

Ma Gui-De 馬貴德. "De Jiao gai shuo" 德教概説 "Introduction to De Jiao", in *De Jiao qi yuan* 德教起源 *Origin of De Jiao*. Bangkok: Zi Zhen Ge, 1997, pp. 166–82. First published in 1940.

———. "De Jiao jiang shu" 德教讲述 "An account on De Jiao", in *De Jiao qi yuan* 德教起源 *Origin of De Jiao*. Bangkok: Zi Zhen Ge, 1997, pp. 183–212. First published in 1949.

RCODJ. Research Committee on the Origin of De Jiao – De Jiao Xun Yuan Zhong Xin Wei Yuan Hui Chu Ban 德教尋源中心委員會出版. *Xun Yuan Ji* 尋源記 *An Account on the Research of Origins*. Bangkok: Zi Zhen Ge, 2001.

Sheng Dian. 圣典 *Holy Canon*. Bukit Mertajam, Malaysia: Lian Yi Hui 联谊会. Association for the Unity and Friendship, 1986.

Song Guang-Yu 宋光宇. "Guan yu shan shu de yan jiu ji qi zhan wang" 关于善书的研究及其展望 "Introduction and Prospect on the Studies of *shan shu*", Taipei, *Xin shi xue* 新史学 New History Studies, Vol. 5–4, 1997, pp. 187–9.

Wang Jian-Chuan 王见川 and Li Shi-Wei 李世伟. "Tai Wan de min jian zong jiao yu xin yang" 台湾的民间宗教与信仰 "Religions and Popular Beliefs of Taiwan". Tai Bei wen xian 台北文献 *Archives of Taipei*, no. 118, 2000, pp. 213–38.

You Zi-An 游子安. *Qing dai shan shu yu she hui wen hua bian qian* 清代善书與社會文化變遷 *Shan shu and sociocultural changes during the Qing dynasty*. Hong Kong: Hong Kong Chinese University, PhD dissertation, 1994.

Zhan Tian-Yan 詹天眼. "De Jiao you lai" 德教由来 "Origin of De Jiao", in *Di si jie De Jiao hui huan qiu da hui luan te kan* 第四届德教会环球大鸾特刊 *The Fourth World Moral Divine Pen Meeting, De Jiao*. Kota Kinabalu: Zi Rui Ge, 1998, pp. 63–6.

Zheng Liang-Xi 郑良锡. "Ma Lai Xi Ya ji luan si shi nian lai gai kuang" 马来西亚乩鸾四十年来溉况 "Forty years of practice of fu ji in Malaysia", in *Di si jie De Jiao hui huan qiu da hui luan te kan* 第四届德教会环球大鸾特刊 *The Fourth World Moral Divine Pen Meeting, De Jiao*. Kota Kinabalu: Zi Rui Ge, 1998, pp. 26–34.

Zhu Qiao Chu Ji. 竹桥初集 *Bamboo Bridge Original Collection*. Kota Kinabalu: Zi Rui Ge, 1998.

Zi Zhen Ge 紫真閣. *De Jiao qi yuan* 德教起源 *Origin of De Jiao*. Bangkok: Zi Zhen Ge, 1997.

Zi Xin Ge 紫新閣. *Cheng li 50 zhou nian jin xi ji nian te kan* 成立50週年釒禧级念特刊 *Special issue commemorating the 50th anniversary of the association*. Singapore: Zi Xin Ge, 2002.

Zi Yun Ge 紫雲閣. *Bin cheng De Jiao hui zi yun ge 47 zhou nian ji xin ge luo cheng ji nian te kan* 槟成德教会紫雲閣闾阁47週咋暨新阁落成记念特刊 *Book commemorating the 47th anniversary of the Penang De Jiao association Zi Yun Ge, and the completion of its new headquarters*. Penang: Zi Yung Ge, 2001.

INDEX